CONTENT AREA READING

CONTENT AREA READING

RICHARD T. VACCA
Kent State University

Little, Brown and Company
BOSTON   TORONTO

Library of Congress Catalog Card No. 80-83799
ISBN 0-316-894885

9 8 7 6 5 4 3 2 1

HAL

Published simultaneously in Canada by Little, Brown & Company (Canada) Limited

Printed in the United States of America

Box 4–11 on page 109: Adapted from "Are You Ready to Go Metric?" by C. William Engel, *Mathematics Student* 21, 1 (October 1973): 1 ff. Used by permission.

Epigraph on page 159: © by E. E. Cummings. Reprinted from his volume COMPLETE POEMS 1913–1962 by permission of Harcourt Brace Jovanovich, Inc. and Granada Publishing Limited.

The teachers, colleagues, and friends listed below have contributed generously to the development of this book.

Chapter 2

Margaret Olson, Title I reading teacher, Joliet, Illinois, prereading activity on "Thanatopsis," p. 32.

Gene Vostinak, science teacher, Tolland Middle School, Tolland, Connecticut, reading guide on health facts, p. 33.

Kathleen Krispin, social studies teacher, Geneva Junior High School, Geneva, Illinois, postreading activity on Southeast Asia, p. 34.

Marietta Raneri, Castleton, New York, cross-tabulation chart for art unit, p. 40.

Camille Fiduccia, English teacher, Westchester, Illinois, contract for fiction unit, p. 46.

(continued on page 383)

Jo Anne,

This one's for you.

Preface

Although "Teach reading in content areas" is the rallying cry for many educators, content specialists have generally turned a deaf ear. Part of their dissatisfaction results from past efforts to impose elementary school and/or clinical assumptions about reading onto the middle and secondary curriculum. Content area reading should not require already beleaguered teachers to become reading teachers as well.

Nevertheless, this book recognizes that content teachers are in the most logical and strategic position to show students how to adapt skills to real reading situations and how to use reading as a vehicle for learning. The purpose of this text, therefore, is to show how reading can become a workable and sensible part of content area methodology.

Workable and *sensible* are the key words. If reading is to find its way into content classrooms, then the emphasis must be on how to help students comprehend what they read. Content teachers do not need to know everything there is to know about the teaching of reading. They do need (and want) to develop skills and understandings which are of intimate and immediate concern to them: content teachers want to know how to facilitate reading comprehension and concept development through their text materials. What they do to show students how to derive meaning from reading is the subject of this book.

Throughout *Content Area Reading* middle and secondary teachers are recognized for their strengths as content specialists. My task in this book is straightforward enough — to show how these strengths can be used to infuse reading into subject matter instruction. "Every teacher, a teacher of reading" need not cause furor and misunderstandings among content teachers. Every teacher is a teacher; let's leave it at that. But as part of our instructional repertoire, there should be the know-how that will enable content to be taught through reading. And in the process, reading will be taught through content.

Although this book offers numerous ideas and suggestions, it is not a cookbook. It presents a system of instruction based on the notion that in order to know how, teachers must know why. While this text deals with nuts and bolts issues, knowing why will enable content teachers to go beyond the techniques and strategies presented here. However, I have avoided dealing with theory in a vacuum. Instead, theory and practice are interwoven and the links between the two clearly made.

Content Area Reading is divided into three parts. Part One, "Preparing for Reading: Teachers and Students," underscores the importance of teacher preparation and student preparation. Teacher preparation involves organizing for and planning instruction. Student preparation highlights the critical nature of prereading instruction. What teachers do to lay the groundwork for concept development and to raise students' expectations in advance of reading has a profound influence on comprehension. Part Two, "Reading and Extending," is the backbone of this book. Each chapter in this section explains the instructional alternatives that will help students respond to meaning in content materials and to extend their understanding of concepts. Part Three, "Evaluating for Instructional Purposes," shows how content teachers can estimate the difficulty of text materials and evaluate the performance of learners to plan instruction.

I have intended this book to be as functional as the reading approach it defines. Every chapter offers practical suggestions, demonstrations, and illustrations that underlie the development of strategies and materials for content area reading instruction. In addition, several features are included to help guide the reading of this text.

The *Organizing Principle* sets the stage by presenting the basic assumption underlying each chapter. These assumptions in a nutshell are as follows:

1. Students learn how to use reading effectively through good teaching, which facilitates comprehension and concept development.
2. Organizing for instruction means planning in advance of action.
3. The study of technical vocabulary lays the groundwork needed to explore and develop concepts.
4. Students reduce the uncertainty that they bring to reading by raising questions about the material to be read.
5. Maturing readers respond to meaning at various levels of comprehension.
6. Teachers can guide maturing readers by helping them to perceive relationships and to distinguish important from less important ideas.
7. How, when, and where questions are used to guide reading determines their effectiveness.

8. Studying helps students to do something with what they have to read.

9. Word meanings and concepts are developed through repeated use and manipulation.

10. The difficulty of text material is the product of factors residing in both the reader and the material.

11. Evaluating for instruction is a continuous process involving observation during teaching and informal assessment on teacher-made inventories.

A *Chapter Overview* accompanies each organizing principle. The overview depicts visually the relationships among the important ideas in each chapter. It is the reader's map to the major concepts which will be developed. As you study the Chapter Overview, ask, "What do I already know about the material to be presented? What do I need to know more about?" These questions will activate reading and inspire a searching attitude.

A third feature of note are the *adjunct questions* which are positioned intermittently in the side margins of this text. These questions serve as organizers. They are posed to help readers focus on important points, analyze and synthesize information.

I wish to thank Mylan Jaixen and Caroline Becker of Little, Brown and Company for walking me through the various stages of writing a book. I am particularly grateful to the reviewers whose suggestions for improving the manuscript were invaluable: Peter Hasselriis, University of Missouri at Columbia; Karl D. Hesse, University of Oregon; Stephen Phelps, State University of New York College at Buffalo; and Leonard Breen, Eastern Montana College.

A special thanks to students and colleagues, too numerous to list, who have contributed immeasurably to my growth as a teacher. And most of all, I want to thank Courtney, who brightens each day, and Jo Anne, my best friend and closest collaborator. Her influence is felt on every page of this book.

Contents

Inservice Guide for Content Area Reading

Working with Content Area Teachers 305

JO ANNE L. VACCA

CONTENT AREA READING

CHAPTER ONE

The Value of Content Area Reading

It is the use of money which determines its value.
ALFRED A. MONTAPERT

ORGANIZING PRINCIPLE

Montapert's words apply easily to reading: it is the use of reading which determines its value. Content area reading instruction shows students how to use reading as a vehicle for learning. Therein lies its value and its promise. The message that is all too clear to today's classroom teacher is that tomorrow's illiterate is the student who has not learned how to learn. Although content is king in many classrooms, it's never absolute. Toffler (1970) put it this way: "education must teach the individual how to classify and reclassify information, how to evaluate its veracity, how to change categories when necessary, how to move from concrete to abstract and back, how to look at problems from a new direction . . ." (p. 414). The organizing principle of this chapter, therefore, is a mixture of philosophy and practicality: *Students learn how to learn from content materials through effective teaching, which facilitates comprehension and concept development.*

Before reading any further, study the Chapter Overview. It's your map to the major ideas in the chapter. The overview shows the relationships that exist among the concepts you will study. Ask yourself, "What do I know already about the information in this chapter? What do I need to know more about?"

I'll never forget the first time I heard Paul Simon's "Kodachrome" on the radio. It was 1973. I had just completed my doctoral studies. The degree in hand, my sights were on new educational horizons. And then I heard

When I think back
On all the crap I learned in high school

1

CHAPTER OVERVIEW

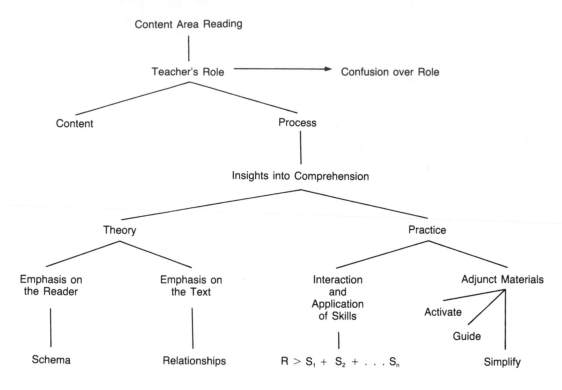

It's a wonder
I can think at all
And though my lack of education
hasn't hurt me none
I can read the writing on the wall.*

Here I was, ready to begin my life's work as a teacher of teachers. I had my fair share of Dewey, Piaget, Bruner, and other learning and educational theorists. Yet it took a pop singer's personal statement about his education to send chills running up and down my spine. I was moved, not so much by the startling lyric ''all the crap I learned in high school'' as by its juxtaposition with ''It's a wonder I can think at all.'' Together, the lyrics hit home. They pretty much said what I had always felt but, up to that point, had not consciously articulated.

You see, I have never known a teacher who didn't believe in earnest that the essence of teaching is to show students how to think through the vehicle of his or her content. *Intention,* however, no matter how earnest, is one thing; effect is another. What really matters is what we *do* in the name of instruction to mediate between intention and effect.

*© 1973 Paul Simon. Used by permission. ''Kodachrome'' is a registered trademark for color film.

To simply tell students to think is not enough. To exhort them to think about what they read or to use reading to learn won't do either, even though

> Reading has the power to carry the (student) further and deeper . . . than any other educational medium . . . he can analyze more thoroughly . . . ; he can compare passages for corroboration or to check seeming inconsistencies; he can stop for reflection . . . ; he can choose a time for reading that will fit in with his mood and personal needs . . . *(Preston, 1968, pp. 241–242)*

Such discussion about what reading can do for students falls flat on its face, unfortunately, when a teacher notices that they "just don't read assigned material anymore." Yet it's not that the majority of students can't read. Most choose not to, primarily because they have never been shown how to explore and interpret text effectively.

How are messages telegraphed against reading?

There must be carefully planned teacher "actions" between good intentions and teachers' ultimate effects in the content classroom. Rieck (1977) reported the findings of interviews with content teachers and their students. These findings show how some teachers unwittingly telegraph messages against reading. English, science, social studies, mathematics, physical education, art, and home economics teachers were asked a series of questions about their actions in relation to reading. On two of the questions asked, here is how they responded:*

1. Do you require reading in your course? 97% yes, 3% no.
2. Do most of your students read their assignments? 58% yes, 42% no.

Approximately three hundred students of the teachers who responded "no" to the second question were then asked these questions:

1. Do you like to read? 52% yes, 38% no, 10% no response.
2. Do you read your assignments in this class? 15% yes, 81% no, 4% no response.
3. Do your tests cover mainly lecture and discussion or reading assignments? 98% lecture and discussion, 2% reading.
4. Are you required to discuss your reading assignments? 23% yes, 70% no, 7% no response.
5. Does your teacher give you purpose for reading or are you only given the number of pages to read? 95% pages, 5% purpose.
6. Does your teacher bring in outside material for you to read

* Billie Jo Rieck, "How Content Teachers Telegraph Messages against Reading,"*Journal of Reading* (May, 1977): 446–447, 647. Reprinted with the permission of Billie Jo Rieck and the International Reading Association.

and recommend books of interest for you to read? 5% yes, 95% no.

7. Does your teacher like to read? 20% yes, 33% no, 47% don't know.

As a result of the contrast between teacher and student responses in the interviews, Rieck (1977) concluded,

> Out loud, these teachers are saying: "I require reading in this course. All students are to read the assignments. Students are to read X number of pages from the textbook." However, their nonverbal attitude said to students: "You really don't have to read the assignments because you aren't tested on them and probably won't have to discuss them. You should read X number of pages but there is no real reason to do so. Reading really isn't important. Outside reading is of little value in this class. My students will have no way to tell whether or not I like to read." *(p. 647)*

What we require and what we actually do can be two different things. What you do to show students how to think through print — how to use reading to derive meaning from content materials — is the subject of this book.

Explain the classroom teacher's role.

Paul Simon's personal reflection on his education is just that — a personal reflection. My purpose is not to debate its accuracy or generalizability. Instead, I referred to the opening lines in "Kodachrome" to raise a point. Teachers who are wedded to a discipline walk a tightrope between content and process. It's certainly a balancing act every time the attempt is made to influence what is learned (content) and how it should be learned (process). Someone once said that teaching a set of ideas without regard to how students are to acquire those ideas is like blowing air into a punctured balloon. The harder you blow . . .

Just the reverse is true when an effort is made to develop skills without meaningful content. Teaching skills for the sake of skills is as purposeless as teaching ancient history in a vacuum. It's all Greek to students.

When it comes to reading, then, a content teacher's job is not to teach skills per se but to show students how to use reading effectively to comprehend and learn from text materials. Therein lies the real value of content area reading instruction.

CLARIFYING THE CONTENT TEACHER'S ROLE ─────────────

As you read this book, keep in mind that the notion that reading be taught in content areas is by no means new. The charge to teach reading through content can be traced to at least the 1920s. But the reading field then was still in its infancy. Content area reading was too ephemeral to have substantial impact on educational practice.

Today, however, the enthusiasm for content area reading can be felt everywhere. Particularly since 1970, the topic consistently dominates the program of the annual convention of the International Reading Association and is a welcome addition to the proceedings of national and state conferences in each of the subject fields. Not a day goes by that a school- or college-based consultant isn't asked to conduct staff development sessions on reading for classroom teachers.

There are good reasons why content area reading has grown in the dramatic fashion that is evident today. Certainly it's reasonable to presume that content teachers are in a very strategic position to show students how to use reading to handle the demands of content materials. But I also believe that content area reading has "grown up" because its technology has caught up with its underlying rationale. To put the matter plainly, there's a lot more known today about how to teach reading in content areas without fragmenting the instructional process. And this makes sense to content teachers.

Both enthusiasm and confusion over content area reading — why the paradox?

Having said this, it's somewhat ironic that the charge to teach content area reading is in many ways still an empty imperative to teachers. Despite the dramatic increase in enthusiasm, content area reading instruction has yet to win wide acceptance by subject matter specialists. That star-crossed cliché "every teacher a teacher of reading" causes confusion and often conveys little meaning. The confusion over teaching reading in content areas is apt to be caused by the traditions associated with subject matter instruction, the misconceptions that content teachers have about reading instruction, and their role expectations in general.

Once traditions and past conceptions of reading instruction are put into perspective, confusion begins to fade and the expectations that classroom teachers hold for teaching reading through content take on new meaning. Let's examine why.

Content as King

Why has content traditionally come first?

Content is the *what* of instruction. And *what* is learned in the presence of a teacher has been the time-honored tradition of schools since the Middle Ages. As Malcolm Knowles (1973) said, in those days novices entered monasteries to prepare for religious life, and as a result, "The teaching monks based their instruction on assumptions about what would be required to control the development of these children into obedient, faithful and efficient servants of the church" (p. 42). Out of this origin developed traditions which have heavily influenced the secular schools of Europe and America.

Schooling in America, for example, can be traced to the Puritans, where it has been pointed out that schools "were definitely instruments of the church at the outset. . . . The schools the children attended were laced with religious experience. Inherent in this vision of the school was the supremacy of content" *(Samples et al., 1977, p. 168)*. Content was king, the teacher the authoritative source. Vestiges of this tradition are still felt whenever a ninth grader, or for that matter a graduate student, looks to the teacher for the "right answer."

In many schools today content is still king — the stuff of learning — in many classrooms where teachers have been prepared to teach a discipline. And that's okay — to be content with content. Sometimes reading specialists in their zeal to get reading techniques across to content teachers forget the centuries-old tradition of a discipline and wind up stepping on toes in the process.

The term *discipline* has an interesting etymological background. Its roots can be traced to the Latin noun *discipulus,* which, in turn, is derived from the verb *discere,* "to know." In other words a discipline can be defined as "knowledge organized for instruction." Bruner (1961) and others proposed that the implicit organization or structure of any discipline is the only proper source of learning content. The student who discovers and understands a discipline's structure will be able to contend with its many detailed aspects. Understanding structure means seeing the big picture, developing the superordinate concepts and powerful ideas that are part of each discipline. Nevertheless, the feeling of having to "get through the curriculum" is still omnipresent for many teachers.

It's not difficult to recognize why teachers don't readily commit themselves to teaching reading. To do so is viewed as one more burden on the llama's back. When a llama is overburdened, it gets ornery. It resists. For many content teachers, reading is perceived as one more distraction from their concept of teaching a discipline.

"I've got too much to cover already." "I've got four weeks to get through this unit."

Lay these very real concerns alongside another artifact of tradition — that teachers tend to teach the way they have been taught — and what emerges is a blockbuster of a mental set to break through. Teachers look to former teachers for their models. When I entered the profession I patterned my teaching style after an eighth grade science teacher, despite three years of methods courses in a teachers' college.

"Teachers tend to teach the way they were taught." How valid is this statement?

What stands out among teachers you have had? Stephen Judy (1978), former editor of *English Journal,* reminisced about two of his.

> Mrs. Beatty taught *English* . . . We read Shakespeare in a small, red-bound edition of "The Merchant of Venice," and although I didn't understand much of the language of the play, I enjoyed

some of the high school "scholarship" — reading footnotes and learning about Quartos and the Folios and the Globe. We diagrammed sentences, which I didn't understand at all, and wrote book reports monthly . . . In retrospect, Mrs. Beatty did many of the things I have come to question in high school English teaching, but I have to say, she did it well and the class made a mark on me.

Leon Sarin was as relaxed as Mrs. Beatty was precise. He taught General Science; or more accurately, he made General Science a forum for whatever was on his mind (and ours). We shot the bull in Sarin's class, talking day after day about books, politics, athletics, drivers' licenses, the internal combustion engine, boy-girl relationships . . . Sarin's universal knowledge impressed me; his class was far removed from the learning we had done in the grades. *(pp. 6–7. Used by permission.)*

Mrs. Beatty and Mr. Sarin were obviously poles apart as teachers. Content was truly king in Beatty's English class. Sarin's approach to general science was decidedly more laissez-faire. Yet both teachers made a lasting impression on Stephen Judy.

Perhaps someone particularly special to you has entered (or will enter) your teaching persona and has influenced (or will influence) your concept of what teaching is about. To impose reading upon that concept of teaching is always difficult until "reading instruction" is clarified.

Misconceptions About Reading

Resistance to content area reading also may occur because of the concepts or, more appropriately, misconcepts that are developed over what reading instruction entails. If, for example, our only experiences with reading instruction are what we can recollect from childhood, what conclusions might we draw? Quite possibly these: (1) reading instruction is reading aloud; (2) reading instruction is learning how to sound out words; (3) reading instruction is doing endless worksheet drills; (4) reading instruction is boring.

Are your childhood impressions of reading instruction similar to the ones described?

Depressing? Outlandish? Johns and Galen (1977) wrote an intriguing article entitled "Reading Instruction in the Middle 50's: What Tomorrow's Teachers Remember Today," in which advanced education majors were asked to record their early impressions of reading. Here's some of what was recalled.

It's amazing how every year "reading" seemed to get farther away from something we were supposed to be enjoying. If it weren't for the good feeling I had when I first started reading, I never would have survived the rest of the progression through formal reading instruction.

> . . . each person took his turn reading aloud. You would nervously fumble with your book . . . When your turn came around you prayed that you wouldn't make any mistakes, for fear of being called ''one of the dummies.''

> While we waited for our turns, most of us became bored and fidgety . . . So I learned to be real sneaky and feel guilty every time I got bored and started reading ahead again.

> I had to stay after school because I was not reading the words on the flash cards correctly.

> The teacher used to catch people off guard and then ask them to read.

> When a child stumbled over a word — our teacher would correct him in a bored and impatient voice. *(pp. 252–254. Used by permission.)*

Times may have changed; the technology for teaching reading has vastly improved since the 1950s. But on a personal note I can tell you this: if you were to ask our daughter Courtney if she likes reading, she would unflinchingly respond, ''I hate it!'' Now, Courtney is an accomplished reader; she devours books. Why, then, would she respond so negatively to the question ''Do you like reading?'' As an elementary student Courtney doesn't distinguish between reading and reading instruction. To her, the question implies ''Do you like your reading period in school?'' She doesn't. Reading books, however, is another story entirely. For Courtney, reading a book is something that she does outside school!

What are your early impressions of reading instruction? Many teachers will have little to do with teaching reading in their disciplines if it means even coming close to doing the things that were done to them in the name of instruction in elementary school.

Happily, it doesn't. Instead, the essence of content area reading is comprehending texts. Most teachers do not need (or want) a comprehensive treatment addressing the many detailed facets related to reading instruction. They do need (and want) to develop skills and understandings that are of immediate and intimate concern to them: they want to know how to facilitate reading comprehension and concept development through text materials. This is the heart of the matter.

Nevertheless, confusion often arises in the minds of content teachers over their role in a schoolwide reading program. The expectations that teachers have about their role and the role of reading specialists contribute to content teachers' dissatisfaction when they are called upon to teach reading through content. Once these expectations are put into perspective, resistance to content area reading is likely to shrink.

The Content Teacher as Process Helper

Although content traditionally has been king to many teachers, process has achieved the stature of prime minister in today's classroom. Showing students how to learn comes with the territory. When textbooks are the vehicle for learning, the teacher has a significant role to perform. In effect, the classroom teacher is a "process helper," bridging the gap that often exists between students and the text.

No doubt a corner has been turned in the perceptions most of us have of reading as a "subject" fit only for the elementary grades. This perception should accompany an even greater awareness that reading cannot be taught entirely as a separate subject at any level of instruction. It defies common sense to think that reading is something taught for one hour every day. Many teachers recognize the dangers inherent in teaching reading as if it were a content area in itself, when in fact reading is a process and should be thought of and taught as such.

Margaret Early, a major voice in secondary reading, has maintained that once the difference between a skills-centered approach to reading, *direct instruction,* and a content-centered approach, *functional instruction,* is explained, the expectations of content teachers will

What are the differences between direct and functional reading instruction?

change, and confusions will begin to fade. Early (1964) suggested that a spiral concept of learning can be adapted to provide insights into the meaning of reading instruction through the grades. In Figure 1–1 two cone-shaped spirals superimposed upon one another signify direct and functional instruction in reading. At the base of the direct instructional cone — in the elementary grades — the spiral is tight and wide to represent heavy emphasis on skills development. As direct instruction continues into the secondary grades, the spiral gradually tapers off to suggest less emphasis.

Direct instruction usually centers around a set of reading skills, arranged according to "scope and sequence" and taught systematically by a reading teacher or specialist. Reading materials are selected for their value in teaching the skills and providing practice and reinforcement once they are taught.

But that's only half the picture. Consider the overlapping spiral which begins narrow in the elementary grades and broadens as it moves through the secondary grades. This spiral represents the functional nature of reading. It emphasizes the application of skills that readers must make to learn content from a variety of sources and materials. A functional approach suggests that classroom teachers are in a better position than

Figure 1–1. *The Total Reading Curriculum: Direct and Functional Instruction*

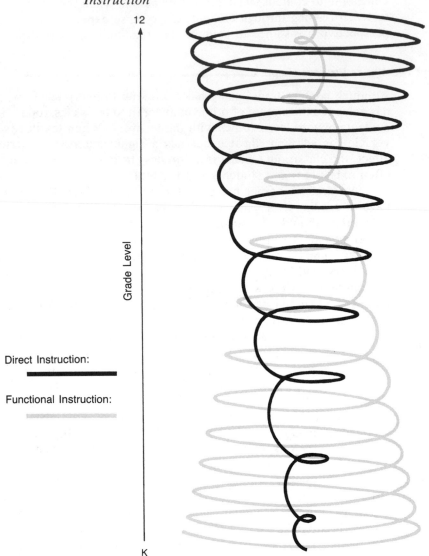

12

Grade Level

Direct Instruction:

Functional Instruction:

K

reading specialists to guide the application of reading skills. Skills aren't taught or applied in isolated drill apart from the mainstream of content area instruction. Nor are "artificial" workbook materials used as a guise for skills development in the content areas. Such materials tend to become exercises in themselves and little else.

An inspection of these overlapping spirals shows that some form of direct teaching of reading skills should continue through the grades but should be superseded by a functional approach to instruction in every subject where reading is an important vehicle for learning. Early (1964) said teachers should draw three implications about their role:

1. They have something important to contribute to the reading development of students, but they need not become reading specialists to contribute it.

2. They should not be held responsible for direct reading instruction, since a qualified reading teacher will be in a better position to deliver a program that meets the specialized needs and abilities of learners at every band in the spiral.

3. A reading program works when reading specialists and content teachers respect and understand each other's roles.

Significant strides in content area reading will be made in the 1980s. More and more students will learn how to read textbooks effectively as content teachers put traditions and old expectations into perspective and build healthy concepts of reading instruction. Progress will depend also on how well teachers use insights into the reading process to plan their actions in the classroom. If comprehension instruction is the heart of the matter, as I suggested earlier, then content teachers will have to know how. But they will also need to know why.

KNOWING WHY LEADS TO KNOWING HOW

Know-how and know-why go hand in hand. This book is designed to deal with nuts-and-bolts issues related to instruction in content area reading. But the book is also based on the premise that if you "know why" you can go infinitely beyond the nuts and bolts proposed here. Moffett and Wagner (1976) were quite right when they said, "To act without understanding is never practical" (p. 2). Others have maintained that nothing is as practical as a good theory.

Why should classroom teachers understand theory?

I will not deal with theory in a vacuum; nor will I deal with practice in a cookbook manner. Instead, I hope to balance theory and practice and avoid the dichotomy that has been created between the two. This dichotomy has led to unfortunate circumstances in the field of education generally and reading specifically. There seems to be a backlash by classroom teachers against anything that smacks of the theoretical. "What can I do on Monday morning?" is the often-heard appeal of those disenchanted teachers who are "fed up" with ivory tower theorists — and, I imagine, with good reason. Teachers are tired of empty theorizing. "Show me what to do on Monday morning" is a legitimate concern. But teachers also want to know why; they just phrase it differently: "Why should I do this rather than that?"

Cunningham and Foster (1978) captured the dilemma created between theory and practice.

It seems that educators have accepted the notion that there must be a long lag between the formulation of theory and basic research with students in classrooms. Such acceptance is manifest in the disdain of some theorists for teachers who "want recipes," and in the disdain of some teachers for theorists who "aren't practical." *(p. 368)*

My concern is to avoid the either-or trap by making connections between classroom practices and their theoretical underpinnings.

Since content area reading has comprehension as its major concern, a question often asked by teachers is how to help students understand what they read. Knowing why is crucial to understanding how. Therefore, let's examine several important insights into reading comprehension.

Insights into Reading Comprehension

We are in the midst of an information explosion that has contributed unprecedented theorizing and research on the process of reading. The assault on reading in the past decade or so has been multidisciplinary. By and large, scholarship in psycholinguistics, information processing, and cognitive psychology has focused on reading comprehension — the search for and interpretation of meaning in print.

How do readers interact with written language?

Positions established by Goodman (1976) and Smith (1978), two of the leading advocates of a psycholinguistic view of reading, have maintained that reading is a language process and not merely the sum of various decoding and comprehension subskills. A reader interacts with print in an effort to understand the author's message. Reading is an active process of deriving meaning.

Suppose you were asked to read the following passage:

The Kingdom of Kay Oss

Once in the land of Serenity there ruled a king called Kay Oss. The king wanted to be liked by all his people.

So onx day thx bxnxvolxnt dxspot dxcidxd that no onx in thx country would bx rxsponsiblx for anything. Zll of thx workxrs rxstxd from thxir dzily lxbors. "Blxss Kzy Oss," thxy xxclzimxd. Now, thx lzw mzkxrs wxrx vxry wvsx. But zs wvsx zs thxy wxrx, thxy dxcvdxd thzt thx bxst form of govxrnmxnt wzs nonx zt zll.

Zs tvmx wxnt qn, thx kvngdqm og Kzy qss bxgzn tq splvt zt thx sxzms znd vt lqqkxd lvkx thvs: Bcx dqufghj klzm nqxp qqt rqst vqxwxxz bqxc dqf ghzj kqlxmnxp.

As you read "The Kingdom of Kay Oss," did the progressive substitution of consonants for vowels stymie your efforts to understand the passage? Probably not. Perhaps it slowed down your rate of reading a bit, but chances are you were still able to interact with the passage and derive meaning from it.

According to advocates of a psycholinguistic view of reading, a reader is a user of language whose task is to make sense out of what he or she reads. To do this, readers make use of their existing knowledge as well as their expectations and interactions with written language. Upon reading about King Kay Oss, you searched for and processed different types of language cues which helped you derive meaning from the passage.

For example, you probably made some use of cues among the letter/sound associations in the passage. Part of your ability to read the phrase "thxy dxcvdxd thzt thx bxst" depended on the recognition of some of the consonants or consonant combinations and the sounds that they represent. However, these letter/sound associations in and of themselves provide no clues to meaning. In order to get at meaning, you had to process other types of information in the passage. Your knowledge of grammar, whether that knowledge is intuitive or overt, undoubtedly helped you anticipate some of the words in the passage which "had to come next." For instance, as you began to read the last paragraph and said to yourself, "As time ———— ————," you probably predicted almost automatically that "went" and "on" would follow. This is partially due to your knowledge of how language works. It is also due to the general knowledge that you brought to bear as you read.

Readers use their knowledge to anticipate the meanings of known words or build meaning for unknown words — or even unknown strings of words. When you read the last paragraph in the passage and perceived, "As time went on, the Kingdom of Kay Oss began to split at the seams and it looked like this:" you probably made the inference that "this" referred to the chaotic string of words that followed. These words convey no letter/sound or grammatical cues. Some of you probably decided that the fablelike nature of the passage dictated a moral at the end. Such a decision is based on what you know already or believe to be so.

How does prior knowledge influence reading comprehension?

The knowledge structures that students bring to learning have important implications for content area reading. We can grasp the importance of prior knowledge in reading by reviewing the findings of the research conducted under the direction of Richard C. Anderson at the Center for the Study of Reading at the University of Illinois. The scientific enterprise undertaken at the Center for the Study of Reading has in large measure developed a support for a *schema theory* of reading and language comprehension. Readers activate existing knowledge structures (schemata) to interpret text. Comprehension involves the matching of what the reader already knows to a new message.

To illustrate this point, I will use a workshop activity. In workshops for content teachers we occasionally read the short story "Ordeal by Cheque" by Wuther Grue (first published in *Vanity Fair* magazine in 1939). The story is extraordinary in that it is told entirely through the bank checks of the Exeter family over a twenty-eight-year span. The workshop participants interact in small groups, with each group assigned the task of reconstructing the meaning of the story. At first glance the participants don't know what to make of the story. "You must be kidding!" is a typical response. After initial puzzlement, however, they begin to "read."

Here is the essential information contained in the first few checks in the story.

Entry Date	Paid to	Amount	Signed by
8/30/03	A baby shop	$ 148.00	Lawrence Exeter
9/2/03	A hospital	100.00	Lawrence Exeter
10/3/03	A physician	475.00	Lawrence Exeter, Sr.
12/10/03	A toy company	83.20	Lawrence Exeter, Sr.
10/6/09	A private school for boys	1250.00	Lawrence Exeter, Sr.
8/6/15	An exclusive military academy	2150.00	Lawrence Exeter, Sr.
9/3/21	A Cadillac dealer	3885.00	Lawrence Exeter, Sr.
9/7/21	An auto repair shop	228.75	Lawrence Exeter, Sr.

Analyze these bits of information and the relationships established among the events depicted by the checks. Are you able to reconstruct what has taken place thus far in the story? Team up with one or two persons and discuss your versions. What do they have in common? What inferences did you make about the characters? Were there differences in your retellings? If so, why?

Here are some typical responses to these questions:

"A baby boy was born. He's named after his father."

"The Exeters must be 'fat cats.' The old man's loaded."

"He spends $83 for toys in 1903! He probably bought out the toy store."

"Lawrence Jr. must be a spoiled brat!"

"Yeah, how can any kid born with the proverbial silver spoon in his mouth not turn out spoiled?"

"Let's not jump to conclusions. Why is he spoiled?"

"Look, the family sent him to a military academy after he screwed up at the private school."

"No, no. It was fashionable in those days to first send your child to a private school until he was old enough for military school. The super-rich send their children to exclusive schools — it's as simple as that."

"Maybe so, but the kid is still a spoiled brat. His father buys him a Cadillac, probably for graduation from the academy, and four days later, it's in the body shop for repair."

"The father overindulges his son. I wonder what will happen to 'Junior' when he has to make it on his own?"

Although readers attempt to reconstruct an author's message, they also attempt to construct meaning as well. In other words, we not only read the lines to determine what an author says, but we also read between the lines to infer meaning and beyond the lines to elaborate upon the message. If the entire display of checks from "Ordeal by Cheque" were in front of you, you would undoubtedly soon find yourself involved in reading: raising questions, predicting, searching for relationships among the pieces of information contained in each check, inferring, judging, and elaborating.

A final insight into reading comprehension merits consideration.

How do relationships in text influence reading comprehension?

Participation in the "Ordeal by Cheque" activity not only reinforces the powerful role that one's prior knowledge plays in interpreting text but also illustrates the importance of the text itself. The conceptual and structural demands in a text selection influence comprehension. Readers must search for and find relationships among pieces of information (often called propositions) and concepts.

Pearson and Johnson (1978) bemusingly wished that the readers of their book *Teaching Reading Comprehension* had encountered "the word *relation* so often that you are near the point of hoping you never see it again. We have used it often, because that is what we think comprehension is about — seeing relations among concepts and propositions" (p. 228). Most authors do not write carelessly or aimlessly. They impose structure — an organization among ideas — on their writings. Perceiving structure in text material improves learning and retention. When students are shown how to see relationships among concepts and propositions, they are in the proverbial driver's seat. That is, they are in a better position to respond to meaning and to distinguish important from less important ideas.

The insights into comprehension presented here will be developed in succeeding chapters within the framework of instructional practices related to content area reading. What these insights tell the classroom teacher is this: readers must "work" with print in an effort to explore and interpret meaning. Reading is first and foremost an interplay, a give and take, between the reader and the text. However, the burden for learning is always on the reader. As a result, content area reading instruction should center around a search for meaning in text materials. The teacher guides comprehension and helps students develop concepts through varied forms of instructional activity — all of which are to be presented in the remainder of this book.

What About Comprehension Skills?

The conventional wisdom in the reading field today is that reading cannot take place unless meaning is involved in the transaction between reader and writer; that comprehension is the bottom line. Yet until recently comprehension has been the least investigated area of reading research over the years — and the least understood by practitioners.

A discussion of reading comprehension is somewhat analogous to Humpty Dumpty's conversation with Alice on the use of a word in *Alice's Adventures in Wonderland:* "When I use a word," says Humpty Dumpty, "it means just what I choose it to mean — nothing more or less." Likewise, in a discussion of *comprehension,* the term has often meant whatever a speaker or writer has chosen it to mean. All too often reading authorities and cognitive psychologists confuse classroom teachers by personalizing comprehension terms with their own unique labels. However, in its broadest sense, particularly for instructional purposes, I will define reading comprehension in ordinary language as the act of exploring and interpreting meaning.

In order to make the teaching of comprehension manageable, the major thrust over the past several decades has been to identify and to isolate the skills commonly thought to be involved in reading comprehension. Davis (1941, 1944, 1968, 1972) spent his professional lifetime determining whether comprehension among mature readers was a unitary process or a set of distinct mental skills. In his 1968 study, Davis used complex statistical analyses to examine the uniqueness of eight skills thought to be discrete:

1. Recalling word meanings
2. Drawing inferences from context about the meaning of a word
3. Finding answers to questions answered explicitly or in paraphrase in the passage
4. Weaving together ideas in the content
5. Drawing inferences from the content
6. Recognizing a writer's purpose, attitude, tone, and mood

7. Identifying a writer's techniques

8. Following the structure of a passage

What are some of the inherent dangers of viewing comprehension skills as independent of one another?

Davis (1972) concluded that reading comprehension is not a unitary mental process: "It is, apparently, a composite of at least five underlying mental skills" (p. 655). These are skills 1, 3, 5, 6, and 8 in the list above. An important contribution of Davis's work is the recognition that discrete skills aren't independent of one another, that comprehension skills are highly interactive. More often than not, however, comprehension has been viewed as a collection of uncorrelated skills. The teaching emphasis usually has been on systematic instruction and practice in each of the individual skill areas.

Proponents of skills instruction in content areas have gone a step further. They affirm that there are comprehension skills that are peculiar to various subject matters. Burmeister (1974), for example, listed "the most commonly needed skills for reading in specific content areas" (p. 80). An analysis of her lists for comprehension reveals among other things a significant amount of overlap among the separate skills *within and across* the content areas of science, mathematics, social studies, and English. How unfortunate it would be if teachers were to conclude that reading comprehension is mainly a pattern of distinct skills that varies from one content field to another and that their job is to teach each of these skills separately.

This skills approach merits caution. There's the implicit danger of imparting to students the sense that reading comprehension is not a thoughtful, cognitive process but rather a series of individual skill performances. What's worse, however, is that this approach to comprehension in content areas runs the risk of fostering the belief that the distinct skills are uncorrelated with one another — that a particular skill, once taught and practiced, can be used independently of the others. This idea just doesn't make sense. Davis (1972), drawing upon psychometric research conducted over several decades, concluded that the concept of comprehension as a body of separate, independent skills should be soundly rejected.

What, then, is an alternative way of viewing "skills instruction" in comprehension? According to Vacca and Johns (1976), reading may be expressed symbolically as

$$R > S_1 + S_2 + S_3 + \ldots S_n$$

In this equation, R (reading) is greater than $S_1 + S_2 + S_3 + \ldots S_n$ (the sum of "teachable" skills). It implies that reading is a meaning-deriving process and places skills within that context. The comprehension process may indeed be a composite of skills, but the skills are so interactive that they cannot be separated from one another during reading.

Goodman and Burke (1972) suggested that individual skills, no matter how identified or labeled, do not necessarily result in effective reading. They explained that:

> You cannot know a process by listing its ingredients or labeling its parts; you must observe the effect of the parts as they interact with each other. Acting together, the parts compose an entity which is uniquely different from the identity of any of the separate parts. Flour, sugar, baking soda, salt, eggs and water can all be listed as ingredients of a cake. Yet the texture, weight, flavor and moistness of a cake cannot be related directly to any one of the ingredients, but only to the quality and result of the interaction. *(p. 95)*

Although it's likely that a composite of comprehension skills does exist, it's just as likely that the interaction among these skills is what really matters.

The content teacher's use of adjunct materials will facilitate skills interaction. Adjunct materials are teacher-made learning devices which bridge the gap between reader and text. Throughout this book I will explain and illustrate the how of developing materials to guide reading in content areas. For now, however, let's take a look at the why of adjunct materials.

Adjunct Materials

Adjunct materials stimulate learning through reading and serve a bridging function. Teacher-made materials which accompany reading assignments help students experience the satisfaction of learning content from texts. A teacher builds in the guidance and structure students need to handle difficult reading materials. Adjunct materials give students a sense of what it means to interact with the text.

How do adjunct materials activate, guide, and, ultimately, simplify reading?

Frase (1971) defined *adjunct aid* as any kind of stimulation that facilitates learning from texts. Since aids are not a natural part of the written text, they are called *adjuncts*. The questions inserted in the margins throughout this book are adjunct aids. Questions are without a doubt the most common form of stimulation that classroom teachers use. However, giving students a batch of questions before or after an assignment provides very little structure or guidance. In Chapter 7 we will study how oral and written questions can be structured effectively to guide reading.

Adjunct materials can provide alternatives to questions. The form and function of these alternatives vary with the reading situation, and, I might add, with the teacher's instructional purposes. Teachers can develop adjunct materials to activate, guide, and, ultimately, simplify the reading of classroom materials.

The prereading activities and materials in Chapters 3 and 4 will help students "get into" reading by establishing purpose and sustaining interest and motivation in an assigned text selection. We will study how adjunct materials can be developed to arouse curiosity and help students make predictions about content before reading. These materials activate schemata. Students clarify and organize what they know, believe, and value in advance of reading. Those readers who have trouble matching schemata to text information or who lack sufficient prior knowledge to bring to bear on an assignment will profit especially from adjunct materials which activate and mobilize reading.

Adjunct guide materials will also help students focus their attention on relevant segments of a text selection. Materials which guide reading show students how to search for and interpret information. The reading guides in Chapters 5 and 6, the use of oral and written questions as explained in Chapter 7, and the study strategies in Chapter 8 emphasize how to find and use information during and after reading.

Adjunct materials as such can prompt the application of and interaction among skills. This is particularly important because students will come to see reading comprehension as a thoughtful process (the way one interacts with text material) and as a product (information gained).

Because they activate, guide, and extend students' response to meaning in text, adjunct materials simplify reading (Herber, 1978). Most students lack the sophistication needed to read text effectively because they are still in the process of maturing as readers. The conceptual and stylistic demands of text are often greater than the levels of reading maturity that students bring to the task. Yet by the time they reach the middle grades, students have a need and a capacity to be self-directing and independent. The whole idea of adjunct materials is to provide enough instructional support for students to gain confidence and to develop strategies to read effectively on their own. To some teachers this may sound like spoonfeeding. Maybe it is. However, spoonfeeding doesn't necessarily mean that you are "giving the content away." It means that you care enough to simplify the tough sledding that is ahead for students when the information in text appears too overwhelming to read. Without some simplification, students' only alternative is often to avoid textbooks altogether.

Some students will find any excuse to avoid reading. Others will read an assignment purposelessly, "getting through" to satisfy the teacher's requirements rather than their own. Nevertheless, most students do want to read but have been turned off by their experiences. If they make no attempt to read they cannot fail or be humiliated. Motivation to read is always a dimension of personality. But it is important to recognize that motivation is also the product of the classroom environment that we create. A teacher can make a "will" reader out of a "won't" reader by applying an important principle of content area reading: Students must experience satisfaction with reading before they will value it as a vehicle for learning and pleasure.

Let's see how.

LOOKING BACK, LOOKING FORWARD

This chapter provided a frame of reference for content area reading instruction. The value of reading in content areas lies in its use as a vehicle for learning. There must be a merger between teaching content (a set of ideas) and process (how to learn those ideas). The teacher's job is not to exhort students to read, but rather to show them how.

Despite the dramatic increase in enthusiasm over content area reading in the 1970s, this aspect of reading instruction has not been received with open arms by content teachers. Teaching traditions as well as teachers' conceptions of reading instruction and their role expectations have contributed to the confusion over what it means to teach reading in content areas. Once the role of the teacher is clarified, confusion will fade.

The value of balancing theory and practice in this book was also discussed. Knowing why will lead to knowing how, because understanding why is the basis for making instructional decisions. In a sense, knowing why provides the "bag" for an infinite number of instructional procedures that go beyond the practical suggestions which will be made in this book. Therefore, some brief but important insights were discussed related to reading comprehension — the heart of content area reading instruction.

What the teacher does to organize the classroom for instruction affects students' motivations. Organizing for instruction means planning in advance of action. The strategies and adjunct materials that we will study must be incorporated within carefully planned lessons, and planning lessons is the subject of Chapter 2. As you read it look for the relationships between lesson organization and classroom organization.

SUGGESTED READINGS

Adler, Mortimer. *How to read a book.* New York: Simon and Schuster, 1972.

Anderson, Richard C. "The notion of schemata and the educational enterprise." In *Schooling and the acquisition of knowledge.* Hillsdale, N.J.: Erlbaum, 1977.

Earle, Richard. *Teaching reading and mathematics.* Newark, Del.: International Reading Association, 1976.

Goodman, Kenneth. "Behind the eye: what happens in reading." In *Reading: process and program*. Urbana, Ill.: National Council of Teachers of English, 1970.

Henry, George. *Teaching reading as concept development*. Newark, Del.: International Reading Association, 1974.

Herber, Harold. *Teaching reading in content areas*. 2nd ed. Englewood Cliffs, N.J.: Prentice-Hall, 1978, chapters 1 and 2.

Lunstrum, John, and Taylor, Bob. *Teaching reading in the social studies*. Newark, Del.: International Reading Association, 1978.

Pearson, David, and Johnson, Dale. *Teaching reading comprehension*. New York: Holt, Rinehart and Winston, 1978.

Smith, Frank. *Understanding reading*. New York: Holt, Rinehart and Winston, 1978.

————. *Comprehension and learning*. New York: Holt, Rinehart and Winston, 1975.

————. *Reading without nonsense*. New York: Teachers College Press, 1979.

Thelen, Judith. *Improving reading in science*. Newark, Del.: International Reading Association, 1976.

PART ONE

Preparing for Reading: Teachers and Students

CHAPTER TWO

Organizing the Content Classroom

Ninety percent of your results come from activities that consume 10 percent of your time.

DEREK A. NEWTON

ORGANIZING PRINCIPLE

Something that isn't worth doing isn't worth doing well. This is especially true of passive and purposeless textbook reading. "Assigning and telling" are poor substitutes for content area reading instruction. Showing students how to read content material is worth doing — and worth doing well. The time it takes to organize the classroom for reading will get the results you want: active and purposeful learning of text materials. If all this is true, then the unifying principle of this chapter is clear: *Organizing for reading instruction means planning in advance of action.*

Lesson planning isn't teaching. Teaching involves putting a plan to work in actual classroom situations. What planning does, however, is give the teacher a blueprint for making decisions.

Your blueprint to the major ideas in this chapter is in the Chapter Overview. Study the interrelationships shown among some of the important ideas in the presentation. What are your expectations for the material to be presented?

The faculty room is a special kind of gathering place. Observe, sometime, the pockets of human activity that form. When they are not talking about students or trading battle stories with one another, it's not surprising to see a group of teachers staking out territory along specialty lines. They delight in talking shop. During any given "free" period English teachers might be heard discussing the current best-seller, social studies teachers hotly debating the latest world crisis, or math teachers just talking algebra.

CHAPTER OVERVIEW

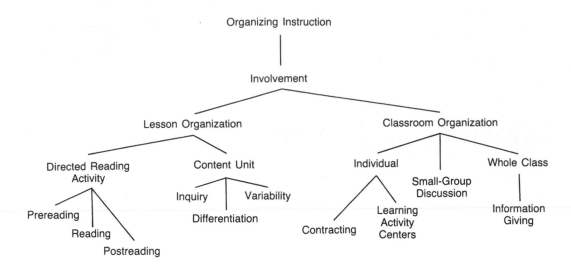

Good teachers know their subject matter. Professional competence is often judged according to how well informed and up to date a colleague is in a particular field. Good teachers also know that an intimate knowledge of a subject in itself isn't a sure ticket to success in the classroom. Another aspect of professional competence lies in "getting content across" to students.

When I first began teaching, I presumed that it was enough to wow my English classes with an impressive analysis of a literary work. It wasn't. I ran students through a miniversion of my favorite college literature seminar, and they in turn almost succeeded in running me into the ground. I quickly learned that there was more to teaching than assigning and telling.

Getting subject matter across to students is always a challenging task. The challenge is more pronounced than ever when reading becomes the vehicle for learning. To be able to show students how to read and learn actively from textbooks is never a small feat. But neither is it an impossible one.

Content teachers should organize instruction from texts for a singular purpose: to involve students actively in the reading of course materials. *Assign-read-answer-discuss* (ARAD) is a common but undistinguished practice that dominates textbook learning. Students are assigned — to read a text selection — so that they can answer several questions — that become the basis for discussion in the next class session. More often than not, ARAD stifles involvement by fostering passive, purposeless reading.

A teacher shouting a reading assignment to students as they hustle out the door at the end of the period probably continues to happen more than we would like to admit. Under these conditions the reading assignment is purposeless. Why read it? The answer students give too frequently is "because it was assigned." The only real purpose for such reading is to get through the material. Getting through is the prime motivation when the assignment lacks any sense of where students are going and how they will get there.

Answering questions at the end of the selection is an important part of the getting-through syndrome. A favorite ploy of some students is to give the teacher a three-liner — an answer to a question that fills up three lines on a sheet of paper. Whether or not the response is thought out or fully developed, three lines suffice.

The class discussion that follows such an assignment usually slips quickly away from students to the teacher. If students can't or won't learn the material through reading, they'll get it through lecture or other means.

Mark Twain wrote in *Life on the Mississippi,* "I'll learn him or I'll kill him!" The same principle applies in spirit to assign-and-tell practices in classrooms. If students learn anything, they learn that they don't have to read course material because there are alternate routes to acquiring the information. The end result is passive reading or no reading at all.

How can passive reading be turned into active reading?

Getting information across through reading demands more than assigning and telling. It requires that students act upon ideas in print. Stauffer (1975) commented that action on the part of students is a basic tenet in all learning. Students who act upon ideas as they read raise questions, make predictions, search for information, and reflect upon an author's message. The teacher's job is to activate and agitate thought. All activities, strategies, and materials presented in this book are valuable only if they serve as springboards to thinking.

Not only must students act on ideas in print, but they must also interact with each other. Social interaction provides the framework within which readers can test, confirm, or reject ideas gained from reading. Students need a social context to articulate emerging concepts. This is why Stauffer (1975) noted: "Interaction means doing things in social collaboration, in a group effort. . . . This kind of interaction can lead to a critical frame of mind. Cooperation becomes co-operation when members of a group operate individually yet jointly upon a common provoked situation" (p. 32).

Readers' interactions with one another permit them to pool knowledge and to compare understandings. And in the process of interacting they will learn something about reading. Moffett and Wagner (1976) put it this way: "A light goes on in the head of a youngster who discovers that his peers understood a story differently from the way he did or that they don't agree about some idea he believed everyone took for granted. . . . The only way he can find out is to try to understand or express something and heed others' reactions'' (p. 34).

Students who act upon ideas and interact with each other are involved in the subject matter. A reader who explains a point or justifies a response in effect shows others how to get information from the reading assignment. Students apply skills during reading; they demonstrate them during discussion.

No less important than the recognition that action and interaction are essential to learning from reading is the recognition that skilled and unskilled readers can work as intellectual equals when the teacher organizes the classroom to emphasize cooperation. A case in point illustrates how two teachers of American history teamed up to stimulate interaction among high, average, and low readers.

The two teachers, both at Lafayette High School in Williamsburg, Virginia, were dissatisfied with their students' performance during an inquiry-based unit on Colonial America (Devan et al., 1975). The students seemed to be unable to form workable hypotheses or to use library skills sufficiently to carry out the inquiry assignment. Their behavior in the media center was poor also. It was obvious to the teachers that the students were taking little interest in the assignment. To make matters worse, the feedback sessions in which students reported the results of their research efforts were little more than student lectures; many of the students just didn't participate.

What did the two teachers do differently?

After evaluating the situation, the two teachers decided that the problems in student performance and behavior were of an instructional nature. They decided they needed a way to stimulate interest and participation. So they devised a new game plan. They organized a new inquiry unit which called for differentiated research assignments on the causes of the American Revolution.

They developed four hypotheses, each related to a different cause of the Revolution and each containing a series of researchable items and events which may or may not have been associated with a particular cause. The distractor items were either completely out of historical context or did not relate to the causes under which they were grouped.

Then to each of several homogeneous groups of high, average, and low readers they assigned one of the hypotheses and a research task to complete. The high group performed at an evaluative or applied level of cognition on their inquiry task, the average group responded to an interpretive level task, and the low readers were to operate at a literal level on its research assignment.

The instructors further structured the inquiry unit by *not* telling the middle or high group about distractor items but telling the lower group of readers, who were assigned to identify and define each item. And throughout the inquiry the low readers were primed — that is, they received intense instruction on which items were related to a given hypothesis and which were not.

The teachers observed that the differentiated approach markedly improved performance during the information search in the media center. But the real payoff came during the feedback sessions when the middle and high groups were assigned to share the results of their inquiries with the low readers. It appeared that the organization of differentiated assignments, coupled with the priming of the low readers, created the "set" necessary for interaction. Here's what happened:

> With the presentation of the first distractor item by the high achieving group, the low achievement students began to question intensely the reporting group, demanding that they delineate and define the precise nature of the relationship existing between the distractor item and the hypothesis it was supposed to support. Discussion became rather heated, and at times, interest was so high that it was difficult to maintain the usual classroom atmosphere. In order to force the reporting group to defend its position, the low achievement group had to deal with the information at the same level of intellectual sophistication as did the reporting group. Instead of functioning at the literal level of comprehension, these low achieving students were now processing information at the applied level. *(Devan et al., 1975, pp. 145–146)*

Organizing the content classroom this way begins with the recognition that many problems related to content area reading *are instructional* in nature. The message behind the preceding illustration is twofold. First, the teacher should analyze conditions as they exist and then plan appropriate frameworks for instruction. Second, even supposedly poor readers will respond successfully to reading material at "higher levels" of comprehension under the proper instructional conditions. One of these conditions, as you might predict, involves the way teachers structure lessons.

LESON ORGANIZATION

What's the first thing that comes to mind when you think of lesson planning?

"That's as old as the ancient mariner."

"Restrictive!"

"Something I did way back when — during student teaching, not since."

"Picky. Picky. Picky."

I don't think any of these things, but neither will I suggest that a lesson plan must have a certain format, that objectives must be written a certain way, and so on and so forth. I will suggest that lesson organization is a blueprint for action, that having a plan in advance of actual classroom teaching is just good common sense.

The ability to organize a single lesson or a unit (a series of lessons) is a thread that runs throughout content area reading. A game plan is essential. Students respond well to structure. They need to sense where they are going and how they will get there when reading content materials. Classroom experiences without rhyme or reason won't provide the direction or stability that students need to enable them to grow as readers.

Why do students need structure?

Lessons should be general enough to include all students, and flexible enough to allow the teacher to react intuitively and spontaneously when a particular plan is put to work in actual practice. In other words, organized lessons shouldn't restrict decisions about instruction that is in progress, but instead should encourage flexibility and change.

Some teachers, no doubt, will still argue that lesson planning is an outdated, educational artifact, that it's too restrictive for today's learners. Yet I'm convinced that "to say that lesson planning is not appropriate is to say that thinking in advance of acting is inappropriate" (Mallan and Hersh, 1972, p. 41). Good lesson planning is a framework for making decisions — nothing more, nothing less.

Planning a Lesson

There's no one way to plan an effective content area reading lesson. Reading authorities have suggested several excellent lesson structures (Stauffer, 1975; Manzo, 1975; Herber, 1978). In this chapter you will examine what has been traditionally called the Directed Reading Lesson (DRL). The DRL offers the content teacher a fairly representative approach for lesson organization. In Chapter 7 you will also learn about two alternatives to the DRL, the Directed Reading–Thinking Activity (DR-TA) and the Guided Reading Procedure (GRP). These will be presented as oral questioning strategies because they rely heavily on teacher-student interactions. But regardless of which type of plan you use, certain provisions must be made for any reading lesson to be effective. What you do before reading, during reading, and after reading is crucial to active and purposeful reading. A discussion of the DRL clarifies this point.

THE DIRECTED READING LESSON

The DRL can help teachers plan a single lesson involving reading. A single lesson doesn't necessarily take place in a single class session; several class meeetings may be needed to achieve the instructional objectives of the lesson. Nor does each

How does a DRL work?

component of a DRL necessarily receive the same emphasis for any given reading assignment; the difficulty of the material, students' familiarity with the topic, and teacher judgment all play a part in deciding upon the sequence of activities you will organize. What the DRL tells you is that readers need varying degrees of guidance. There are prereading, reading, and postreading activities which will improve comprehension as well as increase students' understanding of how that information can be gotten through reading. The components of a DRL can be examined in Figure 2–1.

Figure 2–1. *The Directed Reading Lesson in Content Areas*

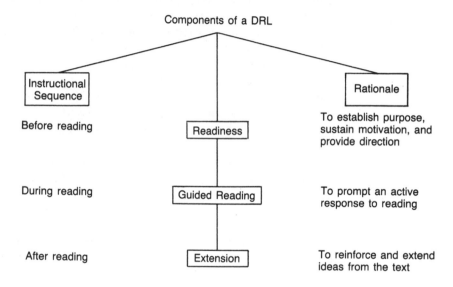

Readiness. A DRL which includes activity and discussion before reading reduces the uncertainty that students bring to an assignment and gets students ready to read. That is, it prepares readers to approach the material in a critical frame of mind so that as they read they will seek answers to questions they have raised about the reading assignment. The major limitation of assigning reading without prereading activity is evident in the observation that Harste (1978) made:

Why create readiness to read?

> The old, but still common practice of giving a reading assignment in preparation for a discussion is, unfortunately, backwards. Because what the reader brings to the process greatly influences what he/she gets out of the process, teachers can ensure more successful processing of print through the reverse procedure — discussion first, reading second. *(p. 22)*

Here is an example of how a teacher of sophomore English encouraged prereading discussion of William Cullen Bryant's poem "Thanatopsis." Before assigning the poem the teacher had students complete the exercise in Box 2–1. After completing the exercise the students formed small groups and discussed their responses to it. The students recognized that they disagreed on certain items; the teacher agitated; she required them to justify their responses. The small-group discussions were lively. Next the teacher polled the whole class so that students would get some idea of the pattern of their responses. The students wondered why some of the statements achieved greater consensus than others. The three students who agreed with statement 5 were asked to reflect upon the reasons for their agreement. Oddly enough, they had totally different answers.

Next the teacher gave some pertinent background information that led to Bryant's writing of the poem. She asked whether anyone knew what the title meant. Then the class analyzed the structure of the word. The teacher made the connection between the exercise the students had completed and the poem. Then she said, "As you read the poem some of the ideas on death that we have discussed will be expressed by the poet. Which ones? Read to find out." Now the stage was set for reading the poem.

Since the 1960s, readiness to read has been studied from many perspectives. Insights have emerged; promising prereading procedures have been developed. How to involve students in prereading discussion is one of the subjects of Part I of this book. The classroom example on "Thanatopsis" gives you a preview of the activities and materials that you will study in Chapter 4. Arousing curiosity and making predictions about upcoming reading material are integral to prereading. In Chapter

---

Box 2–1

ON "THANATOPSIS"

Directions: Read the following statements and check the ones with which you agree. After you have checked the statements discuss your responses with members of your group.

__ 1. Death is inevitable, so there is no need to fear it.

__ 2. Nature can comfort a person facing death.

__ 3. It is important to accept death as a natural occurrence.

__ 4. You should not worry about whether others will mourn your death.

__ 5. Death is like a pleasant dream.

__ 6. A person fears death because it is unknown.

__ 7. Mourning one who dies will not bring that person back to life.

__ 8. When a person dies, others continue their lives as usual.

3 you will study prereading activities which lay the groundwork for concept development through the presentation and teaching of key vocabulary terms.

Guided Reading. A content area reading lesson may also include provisions for guiding the search for and retrieval of information during reading. In other words, students

Why guide reading?

need to be shown how to think through print. Teachers easily recognize the important parts of a text assignment. Most students don't. Instead, they tend to read (if indeed they read at all) every passage in every chapter in the same monotonous manner. Each word, each sentence, each paragraph is treated with equal reverence. No wonder a distance exists between the reading material and the student.

Guidance during reading bridges the gap between students and textbook assignment so that students can learn how to read selectively, to distinguish important from less important ideas, perceive relationships, and to respond actively to meaning.

A junior high science teacher assigned to his class a chapter entitled "Health Facts About Smoking." After some initial prereading discussion he passed out a reading guide to accompany the assignment. First he told the class to preview the guide. Then he directed them to fill in the blanks in the guide as they read the chapter. The postreading discussion focused on the statements in the guide (see Box 2–2).

Box 2–2

HEALTH FACTS ABOUT SMOKING

I. *Directions:* Complete each statement to make it a true one.

1. Smoking affects the various _____ .
2. The most noticeable factor concerning the shorter life span of the American male is _____ .
3. The taste buds are affected by _____ .
4. A smoker's heart must work harder due to increased _____ content.
5. The danger of the respiratory system for the smoker is the _____ , where most _____ .
6. Fingers, teeth, and nails become _____ .
7. If my son weighed less than normal at birth, it was because _____ .

II. Directions: Check those statements you think the author of the chapter would agree with.

— 1. A couple of cigarettes each day can't hurt you.
— 2. Heavy smoking causes damage to the body that can never be repaired.
— 3. Smoking generally affects most of the body's functions.
— 4. Smoking helps you digest food better after a meal.
— 5. Smoking helps you lose weight. This is why skinny people are healthier.

— 6. The life expectancy of children has increased because of better health and medical advances.

— 7. A comparison of smoking trends in various countries shows that American men smoke too much.

III. *Directions:* Check those statements with which you agree.

— 1. The only good cigarette is a dead cigarette.

— 2. You go around life only once, so grab all the "gusto" you can get.

— 3. You die when you die, so smoking can't shorten your life.

Numerous examples of reading guidance like this one are presented in Chapters 5, 6, and 7. In particular you will study how you can develop different kinds of reading guides to facilitate comprehension. You will also explore the effects of questions and questioning procedures on reading performance. The bridges that you build to guide reading require planning, but as students cross over them, you will find that the time spent organizing guidance activities is well worth the effort.

How does the example extend an understanding of concepts?

Extension. Ideas encountered before and during reading may need reinforcement and extension after reading. Postreading activities create the structure needed to refine emerging concepts. For example, a social studies teacher was nearing completion of a unit on Southeast Asia. She asked students to reflect upon their reading by using the activity in Box 2–3 as a springboard to discussion and writing. The writing and follow-up discussion refined and extended thinking about the ideas under study. The questions "Who is best qualified?" and "Who is the specialist in the field?" prompted students to sort out what they had learned. The teacher provided just enough structure by listing topics from various facets of Southeast Asian culture for students to focus thinking and make distinctions.

Box 2–3

SOUTHEAST ASIA

I. *Directions:* A rice farmer, a Buddhist monk, a government official, and a geographer all feel competent to speak on any of the topics listed below. Who really is best qualified? Who is the specialist in each field? On the blank line preceding each topic place the letter of the correct specialist.

(a) rice farmer
(b) Buddhist monk
(c) government official
(d) geographer

___ 1. forested regions of Thailand

___ 2. the life of Siddhartha Gautama

___ 3. amount of rice exported each year

___ 4. monsoon rains in Southeast Asia

___ 5. harvesting rice

___ 6. causes of suffering

___ 7. the art of meditation

___ 8. the Menam river basin

___ 9. amount of rice produced per acre

___ 10. pagodas in Thailand

___ 11. number of Buddhists living in Bangkok

___ 12. virtues of a simple life

___ 13. the rice festival in Bangkok

___ 14. the Temple of the Emerald Buddha

___ 15. attainment of nirvana — perfect peace

II. *Directions:* Pretend you are either the rice farmer, the Buddhist monk, the government official, or geographer. Write a paragraph in which you reveal your professional attitude toward and opinion about the approaching monsoon season.

___

The writing assignment promoted vicarious participation. Getting "into the skin" of a rice farmer, monk, government official, or geographer demanded close, purposeful attention to the specific circumstances of each. It gave students the opportunity to see and weigh an event (the coming of the monsoon season) from a particular bias, vantage point, or point of view. Daigon (1979) noted the advantage of extending thinking through writing from another point of view or in another voice: "The reader must look closely at the role he/she plays, how he/she uses language, and what special interests or moral positions must be taken into account" (p. 119).

Activities such as this one reinforce and extend understanding. In Part II you will study more about the development of adjunct materials and strategies to extend thinking. The idea behind extension is that students "do something" with the concepts that they have read about. This is why postreading discussion is important. The instructional materials and activities you will study are springboards to thinking, but they also form the basis for discussing and articulating ideas developed through reading. Ways to facilitate small-group interactions will be examined later in this chapter.

Planning a Series of Lessons

What's involved in planning a content unit?

While the DRL lends itself to a single lesson from a textbook, a *content unit* organizes instruction around a series of lessons which may include multiple reading materials. This doesn't mean that a predominant source of information such as the textbook will be excluded from a unit of study. Unit planning simply provides more options to coordinate a variety of information sources. Prereading, reading, and postreading activities become an integral part of unit teaching. When you plan a series of lessons in advance, the mesh of activities will give students a sense of continuity, and they won't get a mishmash of unrelated experiences.

Listing instructional materials and resources is an important part of preparation in planning the unit. One reason why a unit is so attractive a means of lesson organization is that the teacher can go beyond the textbook — or for that matter, bypass it. Students often welcome the respite from continuous single-text instruction. Popular books, pamphlets, periodicals, reference books, newspapers, magazines, and audio-visual materials are all potential alternate routes to acquiring information. When a teacher organizes a unit topically or thematically with variable materials, students begin to assume the lion's share of responsibility for learning.

A content analysis is a major part of teacher preparation in the development of a unit of study. The content analysis results in the *what* of learning. It elicits the major concepts and understandings that students should learn from reading the unit materials. Through content analysis, the major concepts become the objectives for the unit. Earle (1976) pointed out that it doesn't matter whether these content objectives are stated in behavioral terms or not. What really matters is that the teacher know which concepts must be taught. Therefore, it's important to decide upon a manageable number of the most important understandings to be gained from the unit. This means setting priorities; it's impossible to cover every aspect of the material that students will read or be exposed to.

A junior high science teacher's content analysis for a unit on the respiratory system yielded these major concepts to be taught:

1. Living things require oxygen.
2. Living things give off carbon dioxide.
3. Living things exchange oxygen and carbon dioxide during respiration.
4. When living things oxidize organic substances, carbon dioxide is given off.
5. When living things oxidize organic substances, energy is given off.
6. Sugars and starches are foods that store energy.
7. The respiratory system of living things is responsible for the exchange of gases.
8. Breathing is a mechanical process of living things and respiration is a chemical process that happens in the cells of living things.
9. The body uses only a certain part of the air that we take in during breathing.

Stating these content objectives forced the science teacher to select reading materials and plan the how of the unit: the instructional activities.

ORGANIZING THE UNIT

The actual organizational framework of a unit will vary. For example,

How does branching out work?

you might organize a unit entirely on a sequence of lessons from assignments from a single textbook. This type of organization is highly structured, and even restrictive in the sense that it often precludes the use of multiple text sources. However, an instructional unit can be planned so that the teacher will (1) use a single textbook to begin the unit and then branch out into multiple-text study and differentiated activities; (2) organize the unit entirely on individual or group inquiry and research; or (3) combine single-text instruction with multiple-text activities and inquiry.

Branching out provides the latitude to move from highly structured lessons to less structured ones. At the same time, the movement from single to multiple information sources exposes students to variable instructional materials that may be better suited to their needs and interests. Figure 2–2 shows the variability of a unit.

Figure 2–2. *Variability of a Content Unit*

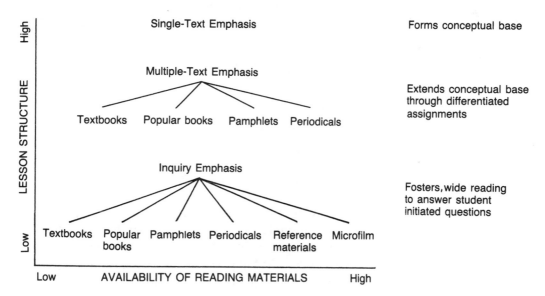

The science teacher organized the respiratory system unit following a branching-out pattern — around laboratory experiments, supplementary readings, and group research projects. The readings came from four information sources. Although students participated in the lab experiments as a whole class, the teacher devised *learning activity centers* for each of the supplementary reading materials:

center 1: Gail G. Milgram, *The teenager and smoking*. New York: Richard Rosen Press, 1972.

center 2: Arthur H. Cain, *The use and abuse of cigarette tobacco*. New York: John Day, 1964.

center 3: Luther Terry and Daniel Horn, *To smoke or not to smoke*. New York: Lothrop, Lee and Shepherd, 1969.

center 4: Bernard Glemser, *All about the human body*. New York: Random House, 1958.

On days when the learning activity centers were in operation, students would open their classroom folders and read the schedules stapled to the inside covers of the folders. This helped determine which center each student was assigned to for a particular day. The centers were equipped with directions for individual and group work. The type of activities varied within each center. Reading guides, vocabulary reinforcement exercises, and outlining activities comprised the bulk of the reading assignments. The centers also included activities for writing and the interpretation of graphic materials. (Learning activity centers are discussed more fully later in this chapter.)

As part of the unit students also participated in group projects. Some projects required little or no reading; others required a great deal. For at least half the class, the classroom library and the school's learning resource center became built-in parts of the unit. Students were allotted class time to plan, research, and present their individual and group projects. Some of the inquiry projects included the following:

1. Your group represents the earth's top scientists. You have been invited to speak at the First Annual Interplanetary Conference on Life Support Systems. How would you explain the human breathing system to nonhuman scientists at the conference?

2. Conduct a cigarette survey of your classmates', neighbors', and teachers' attitudes toward smoking. To do this you must make up a survey questionnaire. Interpret and report the results of the survey to the class.

3. Write letters to the American Cancer Society or the American Lung Association requesting information on the effects of cigarette smoking. Make a classroom display of the literature they send you. Discuss the information in the display with the class.

4. What is SCUBA? How does it work? What is meant by the bends?

5. Research and construct comparison charts of the human breathing system and two other animal breathing systems. Explain to the class how the three animal systems differ and are alike.

6. Construct a model of the human respiratory system. You might use cardboard, papier mâché, or clay.

7. Write a column for the school newspaper on the history of tobacco.

8. If you were a talking fish, how would you explain the secret of breathing underwater to an interviewer from *People* Magazine? Write the explanation in the form of an interview, with questions and responses.

The science unit followed a branching-out pattern, moving from whole-class reading and lab experimentation, to differentiated reading assignments in activity centers, to group inquiry and research projects requiring the use of multiple materials and resources.

A unit of study is a planning tool for teachers; in all likelihood it will grow with use as you modify, refine, or add on instructional activities. In planning, a teacher often finds it difficult to coordinate content objectives with reading materials and resources and instructional activities. Estes and Vaughan (1978) suggested that teachers number the major concepts in the unit and then use a cross-tabulation system.

How does cross-tabulating help to organize the unit?

A unit on spatial relationships for a high school art class provides an example of how a teacher coordinated concept objectives, activities, and materials. First she listed the major concepts to be taught in the unit:

1. Humans are aware of space about them as functional, decorative, and communicative.

2. Space organized intuitively produces an aesthetic result, but a reasoned organization of space can also lead to a pleasing outcome if design is considered.

3. Occupied and unoccupied space have positive and negative effects on mood and depth perception.

4. The illusion of depth can be created on a two-dimensional surface.

5. The direction and balance of lines and/or forms creates feelings of tension, force, and equilibrium in the space that contains them.

6. Seldom in nature is the order of objects so perfect as to involve no focal point or force or tension.

Then she cross-tabulated these concepts with the activities and materials to be used in the unit. See Table 2–1.

Table 2–1. Sample of Cross-Tabulation

		Concepts					
Activities	Materials	1	2	3	4	5	6
1. Structured overview	Collier, Graham *Form, Space, and Vision.* Prentice-Hall, 1963	x	x	x	x	x	x
2. Vocabulary and concept bulletin board		x	x	x	x	x	x
3. Prereading exercise	Chapter 3				x	x	
4. Prereading exercise	Chapters 6 and 7	x	x	x			
5. Reading guide	Chapters 6 and 7	x	x	x			
6. Reading guide	Chapter 11						x
7. Vocabulary exercise	Chapter 3				x	x	
8. Vocabulary exercise	Chapters 6 and 7	x	x	x			
9. Vocabulary exercise	Chapter 11						x
10. Student's "choice" (list of projects for independent study)	Botten, H. *Do you see what I see.* Davis, 1965. Helfman, H. *Creating things that move.* Morrow, 1975. McAgy, D. *Going for a walk with a line.* Doubleday, 1959. Kampmann, L. *Creating with space and construction.* Reinhold, 1971. Le Frevre, G. *Junk sculpture.* Sterling, 1973. Lynch, J. *Mobile design.* Crowell, 1955.	x	x	x			

Activities	Materials	Concepts 1 2 3 4 5 6
11. Hands-On:	Assortment of construction materials needed for activities	
Ink dabs		X X X
Straw painting		X X X
Dry seed arrangement		X X X
Cardboard sculpture		X X
Positive/negative cutouts		X X X
Perspective drawing		X X
Large-scale class sculpture		X
Mobiles		X
Space frames		X
12. Filmstrip	*Calder's Universe.* Miller-Brody Productions #9-MB-808	X
13. Field trip to studio of a sculptress		X
14. Field trip to museum		X X X X X X
15. Learning corner	Displays of artists' works with questionnaires to be filled out about them	X X X

For additional sample units, with descriptions of activities and materials, see Appendix D. These units have been constructed by teachers for their own use. The reading activities in each unit may be unfamiliar to you until you have studied the last two parts of this book.

THE ROLE OF INQUIRY IN THE UNIT

Explain the steps in an individual or group inquiry.

Individual and/or group research is usually the backbone of a unit. The inquiry process forms the basis for differentiating assignments and "opening the shelves" for the study of multiple instructional materials. An individual or group inquiry must be planned carefully to give the right amount of direction to allow students to explore and discover ideas on their own. The inquiry process isn't a "do your own thing" proposition; for budding inquirers need structure. Many a research project has been wrecked on the shoals of nondirection. The trick is to strike a balance between teacher guidance and student self-reliance. The inquiry process must have just enough structure to give students (1) a problem focus, (2) physical and intellectual freedom, (3) an environment where they can obtain data, and (4) feedback situations to share the results of their investigations.

Ideally, an inquiry arises out of the questions that students raise about the subject under study. A puzzling situation may arouse curiosity and interest. Or perhaps the teacher will provoke puzzlement through a discussion of differences in opinion, a reaction to inconsistencies in information in content material, or a response to an emotional issue. There are no set formulas for creating puzzlement or conceptual conflict in students. Table 2–2 lists types of questions that arouse curiosity.

Table 2–2. Questions to Initiate an Inquiry

Type of Question	Example
1. Descriptive	What happened?
2. Comparative	How is _____ different from _____ ? How are they alike?
3. Historical	What has changed from the way it used to be? What can we learn from the past?
4. Causal	What caused _____ to happen? Why did it turn out that way?
5. Prediction	What will happen next? How will it end?
6. Methodological	How can we find out?
7. Value	Which way is best?
8. Application	What does this mean to you? How does this idea apply to other situations?

SOURCE: Adapted from *Three Teaching Strategies for the Social Sciences* by B. R. Joyce, M. Weil, and R. Wald. © 1972, Science Research Associates, Inc.

As a result of questioning, students should become aware of their present level of knowledge and the gaps that exist in what they know. They can use the questioning session to identify a problem. You might ask, "What do you want to find out?" Or you might also decide to assign students research topics and problems as did the science teacher in the unit on the respiratory system.

During the planning stage of an inquiry the emphasis should be on further analysis of each individual or group problem, breaking it down into a sequence of manageable parts and activities. The teacher facilitates by helping students to clarify problems. As students progress in their research, data collection and interpretation become the integral stages of the inquiry. Students will need the physical and intellectual freedom to investigate their problems. They will also need an environment — a library or media center — where they will have access to a variety of information sources including (1) printed materials (books and encyclopedias; magazines, catalogues, directories; newspapers), (2) nonprinted materials (audiotapes; records; films, filmstrips, slides; videotapes, television programs), and (3) human resources (interviews; letters; on-site visitations).

The teacher's role during data collection and interpretation is that of a resource. Your questions will help the student interpret data or perhaps raise new questions, reorganize ideas, or modify plans. "How are you doing?" "How can I help?" "Are you finding it difficult to obtain materials?" "Which ideas are giving you trouble?"

The culmination of the inquiry is a feedback or sharing session. Feedback activities vary. They may include writing or alternative forms of composition. Individual presentations should allow for classroom interaction and participation. Whatever form it takes, sharing is a vital and stimulating result of inquiry.

The inquiry — as well as all other activities within the unit — can be initiated through different grouping patterns. Whole-class, small-group and individual learning are all important means of classroom organization. Certain activities, however, are better suited to a particular grouping pattern than others. The next section explains why.

CLASSROOM ORGANIZATION

Why small groups?

Effective classroom organization uses a combination of individual, small-group, and whole-class experiences. Small groups in particular facilitate active participation and should be a primary form of classroom organization when reading is the vehicle for learning. Students produce more ideas, participate more, and take greater intellectual risks in small-group or team learning situations. First, a small group, with its limited audience, provides more opportunity for students to contribute ideas to a discussion and take chances in the process. They can try out ideas without worrying about being wrong or sounding dumb — a fear that often accompanies risk taking in a whole-class situation. Second, team learning is generally more productive than individual learning. Estes's (1970) comparison of small-group and individual work led him to conclude that "The greater efficiency of groups as compared to individuals is a result of the opportunity for pooling ideas, providing the basis for new associations which one person might never come to alone" (p. 47).

Individualizing

Individual learning shouldn't be confused with individualized instruction. Moffett (1975) contended that individualized instruction often means "learning small things in small steps" (p. 23). Students actually complete the same program "except for some differences in pacing." Individual learning, however, in the context of this book, means providing enough differential guidance to help students read content materials successfully. Individual learning — individualizing — doesn't require a unique program for every member of the class. Nor does it suggest a different text for each student. The teacher can simply make adjustments in the lengths of reading assignments, the time given individual students to complete them, and the instructional activities related to the reading assignments.

The inquiry approach, as we saw, is one means of individualizing. The teacher's use of contracts and learning activity centers provide two additional approaches that will differentiate learning and offer students options.

CONTRACTING

A contract is an agreement between two parties — here, the teacher and the student. Both teacher and students benefit from contracting. Through a contract, the teacher can differentiate instruction according to the competence, enthusiasm, and motivation of each student. For students, contracts foster a sense of commitment and responsibility and encourage them to pursue a variety of topics and interests through variable materials.

How does contracting work?   After introducing a unit and explaining the idea of the contract, the teacher and each student decide upon an acceptable contract between them. The teacher can set the terms of the contract, or teacher and student can set them together. The activities involved in the contract should be challenging but not frustrating. Teacher and student should then decide upon beginning and ending dates, resources needed, reasons for entering the contract, and a plan which includes when and where stages of work are to be accomplished. It is essential that the student understand all responsibilities in assuming the contract. The teacher's role is flexible enough to determine the degree of independence at which each student will function. If a student cannot work independently with certain tasks or materials, you can adjust the situation accordingly, providing the needed guidance and appropriate instruction.

As part of the general agreement, students are given a choice of evaluation options. They can contract to do so many activities for an A, a B, a C, and so on, as their contract grade. A method for evaluating the quality of student work should also be negotiated, as should criteria for final evaluation. Final evaluation may be based on daily conferences, classroom presentation or exhibit, written presentation, or a variety of other means. Evaluation is a vital aspect of the contract. If a student has lived up to his or her share of the bargain, then you must follow through accordingly. A trust can't be betrayed.

As students work to fulfill their contracts the teacher shouldn't remain detached. Your job is to guide, encourage, and give individual instruction depending on the nature of the task and a student's ability to handle it successfully. Such facilitation can best be handled through conferences.

A high school English teacher initiated a six-week literature unit on adolescent growth which she called "New Awareness Through Communication." Within the unit she devised a plan that combined contractual readings with obligatory readings. She introduced the unit to her students, explaining that it would operate partly on a contractual basis. They were required to make a commitment about the amount of reading they would do. Their contract grade would be based upon the number of short stories and novels they read: the more they read, the better their grades. To receive contractual credit for their reading, the students had to report on each of their selections on a five-by-seven-inch index card, writing about some aspect of the unit theme. Each card contained the student's name, the title of the short story or novel, and a discussion of the theme with supporting evidence from the work. The teacher would not accept a plot summary.

Each Monday and Friday for four weeks students had silent reading days to do their contractual reading and complete their index cards. If they needed help in relating a story or novel to the unit theme, they could talk to the teacher.

The terms of the contract were: E = no contractual reading; D = one book, two short stories; C = one book, six short stories; B = one book, ten short stories; A = two books, ten short stories. The contract was to be fulfilled five weeks from date of signing. See Box 2–4.

As you can see, the teacher provided plenty of structure but allowed students options in the quantity and choice of readings. It would have been possible for her to have provided even less structure by letting students decide on their own the terms of their contracts and means of reporting. This teacher chose, however, to operate a half-open classroom.

LEARNING ACTIVITY CENTERS

Learning activity centers (sometimes called stations) "decentralize" the content classroom. They offer an organizational arrangement for differentiating assignments and freeing the teacher to work with students individually or in small groups. For some teachers, decentralizing the classroom means changing their outlooks and attitudes. Yet in many respects a learning center approach will give you the best of two worlds for individualizing. On the one hand, you can devise centers where students explore interests in topics and materials related to a unit of study. Activities may revolve around self-selection of reading materials, listening and viewing, sustained silent reading and writing, inquiry and exploratory study. On the other hand, you can develop activity centers which are more prescriptive in nature. Tasks that are designed with specific content objectives in mind will provide reinforcement and guidance for important concepts and skills to be developed in the unit.

The physical setting is the key to openness with stability in a classroom which organizes instruction around learning activity centers. Decentralization places a premium on classroom space, and how well it is to be utilized. Centers create a physical environment where student movement dramatically increases. Students assume responsibility for their own work; they are for the most part autonomous and self-directing.

Box 2–4

THE CONTRACT

I _____ contract to read _____ novel(s) and _____ short stories as listed below, for a contract grade of _____ .

Novel(s)	*Author*	*Teacher's Initials*
_____	_____	_____
_____	_____	_____
Short stories		
_____	_____	_____
_____	_____	_____
_____	_____	_____
_____	_____	_____
_____	_____	_____
_____	_____	_____
_____	_____	_____
_____	_____	_____

Agreed: _____ (Student)

_____ (Teacher)

This means that the physical arrangement in the classroom should be adapted to reflect the tasks that students are assigned to participate in. Therefore, let the activities themselves determine the physical setup.

Explain the operation of learning activity centers.

The secret to effective operation of learning activity centers lies in teacher organization and scheduling of students to designated activities. Four general organizational objectives must be achieved:

1. Students will operate independently in the classroom. Increased freedom means increased responsibility.

2. Students will be prepared to explain the operation of each activity center in the classroom. The teacher, therefore, should spend some planning time walking students through a demonstration of each center, explaining its purpose and operation to the class.

3. Students will conduct themselves in a manner that reflects a consideration of each individual's right to think and read in a laboratorylike setting. Noise level will increase but students must respect each other's need for concentration.

4. Students will participate in the evaluation of their own progress. As students assume responsibility for their own learning, they should also assume responsibility for self-evaluation.

Activity centers may be philosophically appealing to many teachers, but how does philosophy mesh with the everyday mechanics of operating them in the classroom? How do you start, particularly if you're accustomed to having the whole class do the same thing at the same time?

Start small. Try introducing a limited number of centers at first and then gradually expand your offerings. Also try to visualize the process in which you expect yourself and students to become involved. Vacca and Vacca (1976) developed an organizational chart (Box 2–5) to help teachers visualize the use of learning centers in their classrooms. The chart takes into account several instructional concerns which are likely to become important as you plan centers: type of activity, available reading materials, number of students assigned to each center, and criteria for student placement. The chart may be shortened or lengthened or rearranged to accommodate specific classroom situations.

The first order of business is to decide upon the type of activities in the centers. Get them down on paper. You should make decisions based on curriculum guidelines, the subject under study, and your experience. What activities are feasible and manageable given your talents and resources and the needs and interests of your students? For each center you decide on, plan activities at varying levels of difficulty to ensure that all students can succeed with some of the tasks in each center. Earle and Morley (1974) recommended that you divide tasks into required and optional categories so that students will have some leeway to choose among activities and levels of difficulty. They should also have some freedom to determine the sequence in which they work on individual activities as well as the time it takes to complete work at a center. Activities should be self-directing and self-correcting.

All activities and materials discussed in this book can be incorporated into learning activity centers in any content area. See Box 2–6 for sample learning center activities from Steurer (1978).

Box 2–5

IMPLEMENTATION CHART

	Type of Activity	*Available Materials*	*Number of Students per Class Period*	*Criteria for Student Placement*
1.				
2.				
3.				
4.				
5.				
6.				
7.				

SOURCE: Adapted from J. L. Vacca and R. T. Vacca, "Learning stations: how to in the middle grades." *Journal of Reading* 19 (1976): 563–567. Reprinted with the permission of J. L. and R.T. Vacca and the International Reading Association.

Box 2–6

SAMPLE LEARNING CENTER ACTIVITIES IN CONTENT AREAS

Art:
   Processes/following directions: rearrange mixed-up directions for making an art object.
   Terminology: match pictures with words.

Business education:
   Symbols: match them with words they represent.
   Spelling test: listen to a tape-recorded list of words, write them.
   Graphs and tables: interpret a tax schedule or balance sheet, answering questions.
   Information search: under controlled and timed conditions, glean certain information from a tape.

Driver education:
   Rules of the road: answer test questions for driver's permit.
   Safe-driving attitude survey: take written survey, listen to answers and explanations on tape.
   Road signs: match with words.

Foreign language:
   Phonetics: listen to tape recording of minimal pairs, write on answer sheet "same" or "different."

Dictation: transcribe a passage from a recording.

Listening comprehension: listen to tape, answer written questions.

Gender/case: insert correct article before nouns in sentences, check by listening to tape recording of full sentences.

Health:

Vocabulary: match drug terms with pictures and definitions.

Following directions: from illustrated sheet, learn to do particular exercises (teacher evaluated).

Concepts: answer true/false questions on practices related to eating and drinking.

Home economics:

Nutrition: match foods and proportions to make a balanced menu for four people.

Following directions: make cookies from recipe, evaluate by taste and appearance.

Finances: use newspaper advertisements and checklist to select best buys for indicated items.

Industrial arts:

Concepts: review electrical principles by true/false questions.

Introduction to concepts: take pretest on diagnostic maintenance of autos.

Vocabulary: match items in a box with technical names.

Job overview: fill in job sheet with correct steps, tools, and parts needed to rebuild a carburetor.

Language arts:

Sequence: arrange sentences of a paragraph in logical order.

Main ideas: pick topic sentences from a series of paragraphs.

Mechanics: correct mistakes in punctuation, spelling, or grammar in a paragraph (usually one skill at a time in each paragraph).

Following directions: write a formal letter, evaluate it by a checklist of important letter elements.

Mathematics:

Vocabulary: pair up roots and affixes used in math terms, test them by matching words and meanings.

Word problems: do problems, check each step on answer sheet.

Interpreting graphs: answer questions.

Symbols: match math symbols with words.

Physical education:

Reading comprehension: answer factual and inferential questions on sports articles.

Interpreting diagrams: answer questions on field hockey or basketball play diagrams.

Science:

Reading vocabulary: skim textbook chapter to find certain italicized words, copy those sentences, rewrite in own words (teacher evaluate).

Search skills: find page number where particular questions are answered.

Vocabulary: create technical terms by connecting roots and affixes.

Comprehension: write formulas into sentence form, or rewrite sentences as formulas.

Social studies:

Study: skim a chapter, answer questions about main items.

Historical relationships: arrange related events of French Revolution in proper order.

SOURCE: S. J. Steurer, "Learning centers in the secondary school." *Journal of Reading* 22 (1978): 134–139. Reprinted with permission of S. J. Steurer and the International Reading Association.

Once you decide on the number and type of activity centers, take stock of your materials to see what goes with what. The available materials column in the chart may include teacher-prepared guide exercises, vocabulary reinforcement and extension activities, visual aids, student-made items from previous classes, printed and nonprinted materials.

You will also need to decide the number of students that can participate effectively at one center and to assign students at each center. Three criteria will help you to assign students to centers:

1. Random placement: The types of activities are such that any student in the class can participate in them. For example, the teacher can randomly assign students to the reading area, the workshop area, to most centers that involve listening, viewing, and writing tasks. If the teacher varies the level of sophistication of reading tasks within a center, students can be placed at random.

2. Affective placement: The types of activities depend on students' interests, their ability to work together, personality traits, and so forth.

3. Reading level placement: If multi-level texts are available, the teacher can assign students appropriately.

Scheduling students at the learning activity centers is one of the most time-consuming but crucial tasks of the content teacher. Many teachers have found it efficient to staple a schedule to the inside front cover of each student's folder at the beginning of a new unit involving activity centers. The teacher gives each center a number and lists it on the blackboard or on a dittoed sheet. The first (and possibly the second) day of each student's schedule is blank: You can use this time to explain the directions for and operation of each center, to ask several students to select a center and describe how it functions to the rest of the class, and to have students work at centers of their own choosing. From the second or third day on, students will look at their own schedules at the beginning of a period and each will go to the center indicated for that particular day.

It's best to build a collection of centers over a long period of time, perhaps over a year or two. The commitment to a learning center approach requires a lot of time and energy. You may find centers most useful as an adjunct to more traditional classroom procedures. Steurer (1978) noted that centers "need not replace the teacher-directed format . . . Learning centers add variation to the classroom and provide activities as well as independent study" (p. 134). Centers release teachers from the role of central performer in front of large groups of students so that they can give guidance when needed and provide emphatic instruction when a situation calls for it.

Small-Group Interaction ────────────────────────────────

How does each condition influence learning in small groups?

Organizing reading around small groups shifts the burden of learning from teacher to student. Small groups are particularly well suited to guided reading discussions. However, team learning is complex. Small groups don't run by themselves. Students must know how to work together and how to use techniques they have been taught. The teacher in turn must know about small-group processes. The practical question is "How will individual students 'turn into' groups?" Anyone who has ever attempted small-group instruction in the classroom knows the dilemma associated with the question. Many conditions can confound team learning if plans are not made in advance — in particular, size, composition, goals, performance criteria, and cohesiveness.

GROUP SIZE AND COMPOSITION

The principle of "least group size" (Thelen, 1949) operates whenever you form learning teams. A group should be just large enough to include all the skills necessary to solve a problem or complete a task. A group that's larger than necessary provides less chance for individual participation and greater opportunity for conflict. If too many students are grouped together, there's bound to be a point of "diminishing returns." Group size for content area reading should range from two to six members (depending, of course, on the type of reading task). Since most small group activities will involve discussion and completion of guide materials, four-to-five-member groups are probably best.

Homogeneous grouping is often not necessary for discussion tasks. Both intellectual and nonintellectual factors will influence a small group's performance and the relationship between intelligence and small-group performance, as Davis (1969) attests, is often surprisingly low. (If this sounds like a pitch for heterogeneous discussion groups, it is.) Experiential and social background, interests, attitudes, and personality contribute greatly to the success of a small group. Grouping solely by reading or intellectual ability short-changes all students and robs discussion of its diversity.

Low-powered readers shouldn't be relegated to tasks that require minimal thinking or low-level responses to content material. What quicker way to incite riot and misbehavior than to group together students who are experiencing difficulty in reading? People learn from each other. A student whose background is less extensive than other students' can learn from them. The student who finds reading difficult needs good readers as models. Furthermore the student who has trouble reading may in fact be a good listener and thinker who will contribute significantly to small-group discussion.

The most efficient formation of heterogeneous discussion groups is through random assignment. Students can count off in intervals to yield the appropriate size for each group. For example, a class of twenty-eight can count off in intervals of seven to form four-member groups. Or students can draw numbers from a box: number one through four form a group, five through nine another group, and so forth.

GOALS AND PERFORMANCE CRITERIA

Small-group learning is goal- and task-oriented. The manner in which goals and paths to task completion are perceived affects the volume and quality of involvement by students in the group. If group goals are unclear, members' interest quickly wanes. Goals must also be directly related to the task. Roby (1968) noted that the conditions of the task must be "clearly defined with explicit objectives" and "understood and accepted by individual members" (p. 1).

Therefore, the teacher should explain criteria for task performance. For example, when students work with teacher-prepared guide materials such as those which will be suggested in this book, they should attempt to adhere to criteria such as the following:

1. Read the selection silently and complete each item on the guide individually or with others in the group, depending on the teacher's specific directions.

2. Each item should be discussed by the group.

3. If there is disagreement on any item, a group member(s) must defend his or her position and show why there is a disagreement. This means going back into the selection to support one's position.

4. No one student dominates a discussion or bosses other members around.

5. Each member contributes something to each group discussion.

As students work on reading activities in their groups, the teacher can facilitate performance by reinforcing the criteria that have been established.

COHESIVENESS

Groups lack cohesiveness when learning isn't cooperative but competitive; when students aren't interdependent on each other for learning but work independently. There are no pat answers for developing cohesiveness in small groups. But, the attempts discussed below give insight into how you can achieve cooperative and interdependent learning.

Information Intermix. Capuzzi (1973) reported the success of information intermix. The intermix procedure directs students through a series of interactions with other group members. For example, students form four-member "growth groups" in which each member is given a "concept slip" containing a short excerpt from a text. They are told to learn their concepts and then "teach" them to the rest of the group. The intermix procedure continues in a similar manner with new group formations where members are mutually dependent on one another for their learning.

Jigsaw Puzzle Method. Psychology Today magazine popularized an attempt to ease the effects of busing and racial tension in schools in Austin, Texas, by making students dependent on each other for learning required materials (Aronson et al., 1975). Interdependent learning of text materials was achieved through the jigsaw-puzzle method, an activity that manipulated the way students responded to curriculum-based materials. Here's an example of jigsaw learning in action. A six-paragraph biography on the life of Joseph Pulitzer contained a major aspect of Pulitzer's life in each paragraph. The biography was then cut into six sections with one paragraph given to each member of a learning group. Because each student had no more than one-sixth of the biography, each was dependent on all the others to complete the picture. The jigsaw groups were cooperative because members had to work together to learn the materials for which they were responsible.

Individual-Group Grade System. Vacca (1977) reported the influence of interdependent small groups in a social studies class. The teacher attempted to have students adhere to desired discussion behaviors during their interactions in small groups (these discussion behaviors were basically the same as those discussed in the previous subsection under performance criteria). Each small group earned a performance grade for discussing reading assignments in a six-week instructional unit. Here's how the group members earned their grades.

1. Each member in the group was observed by the teacher to see how well the desired discussion behaviors were exhibited.

2. On Friday of a week, each group earned a color reward worth so many points: green = 1 point; blue = 2 points; black = 3 points; red = 4 points. The color that a group earned was based on how well it had performed according to the criteria for discussion.

3. Each member of the group received the color (and the points that went with it) that the total group earned. This meant that if one or two members of the group did not carry out the appropriate discussion behaviors, the entire group was penalized.

4. The color for each student in the class was charted on a learning incentive chart.

5. Each week the small groups changed composition by random assignment.

6. The points attached to each color added up over the weeks. When the unit was completed, so many points resulted in a performance grade of A, B, C, or D.

A curious thing happened as a result of the reward system. On the Monday of each week that students were randomly assigned to new groups, they immediately went to the learning incentive chart to check the color received the previous week by each of the other members in their new group. Motivation was high. Group pressure was such that individual students who did not receive high points the previous week were intent on improving their performance in the new group.

I believe the main reason for the infrequent use of small groups is the frustration that teachers experience when teams lack cohesion. Uncooperative groups are a nightmare. No wonder a teacher abandons or is hesitant to use small groups in favor of whole-class instruction, which is easier to control. Small-group instruction requires risk taking on the part of the teacher as much as it encourages risk taking among students.

Whole-Class Instruction

As a means of classroom organization, whole-class instruction is significant because of its efficiency. A whole-class presentation is an economical means of giving information to large groups of students. A whole-class presentation can be used to set the stage for a new unit of study. The unit introduction, discussion of objectives, background building, and informal evaluation can all take place within the whole-class structure.

What are some advantages and disadvantages of whole-class instruction?

The chief limitation of whole-class instruction is that it limits active participation among students. While whole-class interaction provokes discussion to an extent, it cannot produce the volume of participation necessary to read and learn actively from content materials. The teacher often reverts to showmanship to enlist the active participation of the majority of students in a whole-class discussion. I often used to wonder why many teachers ended each working day totally exhausted. Although a little showmanship never hurt a lesson, no burden seems more difficult to carry or mentally fatiguing than to feel the need to perform in order to get students involved in learning.

LOOKING BACK, LOOKING FORWARD

Content area teachers can organize for reading by planning instruction that will lead to active textbook learning. Students must act upon ideas in print but also interact with each other when studying, and so lesson organization is an important part of content area reading. The directed reading lesson and the unit plan provide the structure for teaching reading in content areas.

The directed reading lesson makes provisions for prereading, guided reading, and postreading instruction for a single lesson. The unit plan helps you to coordinate a series of reading lessons. It gives you much more latitude to coordinate instructional resource materials and activities. Unit activities can be organized around the whole class, small groups, or individuals. An effective content classroom combines all three grouping patterns to meet the individual and group needs and interests of students.

The next chapter deals with an important part of readiness to read. Content area vocabulary terms — the special and technical words of a subject — are labels for concepts. Vocabulary instruction which precedes reading can lay the groundwork for concept development. Many suggestions for vocabulary study lie ahead. As you read the chapter be prepared to classify information under three major categories: vocabulary presentation, vocabulary building, and vocabulary awareness.

SUGGESTED READINGS

Estes, Thomas, and Vaughan, Joseph, Jr. *Reading and learning in the content classroom*. Boston: Allyn and Bacon, 1978, chapters 9 and 15.

Hanna, Lavone, et al. *Unit teaching in the elementary school*. New York: Holt, Rinehart and Winston, 1963.

Mallan, John, and Hersh, Richard. *No g.o.d.s in the classroom: inquiry into inquiry*. Philadelphia: W. B. Saunders, 1972.

Miles, Matthew. *Learning to work in groups*. New York: Teachers College Press, 1973.

Moffett, James, and Wagner, Betty Jane. *Student-centered language arts and reading, k-13*. Boston: Houghton Mifflin, 1976.

Smith, Carl, Smith, Sharon, and Mikulecky, Larry. *Teaching reading in secondary school content subjects*. New York: Holt, Reinhart and Winston, 1978, chapters 12 and 13.

CHAPTER THREE

Laying the Groundwork for Vocabulary and Concepts

I am a Bear of Very
Little Brain and long
words Bother me.

A. A. MILNE: *WINNIE-THE-POOH*

ORGANIZING PRINCIPLE _____

Vocabulary is as unique to a content area as fingerprints are to a human being. A content area is distinguishable by its language, particularly the special and technical terms which label the underlying concepts of its subject matter. No wonder Dale (1975) noted that to master a content area "is to learn its key concepts; that is, its language" (p. 12).

Yet I wonder how many middle and secondary students feel about long words as does Winnie-the-Pooh. Words — whether they be strange sounding, weird looking, or just plain sesquipedalian in nature — needn't be bothersome to students. There are things that a teacher can do to help students acquire word meanings.

Teaching vocabulary in content areas can't be incidental or accidental. It must be planned. The organizing principle of this chapter suggests why this is so: *The study of content terminology lays the groundwork needed to explore and develop concepts which are an integral part of a unit of study.*

What can a teacher do to lay the groundwork for concept development? Examine the Chapter Overview, then begin the chapter. As you read, refer back to the overview on occasion and flesh it out — that is, relate the instructional options and techniques you will be studying to the various terms. These terms are labels for the key concepts that you will encounter in this chapter.

CHAPTER OVERVIEW

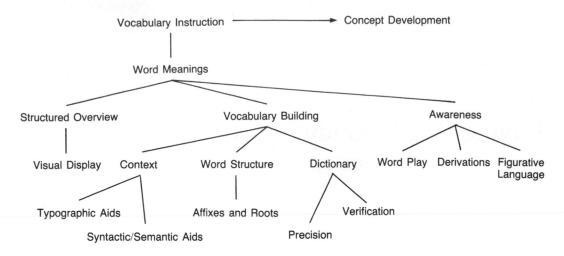

Fridays always seemed to be set aside for quizzes when I was a student. And one of the quizzes most frequently given was the vocabulary test.

"Look up these words for the week. Write out their definitions and memorize them. And then use each one in a complete sentence. You'll be tested on these terms on Friday."

The extent of vocabulary study for me seemed to consistently revolve around the deadly dull routines associated with looking up, defining, memorizing, and using words in sentences that never quite achieved a state of completeness.

Discussions with content teachers over the past decade led me to believe that the predominant approach to vocabulary study today continues to be some form of the look-up–define–memorize–use strategy. Many teachers express the futility of teaching words in such a narrow and paltry manner but ask, "What else is there?"

Classroom teachers often view vocabulary instruction separately from concept development. Vocabulary means teaching a corpus of words rather than grasping word meanings that will lead to the development of concepts. The distinction is subtle but important. Once teachers clarify the relationship between vocabulary and concept development, they are receptive to instructional options and alternatives.

One clarification that's quickly made involves the types of reading vocabulary found in textbooks. Three types of vocabulary are evident. The first type, *general vocabulary,* consists of everyday words having widely acknowledged meanings in common usage. The second, *special vocabulary,* is made up of words from everyday, general vocabulary which take on specialized meanings when adapted to a particular content area. The third type, *technical vocabulary*, consists of words which have usage and application only in a particular subject matter field.

For a number of reasons, special and technical terms are particularly

Why do special and technical vocabulary need to be taught?

bothersome when they're encountered in content material. Your participation in the demonstration in Box 3–1 will help me illustrate why special and technical terms are likely candidates for vocabulary instruction in content areas.

If your responses are similar to those of a number of classroom teachers who have participated in this activity, several predictable outcomes are likely.

First of all, it was relatively easy for you to identify the content areas for several of the lists. Your knowledge and experience probably triggered instant recognition. You have a good working concept of many of the terms on these "easy" lists. You can put them to use in everyday situations that require listening, reading, writing, or speaking. They are your words. You own them.

Second, you probably recognized words in a few of the lists even though you may not be sure about the meanings of individual words. In lists 4 and 9, for example, you may be familiar with only one or two terms. Yet you are fairly sure that the terms in lists 4 and 9 exist as words despite the fact that you may not know what they mean. Dale (1975) commented that your attitude toward these kinds of words is analogous to your saying to a stranger, "I think I've met you before but I'm not sure." Several of the words from the lists may be in your "twilight zone"; you have some knowledge about them, but "their meanings are a bit foggy, not sharply focussed" (Dale, 1975, p. 24). *Polyunsaturated* in list 7 is a case in point for some of us who have heard the word used in television commercials and may even have consciously sought polyunsaturated foods at the supermarket. Nevertheless, my guess is that we would be hard pressed to define or explain the meaning of *polyunsaturated* with any precision.

Finally, in one or two cases a list may have completely stymied your efforts at identification. There simply was no connection between your existing knowledge and any of the terms. You probably are not even sure whether the terms in one list really exist as words. Perhaps list 6 fell into this category?

Your participation in this activity leads to several points about

What does the demonstration point out?

vocabulary instruction and concept development in content areas. The activity is a good reminder that every subject matter field creates a unique language to represent its important concepts. Words are just labels — nothing more or less — for these concepts. All the words on the lists (with the exception of list 6) represent concepts. But, remember, a concept is

Box 3–1

VOCABULARY DEMONSTRATION: WORDS IN CONTENT AREAS

Directions: In each of the ten blanks, fill in the name of the content area that includes all the terms in the list below.

1. _____

nationalism
imperialism
naturalism
instrumentalism
isolationist
radicalism
fundamentalist
anarchy

2. _____

forestry
ornithology
zoology
biology
entomology
botany
bacteriology
protista

3. _____

metaphor
allusion
irony
paradox
symbolism
imagery
simile

4. _____

prestissimo
adagio
larghetto
presto
allegro
largo
andante
tempo

5. _____

centimeter
milligram
deciliter
millisecond
kilometer
decimeter
kilogram
millimeter

6. _____

graffles
folutes
lesnics
raptiforms
cresnites
hygrolated
loors
chamlets

7. _____

polyunsaturated
glycogen
monosaccharide
hydrogenation
enzymes
lyzine
cellulose

8. _____

octagon
hemisphere
decagon
hexagon
bisect
equilateral
quadrilateral
pentagon

9. _____

auricle
ventricle
tricuspid
semilunar
apex
mitral
aorta
myocardium

10. _____

intensity
complementary
hue color neutrals
trial
value
pigments

SOURCE: Adapted from a workshop exercise developed by Robert Baker at Illinois State University.

usually much more than the meaning of a single word. It may take thousands of words to explain a single concept. The systematic study of content area vocabulary, therefore, is a must. Students shouldn't be left to their own devices or subjected to the vagaries of a look-up–define–memorize–use strategy to develop word meanings for key terms.

The definition of a special or technical term can undoubtedly be learned by rote without approaching a conceptual level of understanding. Gagné (1970) said, "An edge might be defined as a 'region of abrupt change in intensity of the pattern of light waves reflected to the eye from a surface.' It should not be supposed that this kind of verbalizing would be very effective in bringing about the learning of a concept" (p. 177). Retaining a definition of a technical term, however, is often a necessary first step in learning abstract concepts. Although you may have been able to define many of the words on the lists, your ability to conceptualize them, to apply them in a variety of ways, may be limited.

Which content area did you identify for list 6? In truth, the terms in this list represent jabberwocky — nonsense. They are bogus words which were invented to illustrate the point that many of the content terms in textbooks look the same way to students that the nonsense words in list 6 looked to you. You were able to pronounce most of them with little trouble but were stymied when you tried to connect them to your knowledge and experience. Students are stymied this way every day. But they are stymied by real words which represent the key concepts of a content area.

The words in these lists were actually taken from middle and high school textbooks. Just think for a moment about the staggering conceptual demands that we place on adolescent learners daily as they go from class to class. Terminology that they encounter in content material is often outside the scope of their normal speaking, writing, listening, and reading vocabularies. Special and technical terms often do not have concrete referents; they are abstract and must be learned through definition, application, and repeated exposure.

This is why teaching vocabulary in content areas is too important to be incidental or accidental. As a teacher you should plan vocabulary study around the reading of course materials in a unit. In doing so you will be able to influence the development of word meanings and concepts before and after reading. This chapter concerns itself primarily with instruction before students encounter vocabulary terms in content material. The emphasis in Chapter 9 is on vocabulary reinforcement primarily after exposure to content terms in unit material.

The prereading phase of vocabulary study provides the opportunity to 1) show students the interrelationships that exist among key concepts, 2) create an interest and awareness in content area words, and 3) illustrate principles that will lead to independence in vocabulary building.

INTRODUCING VOCABULARY RELATIONSHIPS _____

At the start of each chapter I have asked you to organize your thoughts around the main ideas in the text. These ideas are presented within the

Explain the purpose of a structured overview.

framework of a structured overview (or graphic organizer, as it is sometimes called) — a chart which uses content vocabulary to help students anticipate concepts and their relationships to each other in the reading material. These concepts are displayed by arranging key technical terms relevant to the important concepts to be learned. As Figure 3–1 shows, the graphic outline that results shows the hierarchical nature of the concepts to be studied. A concept may be designated as *superordinate, coordinate,* or *subordinate* depending on its relationship to other concepts.

Figure 3–1. *Hierarchical Relationships Among Concepts*

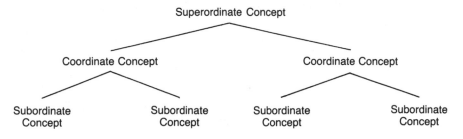

Thelen (1979) illustrated a hierarchical arrangement of mathematical concepts having similar attributes and characteristics. See Figure 3–2.

Figure 3–2.

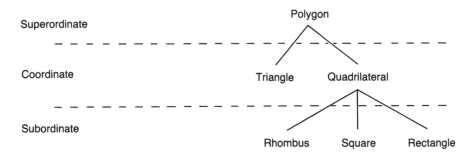

The concept *quadrilateral* is subordinate to *polygon,* coordinate to *triangle,* and superordinate to *rhombus, square* and *rectangle. Polygon* is the most inclusive concept and subsumes all of the others.

A structured overview is a prereading activity which has its roots in Ausubel's theory of meaningful reception learning. A structured overview always shows vocabulary in relation to more inclusive vocabulary concepts. The diagram showing the hierarchical arrangement among vocabulary terms acts as an advance organizer — that is, readers develop a set to learn in advance of the text material. Ordinarily, an advance organizer is a short written passage that students read before reading a larger text selection. The structured overview, however, is a special case of the advance organizer. Let's take a closer look at its construction and application in the classroom.

Constructing the Structured Overview

Describe each step.

Barron (1969) suggested the following steps for developing the structured overview and introducing the vocabulary diagram to students:

1. Analyze the vocabulary of the learning task and list all the words that you feel are important for the student to understand.

2. Arrange the list of words until you have a scheme which shows the interrelationships among the concepts particular to the learning task.

3. Add to the scheme vocabulary terms which you believe the students understand in order to show relationships between the learning task and the discipline as a whole.

4. Evaluate the overview. Have you clearly shown major relationships? Can the overview be simplified and still effectively communicate the idea you consider to be crucial?

5. Introduce the students to the learning task by showing them the scheme and telling them why you arranged the terms as you did. Encourage them to contribute as much information as possible to the discussion of the overview.

6. As you complete the learning task, relate new information to the overview where it seems appropriate.

Suppose you were to develop a structured overview for a text chapter in a psychology elective in a high school social studies program. Let's walk through the steps involved.

1. *Analyze the vocabulary and list the important words.* The chapter yields these words:

hebephrenia	neurosis	personality disorders
psychosis	schizophrenia	catatonia
abnormality	mental retardation	phobias

2. *Arrange the list of words.* Choose the word that represents the most inclusive concept, the one superordinate to all the others. Then choose the words classified immediately under

the superordinate concept and coordinate them with each other. Then choose the terms subordinate to the coordinate concepts. Your diagram may look like Figure 3–3.

Figure 3–3

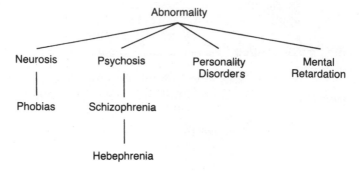

3. *Add to the scheme vocabulary terms which you believe the students understand.* You add the following terms: *antisocial, anxiety, intellectual deficit, Walter Mitty, depression, paranoia.* Where would you place these words on the diagram?

4. *Evaluate the overview.* The interrelationships among the key terms may look like Figure 3–4 once you evaluate the vocabulary arrangement.

Figure 3–4

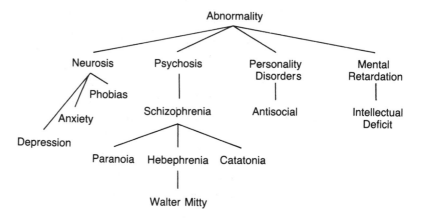

5. *Introduce the students to the learning task.* As you present the vocabulary relationships shown on the structured overview, create as much discussion as possible. Draw upon students' understandings and experiences with the concepts the vocabulary terms label. You might have students relate pre-

vious study or learnings to the terms. For example, *Walter Mitty* is subsumed within *hebephrenia*. If students were familiar with James Thurber's short story "The Secret Life of Walter Mitty," they would have little trouble bringing meaning to *hebephrenia* — a schizophrenic condition characterized by excessive daydreaming and delusions. The discussion might also lead to a recognition of the implicit comparison-contrast pattern among the four types of abnormality explained in the text. What better opportunity to provide direction for the skills to be applied during reading than to have students visualize the pattern. The discussions you will stimulate from the structured overview will be worth the time it takes to construct it.

6. *As you complete the learning task, relate new information to the overview.* This is particularly useful as a study and review technique. The overview becomes a study guide that can be referred to throughout the discussion of the material. Students should be encouraged to add information to flesh out the overview as they develop concepts fully.

Classroom Examples of the Structured Overview ━━━━━━━━━━━━━━━━━━━━

What clues do the classroom illustrations give for constructing a structured overview?

A structured overview can show the relationships in an entire text, in a unit covering several chapters, in one chapter, or in a subsection of a chapter. The classroom scenario that follows provides further insight into its utility as a prereading vocabulary activity.

An eighth grade social studies teacher constructed the structured overview in Figure 3–5 for twelve pages of his text. The purpose of the structured overview was to introduce students to the propaganda terms used in the textbook. Before having the class read the assigned pages, he placed the overview on the board and asked his class to copy it into their notebooks for future reference. Then he explained that propaganda is a word used to describe one way people try to change the opinions of others. He gave an example or two and then asked students to con-

Figure 3–5. *Structured Overview*

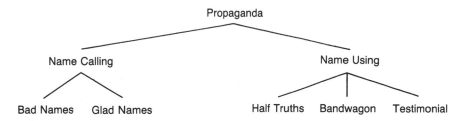

tribute other examples. As part of the development of the concept of propaganda, with the help and participation of students, he derived explanations for all the methods shown in the overview. As these explanations developed, students also saw how each method related to the two categories Name Calling and Name Using. The explanations which developed are as follows:

1. Bad names: calling a person an unpleasant name to make people feel angry or fearful. No facts are given about the person.

2. Glad names: calling a person a pleasant name to make people feel good. No facts are given about the person.

3. Half truths: presenting only good or only bad information about something or someone. Only one side of the story is told.

4. Bandwagon: telling people that "everyone is doing it" to get them to follow the crowd.

5. Testimonial: getting a well-known person to say he or she likes or dislikes something or someone.

The students recorded these definitions in their notebooks. At this point they began to grasp the difference between methods and started to give examples of propaganda they saw being used in advertising. Then the teacher gave them nine sentences and asked them to identify the propaganda method used in each:

1. "Everyone in town is going to vote for Dan Ray."

2. "The present leaders are criminals and should be put in jail."

3. "She is a noble woman, capable in every way."

4. "As a football player, I know how important it is to wear Brand X hair cream."

5. "The young fighter is faster than the champ and will win the fight."

6. "My opponent is a coward, afraid of solving problems."

7. "Before my TV show, I always use Brand X toothpaste."

8. "Come to the fair and see everyone you know."

9. "The new political party is well organized. It will win the election."

Sentences 2 and 6 prompted considerable discussion as to whether the method was bad names, half truths, or both. After completing this exercise the students read the assigned pages of the text. The reading went rapidly, because the students quickly recognized the different methods of propaganda used in the textbook. The class discussion that followed was lively: the students were confident of their decisions and were eager to share them with their peers. According to the teacher, the lesson had a lasting effect on the students: in subsequent lessons not dealing specifically with propaganda they recognized the use of propaganda and shared it with the rest of the class.

So much for the testimonial of one teacher. As you study the following illustrations consider the adaptations that might be made if you were to develop a structured overview for material in your content area.

Business. The overview in Figure 3–6 was developed for a high school class in data processing. It introduced students to the different terms of data processing, delineating causes and effects.

Figure 3–6. *Structured Overview*

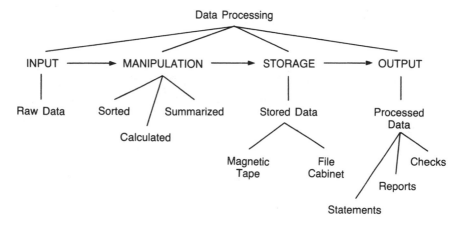

Art. With Figure 3–7 an art teacher showed the relationships among key concepts associated with firing ceramics.

Figure 3–7. *Structured Overview*

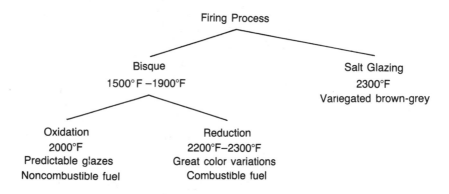

Figure 3–8. *Structured Overview: Ways the Author Develops a Character*

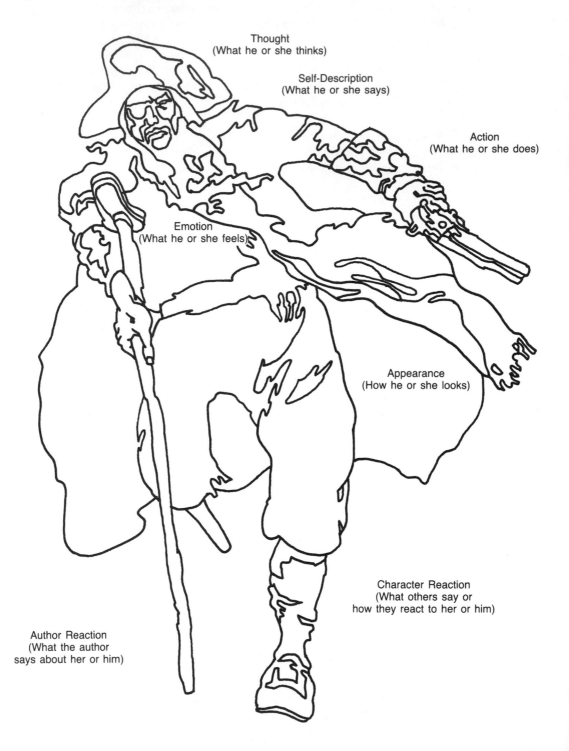

Thought
(What he or she thinks)

Self-Description
(What he or she says)

Action
(What he or she does)

Emotion
(What he or she feels)

Appearance
(How he or she looks)

Character Reaction
(What others say or
how they react to her or him)

Author Reaction
(What the author
says about her or him)

English. A teacher of ninth-grade English students studying character analysis and development in short fiction made the pictorial structured overview in Figure 3–8. During discussion of the overview, students referred to a short story they had read to provide examples.

Science. A biology teacher depicted the chemical nature of human digestion in his structured overview of human digestion (Figure 3–9). The initial discussion considered the distinction between the concepts *physical stimulus* and *hormonal control*. As a result of the class discussion, students developed a framework for organizing the ponderous information in the text chapter.

Figure 3–9. *Structured Overview*

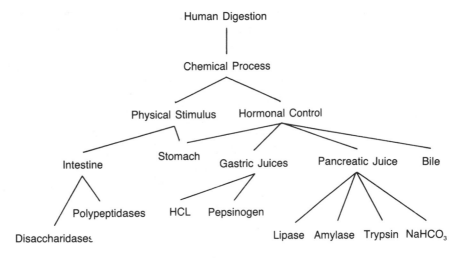

A concluding comment: use the structured overview to show relationships and to teach one or two words in detail before students encounter them in the reading assignment. The words you choose for teaching should represent important concepts. Make every attempt to draw upon students' knowledge and experience. Point out their misconceptions by providing good examples. It's worthwhile to spend a few minutes carefully developing background for a difficult concept that appears on the structured overview.

VOCABULARY BUILDING

Why develop vocabulary-building skills?

You should teach and reinforce vocabulary skills to show students how to inquire into the meanings of unknown words. Demonstrating how to use several basic tools of inquiry — context analysis, structural analysis, and use of the dictionary — builds vocabulary principles which will guide students for a lifetime. With these tools readers can seek clues to word meanings on their own. These clues often reveal enough meaning to allow students to continue reading and not "short-circuit" when they encounter an unknown word.

In short, vocabulary building should show students how to use written language to get clues to meaning during reading. As we saw in Chapter 1, Goodman (1976) contended that reading is a language-based process in which the reader attempts to reconstruct a message which approximates the one the author intended. A reader can therefore be viewed as a user of language whose task is to make sense from what he or she reads.

Do you recall the "Kingdom of Kay Oss" passage from Chapter 1? I used that passage to point out that readers have available three language systems which interact to cue meaning for them as they read: the grapho-phonic system, the semantic system, and the syntactic system. These three systems are formally but briefly described as follows:

1. *The grapho-phonic system.* This system provides readers with graphic (letter) symbols to which they can associate appropriate sounds (phonemes). The grapho-phonic system refers to relationships between letters and sounds. Grapho-phonic cues are within words. In and of itself, this system gives no clues to meaning. Consider the very first time you encountered the word *cat.* You may have tried to associate an individual sound for each letter: *k, a, t.* Or, perhaps more realistically, you perceived a cluster of letters: either *ka-t,* or *k-at,* or *kat.*

2. *The semantic system.* This system enables readers to anticipate words through what is commonly called context, or to build meaning for new words. The semantic system represents cues within the reader, such as his or her conceptual background, knowledge, and experience. Such cues within the reader serve as a basis for deciding whether or not what is read makes sense.

3. *The syntactic system.* This system enables readers to use their intuitive knowledge of grammar to anticipate certain types of words which "must come next" because of the restrictions of English syntax. Syntactic cues are within the flow of language. This system, therefore, refers to relationships that words, sentences, and paragraphs have to each other. Information from syntactic cues aids the reader in dealing with contextual meaning.

Explain the why and how of modeling.

Note that there is information within readers — especially their conceptual background and experience and their knowledge of language. And this is precisely why they can inquire into the meaning of an unknown technical term. Teachers can show students how to use information clues effectively by modeling appropriate meaning-getting strategies. Modeling provides insights into how to use context, a word's structure, or the dictionary to reveal sufficient meanings for difficult terms met in reading.

For example, you can guide students in the use of one or more of the vocabulary building skills before assigning material to be read. If a technical term (or more than one) in the material to be studied lends itself to a short demonstration, the teacher can walk students through the process necessary to derive meaning. As we will see in the following sections, these modeling demonstrations are brief and teacher directed. Often a walk through takes no more than four or five minutes and makes use of visuals such as an overhead transparency or the chalkboard. As students are assigned to read, they are directed to practice and apply the meaning-getting strategy that was modeled.

Let's take a closer look at some of the specifics involved in vocabulary building.

Context Analysis

Getting meaning from context is the major tool at the command of readers. It involves using information surrounding a troublesome word to help reveal its meaning. Every reader makes some use of context automatically. Instruction is needed, however, in cases where the author provides a deliberate context to help the reader with content area terminology that is especially difficult. Dulin (1970) suggested that

> as students progress in school and begin to encounter mature, technical, content-oriented reading materials, a different kind of contexual aid begins to appear. This occurs when an author or editor, consciously anticipating that a new word will be troublesome, purposely provides helpful context. Here the reader faces a true, deliberate context clue . . . and here he must know specifically how to approach it. *(p. 440–441)*

Even though textbook authors may consciously or unconsciously use deliberate contexts for unknown words, constraints in the material itself and/or the reader's own background limit the degree to which context reveals word meaning. The teacher and students must know how context operates to limit meaning as well as to reveal it.

Deighton (1959, 1970) identified several factors which limit the use of context: (1) what a context may reveal to a particular reader depends on the reader's experience; (2) the portion of context which reveals an unfamiliar word must be located reasonably close to the word if it is to act effectively; and (3) there must be some clear-cut connection between the unfamiliar term and the context which clarifies it.

Context analysis, as you have probably concluded, is mostly a matter of inference. Inference requires readers to see an explicit or implicit relationship between the unfamiliar word and its context or to connect what they know already with the unknown term. It can't be assumed that students will perceive these relationships or make the connections on their own. Most developing readers just don't know how to efficiently or effectively use a deliberate context provided by an author.

CONTEXTUAL AIDS

How can contextual aids be used to unlock meaning?

Several authorities have developed classifications for contextual aids (Quealy, 1969). Classification schemes help teachers identify the prevalent contextual aids that authors use in textbooks. These aids provide various kinds of information or clues to help illuminate the meaning of a troublesome word. Three kinds of information in particular are useful to readers: *typographic, syntactic,* and *semantic* aids.

Typographic Aids. Typographic or format aids make use of footnotes, italics, boldface print, parenthesized definitions, pictures, graphs, charts, and the like. A typographic aid provides a clear-cut connection and a direct reference to an unknown word. Many students tend to gloss over a typographic aid instead of using it to spotlight the meaning of a difficult term. The teacher can rivet attention to these aids with minimal expenditure of class time.

For example, consider the way a science teacher modeled a strategy for revealing the meaning of the word *enzymes,* which was presented in boldface type in the text. Before assigning a text section entitled "Osmosis in Living Cells," the teacher asked students to turn to page 241. Then he asked, "Which word in the section on osmosis stands out among the others?" The students quickly spotted the word *enzymes.* "Why do you think this word is highlighted in boldface type?" he asked. A student replied, "I guess it must be important." Another student said, "Maybe because it has something to do with osmosis — whatever that is." The teacher nodded approvingly and then asked the class to see if they could figure out what *enzymes* meant by reading this sentence: "Chemical substances called **enzymes** are produced by cells to break down large starch molecules into small sugar molecules."

The science teacher continued the modeling demonstration by asking two questions: "What are enzymes?" "What do they do?" The students responded easily. The teacher concluded the walk-through with these words: "Words that are put in large letters or boldface print are important. If you pay a little bit of attention to them as we just did, you will have little trouble figuring out what they mean. There are four other words in boldface type in your reading assignment. Look for them as you read and try to figure out what they mean."

Syntactic/Semantic Aids. Syntactic and semantic clues in content materials should not be treated separately, since one (syntactic information) usually triggers the other (semantic associations) for readers. That is to say, the grammatical relationships among words in a sentence or the structural arrangement among sentences in a passage often helps to clarify the meaning of a particular word.

Syntactic/semantic aids are much more subtle for readers than typographic aids. Dulin (1970) emphasized that, "Even bright, generally skillful readers . . . are often unable to utilize this type of context clue to best advantage without help" (p. 444). Table 3–1 presents a summary of the most frequently encountered syntactic/semantic aids.

Table 3–1.   Syntactic/Semantic Contexual Aids

Type of Aid	Explanation	Examples
1. Definition	The author equates the unknown word to the known or more familiar usually by a form of the verb *be*.	*Entomology* **is** the study of insects, and biologists who specialize in this field **are called** *entomologists*. A *critical review* **is** an attempt to evaluate the worth of a piece of writing.
2. Linked synonyms	The author pairs the unknown word with familiar synonyms or closely related words in a series.	Kunte Kinte was the victim of **cruel, evil,** *malevolent,* and **brutal** slave traders. The Congressman from Connecticut possessed the traits of an honest and just leader: **wisdom, judgment,** *sagacity.*

3. Direct description:
  Examples
  Modifiers
  Restatements
	The author reveals the meaning of an unknown word by providing additional information in the form of appositives, phrases, clauses or sentences.	Example clue: Undigested material **such as fruit skins, outer parts of grain, and the stringlike parts of some vegetables** form *roughage.*
		
		Modifier clue: *Pictographic writing,* **which was the actual drawing of animals, people and events,** is the forerunner of written language.
		
		Algae, **nonvascular plants which are as abundant in water as grasses are on land,** have often been called "grasses of many waters."
		
		Restatement clue: A billion

NOTE: Italics denote the unknown word. Boldface type represents information clues that trigger context revelation.

Type of Aid	*Explanation*	*Examples*
		dollars a year is spent on *health quackery.* **In other words, each year in the United States millions of dollars are spent on worthless treatments and useless gadgets to "cure" various illnesses.**
4. Contrast	The author reveals the meaning of an unknown word by contrasting it with an antonym or phrase that is opposite in meaning.	You have probably seen animals perform tricks at the zoo, on television, or in a circus. Maybe you taught a dog to fetch a newspaper. **But learning tricks — usually for a reward — is very different from** *cognitive problem-solving.*
		It wasn't a *Conestoga,* like Pa's folks came in. **Instead, it was just an old farm wagon drawn by one tired horse.**
5. Cause-effect	The author establishes a cause-effect relationship in which the meaning of an unknown word can be hypothesized.	The *domestication* of animals probably began when young animals were caught or strayed into camps. **As a result, people enjoyed staying with them and made pets of them.**
		A family is called *equalitarian,* **because a husband and wife will make decisions together and share responsibilities equally.**
6. Mood and tone	The author sets a mood, whether it be ironic, satirical, serious, funny, etc., in which the meaning of an unknown word can be hypothesized.	A sense of *resignation* engulfed my thoughts as **the feeling of cold grayness was everywhere around me.**
		The *tormented* animal **screeched with horror and writhed in pain** as it tried **desperately** to escape from the hunter's trap.

Teachers need to be explicit in their modeling of strategies that will help students unlock meanings of unknown words through context analysis. Often the chalkboard or an overhead transparency is invaluable in helping students visualize the inquiry process necessary to reveal meaning. For example, if a *definition aid* is used, as in this example from Table 3–1 — "Entomology is the study of insects, and biologists who specialize in this field are called entomologists" — it may be appropriate to first write the sentence on the board. During the modeling discussion, you can then show how *is* and *are called* provide information clues that will reveal meaning for *entomology* and *entomologists*. A simple strategy would be to cross out *is* and *are called* in the sentence and replace them with equal signs (=):

Entomology ~~is~~ the study of insects, and biologists who specialize in this field ~~are called~~ entomologists.

A brief discussion will reinforce the function of the verb forms *is* and *are called* in the sentence.

The definition clue is obviously the least subtle of the syntactic/semantic aids. However, all the aids in Table 3–1 require students to make inferential leaps of varying length. Consider one of the examples from the mood and tone aid: "The tormented animal screeched with horror and writhed in pain as it tried desperately to escape from the hunter's trap." Suppose this sentence came from a short story about to be assigned to a middle grade English class. Assume also that many of the students would have trouble with the word *tormented* as it is used in the sentence. If students are to make the connection between *tormented* and the mood created by the information clues, the teacher will have to ask several effective clarifying questions.

The modeling walk-through begins with the teacher writing the word *tormented* on the board. She asks, "You may have heard or read this word before, but how many of you think that you know what it means?" Student definitions are put on the board. The teacher then writes the sentence on the board, "Which of the definitions on the board do you think best fits the word *tormented* when it's used in this sentence?" She encourages students to support their choices. If none fits, she will ask for more definitions now that students have seen the sentence. She continues questioning, "Are there any other words or phrases in the sentence which help us get a feel for the meaning of *tormented*? Which ones?"

The inquiry into the meaning of *tormented* continues in this fashion. The information clues (*screeched with horror, writhed in pain, desperately*) which establish the mood are underlined and discussed. The teacher concludes the modeling activity by writing five new words on the board and explaining, "These words are also in the story that you are about to read. As you come across them, stop and think. How do the words or phrases or sentences surrounding each word help to create a certain feeling or mood that will allow you to understand what each one means?''

When modeling the contextual aids in Table 3–1, it's important for students to discover the information clues. It's also important for the teacher to relate the demonstration to several additional words to be encountered in the assignment. Instruction of this type will have a significant cumulative effect. Imagine: if students are shown how to use contextual aids for two or three words per week, over the course of an academic year they will have about eighty to one hundred twenty applications in the process.

Structural Analysis

A word itself provides information clues about its meaning. Analyzing a word's structure, therefore, is a second inquiry tool that students can use to predict meaning. Page (1975) noted that a reader encountering an unknown word can considerably reduce the number of feasible guesses about its meaning by approaching the whole word and identifying its parts. When readers use structural analysis in combination with context, they have a powerful meaning-getting strategy at their command.

A long word need not stop cold a reader who encounters it in print. Analyzing a word's structure will often produce enough meaning to allow the reader to continue. Well-timed instruction prior to reading assigned material can show students how to use word structure to advantage.

WHAT A TEACHER SHOULD KNOW ABOUT
WORD STRUCTURE

There are four categories of long or polysyllabic words identified by Olsen and Ames (1972):

*Which categories are best for modeling
structural analysis skills?*

1. Compound words made up of two known words joined together. Examples: *commonwealth, matchmaker.*

2. Words containing a recognizable stem to which an affix (a prefix, a combining form, or suffix) has been added. Examples: *surmountable, deoxygenize, unsystematic, microscope.*

3. Words that can be analyzed into familiar and regular pronounceable units. Examples: *undulate, calcify, subterfuge, strangulate.*

4. Words that contain irregular pronounceable units so that there is no sure pronunciation unless one consults a dictionary. Examples: *louver, indictment.*

Content vocabulary terms from categories 1 and 2 (compound words and recognizable stems and affixes) are the best candidates for prereading instruction. Classroom teachers can readily demonstrate techniques for predicting the meanings of these words, because each of their isolated parts will always represent a meaning unit.

In some instances, a word from category 3 may also be selected for emphasis. However, there is no guarantee that students will bring prior knowledge and experience to words that comprise the third category. Long phonemically regular words lend themselves to syllabication. Syllabication involves breaking words into pronounceable sound units or syllables. The word *undulate,* for example, can readily be syllabicated (un-du-late). However, the syllable *un* is not a meaning-bearing prefix.

Many words from category 3 are derived from Latin or Greek. Many students will find these words especially difficult to analyze for meaning because of their lack of familiarity with Latin or Greek roots. Occasionally a word such as *strangulate* (derived from the Latin *strangulatus*) can be taught because students may recognize the familiar word *strangle.* They might then be shown how to link *strangle* to the verb suffix *ate* (which means "to cause to become") to hypothesize a meaning for *strangulate.* Unfortunately, the verb suffix *ate* has multiple meanings and the teacher should be quick to point this out to students. This procedure is admittedly sloppy, but it has some payoff.

Words from category 2 warrant instruction, as English root words are more recognizable, obviously, than Latin or Greek ones. Whenever feasible, teach the principles of structural word analysis using terms that have English roots. Certain affixes are more helpful than others, and knowing which affixes to emphasize during prereading instruction will minimize students' confusion.

USEFUL AFFIXES

The most helpful affixes are the combining forms, prefixes, or suffixes which have single, invariant meanings. Deighton's (1959, 1970) monumental study of word

Should students memorize affixes?

structure has helped to identify those affixes which have single meanings. (See Appendix A for a summary of Deighton's findings.)

In addition to the single, invariant meaning prefixes, there are many commonly used prefixes which have more than one meaning or have several shades of meaning. Because of their widespread use in content terminology you should also consider these variant meaning prefixes for functional teaching. (See Appendix B for a list of prefixes with varying meanings.)

The tables of affixes are resources for you. Don't be misled into thinking that students should learn long lists of affixes in isolation because they ought to know them to analyze word structure. This approach is neither practical nor functional. Instead I recommend that students be taught affixes as they are needed: to analyze the structure of terms that will appear in a reading assignment.

For example, an English teacher modeled how to analyze the meaning of *pandemonium* before students were to encounter the term in an assignment from *One Flew Over the Cuckoo's Nest*. She wrote the word on the board — pan<u>demon</u>ium — underlining the English base word *demon* and asking students for several synonyms for the word. Student responses included *witch, devil, monster, wicked people.*

Then she explained that *-ium* was a noun suffix meaning "a place of." "Now, let's take a look at *pan*. Sheila, have you ever heard of Pan American Airlines? If you were a Pan Am passenger, name several places that you might visit." Sheila and several other students answered the question as best they could. The teacher then explained than Pan American specialized in flights to all places in the Americas. Further discussion centered around the word *panoramic*. Through this process, relating the known to the unknown, students decided that *pan* meant *all.*

"Now, back to *pandemonium*. A place of all the demons. What would this place be like?" Students were quick to respond. The demonstration was completed with two additional points. The teacher asked the class to find the place in *One Flew Over the Cuckoo's Nest* where *pandemonium* was used and read the paragraph. Then she asked them to refine their predictions of the meaning of *pandemonium*. Next the teacher discussed the origin of the word — which the English poet John Milton coined in his epic poem *Paradise Lost*. Pandemonium was the capital of Hell, the place where all the demons and devils congregated — figuratively speaking, where all hell broke loose.

Using the Dictionary

Context and structural analysis are skills which give insight into approximate meanings of unknown words. Rarely do these skills help to derive precise definitions for key words. Instead, readers use context or word structure to keep themselves in the ballpark — able to follow a writer's communication without bogging down on difficult terminology.

There are times, however, when context and word structure reveal very little, if anything, about a word's meaning. In these instances, or when a precise definition is needed, a dictionary is a logical alternative and a valuable resource for students.

Why is knowing when as important as knowing how?

Knowing when to use a dictionary is as important as knowing how to use it. A content teacher should incorporate dictionary usage into ongoing plans but should avoid a very common pitfall in the process of doing so. When asked, "What does this word mean?" the teacher shouldn't automatically reply, "Look it up in the dictionary."

For some students, "Look it up in the dictionary," is another way of saying "Don't bug me" or "I really don't have the time or the inclination to help you." Of course, this may not be the case at all. However, from an instructional point of view, that hard-to-come-by teachable moment is lost whenever we routinely suggest to students to look up a word in the dictionary.

One way to make the dictionary a functional tool is to use it to verify educated guesses about word meaning revealed through context or structural analysis. For example, if a student asks you for the meaning of a vocabulary term, an effective strategy is to bounce the question right back: "What do you think it means? Let's look at the way it's used. Are there any clues to its meaning?" Or should a difficult word have a recognizable stem and affix(es), take several minutes to guide students through an analysis of word structure to predict meaning.

Once a meaning is hypothesized through one or both of these strategies, students have a choice. If they are satisfied with an educated guess because it makes sense, the ritual of looking up a word in the dictionary ought not be performed. But if students are still unsure of a word's meaning, the dictionary is there.

Of course, the "teachable moment" shouldn't be overdone; it's effective when used sparingly. Sometimes it's perfectly valid just to tell a student a word's meaning when you're asked. Or even to say, "Look it up in the dictionary."

When students go into a dictionary to verify or to determine a precise definition, more often than not they need supervision to make good decisions. Keep these tips in mind as you work on dictionary usage.

1. Help students determine the "best fit" between a word and its definition. Students often must choose the most appropriate definition from several of many. This poses a real dilemma for maturing learners. As they act upon a word, your interactions will help them make the best choice of a definition and will provide a behavior model for making such a choice.

2. If you do assign a list of words to look up in a dictionary, choose them selectively: a few words are better than many. The chances are greater that students will learn several key terms thoroughly than that they will develop vague notions about a large number.

3. Help students with the pronunciation key in a glossary or dictionary as the need arises. However, this does not mean that you will teach skills associated with the use of a pronunciation key in isolated lessons. Instead, it means guiding and reinforcing students' ability to use a pronunciation key as they study the content of your course. Study in Box 3–2 how a social studies teacher created an opportunity to reinforce the use of a pronunciation key as part of an ongoing unit.

AWARENESS

It's worthwhile to spark interest and enthusiasm in the language of a content area. Deighton (1959, 1970) believed that what is needed for vocabulary learning is interest. He argued that "A sense of excitement about words, a sense of wonder, and a feeling of pleasure — these are the essential ingredients in vocabulary development" (p. 59).

Illustrate the power that words have. Take the word *streaking* as an example. That popular pastime on college campuses captured the country by surprise. Streaking, as you recall, became a national phenomenon. Why? One explanation lies in the word itself. Picture, if you can, *meanderers* instead of *streakers*. The word just doesn't work. Yet

Box 3–2

"HOW DO YOU SAY IT?"

Directions: Listed below are the pronunciation spellings for a group of foreign words and names you will be reading in your study of Ivan IV. Using the glossary of your textbook find the actual spelling for the pronunciation spelling. Then sound out and learn the pronunciation of these words. Place the circled letters on the lines below the actual spellings and unscramble them to find the mystery person. Finally, using the glossary and a dictionary, write the pronunciation spelling for the mystery person. Don't forget the diacritical marks.

z ä r´ ə v i c h	_ _ O _ _ _ _ _ _
ē r ē´ n a	_ O _ _ _ _
ḡ r ô z´ n ē	_ _ _ _ _ O _
ē v ä n´	_ O _ _
ä n d r ā´	_ _ _ _ _ O _
k i t ī´ g ə r ô t´	_ _ O _ _ _ _ _ _ _
s h ü´ i s k ē	_ O _ _ _ _ _
t ä r´ t ə r	O _ _ _ _
ä n ä s t ä´ s y ə	_ _ _ _ _ _ _ O _
f y ō´ d ə r	_ O _ _ _
k r e m´ l ə n	_ _ O _ _ _ _
b y e l´ s k ē	O _ _ _ _
z ä r	_ _ _ O
y ü´ r ē	_ _ O _
v ä s ē´ l ē	_ _ _ _ O _

Mystery Person _ _ _ _ _ _ _ _ _ _ _ _ _ _ _ _

Pronunciation Spelling _____ _____ _____

streaking does — its sound, its imagery, all contributed to making this social aberration a little bit more bearable.

How can enthusiasm and interest in words be sparked?

Focus on interesting words whose explanations are likely to arouse students' enthusiasm in other content area terminology. Consider the following "starter" activities.

Creating Word-Enriched Environments

Make bulletin boards and collages where word meanings can be illustrated through headlines, pictures, cartoons, jokes, advertisements, and the like. See Figure 3–10.

Form student committees to preview reading assignments for new and unusual words and to explain them to the rest of the class. For example, an English class committee called the Word Searchers found this passage from *Flowers for Algernon:* "Sculpture with a living element. Charlie, it's the greatest thing since *junkmobiles* and *tincannia*." The Word Searchers introduced the terms *junkmobiles* and *tincannia* to the class. They explained that the two words would not be found in the dictionary. Then the committee challenged the class to come up with definitions that would make sense. To top off the presentation the committee prepared Exhibit A and Exhibit B to demonstrate the words — a mobile made of various assortments of junk and an *objet d'art* made from tin cans, jar lids, and the like.

Word Play

THE READING TEACHER'S LAMENT*
George E. Coon

I tried teaching my students sequencing
skills, but I couldn't keep them in order.

I tried teaching word configuration, but my
lesson never took shape.

I tried teaching my students a lesson using
the kinesthetic approach, but they wouldn't touch it.

I tried a strong phonics approach, but I
found that wasn't too sound.

I wanted to teach my students vocabulary,
but I never found the words to do it.

The Reading Teacher 33 (1979): 154. Reprinted with permission of George E. Coon and The International Reading Association.

Figure 3–10. Collage

I tried using a semantic approach to comprehension,
but my students never caught my meaning.

I did well in teaching palindromes because
I knew them backwards and forwards.

You wouldn't believe my unit on fantasy!

I tried teaching about vowels, but my students
never got the long nor the short of it.

I tried to teach about syllables, but they
broke up the lesson.

I tried working on predicting outcomes, but
they only guessed at the answers.

I tried teaching auditory discrimination, but they
wouldn't hear of it.

So I became a mathematics teacher and
my problems have really multiplied.

On occasion, word play will energize vocabulary study. Students' interest and enthusiasm for content terminology is sparked when they have the opportunity to play with words that are an integral part of their textbook materials.

RIDDLES

Several days before the start of a unit on shelled animals, a science teacher posted on the bulletin board a sign that read Coming Attractions. Each day students received a clue more specific than the one the day before as to what word represented the concept for the next unit of study.

Day 1: What lives from 1 to 75 years . . .

Day 2: on land or water . . . but likes to bury itself in sand . . .

Day 3: prefers warm climates . . .

Day 4: has no backbone . . . comes in many colors . . . a thing of great beauty . . .

Day 5: and whose name begins with m, ends with k, and rhymes with *tusk?*

Answer: m __ __ __ __ __ k

After each clue the teacher encouraged predictions, and discussion followed. She even made a number of resources on marine life available to interested students to extend their search. The students had converged upon the answer by the end of the fifth day. The teacher noted to the class that she was "shell shocked" by their enthusiasm.

IDIOMATIC AND SLANG EXPRESSIONS

Discuss idiomatic and current slang expressions. Dale (1975) contended that "Slang is novel, vivid. It plays tricks with words. It attracts attention — both favorable and unfavorable. To describe the appeal of slang in slang terms is the desire to be with it, in the know, up-to-date" (p. 39). Slang comes from many sources: politics, the jargon of special groups, newspapers, magazines, sports, and so forth. To the extent that slang and idiomatic expressions relate to your subject matter, you might consider introducing them to the class. Students can play with slang words in a variety of ways: (1) making slang dictionaries; (2) interviewing adults about slang expressions that were "in" during their youth; (3) inventing new slang expressions to label events, behavior, phenomena that they were studying. (A business education student once described *high finance* as transactions involving "serious bucks." An English student called writing compositions an exercise in "dirtying paper.")

FIGURATIVE LANGUAGE

Point out instances of figurative language in reading materials. The figurative use of words often transforms colorless textbook writing into vivid prose.

There are several common types of figurative language:

1. Metaphor: an implied comparison which often asserts that one thing is another or that it acts like or has some of the qualities of something else. Examples:

   Meaning is an arrow that reaches its *mark* when . . .

   The *Vietnam War* was a *creeping cancer* which *plagued* the American society.

   The waves cast by a pebble of thought spread . . .

2. Simile: an explicit comparison using *like* or *as*. Examples:

   The *logic of facts* penetrates *like a bullet*.

   A perfect definition of comprehension is *as elusive as the butterfly of love*.

3. Oxymoron: a seeming self-contradiction. Examples:

   hotbed of apathy

   gentle strength

   benign neglect

4. Personification: a figure of speech in which an object or quality or ideal is given some attributes of a human being (more commonly found in verse than in prose). Examples:

The algae danced in the full light of the botanist's microscope.

No computer could brag that it had programmed a human being.

5. Hyperbole: an exaggeration used to emphasize a statement or situation. Examples:

There was something olympian in his snarls and rages, and there was a touch of hell-fire in his mirth.

They felt like sleeping for a year, but the marathon dancers continued numbly across the killing floor.

Word Origins and Histories

A brief discussion of an unusual word derivation or history will usually give students a lasting impression of a word. Piercy (1976) recommended that a teacher accumulate word origins and use them as mnemonic devices. If you do so, there should be a clear connection between the word's "story" and the current meaning.

Students' enthusiasm for language (and therefore for the language of your content area) will increase when they know the derivations behind such words as:

1. *Assassin.* Originally, a drinker of hashish. The members of a secret order founded among a Mohammedan sect in ancient Persia used the drug hashish and, under its influence, secretly murdered people. A cult member was thus referred to as a hashshash. From that origin comes the English word *assassin.*

2. *Bombastic.* Metaphorically, speech stuffed with cotton. From the Latin *bombax* ("cotton") came the word *bombast,* which also meant "cotton." Later the meaning was expanded to include any material used as stuffing for garments. The word *bombast* was eventually used to mean a speaker's "inflated style" — figuratively speaking, speech that is stuffed with high-sounding words.

3. *Muscle.* Metaphorically, the scurrying of a mouse. The Latin word *musculus* means "mouse." The French adapted it because they associated the rippling of a muscle with the movement of a mouse.

4. *Calculate.* Originally, the counting stones of the Romans. The Latin word *calx* means "limestone." The ancient Romans

used little stones called *calculus* to add and subtract. From this derived the English word *calculate* and its many variations.

5. *Broker.* Originally, a vendor of wine. From the French *brochier,* meaning "one who broaches or taps a cask" to draw off the wine. Although the word *broker* was first used to mean a vendor of wine, through the years the term came to mean any small retailer — for example, *pawnbroker.* In modern times, a broker has been associated with the more dignified financial transactions involving stocks and bonds.

6. *Easel.* Metaphorically, the artist's donkey, from the Dutch word *ezel,* "ass or donkey." Figuratively, a small stand or support for the artist's canvas.

(These capsule explanations were adapted from *Picturesque Word Origins* [Springfield, Massachusetts: G. and C. Merriam Company, 1933]. More recent resources for teachers are given in Appendix C.)

You can also spark awareness and interest for words originating from persons or places (*pasteurize, bedlam, maverick, chauvinistic*) or from acronyms — pronounceable words formed from the beginning letters or groups of letters in words that make up phrases (*scuba* stands for *s*elf-contained *u*nderwater *b*reathing *a*pparatus; *amphetamine* for *a*lpha *m*ethyl *ph*enyl *e*thyl *amine; Euromart* for *Euro*pean *Mar*ket; *snafu* for *s*ituation *n*ormal *a*ll *f*ouled *u*p). Interesting words abound. If they appear in a text assignment, don't miss the opportunity to teach them to students.

LOOKING BACK, LOOKING FORWARD

Vocabulary instruction involves more than just looking up, defining, memorizing, and using words in sentences. Vocabulary study lays the groundwork for learning concepts. Teaching vocabulary in content areas combines the acquisition of word meanings with the development of concepts. As part of prereading instruction, teachers can introduce key words through a structured overview, build vocabulary skills to help students recognize word meanings on their own, and spark interest in the language of their disciplines.

A structured overview works on the same principle as an advance organizer. However, unlike the typical advance organizer, which is a short written passage, the structured overview is a graphic display of the important vocabulary terms in the content material. It's a diagram that shows students the relationships among the important concepts they will study.

Another aspect of vocabulary instruction is showing students how to inquire into the meaning of an unknown word in reading material. The teacher should model the inquiry process before students apply it during reading. The teacher can develop insights and principles on using context aids, word structure, and the dictionary to advantage through modeling. As a result of vocabulary building, students will develop a variety of skills which can be applied in reading.

Content area teachers should also spark interest in the languages of their disciplines. They can tell the history and derivation of interesting terms. They can develop word-enriched environments as well as engage students in word play. The study of words should be fun. Enthusiasm for words will lead to further word study in your content area. And this is what the awareness aspect of vocabulary instruction is all about.

In the next chapter we'll study another important aspect of readiness. How does a teacher raise students' expectations about print and set purposes for reading? Curiosity arousal and prediction will reduce the uncertainty that students bring to content material. Let's see why and how.

SUGGESTED READINGS

Burmeister, Lou E. *Reading strategies for middle and secondary school teachers.* 2nd ed. Reading, Mass.: Addison-Wesley, 1978, chapter 6.

Dale, Edgar, and O'Rourke, Joseph. *Techniques of teaching vocabulary.* Palo Alto, Cal.: Field Educational Publications, 1971.

Deighton, Lee. *Vocabulary development in the classroom.* New York: Teachers College Press, 1970.

Hafner, Lawrence. *Developmental reading in middle and secondary schools.* New York: Macmillan, 1977, chapter 5.

Herber, Harold. *Teaching reading in content areas.* 2nd ed. Englewood Cliffs, N.J.: Prentice-Hall, 1978, chapter 6.

Johnson, Dale, and Pearson, David. *Teaching reading vocabulary.* New York: Holt, Rinehart and Winston, 1977.

Piercy, Dorothy. *Reading activities in content areas.* Boston: Allyn and Bacon, 1976, chapter 1.

Robinson, H. Allan. *Teaching reading and study strategies.* 2nd ed. Boston: Allyn and Bacon, 1978, chapter 4.

Roe, Betty; Stoodt, Barbara; and Burns, Paul. *Reading instruction in the secondary school.* Chicago: Rand McNally, 1978, chapter 5.

Shepherd, David. *Comprehensive high school reading methods.* Columbus, Ohio: Merrill, 1973, chapter 3.

Smith, Carl; Smith, Sharon; and Mikulecky, Larry. *Teaching reading in secondary school content subjects.* New York: Holt, Rinehart and Winston, 1978, chapter 7.

Thomas, Ellen, and Robinson, H. Allan. *Teaching reading in every class.* Boston: Allyn and Bacon, 1977, chapter 2.

CHAPTER FOUR

Reducing Uncertainty Through Prediction and Curiosity Arousal

They can because
they think they can.

VIRGIL

ORGANIZING PRINCIPLE ⎯⎯⎯⎯⎯⎯⎯⎯⎯⎯⎯⎯⎯⎯⎯⎯⎯⎯

Positive thinkers always have their goals in front of them. They program themselves for success; they are confident. In other words, they can because they think they can. If there is one imperative in this chapter, it is this: prepare students to think positively about what they will read in textbook assignments.

Preparing students to read can be easily neglected in a classroom teacher's hurry-scurry efforts to cover the content. Yet, the payoffs of prereading instruction are immense. Students will reduce their uncertainty about a reading assignment — bringing to the text what they know and believe already about the subject matter. Expectations about the meaning of assigned material will be raised. As a result of the prereading activities that the content teacher initiates, students will read with anticipation and purpose. Therefore, the organizing principle of this chapter can be stated this way: *A teacher reduces the uncertainty students bring to content material by helping them to raise questions about what they will read.*

Study the Chapter Overview on the next page before you read this chapter. It shows the interrelationships of the major ideas to be presented.

CHAPTER OVERVIEW

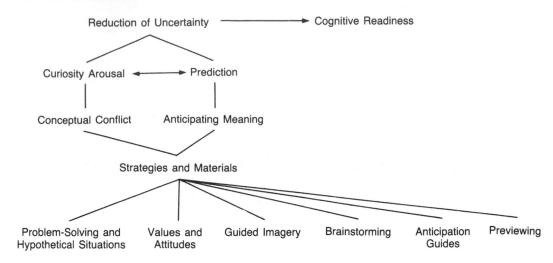

Explanations of reading tend to be complex. Yet as intricate a process as reading may be, it's surely just as magical and mysterious to most of us. After all, who ever really knows a covert process — one that takes place in the head?

Huey (1908) recounted a fascinating tale about the African adventurer Livingstone.

> Livingstone excited the wonder and awe of an African tribe as he daily perused a book that had survived the vicissitudes of travel. So incomprehensible, to these savages, was his performance with the book, that they finally stole it and *ate* it, as the best way they knew of "reading" it, of getting the white man's satisfaction from it. (*p. 2*)

The preliterate natives acted in the only way they knew how. Eating Livingstone's book was a response, somewhat magical, to their uncertainty over the process that we call reading.

Magic and uncertainty go hand in hand. According to Malinowski (1954), people resort to magic in situations where they feel they have limited control over the success of their activities. This is so in primitive cultures such as the African tribe described by Huey or in highly technological societies such as ours.

I believe an element of magic will always be a part of reading, even though it appears second nature to many of us. For most teachers reading just happens, particularly when there is a strong purpose or need to read in the first place. My hunch, however, is that a great deal of uncertainty pervades reading for many students. Reading remains a mystery, a lot of hocus-pocus, for students who believe they have limited control over their chances for success with a reading assignment.

You can do a great deal to reduce the uncertainty that students bring to textbook assignments. In fact, you must. You can take the voodoo out of reading textbook material by helping students link the given — what they know already or the skills they have — with the new — what they are about to learn through reading.

How can the "voodoo" be taken out of reading?

As far as I'm concerned, the basis for effective reading instruction in the content areas may very well come before students read. Hansell (1976) underscored the necessity for prereading instruction when he asserted,

> teachers may help students to read texts, articles, or books by helping them understand the content before they deal with it in print . . . The problem of content teachers then becomes, in the words of an eighth grade teacher in Boston, one of "convincing the students that they know more than they think they do about my subject." (*p. 309*)

In a sense, the *feedforward effect* is what prereading instruction is all about.

Feedforward is different from feedback. Feedback is one of those well-established, valuable concepts in learning. It refers generally to the information learners use to guide their actions. Feedback helps individuals to modify, refine, or redirect behavior so that they will learn. Feedforward, on the other hand, is a relatively new concept. It categorizes a wide range of important acts during learning generally and reading specifically. To my knowledge Stauffer (1975) first offered the term "feedforward" to describe the reader's *anticipation* of what will be learned through print: "Each pupil must learn how to raise questions . . . The feedforward effect of questions raised keeps a reader on course" (p. 34).

Two of the most appropriate questions that students can ask about a reading selection are "What do I need to know?" and "How well do I already know it?" "What do I need to know?" prompts readers to make predictions and set purposes. It gets them thinking about the reading material. "How well do I already know it?" helps readers to search their experience and knowledge to give support to tentative predictions.

The information gained from the questions readers raise before reading will make it easier for them to read in a purposeful manner. The essence of prereading instruction in content area reading, then, is to reduce uncertainty by preparing students to (1) anticipate what will be read, (2) make connections between what they know already and what they will learn, and (3) raise questions whose answers will withstand the test of verification through reading.

THE READER'S KNOWLEDGE OF THE WORLD _____

Comprehension embodies the very complexity (and magic) of reading. The best anyone can do to understand reading comprehension is to examine it indirectly, by inference, as we did with the "Ordeal by Cheque" demonstration in Chapter 1. In recent years two areas of study — *information processing* and *psycholinguistics* — have generated inferences about comprehension that can be applied to what we as classroom teachers do in the name of instruction.

Psycholinguistics combines an understanding of how language works with how people learn. Information processing proposes that the brain functions actively to seek, select, organize, store, and when necessary, retrieve and utilize information about the world (Smith, 1975). A line of inquiry emerging from both fields has examined how knowledge of the world — experience, knowledge, beliefs, attitudes and skills — affects comprehension. What people know, feel, and believe determines the extent to which they will make sense out of events in any situation.

Experiences and knowledge are accumulative and integrated into what cognitive psychologists call *schema* or *cognitive structure*. Ausubel (1978), for instance, believed that a person's wealth of knowledge is organized hierarchically in cognitive structure — that information is stored in the brain in highly generalized concepts, less inclusive concepts, and specific facts. He asserted that cognitive structure — "an individual's organization, stability and clarity of knowledge in a particular subject matter field at a given time" — is a major factor in learning and retaining new information. Learning is easier for a person whose knowledge is clear, stable, and organized. But don't think of cognitive structure as passive. It's dynamic, enlarging, and changing constantly as new information and experiences are assimilated into what you know.

In the introductory remarks to *Comprehension and Learning* Smith (1975) asserted, "The only effective and meaningful way in which anyone can learn is by attempting to relate new experiences to what he knows (or believes) already" (p. 1). There must be a point of contact between the reader's knowledge of the world and the ideas communicated by the textbook author. Reader and text must interact for comprehension and learning to take place. This is why what students know influences the kinds of questions they will ask about content under study.

How does the "Rocky" experiment reinforce the role that knowledge of the world plays in reading?

Anderson and his associates (1977) illustrated the dynamic role that knowledge of the world plays in reading comprehension. As part of an experiment, they asked college-level students to read the following passage:

Rocky slowly got up from the mat, planning his escape. He hesitated a moment and thought. Things were not going well. What bothered him most was being held, especially since the charges against him had been weak. He considered his present situation.

The lock that held him was strong but he thought he could break it. He knew, however, that his timing would have to be perfect. Rocky was aware that it was because of his early roughness that he had been penalized so severely — much too severely from his point of view. The situation was becoming frustrating; the pressure had been grinding on him for too long. He was being ridden unmercifully. Rocky was getting angry now. He felt he was ready to make his move. He knew that his success or failure would depend on what he did in the next few seconds. (*p. 372*)

How did you interpret the passage? Choose one of these statements:

This passage is about a convict planning his escape from prison.

This passage is about a wrestler trying to break the hold of an opponent.

If neither statement works for you, use this space to write your interpretation of the passage:

This passage is about _____

_____

The "typical person," according to Anderson, would interpret the passage as about a convict planning his escape. Nevertheless, the majority of the students in the experiment who had a physical education background and a special interest in wrestling recalled and interpreted the passage as a description of wrestling. The experimenters concluded that "personal history, knowledge, and belief influence the interpretations that they will give prose passages . . . high-level schemata provide the interpretive framework for comprehending discourse . . . language comprehension always involves using one's knowledge of the world" (pp. 376–378).

When understandings such as these are integrated with what you know (and believe) about teaching effectively, you will develop fresh perspectives on content area reading instruction.

CURIOSITY AND PREDICTION

Curiosity and prediction go hand in hand. They are the mainstays of prereading instruction. The more students predict as they read, the more they will read with certainty and confidence; the greater their curiosity, the greater their motivation to read.

Why do conceptual conflicts prepare students for reading?

As instructional tools, prediction and curiosity arousal give students the chance to consider what they know already about the material to be read. Through your guidance they are encouraged to make connections — to relate their knowledge to the text assignment. And further, they will recognize that there are problems — conceptual conflicts — to be resolved that they can best resolve through reading. In short, prediction and curiosity arousal help students raise questions that they can answer only by giving thought to what they read.

I once observed a class of eighth graders form small groups before reading a selection from the book *African Elephants* by B. F. Beebe. The selection, entitled "Today's Stone Age Elephant Hunters," was part of a social studies unit on African life and history. The teacher assigned the groups a hypothetical problem to solve before reading the selection. The problem: if you were a Pigmy, alone and with a spear as your only weapon, how would you hunt and kill an elephant?

The students began to chatter enthusiastically. The problem seemed to be at an intermediate level of familiarity — that is, the hypothetical situation suggested by the question was not outside the students' realm of experience. Nor was it so unfamiliar to the students that the conceptual conflict created by the question would be nonexistent. Rather, they appeared to be intrigued and somewhat perplexed and baffled by the problem yet aroused enough to pursue possible solutions.

The teacher facilitated discussion by keeping the groups on the task — prodding, playing devil's advocate, asking open-ended questions. After several minutes of discussion, the teacher asked each group to share its solution with the whole class. The gist of many of the solutions, as you might expect, was predictable:

"Dig a big hole and lure the elephant into it."

"Climb a tree and wait for the elephant to pass under it."

"Lead the elephant off a cliff."

As each group provided its solution, members of other groups were invited to respond, to find loopholes or additional problems unaccounted for. The teacher, meanwhile, remained nondirective but kept the discussion going, trying to get students to relate their world to the problem. As a result, several of the students shared their knowledge of hunting. Others recognized the element of surprise as the Pigmy's best offense. As one likely future military tactician noted, "When he [the elephant] least expects it, he better expect it."

Next the teacher asked, "Would you like to find out how a lone Pigmy with a spear as his only weapon actually *does* hunt and kill an elephant?" The students leaped on the question. They were off and reading in no time flat.

How *do* Pigmies kill elephants? Read Box 4–1 and find out for yourself.

Creating Conceptual Conflicts

The key to motivation through curiosity arousal is conceptual conflict (Berlyne, 1965). Should students be presented with prereading situations that take the form of puzzlement, doubt, surprise, perplexity, contradiction, or ambiguity, they will be motivated to seek resolution in order to maintain equilibrium, according to Berlyne.

Shablak and Castallo (1977) asserted, "The need within the person becomes one of information-seeking in an attempt to resolve the conflict; to fill the gap between known and unknown" (p. 53). The search for knowledge becomes a driving force. When a question begins to gnaw, searching behavior is aroused; learning occurs as the conceptual conflict resolves itself.

The instructional possibilities for creating conceptual conflict are legion. Several broad strategies can be adapted to arouse curiosity and sustain interest prior to reading content materials.

ESTABLISHING PROBLEMS TO BE SOLVED

The illustration from *African Elephants* indicates a very potent pre-reading technique. The strategy, of course, is to establish a problem, real or hypothetical, to be solved. The teacher's role, generally speaking,

Box 4–1

TODAY'S STONE AGE ELEPHANT HUNTERS
B. F. Beebe

Some pigmies of the western Congo use a system of concealing their scent when hunting elephants. Few of these little jungle dwellers hunt elephants but those that do have chosen about the most dangerous way to secure food in today's world.

Hunting is done by a single man using a spear with a large metal spearhead and thick shaft. After taking the trail behind an elephant herd the hunter pauses frequently to coat his skin with fresh elephant droppings for several days until he has lost all human scent.

Closing on the herd the pigmy selects his prey, usually a young adult. He watches this animal until he is aware of its distinctive habits — how often it dozes, eats, turns, wanders out of the herd and other individual behavior.

Then he moves toward his huge prey, usually at midday when the herd is dozing while standing. The little hunter moves silently between the elephant's legs, braces himself and drives the spear up into the stomach area for several feet. The elephant snaps to alertness, screaming and trying to reach his diminutive attacker. Many pigmy hunters have lost their lives at this moment, but if the little hunter is fast enough he pulls out the spear to facilitate bleeding and ducks for safety.

Death does not come for several days and the hunter must follow his wounded prey until it stops. When the elephant falls the pigmy cuts off the tail as proof of his kill and sets off for his village which may be several days away by now.

SOURCE: B. F. Beebe, *African Elephants.* McKay, 1968, 91–92.

---

becomes one of (1) providing the time to discuss the problem, raising questions, and seeking possible solutions prior to reading, and then (2) assigning the reading material that will help lead to resolution and conceptual development.

Collette (1973) offered two excellent illustrations (Box 4–2) of curiosity arousal which helped to "feed" students into the reading of science materials.

These are two examples of the "teachable moment." They have an important touchstone in that each connects the real world to rather abstract concepts. To be sure, there is a mismatch between cognitive structure (what the students know already) and what is to be learned. But the mismatch creates a gap that can be closed. Curiosity is therefore aroused, and the desire to seek information stimulated.

In Boxes 4–3 and 4–4 notice how the hypothetical problem situations created serve as springboards to learning. Each situation thrusts readers into a role and a circumstance which forces them to rely on their knowledge and experience. Box 4–3 provided the prereading activity appropriate to study the textbook unit on Colonial life and the development of early settlements. The example in Box 4–4 readied students to deal with basic issues in the story "Alas Babylon."

As a concluding example, note in Box 4–5 how an auto mechanics teacher created a hypothetical problem to prepare students for reading a text selection on the mechanics involved in "clutch" situations.

Box 4–2

A popular high school couple were overcome by exhaust fumes in a parked car but were revived through prompt action by the police. Mrs. Dunning mentioned the event to her biology classes the following day. Pupils immediately began raising questions about the effects of carbon monoxide, the time needed for recovery, and the like. Mrs. Dunning helped the students clarify their questions, organized them into groups, and used various available references to find answers.

An unusual fall thunderstorm killed one of two men who sought shelter under a tree. The ninth grade students immediately were curious about the reason for the death of only one man while his companion only a couple of feet away was unharmed. The science teacher explained that man did not know much about the action of lightning and suggested that the pupils make a list of questions that would likely be answered by looking in books and other references.

SOURCE: Collette, Alfred T. *Science teaching in the secondary school.* Boston: Allyn and Bacon, 1973, 574–575. Used with permission of the author.

Box 4–3

Suppose the time is 1680, and the place Massachusetts. Imagine that you are early European settlers. You will want to try to think as you believe they may have thought, act as they might have acted. You and your group have petitioned the Great and General Court to be allowed to form a new town. After checking to make sure you are of good character and the land is fertile and can be defended, the court says yes. They grant you a five-mile square of land. As proprietors of this land, you must plan a town. Use the outline map for your planning. What buildings would you put in first? Second? Third? Later? Why? How would you divide the land among the many people who want to live there? Why? As proprietors would you treat yourselves differently from the way you treated the others? Why? How would you run the government?

Name of town: _____   Scale: 1 inch = 1 mile

EXAMINING VALUES AND ATTITUDES

Conceptual conflict and prereading discussion can be sparked through an examination of the values and attitudes that students bring to reading assignments. Values clarification activities (Simon et al., 1972) can be adapted nicely to feed students into reading.

How can values clarification be adapted to your content area to activate reading?

Study two exercises that were developed for a secondary school English and social studies class. The attitude inventory in Box 4–6 led to a lively discussion that preceded a literature unit on crime and criminals. Box 4–7 helped to connect students' beliefs and feelings about war to the study of American involvement in the Mexican War.

Box 4–4

ALAS BABYLON

Directions: The year is 1944. We are on the verge of a nuclear disaster. Through inside sources you learn that the attack will occur within five days. Below is a list of preparations you might consider making before the nuclear attack occurs. Assuming that your town and house will not be destroyed by the bomb and that you have time to complete only twelve of these items, which will you choose? Within your group number from 1 to 12 the items you think are most important to your survival.

__   a. buy a gun and ammunition to protect against looters

__   b. cash in all savings bonds and take all the money out of your checking and saving accounts

__   c. build a fireplace in your house

__   d. buy firewood and charcoal

__   e. buy extra tanks of gasoline and fill your car up

__   f. purchase antibiotics and other medicines

__   g. dig a latrine

__   h. buy lumber, nails, and various other supplies

__   i. plant fruit trees

__   j. notify all your friends and relatives of coming nuclear attack

__   k. invest in books on canning, making candles, and soap

__   l. buy a few head of livestock from a farmer

__   m. buy fishing equipment and a boat

__   n. buy seeds of several different kinds of vegetables for a garden

__   o. make friends with a farmer who has a horse and wagon

__   p. shop at antique stores for kerosene lamps and large cooking pots

__   q. buy a safe in which to hide your money

__   r. buy foodstuffs

BRAINSTORMING

Brainstorming is another way to arouse curiosity before reading. The brainstorming technique involves two basic steps which can be adapted easily to content objectives: (1) identify a broad concept that reflects the main topic to be studied in the assigned reading and (2) have students work in small groups to generate a list of words related to the broad concept in x number of seconds.

These two steps help you instantly discover what knowledge of the world your students possess about the topic they are going to study. From a diagnostic standpoint, you will have a quick and easy indicator of the knowledge and experience students bring to the lesson. Furthermore, Herber (1978) suggested:

> The device of having students produce lists of related words is a useful way to guide review. It helps them become instantly aware of how much they know, individually and collectively, about the topic. They discover quickly that there are no right or wrong answers . . . Until the students reach the point in the lesson where they must read the passage and judge whether their predictions are accurate, the entire lesson is based on their own

Box 4–5

THINKING IN A CLUTCH SITUATION

Directions: You are the only mechanic on duty when a four-wheel drive truck with a V-8 engine pulls in for repair. The truck has high mileage, and it appears that the problem may be a worn clutch disc. What tools do you anticipate needing? What procedures do you follow? Classify your answers to these questions under the two headings below.

Tools Needed   *Procedures*

knowledge, experience and opinion. This captivates their interest much more than the more traditional, perfunctory review. (*p. 179*)

How can brainstorming be adapted to your content area?

When the brainstorming activity is over, you can make adaptations to stimulate curiosity and arouse interest in the topic to be read. Consider, for instance, these two applications: (1) Have students in small groups arrange their lists of words into subcategories. They must be prepared to identify the subcategories and the logic behind each arrangement. (2) Once the brainstormed word lists have been compared and discussed, have students make predictions about the content to be studied. You might ask, "Given the list of words and subcategories that you have developed, what do you think the reading assignment will be about?

Box 4–6

CRIME: AN ATTITUDE INVENTORY

Directions: Using the numbers 1 through 20, rank each of the following behaviors from most wrong to least wrong. In other words, determine which are most "criminal" according to your values, and rank the rest in descending order. If you feel that some are not wrong at all, just circle the letters of those items. Number 1 = most criminal; Number 20 = least criminal.

___ a. a man drives his car after he's had eight drinks in a short amount of time

___ b. a woman kills her husband during an argument

___ c. a teenager uses a false ID to buy liquor

___ d. a businessman "bugs" the office of a competitor

___ e. a twelve-year-old steals a record from a discount department store

___ f. a woman constantly beats her child

___ g. a golfer cheats on his score at the sixth hole

___ h. an eighteen-year-old knowingly buys a "hot" tape deck at a fraction of its real value

___ i. a mugger breaks the arm of an old man in the park

___ j. a married man has an affair with another woman

___ k. a man falsely reports his income in order to pay less income tax

___ l. a doctor unplugs the machine of a patient he thinks has no chance of recovering

___ m. a man steals $100,000 from a bank through armed robbery

___ n. a major industry pollutes air and water

___ o. a starving man steals five dollars from a church collection

___ p. a teenager smokes marijuana

___ q. a shopowner burns his shop to collect insurance

___ r. a woman attempts to commit suicide

___ s. a pusher deals heroin to kids on the street

___ t. a college student turns in a research paper he has bought instead of written himself.

How does the title of the selection relate to your subcategories? Why do you think so?"

A high school teacher in New Haven, Connecticut, initiated a brain-storming activity with a class of "slow learners." The students, working in small groups, were asked to list in two minutes as many words as possible that were related to the Civil War. Then the groups shared their lists of Civil War words. The teacher then created a master list on the board from the individual entries of the groups. He also wrote three categories on the board — North, South, Both — and asked the groups to classify each word from the master list under one of the categories.

Box 4–7

WAR WITH MEXICO

Directions: During the next two days you will be reading about President Polk's war message in which he gave his reasons for asking Congress to declare war against Mexico. Before beginning that assignment, it is important to examine your beliefs and feelings about war. For each statement, put a check mark along the continuum to indicate the extent to which you "agree" or "disagree."

Strongly agree   Strongly disagree

1. A nation must protect the property of its people, even if war is necessary.

2. If a country expects to be attacked by a foreign power, it is justified in attacking that power first in its own defense.

3. Only when a nation is invaded does it have the right to go to war.

4. The government of the U.S. must defend American-owned businesses in foreign countries.

5. Even though some Americans may oppose war with another country, once war is declared each person should give the government his or her full support.

6. When two countries are at war, there should be no distinction between the civilian population and the military.

7. There are situations facing a nation where war is the only alternative.

8. A nation has the right to resort to war to obtain the natural resources it lacks and needs for its own well-being.

9. When called upon to approve a declaration of war, a Congressman should decide the matter according to his conscience rather than according to the wishes of his or her constituents.

10. During time of war, a person should put his country ahead of his or her personal beliefs.

Here's how one group responded:

North	South	Both
blue	grey	soldiers
Lincoln	farms	armies
Grant	Rebel	guns
factories	Booth	cannons
Yankee	slavery	Gettysburg Address
Ford Theater		roots
We won		death
		horses
		assassination

Note that in this example the teacher provided the categories. He recognized that students needed the additional structure to be successful with this particular task. The activity led to a good deal of discussion and debate. Students were put in the position of "authority," sharing what they knew and believed already with other classmembers. As a result of the activity, they were asked to raise questions about the Civil War that they wanted to have answered through reading and class discussion.

GUIDED IMAGERY

Guided imagery is another alternative for your teaching repertoire during
How does guided imagery work?
prereading preparation. The strategy is simple; it allows students to explore concepts visually. Guided imagery is described here as a feedforward activity, although it can be incorporated into a variety of instructional situations for a variety of purposes.

Samples et al. (1977, p. 189) recommended guided imagery, among other things, as a means for:

1. building an experience base for inquiry, discussion and group work

2. building self-image

3. exploring and stretching concepts

4. solving and clarifying problems

5. exploring history and the future

6. exploring other lands and worlds

7. creative writing

Guided imagery works like this. The teacher, according to Samples et al., structures a daydream: "You use *words* to get into the process — but once there, images take over" (p. 188). Box 4–8 is an illustration. After you read it, close your eyes and do it.

Box 4–8

GUIDED IMAGERY: THE SPACE TRIP

Close your eyes . . . tell all your muscles to relax. You are entering a space capsule ten minutes before takeoff. Soon you feel it lift off . . . you look over at your companions and check their reactions. Now you are ready to take a reading of the instrument panel. As you relay the information to ground control, it is eleven minutes into the flight . . . you settle back into your chair and tell your fellow astronauts about your thoughts . . . about what you hope to see when the vehicle lands . . . about what you might touch and hear as you explore the destination. Finally, you drift off to sleep . . . picturing yourself returning to earth . . . seeing once again your friends and relations. You are back where you started . . . tell your muscles to move . . . open your eyes.

You may wish to have students discuss their "trips" which, of course, parallel in some way the content of the reading selection to be assigned. In the classroom where this example was devised, students in a literature class participated in the imagery discussion prior to reading a short story on space travel. Discussion questions included: "How did you feel just before entering the space capsule?" "What were the reactions of your companions?" "Where did your exploration take you?" "Were there things that surprised you on the trip? Colors? Sounds?"

Samples et al. (1977) provided these tips as they explained the imagery strategy:

> Relaxed positions are helpful. . . . As few distractions as possible will make the first few experiences easier. A soothing but audible voice is best. For those who can't get themselves to participate, an alternative quiet activity will cut down on embarrassed giggles. Leave lots of "empty" space both in terms of specific content and time to visualize . . . (*p. 188*)

Guided imagery isn't for everyone. Some teachers will find themselves uncomfortable using it; others will not. As a prereading alternative, however, it gives you an additional option that will help students connect, in this case, what they "see" to what they will read.

Making Predictions

Prediction is a sure aid to reading comprehension. For one thing, strategies and materials for prediction activate thought about the content before reading. Students must rely on what they know through previous study and experience to make educated guesses about the material to be read.

Why an educated guess? Smith (1978) defined prediction as the prior elimination of unlikely alternatives. He suggested that

Readers do not normally attend to print with their minds blank, with no prior purpose and with no expectation of what they might find in the text. . . . The way readers look for meaning is not to consider all possibilities, nor to make reckless guesses about just one, but rather to predict within the most likely range of alternatives. . . . Readers can derive meaning from text because they bring expectations about meaning to text. (*p. 163*)

You can facilitate student-centered purposes by creating anticipation about the meaning of what will be read. Questioning stimulates prediction. Ortiz (1977) suggested a set of questioning exercises which can be adapted to most content areas. The most applicable among these suggestions are the following*:

1. Write the first sentence of a short story, an essay or article on the chalkboard or on a piece of paper. Ask students to write at least ten questions about the sentence. Then have them read the piece and write or be prepared to tell which, if any, of their questions were answered.

2. Choose a difficult passage, preferably nonfiction. Have students ask questions for each sentence or for the first sentence of every paragraph. Have them read the entire piece and be prepared to write or tell which, if any, of their questions were answered. (You might suggest that among their questions should be, "Do I understand this sentence?" or "Am I clear about the meaning of this paragraph?" before going on to read more.) If they have questions which are not answered by the text, they may find the answers elsewhere. Discuss this possibility with them. As another exercise, arrange for them to seek answers by consulting other sources.

3. Tell a story aloud, stopping in the middle of an exciting part. Record your students' responses.

4. Choose an exciting story which you are quite sure will interest your students. Direct them to read it silently and observe whether they ask any questions. Have them put an "X" whenever (if ever) they notice themselves asking questions. Have them discuss their experiences.

5. Give students the first sentence of a prose piece. Don't show them the rest of the passage. Ask them to write as many questions as they can about the sentence. Then have them write a prose piece in which they answer these questions. Afterwards have them read the original piece and ask them to compare the content of their writing with that of the original. (This strategy helps students become aware of how much of themselves they bring or can bring to a piece of writing.)

*Rose Katz Ortiz, *Journal of Reading* 21 (November 1977): 113–114. Reprinted with permission of Rose Katz Ortiz and the International Reading Association.

In Chapter 7, questioning strategies which include prediction will be presented. For now, however, let's examine two distinctive approaches which can help students anticipate meaning prior to reading content assignments.

ANTICIPATION GUIDES

What are the implications of anticipation for content area reading?

An anticipation guide is a series of statements to which students must respond individually before reading the text. Their value lies in the discussion that takes place after the exercise. The teacher's role during discussion is to activate and agitate thought. As students connect their knowledge of the world to the prediction task, you must remain open to a wide range of responses. Draw upon what students bring to the task, but remain nondirective in order to keep the discussion moving.

An Anticipation Guide Demonstration. Sidney Harris wrote an article for his "Strictly Personal" column concerning an air crash that killed seventy-five persons returning from a college football game. Complete the anticipation guide Box 4–9 and then read the article.

Box 4–9

ANTICIPATION GUIDE DEMONSTRATION: CRASH WAS NO TRAGEDY

Directions: Before you read Harris's article, check those incidents you think Harris will classify as tragedies in the column headed You. Discuss your responses with class members, providing reasons for your choices. After reading the article, check in the column headed Harris those incidents that Harris would label as tragedy.

You	Harris	
___	___	1. In his desire to remain in office, a law and order president authorizes breaking the law (for political and national security reasons) and is ultimately driven from office.
___	___	2. During the Master's Tournament, a golfer leading by ten strokes on the sixteenth hole of the last round is struck and killed by lightning.
___	___	3. In Guatemala, an earthquake kills sixteen thousand persons and leaves five times as many homeless.
___	___	4. A mass murderer slips and falls to his death as police close in on him.
___	___	5. A community spends one million dollars to upgrade its football program instead of its airport, and then its football team dies in a crash at that airport.
___	___	6. An understudy for an ill leading lady breaks her leg hurrying to meet her cue in her debut in a leading role.
___	___	7. A father and mother of three die in a head-on auto accident on the way

home from a New Year's Eve party. The father was heard to brag about his capacity for alcohol and his ability to drive after drinking heavily.

_____ _____ 8. A soccer team crashes in the Andes and those who are left are forced to eat the flesh of the victims in order to have a chance to live. Only seven of thirty-six survive.

_____ _____ 9. As his defenses crumble before the onslaught of the allies, a ruthless dictator shoots and kills himself and has his body cremated.

_____ _____ 10. The week before the Master's Tournament, the golfer in statement 2 laughed at a near miss and asserted that as long as he wore a bandaid on his arm, nothing could happen to him. He refused to get off the course during a violent thunderstorm.

Crash Was No Tragedy
Sydney J. Harris

We say that differences in words are "just semantical" and so we fail to understand the important distinctions between words that we use interchangeably. But if we use the wrong word, it is hard to think properly.

For a few days last November, the newspapers were filled with the story of "the Marshall University air tragedy" that killed 75 persons returning from a football game to Huntington, W. Va.

If I said it was not a *tragedy* but a *catastrophe*, you would retort that I was quibbling about words, or that I am being shallow and unfeeling. I think I can show you that you would be wrong on both counts.

An airplane crash is a catastrophe (literally, from the Greek, an "overturning"), like a sudden flood, a fire, a falling girder. Such accidents are part of the natural order and of the human condition; they result from the contingency of things, and are sad or shocking or pitiful — but they are not tragic.

There was, however, a tragic element in the Marshall University air crash; and we can recognize it only if we comprehend the difference between the two words. The tragedy lay in the community's frantic effort to have a winning football team, coupled with its indifference to an unsafe airport.

The school's and the city's hunger for football fame prompted the formation of a booster organization, the Big Green Club, made up of wealthy local business and professional men, who collected funds to help pay for the college's athletic program.

Two years ago, the athletic department's budget began to boom. A new coach was hired, players were recruited from other states, and the college's president resigned under pressure from sports buffs. Vigorous lobbying attempts were made in the state legislature to obtain $1 million for the building of an athletic field and facilities.

Meanwhile, the president of the Tri-State Airport Board confessed the day after the crash: "I've been sleeping with this possibility for the last eight years."

He blamed the lack of funds for the airport failure to have either radar or a warning light system — which would cost about $1 million, the price of the proposed athletic field.

In the classic Greek conception of tragedy, *hubris*, or false pride, is followed by *hamortia*, or sin, and this in turn is followed by *nemesis*, the fate that catches up with human pride and folly.

When having a victorious football team means more to the citizens than having a safe airport, then community *hubris* is riding for a terrible fall.

The players paid with their lives for this sin, but only if we understand the true nature of their "tragedy" will they not have died in vain.

SOURCE: *Strictly Personal* by Sydney J. Harris. © 1970 Field Enterprises, Inc. Courtesy of Field Newspaper Syndicate.

This demonstration shows how strongly anticipation is founded on what the reader brings to the reading selection. Your response to each statement reflects what you know and believe already about the two concepts tragedy and catastrophe. Notice that the opportunity to discuss your responses with other class members may have broadened your conceptual base or helped to further articulate and clarify the difference between the two terms.

By contrasting You and Harris, you probably read the selection more attentively, with purpose, to determine how accurate your predictions were and how similar or different your choices were from those of the author.

If there are differences between your choices for tragedy and Harris's, you have the opportunity to justify the reasons for your choices against those Harris provided. What better critical reading experience could you have?

Classroom Examples of Anticipation Guides. Anticipation guides may
How can an anticipation guide be adapted to your content area? vary in format but not in purpose. In each case, the reader's expectations about meaning are raised prior to reading the text. There are no set guidelines to constructing anticipation guides. However, you may want to keep these tips in mind. First, analyze the material to be read. Determine the major ideas — implicit and explicit — with which students will interact. Then, write those ideas in short, clear declarative statements. These statements should in some way reflect the world that the students live in or know about. Therefore, avoid abstractions whenever possible. Finally, put these statements into a format that will elicit anticipation and prediction making.

Study Boxes 4–10 (social studies) and 4–11 (math). Then consider ways you can develop guides for material in your content area.

PREVIEWING

The technique of previewing gives students some idea of what a text
Why does previewing reduce uncertainty? selection is about in advance of reading it. It prepares them for what is coming. Students' tendency, of course, is to jump right into an assignment, often without rhyme or reason, and plow through it. Not so, however, when they learn how to preview material. This prereading technique helps them to raise questions and set purposes which will lead to more efficient processing of information.

When students raise questions about content material that they preview, they are likely to examine the extent of their own uncertainty and to find out what they don't know about the information they will acquire during reading. As a result of previewing and questioning, students become involved in a search for answers during reading. However, previewing and questioning require active participation by students; this is why high-powered as well as low-powered readers have trouble previewing on their own. They need teachers who will guide the preview and activate questions. Where does the teacher start?

Textbook Aids. Previewing works well when content materials contain textbook aids which are organizational, typographic, or visual in nature. Textbook writers use these aids as guideposts for readers.

How can teachers help students to preview various kinds of textbook aids?

Certain organizational aids such as the table of contents, preface, chapter introductions and/or summaries, and chapter questions give readers valuable clues about the overall structure of a textbook or the important ideas in a unit or chapter. Previewing a table of contents, for example, not only creates a general impression but also helps readers to distinguish the forest from the trees. The table of contents in Box 4–12 might well be used by a business teacher to give

---

Box 4–10

THE COMMON SOLDIER OF THE CIVIL WAR

Directions: Johnny Reb and Billy Yank were common soldiers of the Civil War. You will be reading about some of their basic differences in your textbook. What do you think those differences will be? Before reading your assignment, place the initials JR in front of the phrases that you think best describe Johnny Reb. Place initials BY in front of those statements which best describe Billy Yank. Do not mark those statements common to both sides.

___ 1. more likely to be able to read and write

___ 2. best able to adjust to living in the open areas

___ 3. more likely to be from a rural setting

___ 4. took a greater interest in politics

___ 5. more deeply religious

___ 6. often not able to sign his name

___ 7. disliked regimentation of army life

___ 8. more likely to speak more slowly and with an accent

___ 9. more probably a native American

___ 10. more likely to be on the side with the greater percentage of foreign-born soldiers

___ 11. common man in the social order

students a feel for the overall theme or structure of the course material so that students will get a sense of the scope and sequence of ideas at the very beginning of the course. The business teacher can also use this opportunity to build background and discuss the relatedness of each of the parts of the book. He or she might raise these questions: "Why did the authors sequence the material this way?" "Why do the authors begin with 'Planning and Decision Making' in Part One?" "If you were the author, would you have arranged the major parts in the text differently? Why?"

The table of contents can also be used to introduce a chapter or unit. The business teacher might ask students to refer to Part One on the table of contents. "What do you think this part of the book is about?"

Box 4–11

METRIC MEDITATION

Directions: Consider the following statements and determine which are likely and which are unlikely. Check the column under Likely if you think the statement could be true. Check the column under Unlikely if you think the statement could not be true. Do this by yourself. We will then compare answers.

Likely   Unlikely

_____	_____	1. The basketball player is 3 meters tall.
_____	_____	2. The bicycle was traveling 20 kilometers per hour.
_____	_____	3. He drank a liter of pop in one gulp.
_____	_____	4. The temperature dropped to 25° Celsius and it started to snow.
_____	_____	5. The football player had a mass of 120 kilograms.
_____	_____	6. The pencil had a mass of 100 grams.
_____	_____	7. His foot is 5 decimeters long.
_____	_____	8. The area of a postage stamp is 20 square centimeters.
_____	_____	9. He purchased 250 milliliters of pop for 20 cents.
_____	_____	10. The beauty contestant measured 90-60-90 centimeters.

Now you can determine your metric rating.

I will read the ones which are likely. If you agreed, give yourself one point. For each of the others you marked unlikely give yourself one point. Count the number of points and find your metric rating on this chart:

Points: Metric Rating
0 – 3   A miserably messy metric measurer
4 – 7   A moderately mediocre metric measurer
8 – 10   A miraculously meticulous metric measurer

At the end of our unit of study we will check our metric rating again.

"Why do you think so?" Key words can also be highlighted for discussion: "What do you think the author means by *values?*" "What does *budgeting* mean? What does it have to do with *financial planning?*" Open-ended questions such as these help readers to focus attention on the material.

As students zero in on a particular chapter, they can make use of additional organizational aids such as the introduction and/or summary or the questions at the end of the chapter. These aids often create a frame of reference for the important ideas in the chapter.

Typographical and visual aids within a chapter are also invaluable devices for previewing. Students can survey chapter titles; headings and subheadings; words, phrases, or sentences in special type; and pictures, diagrams, illustrations, charts, and graphs in advance of reading to get a general outline — an agenda, so to speak — of what to expect.

Box 4–12

PREVIEWING A TABLE OF CONTENTS

CONTENTS

SOURCE: Jelley, Herbert, and Herrmann, Robert. *The American Consumer: Issues and Decisions*, 2nd ed. New York: McGraw-Hill, 1978. Reproduced with permission.

In general, students should follow these guidelines when previewing:

1. Read the title. Convert it to a question.
2. Read the introduction/summary and questions. What seem to be the author's main points?
3. Read the heads and subheads. Convert them to questions.
4. Read print in special type. Why are certain words, phrases, or sentences highlighted?
5. Study visual materials such as pictures, maps, and diagrams. What do the graphics tell you about the chapter's content?

The teacher orchestrates the preview. Initially, you might want to model effective previewing/questioning behaviors. This entails walking students through the process. Aukerman (1972) suggested using an overhead projector and transparencies for this purpose. Select several pages from the assigned reading and develop transparencies in which you annotate the type of questions which students should ask while previewing. Then share the overhead transparencies with the class, explaining the reasons for your annotations. You might then have students open their textbooks to another section of the chapter. Ask the kind of questions that will encourage them to pay attention to the organizational, typographical, and visual aids in the assigned material. Finally, encourage students to raise their own questions while previewing.

Skimming. A natural part of previewing is to learn how to skim content material effectively. Skimming involves a quick perusal of the material to see what the reading assignment will be about. One recommendation is to show students the importance of reading the first sentence (usually a topic statement or important idea) of every paragraph. In this way, they will get a good sense of what is coming.

Why skim material quickly?

In addition, an effective motivator for raising students' expectations about the material is to have them skim an entire reading selection rapidly — in no more than one or two minutes. Encourage students to zip through every page and not to get bogged down on any one section or subsection. The class must then reconstruct what they have skimmed. Ask them to recall everything that they have read. You and they will be amazed at the quantity and quality of the recalls.

A Brief Word About SQ3R. Previewing and questioning comprise the first two steps of SQ3R, an often prescribed study strategy for content area reading. SQ3R stands for:

Survey. Students preview the material as described above to create a framework for organizing information as they read the material.

Question. The reader raises questions with the expectation of finding answers in the material to be studied.

Read. The reader next attempts to answer the questions formulated in the previous step.

Recite. The reader then deliberately attempts to answer out loud or in writing the questions formulated in the second step.

Review. The reader finally reviews the material by rereading portions of the assignment in order to verify the answers given during the previous step.

SQ3R is called a "study system" because of its interlocking steps. Robinson (1961) originated SQ3R as an independent study tool for college students nearly three decades ago. Most secondary school students may find it difficult to SQ3R on their own. In fact, I personally have never known a secondary student to SQ3R on a regular basis. Maturing readers need more structured guidance to study reading assignments than SQ3R, when attempted independently, can offer.

In this chapter we explored the value of previewing or surveying and questioning. But as the case may be, the content teacher orchestrates the survey and activates the questions. At various points in this book we will also explore the value of reading to answer questions, selective reading and rereading, and review. Again, the emphasis will be on what the teacher does to guide reading. And this is as it should be for maturing readers.

LOOKING BACK, LOOKING FORWARD

Teachers can reduce the uncertainty that students bring to reading material by helping them raise questions and anticipate meaning. The reader's knowledge of the world is the given in any kind of a classroom situation that requires reading. The teacher must make full use of this given by showing students how to connect what they know already to the new — the ideas presented in the content material. Prediction and curiosity arousal are two important instructional tools for this purpose.

A teacher arouses curiosity for reading material by creating conceptual conflict. Students will read to resolve conflicts arising from problem solving and hypothetical situations, an examination of values and attitudes, brainstorming, and guided imagery.

Prediction and curiosity arousal go hand in hand. The questions students raise as a result of predicting will feed them into the reading material and keep them on course. Anticipation guides and previewing techniques are two strategies for stimulating predictions about the content under study.

We're ready now to move to Part II, Reading and Extending. In many ways this unit may be considered the backbone of content area reading instruction. We'll explore the strategies and materials that can be adapted to guide reading and develop understandings through content materials. The next chapter introduces the notion of levels of comprehension and then shows how teachers can develop three-level reading guides to bridge the gap between students' reading abilities and textbook difficulty.

SUGGESTED READINGS

Estes, Thomas, and Vaughan, Joseph, Jr. *Reading and learning in the content classroom*. Boston: Allyn and Bacon, 1978, chapter 10.

Friedman, Myles, and Rowls, Michael. *Teaching reading and thinking skills*. New York: Longman, 1980, chapter 2.

Herber, Harold. *Teaching reading in content areas*. 2nd ed. Englewood Cliffs, N.J.: Prentice-Hall, 1978, chapter 7.

Macklin, Michael. "Content area reading is a process of finding personal meaning." *Journal of reading* 22 (1978): 212–213.

Olshavsky, Jill, and Kletzing, Karen. "Prediction: one strategy for reading success in high school." *Journal of reading* 22 (1979): 512–516.

Olshavsky, Jill. "Reading as problem solving: an investigation of strategies." *Reading research quarterly* 12 (1976-1977): 654–674.

Smith, Frank. *Comprehension and learning*. New York: Holt, Rinehart and Winston, 1975.

Vacca, Richard. "Readiness to read content area assignments." *Journal of reading* 20 (1977): 387–392.

PART TWO

Reading and Extending

CHAPTER FIVE

Guiding Levels of Comprehension

*Training is everything. The
peach was once a bitter
almond; cauliflower
is nothing but cabbage
with a college education.*

MARK TWAIN

ORGANIZING PRINCIPLE

Growth *in* reading. Growth *through* reading. These are the major themes of content area reading instruction. From the very first day that a child picks up a book, he or she is reading to learn and learning to read. It's a two-way street from the very beginning. This dual process of reading to learn and learning to read never ends. When the philosopher Goethe was in his eighties he supposedly said, "The dear people do not know how long it takes to learn to read. I have been at it all my life and cannot say that I have reached the goal." Reading is an act of maturity. And each of us in a significant way can contribute to the reading maturity of students within the context of subject matter instruction.

The organizing principle of this chapter suggests a major contribution that content teachers can make to students' reading maturity: *You can guide maturing readers to respond to meaning at various levels of comprehension.* Through the use of three-level reading guides, teachers will give students a feel for what it means to comprehend at literal, interpretive, and applied levels.

Before continuing on in this chapter, study the Chapter Overview, which shows the relationships among the important ideas you will encounter.

CHAPTER OVERVIEW

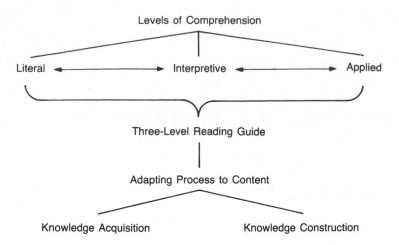

Good readers adapt. They read differently at different times because they read different materials for different purposes. One way to look at reading, albeit simplified, is to suggest that it's a dynamic interplay, a give-and-take process, between the reader's knowledge and skills and the conceptual and stylistic demands implicit in content material.

When I was in the midst of doctoral studies I remember laboring perhaps five or six hours at a stretch over several pages of reading material in Statistics III — a fate endured by most students who managed to survive Statistics I and II. I can recall, however, reading *The Exorcist* in its entirety in about the same length of time. Interestingly, the Statistics III textbook and *The Exorcist* had the same accumulative effect: each scared the daylights out of me. The point of these remembrances, nonetheless, is that as readers we adapt.

Gibson and Levin (1975) maintained that mature readers develop and use varying strategies for dealing with different kinds of reading material. In Chapter 4, I built a case for reducing uncertainty about content material before students read. Content teachers can set purposes for reading and sustain motivation through prediction and curiosity arousal. Purpose helps to determine how readers will adapt themselves to content materials. There's little new about this particular revelation. The Roman writer Seneca remarked centuries ago, "When a ship does not know what port to sail toward, no wind is favorable."

The instructional implications of purpose in reading are best supported by Stauffer (1975), who claimed that the quality of prereading

Why does text content also influence reading comprehension?

instruction classroom teachers incorporate into their lessons influences how well students will comprehend: "What the reader does before he reads largely determines what he will achieve" (p. 5).

To some degree, however, the content of the text also determines how readers will adapt. The conceptual demands of the material interact with the reader's purpose and the knowledge of the world that he or she brings to a particular reading task. Teachers are more likely to guide reading when they are aware of the conceptual demands of the material they assign than when they are not. If you know what students should gain from reading, you will be in a better position to influence how they will gain it.

Guiding reading is the focus of the next three chapters. This chapter emphasizes the development of *three-level guides*. Chapter 6 continues the discussion by examining the use of *pattern guides* and *concept guides*. Chapter 7 explores the role of questions and questioning.

GUIDING COMPREHENSION

During the past two decades a substantial body of information has been reported on the skills and strategies that people use and adapt in reading. The emphasis from a practical and theoretical view in general has been on what a reader does during learning.

Likewise, guiding comprehension of content material depends on what you do within the structure of planned lessons. The success of guided reading is a function of how well you manipulate students' thinking during reading. I used to feel that the term "manipulate" sounded somewhat harsh because of its negative connotations. Perhaps "stimulate" or "orchestrate" are more pleasing terms. Yet, in a very positive sense good teaching is a matter of manipulation. Showing students how to do what they are required to do is the name of the game. Guiding reading comprehension in content areas means making sure students know how to adapt skills and strategies to your reading material.

I have contended that what you do to guide reading is terribly

Why use reading guides?

important. What, then, are some of the things that you can do? For openers, consider the use of reading guides. A reading guide bridges the chasm between students and textbook; it narrows the gap between the levels of reading maturity students bring to content material and the conceptual demands of the material itself. Reading guides will make life in the classroom easier for students. Don't think by "easier" that I mean "less challenging" or "less productive" or that guides represent a panacea. Experience and research suggest just the opposite. Reading guides are used in content classes primarily because the text material is difficult and important enough to warrant guidance. The judicious use of these adjunct materials will make learning easier.

Levels of Comprehension

Describe each level of comprehension.

Because reading is a thoughtful process, it embraces the idea of levels of comprehension. Readers respond to meaning at various levels of abstraction and conceptual difficulty. Herber (1978) argued that the levels construct is a simple treatment of comprehension. Content area reading is not complicated by teaching snippets of comprehension skills separately. This is precisely the reason why so many content area teachers with minimal training (or interest) in the detailed aspects of reading instruction find the three-level process useful. Although skills are assumed to operate in each level, the emphasis is clearly on how comprehension skills interact within and among the three levels. Figure 5–1 shows the major aspects of levels of comprehension.

Figure 5–1.

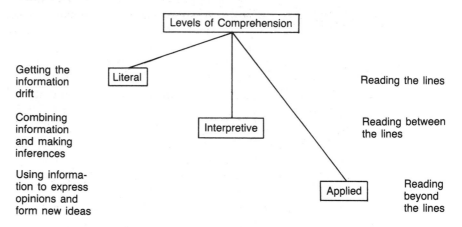

INFORMATION DRIFT AND THE LITERAL LEVEL

The literal level is another way of saying students can "read the lines" of your content material. They can stay with print sufficiently to get the drift of the author's message. In simple terms, a literal recognition of that message determines what the author says.

Try to recall your freshman year in college when you probably learned the universal strategy of coping with the literal level of your first five-pound text. Probably after careful observation of a "model," that stoic sophomore or junior struggling with a textbook in a library carrel, you rushed to the nearest bookstore and purchased your first felt-tip marker. Its ink was pink or yellow, wasn't it? Then you began to get the drift as you underlined the essential information in your text readings.

If you were like me, your yellow felt-tip pen soon became as comfortable as Linus's blanket. The only trouble, of course, is that soon into the business of underlining, you moved from selective markings to full-scale assaults on the printed page. You probably began to change entire pages of white background to yellow background as your marker ran amuck with indiscriminate frenzy. You were learning. Or so you thought.

The trouble is that searching for important literal information isn't an easy chore, particularly if readers haven't matured enough to know how to make the search, or even worse, haven't determined why they are making it in the first place. Most students can and will profit handsomely from being shown how to recognize the essential information in text.

INFERENCE AND THE INTERPRETIVE LEVEL

Knowing what the author says is necessary but not sufficient in constructing meaning from print. Good readers search for conceptual complexity in material. They "read between the lines." They focus not only on what authors say, but also on what authors mean by what they say. Herber (1978) clarified the difference between literal and interpretive levels this way: "At the literal level readers identify the important information. At the interpretive level readers perceive the relationships that exist in that information, conceptualizing the ideas formulated by those relationships . . ." (p. 45).

The interpretive level is laced with inferences about the author's intended meaning. How the reader "teases out" implied ideas by combining information is integral to the interpretive process.

KNOWLEDGE CONSTRUCTION AND THE APPLIED LEVEL

How is reconstructing an author's message different from constructing knowledge about that message?

From time to time throughout the book you have probably been trying to read me — not my words but *me*. And, in the process of reconstructing my messages, you probably raised questions similar to these: So what? What does this information mean to me? Does he make sense? Can I use these ideas for content instruction? Your attempt to seek significance or relevance in what I say and mean is one signal that you are reading at the applied level. You are reading beyond my lines. You are essentially constructing knowledge.

Reading at the applied level is undoubtedly akin to the act of discovery. It underscores the creative nature of reading comprehension. Bruner (1961) explained that discovery "is in its essence a matter of rearranging or transforming evidence in such a way that one is enabled to go beyond the evidence so reassembled to additional new insights" (p. 21). By guiding students at the applied level you will show them how to synthesize information — lay that synthesis alongside what they know already — to express opinions about and to draw additional insights and fresh ideas from content material.

A THREE-LEVEL GUIDE DEMONSTRATION

I came across an article in the newspaper several years ago with some significance about teachers' actions. First preview the three-level guide in Box 5–1 and then read the fictitious selection that I developed based on the newspaper item. After reading the selection, complete the guide.

Box 5–1

THREE-LEVEL GUIDE TO "GUEST LECTURER"

I. *Directions:* Check the items you believe say what the author says. Sometimes the exact words will be used; other times other words may be used.

__ 1. Letters of reprimand were to be written for two teachers and their department head.

__ 2. The school committee decided the teachers made an error in judgment.

__ 3. The teachers were finally suspended for three days.

__ 4. Students and parents generally felt the "lecture" was a mistake.

__ 5. School officials approved the prostitute's visit beforehand.

__ 6. Control over the program will be tightened in the future.

II. *Directions:* Put a check on the line beside any of the statements below which you think are reasonable interpretations of the author's meaning.

__ 1. Emotion rather than reason prevailed among some members of the community.

__ 2. Parents and students seemed to view the controversy differently.

__ 3. A few vocal parents led the attack against the teachers.

__ 4. The prostitute's lecture is another example of teachers and students trying to take over the schools.

__ 5. The teachers involved in the controversy were glad to be reprimanded and not suspended.

III. *Directions:* To apply what you read means to take information and ideas from what you have read and connect them to what you know. Place a check in the blank beside any statements below which are supported by statements in Level 2 and by previous experience or study. Be sure you can defend your answers.

___ 1. A prostitute can contribute to one's formal education.

___ 2. Schools should be run more *for* students than *by* them.

___ 3. Ends justify means.

___ 4. Ideas and actions alien to the status quo usually precipitate aggressive reaction and restrictive requirements.

Guest Lecturer

The tension in the air could be sliced with a knife. The hearing had lasted nearly five hours. More than two hundred people, many of them students, were in the meeting room where the session was held. Bob Herring and Ray Weatherman, the two American history teachers, sat attentively. They didn't blink an eyelash at the verdict: letters of reprimand were to be written for the two teachers and their department head.

The Hard Rock School Committee had concluded that the teachers made an error in judgment but didn't deserve to be suspended. Little did Bob and Ray realize the community turmoil that would be created when they invited a guest lecturer, a young prostitute, to speak to their high school class. The class was an innovative social studies elective, "Economics and Politics in the Community." The teachers didn't suspect that their guest lecturer would get some residents of Hard Rock so "bent out of shape."

"I want them suspended," bellowed Anton Slipman to the cheers of some of the parents in the room. "What does a teacher have to do to get suspended?" Slipman wondered. As a member of the school committee, he continued his tirade against the teachers. "This is the most outrageous thing to happen in Hard Rock since I can remember." More cheers. Slipman was hot. "At least forty, maybe fifty, people in the community have contacted me. They're as upset as I am." And they all must have been in the room.

One parent stood up and shouted, "I'm going to send my children to a private school if things keep up the way they have been going." Another added, "I want to know who's running the schools. The students? The teachers? What's going on?"

Mr. Prufrock, the department head of social studies, squirmed restlessly in his chair during the entire session. He was the teachers' supervisor. Why didn't he stop them from inviting the prostitute? Although he had listened to part of the guest lecturer's talk, he claimed that he and the principal had not sanctioned the lecture beforehand.

Bob Herring and Ray Weatherman explained in detail the objectives of the controversial course. Weatherman, the more vocal of the two, said, "Prostitution is a victimless crime, just like bookmaking and homosexuality. The only victim is the law that is broken." Some gasps were heard in the room.

Dr. Picasso, the school superintendent, acknowledged that students in the class had talked to alcoholics and drug addicts as part of the program, and they even saw an X-rated movie called "Without a Stitch." But he said, "Having a prostitute speak to students overstepped the bounds and contradicted the mission of the school."

Most of the students who testified at the hearing agreed that the guest lecturer had provided them with a good learning experience. One girl accused the school committee of being overprotective. "If we don't learn about these things in school, where are we going to learn about them — on the street?" Slipman, however, warned the girl, "These schools aren't going to be run for what you want."

In the end, Slipman lost the fight for suspension of the two teachers and the department head. The attorney for the teachers promised to fight the reprimand. The superintendent of schools indicated in a memorandum to the school committee that controls over the controversial course would be tightened.

And the students? They attended school the next day.

Comments on the Demonstration

What does the demonstration suggest about first previewing a reading guide?

First of all, note that the three-level format gave you what Herber (1970) has described as a "conscious experience" with comprehension levels as a process. Consider also that as you walked through the process you responded to and manipulated the important explicit and implicit ideas in the material. You may have sensed the relatedness of ideas as you moved within and among the levels.

Why did I direct you to first preview the guide and then read the material? Because previewing helps create a predisposition for reading the material. As you recall from Chapter 4, previewing helps to reduce the reader's uncertainty about the material to be read. You know what is coming. When I asked you to read the guide first, I hoped to raise your expectations about the author's message. In a sense, previewing the reading guide fulfills the same purpose as the materials and strategies suggested in Chapter 4. By encountering some of the ideas before reading you are in a more flexible and adaptive position to direct the search for information that may be relevant in the reading material.

You probably noted also that the declarative statements did not require you to produce answers to questions. Rather, you had to make decisions among likely alternatives. Herber and Nelson (1975) supported the notion that it's easier to recognize possible answers than to produce them. This is why you weren't asked to respond to a set of questions at each level. In Chapter 7, the role of questions and questioning will be discussed.

Notice too that in a very positive way the statements can serve as springboards for discussion and conversation about the content. Were students to react to guides without the opportunity to discuss and debate responses, the adjunct material would soon deteriorate into busy work and paper shuffling.

A final comment: your maturity as a reader probably is such that you didn't need structured guidance for this selection, particularly at levels I and II. If you make the decision that certain segments of your text can be handled without reading guidance, then don't construct guide material. A three-level guide is a means to growth in reading and growth through reading. It is not an end in itself. Were I to use "Guest Lecturer" in a class for adult learners, I probably would provide prereading instruction to activate interest in and thinking about the content before reading and then follow with a guide at level III — thus providing just enough structure to suit my purposes.

Cautions and Observations

Don't be misled by the apparent discreteness among comprehension levels. Don't, as Dale (1969) pronounced, suffer from "hardening of the categories." The term *levels* implies a cognitive hierarchy that may be more apocryphal than real. A reader doesn't necessarily read first for literal recognition, then interpretation, and finally application — although that may appear to be a logical sequence. Many readers, for example, read text for overarching concepts and generalizations first and then search for evidence to support their inferences.

Most important is that you recognize that in reading, levels are probably interactive and inseparable (just as skills are within levels). Nevertheless, the classroom teacher attempts to have students experience each aspect of the comprehension process as they read content material. In doing so, students adapt skills and strategies as they interact with the material. They get a feel for the component processes within reading comprehension. They come to sense in an instructional setting what it means to make inferences; what it means to use information as the basis for those inferences; and what it means to rearrange or transform acquired understandings into what they know already in order to construct knowledge.

Why use a reading guide judiciously?

The reading guide is not meant to be used with every text assignment every day. If it were to be, it would soon be counterproductive. One math teacher's evaluation of a three-level guide crystallizes this point: "The students said the guide actually helped them organize in their minds the author's ideas and helped them to understand the material. I think the guide was successful but I would not use it all the time because many of the assignments don't lend themselves to this type of activity." The three-level reading guide is but one instructional aid which helps students grow toward mature reading and independent learning.

Merlin the magician doesn't wave his magic wand to ensure the effectiveness of three-level guides. They can be facilitative only when students know how to work in groups and know how to apply techniques that have been taught clearly. The heart of the matter is what the teacher does to make guided reading work.

Finally, I urge you also to consider guides as tools, not tests. Their real value ultimately lies in providing for the adaptation and application of skills to subject matter material. But I hasten to emphasize one more time that individual skills and levels are likely to be interactive and inseparable from one another. Think of each statement in a reading guide as a prompt that will initiate that interaction and reinforce the quality of the reader's response to meaning in text material.

CONSTRUCTION OF THREE-LEVEL GUIDES ━━━━━━━━

Explain the guidelines for constructing a three-level guide.

There are no set procedures for constructing three-level reading guides. Before constructing a guide, however, the teacher has to make at least two important decisions. First, you should examine content material to decide what information to emphasize. Given your content objectives, what are the important ideas that should be emphasized? Second, Earle (1969) suggested you decide how much assistance students will need to succeed. What are the students' competencies? The depth of understanding that you expect them to achieve? The difficulty of the material?

Having made these decisions you may wish to consider these guidelines:

1. Begin construction of the guide at level II, the interpretive level. Analyze the text selection, asking yourself, "What does the author mean?" Write down in your own words those inferences that make sense to you and fit your content objectives. Make sure your statements are written simply and clearly. (After all, you don't want to construct a guide to read the guide.)

2. Next, search the text for propositions, explicit pieces of information, needed to support the inferences you have chosen for level II. Put these into statement form. You now have level I, the literal level.

3. Decide whether you want to add a distractor or two to levels I and II. There is some debate whether distractors detract from the guided experience (Herber, 1978). My suggestion is that you follow your instincts. I have found that a distractor can maintain an active response to the information search, mainly because students sense that they cannot indiscriminately check every item and therefore focus the information search more carefully. Others, however, feel that a distractor reinforces a "right-wrong" mentality and should not be used.

4. Develop statements for level III, the applied level. Such statements represent additional insights or principles that can be drawn when relationships established by the author are combined with other ideas outside the text selection itself but inside the heads of your students. In other words, help students connect what they know already to what they have read.

5. Be flexible and adaptive. Develop a format that will appeal to you and your students. Try to avoid crowding too much print on the reading guide.

CLASSROOM EXAMPLES

The format of the guide should vary. The classroom examples that follow serve only as models. As you study these illustrations, think of ways that you will be able to adapt and apply the three-level construct to your content materials.

Why are these classroom examples only "models"?

English ───────────────────────────────────────

The three-level guide in Box 5–2 was designed for eleventh graders as part of a modern American poetry unit. The purpose of the guide was to have students experience an E. E. Cummings poem at different levels of complexity. Although the English teacher considered the class to be able readers, he felt that his students needed assistance to deal effectively with the poet's unusual style as well as his explicit and implicit meanings.

Preview the three-level guide for Cummings's poem, read through the poem, and then complete the guide. Where an alternative choice says "other," develop a statement that reflects an idea within the specified level of comprehension. If possible, compare your statements with others' statements.

Box 5–2 ───────────────────────────────────────

THREE-LEVEL GUIDE FOR CUMMINGS POEM

l(a
E. E. Cummings[*]

l(a

le
af
fa

ll

s)
one
l

iness

I. *Directions:* Check the statements that say what the poet said.

___ 1. Fall has arrived.

___ 2. Loneliness

___ 3. A leaf falls.

___ 4. Oneliness

II. *Directions:* Check each statement below you believe represents what the poet meant by what he said.

___ 1. Loneliness is like the falling of a leaf.

___ 2. Loneliness is a quiet time.

___ 3. To be one is to be lonely.

[*] © 1958 by E. E. Cummings. Reprinted from his volume COMPLETE POEMS 1913–1962 by permission of Harcourt Brace Jovanovich, Inc. and Granada Publishing Limited.

— 4. An occurrence in nature is similar to what occurs in humankind.

— 5. (Other) _____ .

III. *Directions:* Check those statements which you believe express ideas you can support based on what you know and your interpretation of the poem.

— 1. Oneliness is not a human characteristic.

— 2. Loneliness can be a beautiful time.

— 3. No man is an island.

— 4. Loneliness is a slow death.

— 5. Nature teaches us about ourselves.

— 6. (Other) _____

A poem presents a problem at the interpretive and applied levels. Is it possible, or even desirable, to separate the poet's intended meaning from your personal response to that meaning? You may decide to combine levels II and III when developing a reading guide for a poem. The guide will then prompt two levels of thinking — explicit and implicit responses to meaning.

By way of contrast, note how a seventh grade English teacher developed a sequence of reading guides for sections from *Flowers for Algernon* (Box 5–3).

Box 5–3

FLOWERS FOR ALGERNON

Directions: Charlie Gordon's values should be easy to identify, but as the text says, Charlie gets a chance to live in two worlds. Watch for changes in people's values as Charlie goes through his changes. Follow the directions for each part of the reading guide after or while reading each of the four sections.

I. Pages 172–176

A. Check statements that are true. They may or may not be in exact words.

— 1. Charlie wants to be smart.

— 2. Charlie sees nothing in the ink blots.

— 3. Miss Kinnian recommends Charlie to the doctors.

— 4. Charlie beats Algernon in every maze test.

— 5. Charlie has good motivation.

— 6. Charlie likes his friends at the factory.

B. Check statements that are true. They may be reasonable interpretations of the facts.

— 1. Charlie has no imagination.

— 2. Charlie is honest.

— 3. Drs. Nemur and Strauss hope to create a new breed of intellectual supermen through their surgical techniques.

— 4. The doctors triple Algernon's intelligence through surgery.

— 5. The hospital people are very patient with Charlie.

— 6. Charlie's friends at the factory really like him.

— 7. To "pull a Charlie Gordon" is to do something really stupid.

C. Check statements that might apply to your own experience in real life, or statements that are supported by the story so far.

— 1. Some people make fun of the mentally retarded.

— 2. It is possible to surgically increase intelligence.

— 3. Some people have the patience and desire to help the mentally retarded.

— 4. Motivation is important to learning.

II. Pages 177–184

A. Check statements that show Charlie is making progress.

— 1. That crazy TV kept me up all night. How can I sleep . . .?

— 2. I beat Algernon!

— 3. I showed them (how I mop out the toilet) and everyone laughed . . .

— 4. I think their must be somebody else on this island because there's a picture with his funny umbrella looking at footprints.

— 5. I want to find out more . . . but . . . that's all ther is. Why.

— 6. . . . all my friends are smart people but there good.

— 7. (Punctuation, is; fun!)

— 8. I read the grammar book last night and it explanes the whole thing.

— 9. I'm ashamed.

B. Check statements that you think are logical inferences about the story.

— 1. Miss Kinnian feels sorry for Charlie.

— 2. Joe Carp and Frank Reilly feel sorry for Charlie.

— 3. Mrs. Flynn, Charlie's landlady, is suspicious of him.

— 4. An IQ measures how much intelligence a person has.

— 5. Dr. Nemur values success most highly.

— 6. Dr. Strauss values money most highly.

— 7. Mr. Donnegan fires Charlie for ruining the factory's production schedule.

— 8. Fanny Girden admires Charlie for his intelligence.

C. Check statements you think could apply to real life, based on the story.

— 1. Ignorance is bliss.

— 2. Knowledge is evil.

— 3. Intelligence can drive a wedge between people.

— 4. IQ is an important measuring tool.

— 5. People hate and fear things they don't understand.

III. Pages 188–192

A. Check statements that are true in the story.

  — 1. Algernon loses his intelligence.

  — 2. Charlie begins to forget.

  — 3. Dr. Strauss feels guilty.

  — 4. Mrs. Flynn helps Charlie.

  — 5. Charlie becomes a lathe operator at the factory.

  — 6. Charlie doesn't like Miss Kinnian any more.

  — 7. Joe Carp and Frank Reilly defend Charlie.

  — 8. Charlie moves to an apartment closer to the hospital.

B. Check inferences based on the facts you have noted.

  — 1. Charlie knows that what happened to Algernon will happen to him.

  — 2. Miss Kinnian feels guilty.

  — 3. Mr. Donnegan respects Charlie.

  — 4. Joe Carp and Frank Reilly have learned not to mistreat Charlie.

  — 5. Charlie is happier with an IQ of 68.

C. Check statements you think would be good conclusions applied to life.

  — 1. It's easy to make friends if you let people laugh at you.

  — 2. People of honest feelings and sensibility think nothing of abusing a man born with low intelligence.

  — 3. Even a feebleminded man wants to be like other men.

  — 4. Intelligence is more important than personality.

  — 5. A strong sense of values is more important than intelligence.

  — 6. Sensitivity has nothing to do with intelligence.

  — 7. Smart people are better than dumb people.

Because Daniel Keyes' novel was taught to junior high school readers, the statements for the guide to it are less abstract and complex than those in the guide to Cummings's poem. The teacher introduced *Flowers of Algernon* as part of a unit on values. He had given the students a great deal of readiness — simulation games and values clarification exercises — before introducing the novel. He developed the reading guides to initiate discussion and extend the students' thinking about their own values.

Math

The nature of the mathematical content determines the form of the guide. Word problems in particular illustrate this point. For example, Riley and Pachtman (1978) explained: "Mathematical word problems constitute a new area of difficulty for the student. Unlike the language of narrative material, the language of word problems is compact. Mathematic concepts and relationships are often 'hidden' or assumed and therefore not readily apparent to the student'' (p. 531). Riley and Pachtman suggested how the three-level guide can be adapted to meet the reading demands implicit in solving word problems. The procedure is as follows: (1) Level I = the facts of the problem; (2) Level II = the mathematical ideas or concepts underlying the problem; (3) Level III = the numerical depictions related to the problem. Study Box 5–4 which illustrates the adaptations which can be made when reading word problems in math.

Box 5–4

WORD PROBLEM READING GUIDE

Problem: Tom has collected 239 empty cans for recycling. He puts 107 into a big box. How many must he put in each of two smaller boxes if he uses the rest of the cans and puts the same number in each box?

I. Facts of the Problem

Directions: Read the word problem above. Then under column A check those statements that contain the important facts of the problem. Look back at the problem to check your answers. Under column B check those statements you think will help you solve the problem.

A (Facts)	B (Will help)	
_____	_____	107 cans went into the big box.
_____	_____	The cans were for recycling.
_____	_____	Tom had collected 239 empty cans.
_____	_____	Tom had one big box and two smaller ones.
_____	_____	Tom put the cans into three boxes.
_____	_____	The cans were empty.
_____	_____	107 cans had to be put into two smaller boxes.

II. Math Ideas

Directions: Check the statements that contain math ideas about this problem. Look back to column B of part I to prove your answers. (You may change your answers in part I if you wish to.)

___ Division is putting an amount into equal groups.

___ To find the total amount of a group we add the parts.

___ When we take an amount away we subtract to find the amount left.

___ Adding groups with the same amount in each group is multiplying.

___ Subtracting is separating a group into two parts.

— When we put an amount into groups of the same size we divide the amount by the number of groups.

III. Numbers

Directions: Below are possible ways of getting an answer. Check those that will work in this problem. Look back to Column B of part I and to part II to prove your answers. (You may change some of your answers in parts I and II if you wish to.)

_____ (239 ÷ 2) + 107
_____ (239 − 107) ÷ 2
_____ 107 ÷ 2
_____ 239 ÷ 2
_____ 239 − 107
_____ 107 + 239

Now that you have responded to each part of the guide, you may compute the answer to the problem.

Box 5–5 shows how junior high school students who were in a "below average" math group were given three-level guidance. Again, observe how the statements were written to meet the competencies of the students.

Box 5–5

FRACTIONS

I. What did the material say?

Directions: Check each statement below that you can find on the pages you just read.

— 1. 49/52 is a fraction.
— 2. A fraction has two numbers.
— 3. A fraction is a whole of a part.
— 4. 50¢ = 1/2 of a dollar.
— 5.
— 6. Fraction = $\frac{\text{Parts Used}}{\text{Total Parts}}$
— 7. You must use two numbers to write a fraction.

II. What does the material mean?

Directions: Check each statement below that you think is true and can defend.

— 1. Fractions are important in your life.

— 2. You can make a fraction by putting the number 3 inside the circle: $\frac{\bigcirc}{4}$

___ 3. You can make a fraction by putting the number 8 inside the circle: $\dfrac{\bigcirc}{8}$

___ 4. ◑ = 1/3

___ 5. 3/5 means ●●●○○.

III. How can you use fractions?

Directions: Check each item you agree with.

___ 1. You are on an elevator with seven persons. Two out of the seven are men. 2/7 of the people are men.

___ 2. Start with 8. Take half of it. Take half of the answer, then half of the last answer. Keep on doing this. Pretty soon you will reach zero (0).

___ 3. Hank Aaron had three hits in five at bats. You can say this by writing a fraction.

Social Studies

A ninth grade teacher developed the three-level guide in Box 5–6 to show students how to read a textbook section entitled "Building the First Cities." He directed the students to complete the three-level guide *as* they read the assignment. Examine the variation at the literal level. Completing the guide as you read helps you read selectively and focus on essential information.

Box 5–6

THREE-LEVEL GUIDE: BUILDING FIRST CITIES

I. *Directions:* For the statements below, tell which of the four cities listed is being described exactly by the author. Use this letter code:

    B = Boston
    C = Charleston
    N = New York
    P = Philadelphia

___ 1. the first seaport to be settled

___ 2. rice the main crop

___ 3. many settlers businessmen

___ 4. a busy and beautiful city

___ 5. planned streets

___ 6. theaters here

___ 7. much fishing here

___ 8. a library here built by Ben Franklin

___ 9. the first public schools here

___ 10. planters as leaders here

___ 11. the University of Pennsylvania and religious freedom here

___ 12. many dinners and dances for rich people

___ 13. the largest city for one hundred fifty years

___ 14. a hot, humid city

II. *Directions:* On the basis of what you've read, check each of the statements below about our first four major cities with which the author would agree:

___ 1. Early American cities had some paved streets.

___ 2. Cities were places where news and ideas were exchanged.

___ 3. Minorities were rarely seen in the cities.

___ 4. People of all religions were welcomed everywhere.

___ 5. The common people were allowed a voice in controlling all of the earliest cities.

___ 6. Trade was necessary for the survival of the cities.

___ 7. Entertainment was available in some cities.

___ 8. The early cities were inhabited by different national groups.

III. *Directions:* Check the statements below that you agree with:

___ 1. The early cities were like people: to be healthy they had to be busy with work to do.

___ 2. The early city could be pictured as "a strong young man wearing work clothes."

___ 3. The early city could be pictured as "a middle-aged man wearing a clean, pressed suit."

___ 4. Transportation + money = city problems.

Science and Health ━━━━━━━━━━━━━━━━━━━━━━━━━━━━━━━━━━━━━

The simplicity of Box 5–7 speaks for itself. A fifth grade teacher constructed it as part of a health unit. Students completed the guide individually and then discussed their responses in small groups.

Box 5–7

HEALTH AND GROWTH: "HOW DO YOU GROW UP?"

I. What did the author say?

Directions: Place a check on the line in front of the number if you think a statement can be found in the pages you read.

___ 1. Every human being has feelings, or emotions.

___ 2. Research workers are studying the effects of repeated use of marijuana on the body.

___ 3. You should try hard to hide your strong emotions such as fear or anger.

___ 4. Your feelings affect the way the body works.

— 5. You are likely to get angry at your parents or brothers or sisters more often than at other people.

II. What did the author mean?

Directions: Check the statements below that state what the author was trying to say in the pages you read.

— 1. Sometimes you act in a different way because of the mood you are in.

— 2. Emotional growth has been a continuing process since the day you were born.

— 3. The fact that marijuana hasn't been proven to be harmful means that it is safe to use.

— 4. Each time you successfully control angry or upset feelings you grow a little.

III. Do you agree with these statements?

Directions: Check those statements that you can defend.

— 1. Escaping from problems does not solve them.

— 2. Decisions should be made on facts, not fantasies.

— 3. Getting drunk is a good way to have fun.

Study the adaptations made on Box 5–8, a three-level guide for a relatively sophisticated group of seniors as compared to those in Box 5–7. This new guide is difficult and different. It requires the students to manipulate information and participate actively in the reading assignment.

Box 5–8

DIFFUSION THROUGH A MEMBRANE

I. Observations

Directions: Check all items below which you observed through the lab experiment.

— 1. When you add Lugol (iodine) to a starch solution the solution turns black.

— 2. When you add Lugol to a glucose solution the solution turns orange.

— 3. When you add Benedict to a glucose solution the solution turns black.

— 4. When you add Benedict to a glucose solution the solution turns orange.

— 5. The bag containing the glucose and starch solution is slightly fuller.

— 6. Glucose molecules passed through the semipermeable membrane.

— 7. Starch molecules can pass through the semipermeable membrane.

— 8. Iodine molecules (Lugol solution) can pass through the semipermeable membrane.

— 9. Benedict molecules can pass through the semipermeable membrane.

— 10. The purpose of using the two test tubes containing the water-Benedict solution and the water-Lugol solution is to see and compare the difference in color of the solutions in other test tubes.

II. Interpretations

Directions: Fill in the blanks to make the following interpretations of the previous experiment correct.

1. Benedict solution is used to indicate the presence of _____ in a solution.
2. Lugol is used to indicate the presence of _____ in a solution.
3. _____ molecules and _____ molecules can pass through a semipermeable membrane.
4. _____ molecules cannot pass through a semipermeable membrane because they are too big.
5. The two test tubes containing a _____ solution and a _____ solution were used as controls for this experiment.
6. The bag containing the glucose and starch solution is fuller because more _____ diffused in than diffused out.

III. Implications

Directions: Using information from the previous experiment and from principles A, B, or C below, check the situations described below which you feel could occur. Be ready to explain your answers in terms of the principles and what you observed in the lab.

Principles

A. A substance moves from a region of greater concentration to a region of lesser concentration until there is an equal distribution of molecules on both sides (diffusion).
B. Smaller particles go through the cell membranes more easily and thus faster than do large particles.
C. A solution similar in nature to a solution lost by a cell will be absorbed faster than a dissimilar solution.

__ 1. Road construction causes a landscaper's tree farm once composed of dry fields to become swampy. Within a few weeks several of the trees die.
__ 2. An industrious gardener overfertilizes his plants. As a result he has a very productive garden and is able to share a lot of his produce with his neighbors.
__ 3. The body responds faster to medicine taken orally than it does to medicine taken intravenously.
__ 4. A person with only a slight case of diabetes may take insulin orally; whereas a person with a severe case of diabetes must inject insulin.
__ 5. It is impossible for a doctor to determine through a blood test whether a person has been drinking excessively, because alcohol molecules do not permeate blood cells.
__ 6. When a surgeon is transplanting an organ, it is important to keep the organ being transplanted in an isotonic solution.
__ 7. After an athlete has been working out for an extended period of time, her body cells respond faster to Gator-Ade than water.

And, as a concluding classroom example, you can see how foreign language students will also experience the process of levels of compre-

hension. The Spanish teacher who constructed Box 5–9 marveled at how
well the guide helped to focus attention on the reading selection.

Box 5–9

THREE-LEVEL READING GUIDE

I. Leer paginas 183 y 184, "A un colegio."
Instrucciónes: Ponga una marca en cada una de las frases que usted cree que el autor de
esta lectura dice. A veces las frases son iguales; en otros casos algunas palabras diferentes se
pueden usar.

— 1. Todas las escuelas de Hispanoamerica son públicas.
— 2. Jaime y Carmen son hermanos.
— 3. Carmen va a una escuela pública.
— 4. La escuela de Carmen está en una antigua residencia.
— 5. El colegio se llama Colegio San Martín.
— 6. Carmen y Jaime van a la escuela en tren.
— 7. En Hispanoamerica todos los muchachos y las muchachas van a la escuela juntos.
— 8. El ambiente de las escuelas es bastante informal.
— 9. Jaime se levanta temprano.
— 10. La familia de Carmen y Jaime desayunan juntas.
— 11. En Sur America el colegio es lo mismo que nuestro "high school."
— 12. En muchos paises hispanoamericanos, si las familias tienen dinero, suelen mandar a
       sus hijos a escuelas particulares.
— 13. En muchos colegios, los alumnos no van de un aula a otro.

II. *Direcciónes:* Varias frases están escritas en seguida que representan lo que quiere decir el
autor y que son interpretaciónes con razón de la lectura. Ponga los numeros de las frases de
la primera parte que usted cree son combinados a formar las ideas de la segunda parte:

— a. En Sur America hay escuelas públicas y particulares.
— b. Las familias que tienen los fondos mandan a sus hijos a escuelas particulares.
— c. Las escuelas de casi todas las partes de Hispanoamerica son mas formales que las de
     los EEUU.
— d. En muchos paises de Hispanomerica los alumnos solo van a las escuelas los años
     primarios.
— e. En algunos paises hay más alumnos que escuelas donde pueden asistir.

III. *Direcciónes:* Ponga una marca en las frases que usted cree pueden ser soportadas por las
ideas del autor o por otras ideas de información que usted tiene.

— a. Las escuelas en Sur America son más difíciles que las nuestras.
— b. La educación de los pueblos es menos que en los EEUU.
— c. La populación de Sur America es mucha, y no hay escuelas para todos.
— d. Si la gente tiene buena educación, hay mejor gobierno en el pais.

LOOKING BACK, LOOKING FORWARD ━━━━━━━━━━━━━━━━━━

One important way to guide comprehension is through a three-level reading guide, which a teacher constructs to bridge the gap between students' competencies and the difficulty of text material. The three-level guide stimulates an active response to meaning at the literal, interpretive, and applied levels. It helps readers to acquire and construct knowledge from content material that might otherwise be too difficult for them to read.

Levels of comprehension interact with one another during reading; in all probability levels are inseparable among mature readers. Nevertheless, for instructional purposes, students should experience each level in order to get a feel for the component processes involved in comprehending. Furthermore, three-level guides will help students develop a good sense of the conceptual complexity in text material.

Classroom examples of three-level guides were presented with the expectation that they might serve as models for teachers. Guidelines were also listed for constructing this particular form of guided reading.

In the next chapter the discussion on guiding comprehension continues. Two additional types of reading guides will be considered; the first is called a pattern guide, the second a concept guide. These two reading guides give you additional options for guiding comprehension through teacher-prepared materials.

SUGGESTED READINGS ━━━━━━━━━━━━━━━━━━━━━━━━━━━

Earle, Richard. *Teaching reading and mathematics.* Newark, Del.: International Reading Association, 1976.

Estes, Thomas, and Vaughan, Joseph, Jr. *Reading and learning in the content classroom.* Boston: Allyn and Bacon, 1978, chapter 11.

Gray, William. "The major aspects of reading." In Helen Robinson, *Development of reading abilities.* Supplementary Educational Monograph Series, no. 90. Chicago: University of Chicago Press, 1960, pp. 8–24.

Hafner, Lawrence. *Developmental reading in middle and secondary schools.* New York: Macmillan, 1977, chapter 6.

Herber, Harold. *Teaching reading in content areas,* 2nd ed. Englewood Cliffs, N.J.: Prentice-Hall, 1978, chapter 3.

Robinson, Helen. "The major aspects of reading." In H. Allan Robinson, *Reading: seventy-five years of progress.* Supplementary Educational Monograph Series, no. 96. Chicago: University of Chicago Press, 1966, pp. 22–32.

Thelen, Judith. *Improving reading in science.* Newark, Del.: International Reading Association, 1978.

Vacca, Richard, and Meagher, Judith, eds. *Reading through content.* Storrs, Connecticut: University Publications and the University of Connecticut Reading–Language Arts Center, 1979.

CHAPTER SIX

Perceiving Organization in Text Materials

There are generalizations which
provide examples for supergeneralizations,
just as there are rajas and maharajas . . .
STRANG, McCULLOUGH, AND TRAXLER

ORGANIZING PRINCIPLE

The reading guide was described as a bridge between the textbook and students. It helps close the distance between students' reading abilities and the conceptual demands of the material. The real benefits of reading guides are in their capacity to influence gains in knowledge and the development of processes needed to acquire and construct such knowledge from reading material.

A process that is integral to mature reading is the ability to perceive text organization. Recognizing the structure of ideas in content material enhances reading comprehension. A reading guide can be adapted to help students see the way an author fits together ideas. Therefore, the organizing principle of this chapter is similar to that of the previous chapter: *You can guide maturing readers by helping them perceive relationships and distinguish important from less important ideas.*

As you study the Chapter Overview notice that the pattern guide and the concept guide are presented as alternatives along with the three-level guide. Consider the differences as well as similarities among the three types of reading guides.

Reading guides have immediate and long-term payoffs. They are firmly grounded in the here and now, working to aid students to understand the text material better than they would if left to their own resources. But reading guides also pay "annual dividends compounded

CHAPTER OVERVIEW

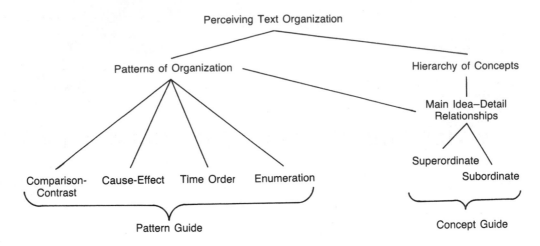

quarterly." A reading guide trains. It shows students how to handle material effectively and efficiently over time so that they will develop the maturity to eventually read on their own.

In the previous chapter the three-level guide was presented as a way of stimulating students to respond to meaning during reading at three levels of comprehension. This chapter introduces you to the *pattern guide* and *concept guide*.

The pattern guide creates an experience for students similar to that of the three-level guide. But you can see the difference between the two guide materials at the literal level. A pattern guide helps students perceive and use the major text relationships that predominate in the reading material. Although the three-level guide focuses on a recognition of the relevant information in the material, text organization is implicit.

A third form of reading guidance, the concept guide, allows students to distinguish important ideas from less important information. With it they will learn to associate and categorize information under major concepts in the material.

TEXT ORGANIZATION

Common sense tells us that most reading materials should have structure, or organization among the ideas. Authors aren't in the business of presenting ideas aimlessly — at least they shouldn't be. Mature readers follow the way an author structures ideas and fits together information. They look for text organization in everything they read. A good reader recognizes that there are relationships among ideas and also that some ideas are more important than others.

As early as 1917, Thorndike concluded that many children fail to

Why perceive text organization?

read successfully because they "have been unable to organize and use" information in written material. His now classic dictum on the nature of reading, that it "involves a weighing of each of many elements in a sentence, their organization in the proper relation to one another" (p. 323), provides a sturdy support for those who underscore the need for recognizing text organization during reading. The perception of organizational patterns — relations — in single sentences, in paragraphs, and in long text passages has been considered basic to comprehension by many authorities in the field of reading.

Smith (1964), for example, warned that "If a student . . . failed to identify these patterns and continues to use the same approach in reading . . . his resulting understanding and concepts discussed in class will undoubtedly be extremely limited" (p. 37). Niles (1964) claimed that there are three abilities that clearly differentiate between the good and the poor reader, among them the "power to find and understand various kinds of thought-relationships that exist . . . in single sentences, in paragraphs and in selections of varying length" (p. 5).

Shepherd (1973) and Robinson (1975) provided a number of elaborate classifications by which teachers could identify patterns in the

How might elaborate classifications work against students?

writings of their disciplines. They also provided excellent detailed analyses of how patterns work in individual paragraphs or short segments of text. While the many elaborate classifications and close distinctions have value, particularly in the experimental study of text structure per se, I believe they can be counterproductive to content area reading instruction. I agree with Niles (1965), who maintained "that elaborate classifications are not only unnecessary but actually a hazard to meaningful teaching" (p. 60).

First of all, elaborate classification often leads to overlap and to the labeling of patterns which essentially depict similar kinds of thought relationships. This labeling can only tend to confuse teachers with minimal background in reading instruction who are genuinely interested in helping students read better. Content teachers often seek the main ideas of reading instruction without the details; elaborate analyses tend to scare them off. Furthermore, if they were to implement detailed analyses of specific paragraphs à la a reading specialist, they would soon become disillusioned. And so would the students. This is why Niles (1965) was right on the mark when she explained that while the combination of patterns in a content reading selection "may confuse the researcher, who is frustrated in attempts to classify or describe, it is not of great significance in the teaching process" (p. 60).

What is essential in perceiving text organization, according to Niles, bears repeating: "The important goal is to teach the student enough so that he forms the habit of looking for order or structure in everything he reads and knows what to do with it when he finds it" (p. 61).

I might also emphasize that students will often read and understand content material without consciously perceiving patterns of organization. However, if the author uses a predominant pattern — and it is recognized — comprehension will undoubtedly be enhanced. Let's see why.

Patterns of Organization

A case can be made for four patterns that seem to predominate over a reading selection of several or more pages of textbook writing: enumeration, time order, comparison-contrast, and cause-effect. Here is a simple definition for each of the patterns:

Explain the different organizational patterns?

1. Enumeration: Listing bits of information (facts, propositions, events, ideas), usually qualifying the listing by criteria such as size or importance.
2. Time Order: Putting facts, events, or concepts into a sequence, using references to time (like dates) to order them.
3. Comparison-Contrast: Pointing out likenesses (comparison) and differences (contrast) among facts, people, events, concepts, etc.
4. Cause-Effect: Showing how facts, events, or concepts (effects) happen or come into being because of other facts, events, or concepts (causes).

Most textbook authors give readers clues or signals that will help them figure out the pattern they are using. Readers will become aware of the pattern if they are looking for the signals. A signal may be a word or a phrase that helps the reader follow the writer's thoughts.

Study Figure 6–1 for signals that authors use to call attention to the organizational patterns just defined.

Identifying and Using Patterns

Try your hand at identifying the predominant organization in each of the following segments of material.

1. There are several points in the fight for freedom of religion. One point was that religion and government should be kept apart. Secondly, Americans did not want any form of a national church as was the case in England. Finally, Americans

Figure 6–1.

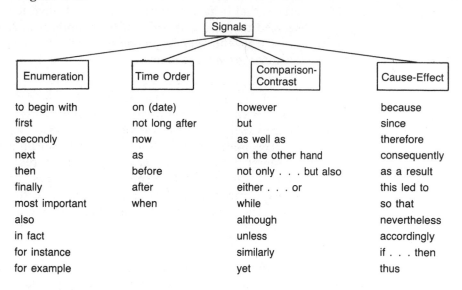

made sure that no person would be denied his or her religious beliefs.

Pattern: _____

2. The fire was started by sparks from a campfire left by a careless camper. Thousands of acres of important watershed burned before the fire was brought under control. By then the trees and the grasslands on the slopes of the valley were gone. Smoking black stumps were all that remained of tall pine trees.

Pattern: _____

3. Castles were built for defense, not comfort. In spite of some books and movies that have made them attractive, castles were cold, dark, gloomy places to live. Rooms were small and not the least bit charming. Except for the great central hall or the kitchen, there were no fires to keep the rooms heated. Not only was there a lack of furniture, but what there was was uncomfortable.

Pattern: _____

4. As part of an experiment, young monkeys were taken away from their mothers when they were born and each was raised in complete isolation. When these monkeys were brought together for the first time, they didn't want to play with each

other as monkeys usually do. They showed no love for each other. And in fact they never learned to live together. It seemed that living apart from their mothers and from each other from the very beginning had some unusual side effects on these growing monkeys.

Pattern: _____

5. John F. Kennedy was the Democratic candidate for President when in October 1960 he first suggested there should be a Peace Corps. After he was elected, Kennedy asked his brother-in-law, Sargent Shriver, to help set up a Peace Corps. In March 1961 Kennedy gave an order to create the organization. It wasn't until September that Congress approved the Peace Corps and appropriated the money to run it for one year. The Peace Corps is still running strong today.

Pattern: _____

The pattern in paragraph 1 was mainly a listing of points. Therefore, enumeration is the most appropriate choice. If you identified paragraph 2 as cause-effect consider yourself "correct." Notice, nevertheless, that the cause (sparks from a campfire) led to a listing of effects (watershed burned, trees and grassland gone, and so forth). An enumeration of several related causes may also result in only one effect. Patterns such as cause-effect and comparison-contrast may very well contain elements of other patterns such as enumeration or time order. The predominant relationship, however (in this case between a cause and its effects), is what is important. Paragraph 3 is organized around a comparison-contrast relationship. Note the signals: "in spite of," "not only . . . but," "except for." The pattern that predominates in paragraph 4 is cause-effect again. The experiment (the cause) created a series of peculiar behaviors (the effects) among the baby monkeys. Paragraph 5 involves a time sequence; therefore, the pattern in this passage is *time order*.

Why is identifying patterns not enough?

An important point to teach students about perceiving text organization is that recognition per se is not enough. You must show students how they can use the structure of relations in content material to facilitate interpretative responses. For example, study in Figure 6–2 how the relationships between the ideas in paragraph 3 and the ideas in paragraph 4 lead to a more inclusive idea or inference.

How, then, might you simplify the search for structure in reading materials as you teach your content? First, you should try to keep to a minimum the number of patterns that students identify and use. Second, your goal should be to guide students to recognize a single pattern that predominates over long stretches of print, even though you recognize that individual paragraphs and sentences are apt to reflect different thought relationships within the text selection.

Figure 6–2.

Paragraph 3

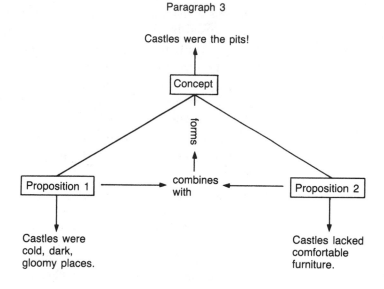

Castles were the pits!

Concept

forms

Proposition 1 → combines with ← Proposition 2

Castles were cold, dark, gloomy places.

Castles lacked comfortable furniture.

Paragraph 4

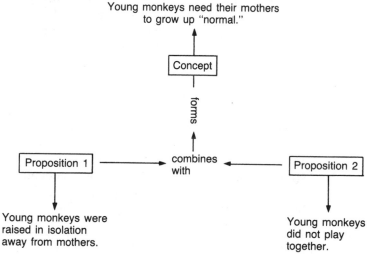

Young monkeys need their mothers to grow up "normal."

Concept

forms

Proposition 1 → combines with ← Proposition 2

Young monkeys were raised in isolation away from mothers.

Young monkeys did not play together.

PATTERN GUIDES

How does a pattern guide work?

A pattern guide is a variation of the three-level guide. The difference between the two lies in the literal level: rather than have students respond to relevant information per se, you can create guide material which allows them to experience how the information fits together. Research and experience

(Vacca, 1975, 1977; Herber, 1978) indicate that the following teaching sequence works well in content classes:

1. Examine a reading selection and decide upon the predominant pattern used by the author.
2. Discuss this pattern and how to interpret the author's meaning as part of the total lesson.
3. Provide guidance in the process of perceiving organization through a pattern guide followed by small-group or whole-class discussion.
4. Provide assistance in cases where students have unresolved problems concerning either the process and/or the content under discussion.

This sequence is deductive. Once you decide that a particular text selection has a predominant pattern, share your insights with the class. Perceiving text organization is undoubtedly one of the most sophisticated activities that a reader engages in. Chances are that most readers will have trouble recognizing text organization independently. By discussing the pattern before they read, students will develop a frame of reference which they can apply during reading.

The pattern guide itself tears the text organization apart. The students' task, then, is really that of piecing together the relationships that exist within the predominant pattern. Interaction among class members as they discuss the guide heightens their awareness of the pattern and how the author uses it to structure information. Students learn from one another as they share their perceptions of the relationships in the reading selection.

The final step in the teaching sequence is crucial. I'll repeat my admonition from the previous chapter not to use a reading guide rigidly. Therefore, as students work on or discuss a pattern guide, provide feedback that will keep them going, that will clarify and aid in rethinking the structure of the material, that will get students back into the material. In this way the tendency to "stifle," as Archie Bunker might say, will be minimized.

Classroom Examples

Note the variations in the first two classroom examples of pattern guides.

How do the examples differ from one another?

Each was developed by a teacher to help students recognize the cause-effect pattern. In presenting the guides to their classes, the teachers followed the four-step teaching sequence just outlined. Study each illustration as a model for preparing your own guides based on causes and effects.

AUTO MECHANICS

The students in this auto mechanics class — part of a high school vocational arts program — were described by the teacher as "nonreaders." Most activities in the course are "hands on," as you might expect, and although the students have a textbook, it's seldom used.

But the auto mechanics teacher felt that the textbook section on transmissions warranted reading because of the relevance of the material. To help the students follow the author's ideas, the teacher constructed the pattern guide in Box 6–1.

The students worked in pairs to complete the guide. When some had trouble locating certain effects in the assignment, the teacher told them what page to study. As a result of the guided recognition of cause-effect, the teacher felt that students would better be able to handle interpretation and application through class discussion followed by a hands-on activity.

SOCIAL STUDIES

A junior high school teacher prepared a matching activity to illustrate the cause-effect pattern for students who were studying a unit entitled "The American Indian: A Search for Identity." One reading selection

---

Box 6–1

POWER MECHANICS

Directions: In your reading assignment on transmissions find the causes that led to the effects listed. Write each cause in the space provided.

1. Cause: _____
   Effect: Grinding occurs when shifting gears.
2. Cause: _____
   Effect: Car speed increases but engine speed remains constant while torque is decreasing.
3. Cause: _____
   Effect: Car makers changed over to synchronizing mechanisms.
4. Cause: _____
   Effect: Helical gears are superior to spur gears.
5. Cause: _____
   Effect: Some cars cannot operate correctly with three-speed transmissions and require extra speeds.
6. Cause: _____
   Effect: Most manuals have an idler gear.
7. Cause: _____
   Effect: All cars require some type of transmission.

---

from the unit material dealt with Jenny, an adolescent member of the Blackfoot tribe, who commits suicide.

The teacher asked, "Why did Jenny take her life?" The question led to prereading discussion. The students offered several predictions. The teacher then suggested that the reading assignment was written in a predominantly cause-effect pattern. He discussed this type of pattern, and students contributed several examples. Then he gave them the pattern guide to complete as they read the selection — Box 6–2.

The class read for two purposes: to see whether their predictions were accurate and to follow the cause-and-effect relationships in the

---

Box 6–2

JENNY

Directions: Select from the causes column at the left the cause which led to each effect in the effects column at the right. Put the number of the cause in the proper space in the answer box.

Causes	Effects
__ 1. Jenny took an overdose of pills (p. 9).	a. Unemployment rate for the Blackfeet is about fifty percent.
__ 2. The buffalo herds were destroyed and hunger threatened (p. 10).	b. The first victim of this life is pride.
__ 3. Indians remained untrained for skilled jobs (p. 10).	c. Blackfeet became dependent on the white man's help for survival.
__ 4. The temperature reaches 50 degrees below zero (p. 10).	d. Blackfeet turn to liquor.
__ 5. There are terrible living conditions (no jobs, poor homes, and so on) (p. 10).	e. The Indian is robbed of his self-confidence.
__ 6. Pride and hope vanish from the Blackfeet (p. 11).	f. They are always down-graded.
__ 7. Because we're Indians (p. 12).	g. Eighty percent of the Blackfeet must have government help.
__ 8. The old world of the Indians is crumbling, and the new world of the white rejects them.	h. Hope is a word that has little meaning.
__ 9. The attitude of the Bureau of Indian Affairs (p. 13).	i. She killed herself.

a	b	c
d	e	f
g	h	i

_____

material. The guide has a "magic square" attached to it. The magic square is a motivational device. As students put the appropriate number of each cause in the proper space in the answer box, they find that each row and each column add up to the same number. This is the magic number. (For a full discussion of the magic square technique, see Chapter 9.)

The social studies teacher used the magic square not because it was a gimmick but because he recognized that the material was difficult. He felt that this motivational device would help his eighth graders sustain their efforts at reading. He also included page numbers after most of the causes listed on the guide. This helped students focus their attention on the relevant portions of the text. First the students read the selection silently, then they worked in groups of four to complete the pattern guide.

Do you recall the passage from Chapter 4 on how a Pigmy hunter kills an elephant? Notice how Part I of the next guide, Box 6–3, aids you to recognize the sequence of events associated with the Pigmy's hunt. The sequence then forms the basis for the interpretive and applied levels of comprehension. Refer to the passage on page 95 as you work through the pattern guide.

Box 6–3

TODAY'S STONE AGE ELEPHANT HUNTERS

I. Recognizing the Sequence

Directions: The Pigmy hunter follows ten steps in hunting and killing an elephant. Some of the steps are given to you. Decide which steps are missing and write them in the spaces provided.

The Pigmy hunter:
 1. takes the trail of an elephant herd.
 2. _____
 3. selects the elephant he will kill.
 4. _____
 5. moves in for the kill.
 6. _____
 7. _____
 8. pulls out the spear.
 9. _____
10. cuts off _____

II. What Did the Author Mean?

Directions: Check the statements you think suggest what the author is trying to say.

— 1. The Pigmy hunter is smart.

— 2. The Pigmy hunter uses instinct much as an animal does.

— 3. The Pigmy hunter is a coward.

III. How Can We Use Meanings?

Directions: Based on what you read and what you know, check the statements you agree with.

— 1. A person's ingenuity insures survival.

— 2. Where there's a will there's a way.

— 3. There are little differences between primitive and civilized people.

This guide was developed for low-powered readers, and so several steps in the sequence are given. The teacher provided just enough structure to make the guide challenging.

ENGLISH

This comparison-contrast pattern guide shows how the format of a guide will differ with the nature of the material (in this case, narrative) and the teacher's objectives. In Box 6–4, juniors in an English class use the pattern guide to discuss changes in character from the story "A Split Cherry Tree."

Box 6–4

"SPLIT CHERRY TREE": CHARACTER CHANGE

Directions: Consider Pa's attitude (how he feels) toward the following characters and concepts. Note that the columns ask you to consider his attitudes to these things (twice — the way he is at the beginning of the story (pp. 147–152) and the way you think he is at the end of the story. Whenever possible, note the page numbers where this attitude is described or hinted at.

At the beginning of the story what is Pa's attitude toward:		At the end of the story what is Pa's attitude toward:
	Punishment	
	Dave	
	Professor Herbert	

	School	
	His own work	
	His son's future	
	Himself	

Constructing Pattern Guides

Combining information is an important intellectual act requiring analysis followed by synthesis. It isn't enough, in most cases, to exhort students to "read for cause-effect" or "study the sequence." You must show them how to perceive organization over long stretches of print. Pattern guides will help you do this.

How do you construct a pattern guide?

When you decide to guide the search for organization in content material, I suggest that you first separate or break down the pattern for your students so that they can then rebuild the text structure by putting the pattern back together as they work through and discuss the guide.

As you consider developing a pattern guide you may find it useful to follow these three steps:

1. Read through the text selection, identifying a predominant pattern.
2. Develop an exercise in which students can react to the structure of the relationships represented by the pattern.
3. Decide on how much you want to provide in the pattern guide. If it suits your purposes you may develop sections of the guide for the interpretive and applied levels. Or you may decide that these levels can be handled adequately through questioning and discussion once students have sensed the author's organization through the guided reading activity.

Pattern guides help students to follow relationships among ideas. They are most suitable for expository materials, where a predominant pattern of organization is likely to be apparent. Although students sense the way important ideas are connected to one another when they use a pattern guide, they should also recognize that some ideas are more important than others in the organization of text. Enter the concept guide.

CONCEPT GUIDES

Why concept guides?

Concept guides extend and reinforce the notion that information is hierarchically ordered in factual material, that some ideas are subordinate to others. The work of Fredericksen (1975) and Meyer (1975) epitomizes the recent surge in research and theoretical development in the cognitive science of *discourse analysis* — the study of text organization in written material. Meyer (1975) described the *content structure* of a passage as specifying relationships and showing how some ideas in the passage are subordinate to other ideas: "Most of the ideas located at the top levels of the content structure have many levels of ideas beneath them . . . These top level ideas dominate their subordinate ideas. The lower level ideas describe or give more information about the ideas above them in the structure" (pp. 13–14). In other words, the so-called top-levels of content structure contain main ideas, and the bottom levels contain the details.

Main idea–detail relationships can be described as a distinct pattern of organization. Herber (1978) explained the main idea pattern this way.

> "Main idea" is sometimes identified as an additional organizational pattern. True, it is a pattern, but . . . Its construct is so broad that it subsumes each of the other patterns. For example, a *cause* might be the "main idea" of a paragraph and the *effects,* the "details"; or a *comparison* might be the "main idea" and the *contrasts,* the "details"; or a stated objective might be the "main idea" and the *enumeration* of steps leading to that objective, the "details." (*p. 78*)

The point, of course, is this: Within any pattern of organization there are likely to be certain concepts that are more important than others.

This is why students need to be shown how to distinguish important information (the main ideas of a passage) from less important information (the details). The three-level guides and pattern guides that we have been studying do this to some degree. The concept guide also serves this purpose.

How does a concept guide work?

Based on his own research, Baker (1977) claimed that concept guides help students associate and categorize subordinate information under major concepts. Therefore, the first step in constructing a concept guide is to analyze the text material for the main ideas. Then for each main idea, identify less inclusive concepts and relevant propositions which are supportive of it.

Baker suggested the use of concept guides as a postreading activity. Study Box 6–5, one of the guides that he developed.

Box 6–5

INDIA'S ECONOMY

I. *Directions:* Check each of the following statements you think is true based on what you have learned from your textbook reading, outside reading, class discussions, and lectures.

____ 1. Approximately 10 percent of India's people are *subsistence farmers* enjoying *private land ownership.*

____ 2. One of India's *government programs* is the attempt to increase agriculture production.

____ 3. Since India became independent in 1947, *land reform* has been instituted to give the peasants more land.

____ 4. The Indian government has attempted to speed up industrialization through *five-year plans.*

____ 5. Because of a lack of necessary *capital* to finance industrial growth, India has had to borrow money.

____ 6. India lacks the necessary *mineral resources* needed for industrial growth.

____ 7. India's major *agricultural products* include rice, wheat, jute, tea, sugar cane, and cotton.

____ 8. The average annual *per capita income* in India is about $70,000.

____ 9. Cotton and textile industries produce the largest number of *manufactured products* in India.

____ 10. India generally has an *unfavorable balance of trade.*

____ 11. India's *major exports* include burlap and tea; her *major imports* include rice and various foodstuffs.

II. *Directions:* Take each of the underlined words and phrases from Part I and place each under the heading to which it most closely relates. Place a check next to any word or phrase listed under more than one heading.

     Agriculture   *Industry*   *Trade*   *Standard of Living*

III. *Directions:* Based on the information just organized and your own knowledge, check any of the following statements for which you can give an example.

____ 1. Economic growth is determined largely by private enterprise.

____ 2. Government has a strong influence over economy.

____ 3. Industrial production is a major source of a nation's wealth.

____ 4. To maintain a favorable balance of trade a country must export more than it imports.

SOURCE: Adapted from Baker, Robert. "The effects of informational organizers on learning and retention, content knowledge, and term relationships in ninth grade social studies." In H. L. Herber and R. T. Vacca, *Research in reading in content areas: third report,* 148–149. Syracuse, N.Y.: Syracuse University Reading and Language Arts Center, 1977.

Part I of Baker's concept guide is similar to the literal level task in a three-level guide. In Part II of the guide, however, students are required to categorize information under coordinate concepts related to India's economy, which makes them aware that some ideas are more important than others. The reader associates specific pieces of information and then groups them together to aid conceptual learning and retention. The culmination of this activity leads to Part IIA in Baker's guide. Students are asked to support major ideas (superordinate concepts) that are integral to the content material.

Classroom Examples

There are many modifications that you can make in developing concept guides for your content area. Here two sample guides are described.

How can concept guides be modified for your content area?

A high school photography instructor wanted his students to distinguish between two important concepts related to picture composition: the rules of composition and the techniques of composition. Note how the concept guide in Box 6–6 helps to achieve this purpose.

Box 6–7 shows how a seventh grade social studies teacher modified the concept guide somewhat differently to fit his content objectives.

Box 6–6

CONCEPT GUIDE: "PICTURE COMPOSITION"

I. *Directions:* As you read Chapter 12 in the textbook (pages 135–152), check the statements below which are specifically supported by the reading.

___ 1. Composition may be defined as a pleasing arrangement of subject matter in the picture area.

___ 2. Light is to the photographer as paint is to the artist.

___ 3. There are no fixed rules which will insure good composition in every picture.

___ 4. There are only principles which may be applied to help in achieving pleasing composition.

___ 5. Pictures should never tell a story.

___ 6. Simplicity is the secret of many good pictures.

___ 7. Choose a subject that will lend itself to a simple pleasing arrangement.

___ 8. Check your camera angle carefully.

___ 9. Camera angle is unimportant.

___ 10. Poor background and foreground are errors of amateur photographers.

— 11. The "Golden Section" is a subject placement guide.

— 12. In photo composition one should pay heed to balance.

— 13. Two subjects of different sizes should be farther apart than two subjects of equal size.

— 14. There are four basic line forms in photography.

— 15. Use horizontal lines to show peace and tranquility.

— 16. Vertical lines show strength and power.

— 17. The diagonal line is said to represent action, speed, and movement.

— 18. The Hogarth Curve is said to be the most beautiful line in the world.

II. Categorize those statements you have checked under one of the columns listed below.

Rules of Composition   *Techniques*

Box 6–7

THE INCAS OF PERU: "ENLARGING THE EMPIRE"

I. *Directions:* Read the chapter "Enlarging the Empire" in your textbook. As you read, check the statements below which say what the author said.

— 1. But unlike the nation as a whole, the capital housed no commoners.

— 2. The general, finding himself near an area with many villagers, ordered his men to rob the villagers of their gold and jewelry and burn the fields.

— 3. These assignments did provide the necessary labor for public works, and they also took troublemakers away from their own people for a while.

— 4. By means of this pyramid of authority, orders were transmitted to all parts of the empire.

— 5. Such methods and policies were a new experience for commoners. But their lives did not change much.

— 6. Crimes against the state were the most serious and were punishable by death.

— 7. Noblemen received special food, fine clothing, and many wives.

— 8. He (Panchacutec) would quickly promote to important positions men who were able and trustworthy.

— 9. For example, the people wanted to barter for extra food and goods with their neighbors, instead of traveling all the way to the marketplace in Cuzco.

II. *Directions:* Place the number of each statement you checked in the box next to the concept that it supports. A statement may be used more than once.

Concepts	*Supporting Ideas*
1. Great empires are highly organized.	_____
2. Some people are more privileged than others.	_____
3. Unnecessary destruction during war should be avoided.	_____
4. Societies run smoothly when people are busy.	_____
5. Rewards and punishments keep people in control.	_____

This guide provoked a good deal of discussion among the students. The teacher extended students' thinking after they discussed their responses to the guide by asking them to circle the numbers of those concepts in Part II which they felt described life in the United States today. Students worked in small groups and had to support their decisions with specific reasons; thus the concept guide became a springboard for thoughtful conversation and discussion. Comprehension processes will develop in situations that require not only active responding but also interaction among the respondents.

LOOKING BACK, LOOKING FORWARD

Reading guides show students how to acquire information during reading. The pattern guide gives students a feel for what it means to recognize and use patterns of organization in content materials. A concept guide helps students distinguish major from minor ideas.

A case was made for four dominant patterns of organization in content material. Detailed and elaborate classifications are the work of the researcher and theoretician. A teacher, however, aims for simplicity in presenting patterns to maturing readers. Students begin to develop the habit of searching for organization in everything they read when they have the opportunity to perceive patterns that predominate over long stretches of print. The concept guide is based on the cognitive principle that concepts are ordered hierarchically and helps students recognize that some ideas are more important than others.

The reading guides presented in this chapter and the previous one served as models. The value of these models rests with content teachers' ability to adapt them to their materials. In the next chapter the discussion on guiding and extending reading continues. When, where, and how should you use questions and questioning to guide reading in the classroom?

SUGGESTED READINGS

Estes, Thomas, and Vaughan, Joseph, Jr. *Reading and learning in the content classroom.* Boston: Allyn and Bacon, 1978, chapter 11.

Herber, Harold. *Teaching reading in content areas.* 2nd ed. Englewood Cliffs, N.J.: Prentice-Hall, 1978, chapter 4.

Herber, Harold, and Vacca, Richard, eds. *Research in reading in content areas: third report.* Syracuse, N.Y.: Syracuse University Reading and Language Arts Center, 1977.

Meyer, Bonnie. "Organizational patterns in prose and their use in reading." In M. Kamil and A. Moe, *Reading research: studies and application,* pp. 109–117. Twenty-eighth Yearbook of the National Reading Conference. Clemson, S.C.: National Reading Conference, 1979.

Niles, Olive. "Organization perceived." In H. Herber, *Developing study skills in secondary school,* Newark, Del.: International Reading Association, 1965.

Robinson, H. Allan. *Teaching reading and study strategies.* 2nd ed. Boston: Allyn and Bacon, 1978, chapter 5 and part II.

Shepherd, David. *Comprehensive high school reading methods.* 2nd ed. Columbus, Ohio: Charles E. Merrill, 1978, chapter 4.

Vacca, Richard. "A means of building comprehension in social studies." In H. Herber and R. Barron, *Research in reading in content areas: second report,* pp. 75–83. Syracuse, N.Y.: Syracuse University Reading and Language Arts Center, 1973.

Vacca, Richard. "Development of a functional reading strategy: implications for content area instruction." *Journal of educational research* 69 (1975): 108–112.

SUGGESTED READINGS

CHAPTER SEVEN

Questions and Questioning

Always the beautiful
answer who asks
a more beautiful
question.

E. E. CUMMINGS

ORGANIZING PRINCIPLE

Questions are the tools of our trade. They dominate instructional time in most classes. Reflect for a moment on the number of times you have asked students to respond to oral and written questions. If you have yet to teach, recall the number of times that you have been asked questions by instructors. Questions are important. When used effectively in lessons that require reading, oral or written questions stimulate thinking and light the way to productive learning and retention of content material.

It has been said that a good question is half the answer. What, then, is a bad question? Probably a question in and of itself is neither good nor bad. Questions are tools in the hands of the teacher, but they are only as good as the context in which they are asked. The organizing principle of this chapter says this to teachers: *How, when, and where questions are used to guide reading determine their effectiveness.*

Study the Chapter Overview to get a sense of the conceptual framework of this chapter.

The bright side of questions is that they work. The issue, according to Pearson and Johnson (1978), "is not whether or not to use questions, but how, when, and where they ought to be used" (p. 154). The issue of how, when, and where is all the more intensified when the "darker" side of questions is considered. Questions can be tools, but they can also become weapons which interfere with learning from content materials.

CHAPTER OVERVIEW

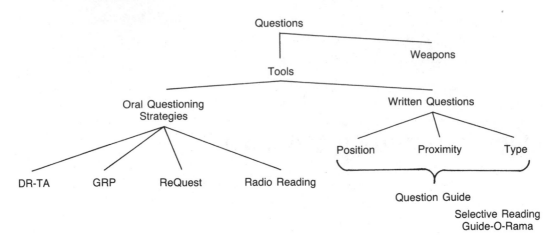

When do questions become weapons? Most students, young and old alike, know in their hearts that questions can be used menacingly by the teacher, even though they are posed in the name of learning objectives. Samples et al. (1977) in fact characterized questions as conversational acts of aggression. Questions can put people on the defensive — freezing up a learning opportunity rather than making the most out of it.

Do you recall ever being put on the spot by a question? In that interminable second or two between question and response, between pounding heart and short gasps for air, do you remember asking yourself, "What's *the* right answer — the one this instructor expects?"

Peppermint Patty in the *Peanuts* cartoon below exposes one instance in particular when a question becomes a weapon to be feared by students. When questions are used to foster a "right answer only" atmosphere in class they will not focus thinking about what has been read, nor will they prompt the processes by which students construct knowledge from text material. Instead they make the response — the correct answer — the all-important concern. Some students even become the classroom "answer machines." (An "answer machine" is easily recognizable. Usually one arm is several inches longer than the other — from constantly shooting the arm skyward in a quick, jerky motion to gain attention during a question-answer interchange.) The danger is this: when we play a Right Answer Only game we run the risk of losing most of the class during discussion by actively seeking responses from students who will give us what we want to hear — the right answer.

Closely related to the Right Answer Only game is the sometimes familiar scenario labeled by Pearson and Johnson (1978) "Guess What's

in My Head.'' Guess What's in My Head unfolds in classrooms from primary through graduate schools. The game is often initiated unwittingly by the teacher. The ground rules, nevertheless, are easy to figure out: ''. . . the teacher has a specific response in mind. And each time a student fails to give the desired response, the teacher says, 'uh huh,' or 'okay?' and calls on another volunteer until finally someone has accurately guessed what is in the teacher's head'' (Pearson and Johnson, p. 186).

Unfortunately, some students soon learn to play Guess What's in My Head with consummate skill. They will read everything but the material to answer ''correctly.'' They scrutinize the teacher's gestures for the slightest of indications that they are on the right track. As they respond to body language and facial gestures, these students skillfully verbalize under, over, and around a question until they strike the responsive chord they seek — a nod of approval.

Judy Blume, the popular author of early adolescent literature, is devastating in this parody from her novel *Blubber* of a Guess What's in My Head teacher (Box 7-1).

Box 7-1

When she finished her song she was right next to Wendy. "Wendy . . . can you tell me what was coming out of my mouth as I sang?"

"Out of your mouth?" Wendy asked.

"That's right," Miss Rothbelle told her.

"Well . . . it was . . . um . . . words?"

"No . . . no . . . no," Miss Rothbelle said.

Wendy was surprised. She can always give teachers the answers they want.

Miss Rothbelle moved on. "Do you know, Caroline?"

"Was it sound?"

"Wrong!" Miss Rothbelle said, turning. "Donna Davidson, can you tell me?"

"It was a song," Donna said.

"Really Donna . . . we all know that!" Miss Rothbelle looked around. "Linda Fischer, do you know what was coming out of my mouth as I sang to the class?"

Linda didn't say anything.

"Well, Linda . . ." Miss Rothbelle said.

"I think it was air." Linda finally told her. "Either that or breath."

Miss Rothbelle walked over to Linda's desk. "That was not the correct answer. Weren't you paying attention?" She pulled a few strands of Linda's hair. . . .

She walked up and down the aisles until she stopped at my desk. . . .

"We'll see if you've been paying attention . . . suppose you tell me the answer to my question."

I had no idea what Miss Rothbelle wanted me to say. There was just one thing left that could have been coming out of her mouth as she sang, so I said, "It was spit."

"What?" Miss Rothbelle glared at me.

"I mean, it was saliva," I told her.

Miss Rothbelle banged her fist on my desk. "That was a very rude thing to say. You can sit in the corner for the rest of the period." . . .

At the end of music period Robby Winters called out, "Miss Rothbelle . . . Miss Rothbelle . . ."

"What is it?" she asked.

"You never told us what was coming out of your mouth when you sang."

"That's right," Miss Rothbelle said. "I didn't."

"What was it?" Robby asked.

"It was melody," Miss Rothbelle said. Then she spelled it. "M-e-l-o-d-y. And every one of you should have known." She blew her pitchpipe at us and walked out of the room.

SOURCE: Copyright © 1974 from the book *Blubber* by Judy Blume. Reprinted with permission of Bradbury Press, Inc., Scarsdale, N.Y. 10583.

Questioning becomes another form of weaponry in classrooms when it turns into an "interrogation session." This is usually the case when questions are used to check on whether or not students have read the material. When questioning becomes interrogating, the teacher's goal usually is veridicality ("the truth, the whole truth, and nothing but the truth"). The teacher fires one question after another, typically pausing no more than a second or two between queries. The questions are mostly low level in that they require verbatim text responses from students. Interrogation questions will test comprehension rather than guide its development.

Questions can also be assumptive. That is to say, a question posed by the teacher assumes that students have the skills required to answer the question in the first place. This, of course, may not be the case for some students. As Herber and Nelson (1975) suggested, "Using questioning to direct students' search for information or ideas assumes at least some competency and independence in the process essential for the search" (p. 514). A question becomes a weapon when the student's lack of maturity as a reader is not taken into consideration.

My purpose for beginning this chapter on what seems to be a sour note is calculated. Too often the benefits of questions and questioning are extolled with little attention paid to these negative effects. While I hope that these conditions don't exhaust instructional time in most classes, they do represent the most common misuses of questions, particularly in teaching situations which require reading. Even the most effective teachers on occasion turn a question into a weapon, out of lack of awareness more than anything else. Awareness will make the difference in most cases.

So much for the bad news about questions. The good news is that questions and questioning can become stimulants for thinking and can be incorporated functionally into reading in content areas. The remainder of this chapter looks at ways in which you can accomplish this.

ORAL QUESTIONING

Oral questions are sometimes calculated, sometimes spontaneous. They dominate the teaching strategies observed in classrooms from kindergarten through college. Taba's (1967) work illustrated quite clearly that "the most marked single influence" on thinking seemed to rest with the impact of questioning in the classroom. In this section I will describe four questioning strategies which influence thinking during reading. These strategies are equally at home with narrative or expository prose. They are (1) the *directed reading–thinking activity* (DR-TA), (2) the *guided reading procedure* (GRP), (3) *reciprocal questioning* (ReQuest), and (4) *radio reading*.

Originated by Stauffer (1969), the DR-TA allows a teacher to serve as an intellectual agitator by directing reading with the frequent use of three questions: "What do you think?" "Why do you think so?" "Can you prove it?" The activity begins by having students predict meaning based on a selection's title. Then the teacher intersperses the cycle of questions at logical points in the text. As the students refine their predictions and support their responses, they reach a point where the teacher encourages them to read the remaining portion of the selection. Discussion follows.

The GRP was developed by Manzo (1975) as an alternative for directed reading. The GRP is grounded in the belief that acquisition of explicit information and accuracy in literal comprehension are legitimate instructional objectives which must precede discussion at higher levels of comprehension. The GRP prepares students to recall literal information better than they may have believed possible. Once this phase of the procedure is accomplished, students are encouraged to organize information around the important ideas implicit in the material, responding at interpretive and applied levels of comprehension in follow-up discussion of the material.

ReQuest is another strategy devised by Manzo (1969) to help readers cope with text material. The procedure simply calls for both teacher and students to take turns asking each other questions about common portions of a selection they have read. When students reach a point where they can predict a selection's outcome, they complete their reading and engage in extended discussion of the material.

Radio reading was developed by Greene (1979) to utilize oral reading to emphasize the importance of the communication of ideas rather than accuracy of pronunciation. Only the reader has an open text; others in the group act as listeners and do not look at a book. Upon completion of a portion of a selection, the reader leads a discussion of what was read. The discussion centers around questions that the reader poses to the listeners, thus establishing a communication network between reader and listeners.

As you study these four questioning strategies in detail, note the specific differences as well as the commonalities among them. Each strategy can be adapted to meet the demands inherent in any subject matter material, narrative or expository. Think about the kinds of adaptions you will have to make to meet particular needs.

The Directed Reading–Thinking Activity (DR-TA)

The DR-TA fosters critical awareness by moving students through a process that involves prediction, verification, judgment, and ultimately extension of thought. The teacher directs reading and agitates thinking; therefore, the teacher should pose open-ended and/or directive questions which prompt interpretation and application.

What are some of the dynamics of a DR-TA?

The atmosphere created during a DR-TA questioning episode is paramount to the strategy's success. You must be supportive and encouraging so as not to inhibit students' free participation. Never refute any predictions that students offer — to do so is comparable to pulling the rug out from under them.

"Wait time" is also important. When you pose an open-ended question, is it reasonable to wait no more than two, three, five, or even ten seconds for a response? If silence pervades the room for the several seconds or more that have lapsed from the time a question has been asked, simply wait a few more seconds. Too often, the tendency is to slice the original question into smaller parts. Sometimes a teacher starts slicing too quickly out of a sense of frustration or anxiousness (after all, three seconds of lapsed time can seem an eternity in the midst of a questioning foray) rather than the students' inability to respond. Silence may very well be an indication that hypothesis formation or other cognitive activities are taking place in the readers' heads. So, wait — and see what happens.

To prepare for a DR-TA with narrative or expository material, first analyze the content. What do you see as relevant concepts, ideas, relationships, information in the material? The content analysis will help you decide on logical stopping points as you direct students through the reading.

STEPS IN THE DR-TA

As I mentioned earlier, you set the climate and direct the DR-TA by the frequent use of three questions:

What do you think?

Why do you think so?

Can you prove it?

The following may be considered general steps in the DR-TA:

1. Begin with the title of a narrative or with a quick survey of the title, subheads, illustrations, and so forth in expository material. Ask: "What do you think this story (or section) will be about?" Encourage predictions. Ask: "Why do you think so?"

2. Ask students to read silently to a predetermined logical stopping point in the text.

3. Repeat questions as suggested in step 1. Some predictions will be refined; new ones will be formulated. Ask: "How do you know?" to encourage verification. Redirect questions.

4. Continue silent reading to another suitable point. Ask similar questions.

5. Continue this way to the end of the material.

How do you apply the DR-TA? This is precisely the question that Homer (1979) asked. Her plan specifies the following procedures:

1. Identifying Purposes for Reading — individual or group purposes set by students based on some limited clues in material and their own background of experience.

   a. "From only reading the chapter title (subtitles, charts, maps, etc.) what do you think the author(s) will present in this chapter (passage, next pages, etc.)?"

   b. Record speculations on chalkboard and augment by the query, "Why do you think so?"

   c. Encourge discussion. If speculations and statements of proof yield an inaccurate or weak knowledge base, review through discussion. Frequently terminology will be introduced by students in their predictions (especially from those more knowledgeable). The teacher may choose to capitalize on such situations by further clarifying significant concepts, etc. If done, this should be accomplished in a way that enhances pupil discussion and inquiry through discovery techniques.

   d. A poll can be taken to further intensify the predictive process. A debate-like setting may naturally ensue at this point pending the outcome of the poll count. Additional proof may be needed from available reference books.

2. Adjustment of Rate to Purposes and Material — Teacher adjusts amount of reading depending upon the purposes, nature, and difficulty of the reading material; skimming, scanning, and studying are involved.

a. "Read to find out if your predictions were correct." The reading task may be several pages within a chapter, an entire chapter, a few passages, etc. If the teacher designates numerous stopping points within the reading task, then the same steps for "identifying purposes" should be executed at each stopping point.

3. Observing the Reading — The teacher observes the reading by assisting students who request help and noting abilities to adjust rate to purpose and material, to comprehend material, and to use word recognition strategies.

4. Developing Comprehension — Students check purposes by accepting, rejecting, or redefining purposes. This can be accomplished by providing discussion time after having read a predetermined number of pages or by encouraging students to rework predictions as they read. Revised predictions and hypotheses can be written on paper by the students during the reading.

5. Follow-up Activities: Discussion, Further Reading, Additional Study, Writing — Students and teacher are identifying these needs throughout the strategy.

a. After the reading students should be asked a) if their predictions were inaccurate, b) if they needed to revise or reject predictions during the reading, c) how they know revision was necessary, d) what were their newly created predictions.

b. Discussion in small groups is most constructive for this step. A recorder can be appointed by the group. It is this person's responsibility to share the group's reading-thinking processes with the total class. These should be compared with original predictions.

c. The teacher should ask open-ended questions that encourage generalization and application relevant to students' predictions and significant concepts presented. In any follow-up discussion or questioning the demand for proof should always prevail. "How do you know that?" "Why did you think so?" "What made you think that way?" Encourage students to share passages, sentences, etc. for further proof.

A DR-TA TRANSCRIPT OF AN ACTUAL LESSON

Greenslade (1980) illustrated a DR-TA in action with a transcript of an actual social studies lesson. Note the interactions among teacher and students as they walk through a text assignment on a unit entitled "The Great Depression of the 1930s.*"

Looking at the title and thinking about what you might already know about the subject, what do you think this unit will be about?

Something that happened back in the twenties.

What kinds of things about the twenties?

Troubles in the twenties.
Prosperity means troubles.

(Students read silently.)
Now what do you think?

People were paid during the war and they could buy more goods.
They could buy now and pay later.

Have you changed your mind about the meaning of the word prosperity?

Yes, it means good things.

Why have you changed your mind?

Well, I read the book and it means a different thing. The people are having good things happen.

What kinds of good things?

Food was cheaper.
Gas was cheaper.

Why do you think things were cheaper?

Well, they really weren't, because the people didn't have as much money to buy them.
You could buy now and pay later.

Why do you think that buy now, pay later is important here?

Well, you wouldn't have to pay for the food or goods all at once. You could pay a little each month.

Do you think that is a good thing or a bad thing?

Good. *(All)*

Why?

If you need something now but don't have the money you could get it anyway and pay for it by the month.

*Greenslade, Bonnie. "Awareness and Anticipation: Utilizing the DR-TA in the Content Classroom," *Journal of Language Experience* 2 (1980): 21–28. Used with permission of the author.

Do you think the prosperity will continue?

Probably.

No.

Why?

I don't know.

Well, the way things are today, it couldn't have continued.

Prices went way up.

Are we prosperous today?

No.

Things started going down when prices started going up.

What do you expect to read next?

That prices start to go up.

And keep going up.

Rising prices will ruin the prosperity.

(Students read silently.)
Now what do you think?

We were right, because it says that wages went from $13.00 in 1925 to about $25.00.

The prices are rising.

What makes you think prices are rising?

It's the wages that are rising, not prices.

Well, when pay goes up, prices go up too.

What do you expect to find next?

There will be more things to buy.

Why?

Because if factories hire more workers then they're able to make more of the products they're manufacturing.

Where will this lead?

To more inflation.

Why?

Prices will rise higher and higher.

That's what happens today.

It's been going up since then.

(Students read silently.)
Based on new information, what do you think now?

I was wrong. Everybody needs jobs now.

Everybody is bankrupt.

The banks tried to get their money from the investors and they didn't have it. They couldn't get their money back.

What happened?

They started closing.
They were losing all their money.
By 1932 the banks were closing.
People had borrowed money and couldn't pay it back so they
had to close up.

What is going to happen next?

Inflation is going to go higher.

Why?

Because the production went down and they need more money.
They'll have to raise the prices.
Stores need more money to stay open.

Where will the money come from?

Not from the banks. They're all closed.
They can fire workers and save money.
But the factories are already bankrupt.
You can't save money you don't have.

What else will happen?

The people will be in trouble.

How?

They won't have the products the factories make.
They won't have money to buy the goods because they won't
have jobs.
They won't have money to buy food.

(Students read silently.)
Have any of your predictions been confirmed?

It says children had torn clothes at school.
Children were asking for food from the schools.
Stores offered to give away food and so many people wanted
some that there was a riot.
The government should have given everybody enough to live on.

Why do you think that?

Nobody should have to starve.
It was the government's fault that the problem started.

Why do you say that?

Because they were involved in a war and the depression started
because of changes after the war.

Did you find that information in the text?

No, but I thought it implied it. It said people had lots of money
to spend after the war and began to overbuy.

It says that American factories produced huge amounts of supplies for our troops and our allies during World War I. Everybody had jobs.

Everybody saved their money during the war because there
really wasn't much to buy. It was all going to the war. After the
war, they were so happy they began to buy just for the heck of
it.

They started to buy on credit and then they got in trouble.

When the bills came they couldn't pay.

Then the banks went bankrupt. They lost all their money because nobody could pay them.

As you can see, the DR-TA begins with divergent responses and
moves toward convergence as students refine predictions and acquire
additional information revealed in the reading. Contrast the DR-TA with
the next questioning strategy, the Guided Reading Procedure.

Guided Reading Procedure (GRP)

The GRP emphasizes close reading. It requires that students gather information and organize it around important ideas, and it places a premium
on accuracy as students reconstruct the author's mes-

*What are some of the
dynamics of a GRP?*

sage. With a strong factual base, students will work
from a common and clearer frame of reference. They
will then be in a position to elaborate thoughtfully on the text and its
implications.

STEPS IN THE GRP

The GRP is a highly structured activity and therefore should be used
sparingly as a training strategy — perhaps once a week at most. These
steps are suggested:

1. Prepare students for reading: clarify key concepts; determine
   what students know and don't know about particular content
   to be studied; build appropriate background; give direction to
   reading.

2. Assign a reading selection: five hundred to nine hundred
   words in middle grades (approximately five to seven minutes
   of silent reading); one thousand to two thousand words for
   high school (approximately ten minutes). Provide general purpose to direct reading behavior. Direction: read to remember
   all you can.

3. As students finish reading, have them turn books face down.
   Ask them to tell what they remember. Record it on the chalkboard in the fashion in which it is remembered.

4. Help students recognize that there is much that they have not remembered or have represented incorrectly. Simply, there are implicit inconsistencies which need correction and further information to be considered.

5. Redirect students into their books and review the selection to correct inconsistencies and add further information.

6. Organize recorded remembrances into some kind of an outline. Ask guiding, nonspecific questions: "What were the important ideas in the assigned reading?" "Which came first?" "What facts on the board support it?" "What important point was brought up next?" "What details followed?"

7. Extend questioning to stimulate an analysis of the material and a synthesis of the ideas with previous learnings.

8. Provide immediate feedback, such as a short quiz, as a reinforcement of short-term memory.

A GRP ILLUSTRATION

Eighth graders were assigned a reading selection from the music education magazine *Pipeline*. The selection, "Percussion — Solid as Rock," concerns the development and uses of percussion instruments from ancient to modern times.

The teacher introduced the selection by giving some background. She then asked students to remember as much as they could as they read the assignment silently. The teacher recorded the collective memories of her students on a transparency, projecting responses onto an overhead screen. Then she asked, "Did you leave out any information that might be important to know about?" Students were directed to review the selection to determine if essential information was missing from the list on the screen. The teacher also asked, "Did you mix up some of the facts on the list? Did you misrepresent any of the information in the author's message?"

These two questions are extremely important to the overall GRP procedure. The first question — "Did you leave out any information that might be important?" — encourages a review of the material. Students sense that some facts are more important than others. Further questioning at this point will help them distinguish essential from nonessential information. The second question — "Did you misrepresent any facts?" — reinforces the importance of selective rereading and rehearsal because of the limitations imposed by short-term memory.

Next the teacher asked the class to study the information recorded on the screen. The teacher requested the students to form pairs and then assigned the following task: "Which facts on the overhead can be grouped together? Organize the information around the important ideas in the selection. You have five minutes to complete the task."

Upon completion of the task the teacher encouraged students to share their work in whole-group discussion. Their groupings of facts were compared, refined, and extended. The teacher served as a facilitator, keeping the discussion moving, asking clarifying questions, provoking thought. She then initiated the next task: "Let's organize the important ideas and related information. Let's make an outline."

Figure 7–1 shows what the students produced.

Figure 7–1. *Outline of "Percussion — Solid as Rock"*

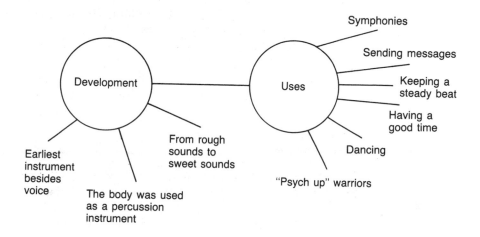

Outlining the mass of information will make students aware of the text relationships developed by the author. Producing the author's organizational structure leads to more efficient recall at a later time and lays the groundwork for interpreting and applying the author's message. Once this commmon framework is developed, your questioning should lead to more divergent and abstract responding by the students.

The discussion "took off" after the outline was completed. The teacher asked several applied questions that helped students associate their previous experiences and beliefs about drumming to the content under discussion. Cognitive performance centered on evaluation and application as students linked what they knew to what they were studying.

The final suggested step in the GRP is a short quiz — mainly to demonstrate in a dramatic way how successful the students can be with the reading material. The quiz should be viewed as positive reinforcement, not an interrogation check. Most of the students in this class earned perfect or near-perfect scores on the quiz — and this is as it should be.

How does a GRP differ from a DR-TA?

A final comment: what are the differences between the GRP and DR-TA? What do the strategies have in common? The DR-TA and GRP mainly differ in their approach to text material. The DR-TA keeps discussion on an open-ended, broad question plane throughout the activity. The DR-TA is a "top-down" strategy in that students move from divergent to convergent responses as reading progresses.

The GRP, on the other hand, might be called a "bottom-up" strategy because students begin at the literal level and move progressively toward higher levels of comprehension.

Both the DR-TA and the GRP are teacher directed. Both require active participation. Both serve a training function as students acquire content understandings. Both procedures work.

Which should you use? Consider tinkering with both strategies over a period of time. Refine your approach to each. You will find that both your content analysis to determine the nature of text material and your instructional objectives will help to answer the question regarding which one to use.

Reciprocal Questioning (ReQuest)

Why use the ReQuest procedure?

ReQuest was originally devised as a "one-on-one" remedial procedure involving the student and teacher. Yet this strategy can easily be adapted to content classrooms to help students think as they read. ReQuest encourages students to ask their own questions about the content material under study. Self-declared questions are forceful. They help students establish reasonable purposes for their reading. Betts (1950) described a "highly desirable learning situation" as one in which the student does the questioning: "That is, the learner asks the questions, and sets up the problems to be solved during the reading activity" (p. 450).

ReQuest fosters an active search for meaning. The rules for ReQuest, as described by Manzo (1969), follow:

> The purpose of this lesson is to improve your understanding of what you read. We will each read silently the first sentence. Then we will take turns asking questions about the sentence and what it means. You will ask questions first, then I will ask questions. Try to ask the kind of questions a teacher might ask, in the way a teacher might ask them. You may ask me as many questions as you wish. When you are asking me questions, I will close my book (or pass the book to you if there is only one between us). When I ask questions, you close your book. . . . Any question asked deserves to be answered as fully and honestly as possible. It is cheating for a teacher to withhold information or

play dumb to draw out the student. It is unacceptable for a student to answer with "I don't know," since he can at least attempt to explain why he cannot answer. If questions are unclear to either party, requests for rephrasing or clarification are in order. The responder should be ready (and make it a practice) to justify his answer by reference back to the text or to expand on background that was used to build or to limit an answer. Whenever possible, if there is uncertainty about an answer, the respondent should check his answer against the text. *(pp. 124–125)*

STEPS IN REQUEST

What are some of the dynamics of ReQuest?

Although the rules for ReQuest were devised for one-on-one instruction, they can be adapted for the content classroom. If you decide to use ReQuest in your class, consider these steps:

1. Both the students and the teacher silently read a common segment of the text selection. Manzo recommends one sentence at a time for poor comprehenders. However, text passages of varying length are suitable in applications to a classroom. For example, both teacher and students begin by reading a paragraph or two.

2. The teacher closes the book and is questioned about the passage by the students.

3. Next there is an exchange of roles. The teacher now queries the students about the material.

4. Upon completion of the student-teacher exchange, the next segment of text is read. Steps 2 and 3 are repeated.

5. At a suitable point in the text, when students have processed enough information to make predictions about the remainder of the assignment, the exchange of questions stops. The teacher then asks DR-TA-type questions: "What do you think the rest of the assignment is about?" "Why do you think so?" Speculations are encouraged.

6. Students are then assigned the remaining portion of the selection to read silently.

7. The teacher facilitates follow-up discussion of the material.

You can modify the ReQuest procedure to good advantage. For example, consider alternating the role of questioner after each question. By doing so you will probably involve more students in the activity. Once students sense the types of questions that can be asked about a text passage, you may also try forming ReQuest teams. A ReQuest team composed of three or four students is pitted against another ReQuest team. Your role is to facilitate the multiple action resulting from the small-group formations.

My own experiences with ReQuest suggest that students may consistently ask factual questions to "stump" the teacher. Such questions succeed brilliantly, because you are subject to the same restrictions imposed by short-term memory as the students. That you "miss" an answer or two is actually healthy — after all, to err is human.

However, when students ask only verbatim questions because they don't know how to ask any others, then the situation is unhealthy. The sad fact is that many students don't know how to ask questions that will stimulate interpretive or applied levels of thinking. Therefore, your role as a good questioner during ReQuest is to provide a model that students will learn from. Over time you will notice the difference in the quality of student questions formulated.

Radio Reading

Does oral reading have a place in content areas? The answer is, "Yes, if . . ."

When students are required to read orally in content area classes, the result is often a tortured and senseless rendition — an extended version of round robin reading, still commonly practiced in elementary classes. Try to recall this scenario as you probably lived it as a secondary school student a few years ago:

Your teacher directs you to turn to a particular page in the textbook. "We're going to read orally. Jane, please begin." Jane gulps, then starts. Bill, who sits behind Jane, figures he'll be asked to read next. He starts rehearsing the paragraph ahead of Jane's. Meanwhile, Pauline sits in the third row, second seat. She resourcefully counts off eight paragraphs; her lips move visibly as she also rehearses. And who in the class is listening to Jane read? The teacher, of course, along with about ten students, is ready to come to Jane's rescue when she falters on a word too difficult to pronounce.

In round robin reading each class member follows along with the reader until his or her part comes up. Because of the stress and storm that oral reading creates in most adolescents, few students actually listen to the reader except to correct mispronounced words. Most class members have determined quite cleverly which part of the text to be responsible for when their turn comes to read. Didn't you hate it when the teacher upset the usual routine for calling on readers?

What role should oral reading play in content areas?

Round robin literally is sense*less* at any level of instruction. It lacks sense because hardly anyone ever pays attention to the author's message when engaged in the activity. A legitimate purpose for oral reading, as a result, is destroyed.

The main instructional objective for oral reading in a content area class is to communicate ideas to others. Artley (1972) noted that oral reading has a worthwhile function if it is used "to interpret what the writer says or feels to concerned listeners" (p. 47). To this end, radio reading is a powerful alternative to round robin methods. Furthermore, radio reading will promote good questioning behaviors because reading orally will be viewed as a communication process by students rather than a tedious exercise in frustration.

What are some of the dynamics of radio reading?

Radio reading maximizes communication between the reader and class members who must listen attentively. The ground rules are quite simple: the reader reads and the listeners listen. When the reader completes reading, the listeners respond by discussing what was comprehended. Therein lies the potential of radio reading as a questioning strategy.

Vacca (1976) recommended that the reader initiate discussion by asking questions of the audience. Typically, questions will be literal. Vacca, therefore, suggested that the teacher also take part as a radio reader "to model higher level questioning techniques when it is her (or his) turn" (p. 29).

STEPS IN RADIO READING

Radio reading works smoothly when used in small groups with four to six members. An instructional sequence which has proved successful follows:

1. Assign the text selection to be read. Provide prereading preparation as needed.

2. Form small groups. Each group member selects a segment of text to read. Several minutes are given for rehearsal and the formulation of questions for discussion.

3. Begin radio reading. As the reader reads, listeners have their books closed.

4. Initiate discussion of what was read. The radio reader asks each member of the group a question or two to prompt the discussion. If a question is unclear, the listener can ask for a restatement.

5. Each listener takes a turn as reader.

When small groups are used, charting responses to the reader's questions sustains the process, especially among middle school students. Box 7–2 shows a score sheet that was devised for this purpose. A "secretary" in each group marks a plus or minus beside each person's name on the score sheet to indicate a satisfactory response to the reader's question. It is the reader's prerogative to decide whether or not an answer is satisfactory.

Radio reading has been used also as a whole-class activity. Unfortunately, active participation by most of the class members is drastically reduced, particularly during discussion. If you decide, nevertheless, to use radio reading with the whole class, plan it in advance. Designate your radio readers ahead of time so that they will have an opportunity to rehearse their portion of text and to give thought to the questions they will ask. Make sure that each student has the chance to read — don't always choose the best oral readers. In fact, a great motivational technique is to set up a microphone to amplify the reader's message to his or her listeners — thus adding a touch of authenticity to the radio motif.

There are several predictable student responses to difficult words while reading orally. First, many readers will respond to radio reading smoothly, requesting pronunciation help only when it appears absolutely

Box 7–2

Radio Reading   Secretary_____

                                                   Date _____

List the names of those in the group. Mark a + or — in columns for each question. Mark an R in the box for the reader.

		Questions						
		1	2	3	4	5	6	7
1.	_____							
2.	_____							
3.	_____							
4.	_____							
5.	_____							

The secretary will fill in this sheet correctly and hand it to the teacher before the end of the period.

necessary to do so. Other students, however, will request help for a difficult word even though the teacher believes they have the word attack skills to decode it. Greene (1979) suggested there is only one legitimate behavior in this situation: tell the reader the requested word.

> It is not appropriate for the listener to play games with the reader. All responses such as "look at it again," "look at the first letter," "sound it out," "you had it yesterday," "see if you remember it," "it rhymes with ———," are strictly forbidden. Radio reading involves a contract between the reader and the listener. If the reader asks for a word it is immediately supplied.
> *(p. 106)*

The contract between reader and listeners is built on the premise that oral reading is a communication process. Therefore any attempts to short circuit communication through word attack games should be avoided.

A third response is for the reader not to request help when assistance is actually needed. If the reader produces a reasonable substitute for a difficult word, this is acceptable and highly desirable behavior. If the reader attempts to pronounce the word but botches it terribly, this should be accepted by the listeners if it does not hinder communication of an important idea. During questioning, a listener can request a re-reading of that point in the text where mispronunciation took place. The correct pronunciation is then supplied by one of the listeners or the teacher.

A final comment: Activities such as radio reading or ReQuest help students to develop questioning competencies. As emphasized earlier, your model as a good questioner is important to the development of these competencies. You might also consider setting aside a few minutes periodically to teach students about question asking. Begin with questions which prompt responses at a literal level and progress gradually to applied level questions. Contrasting examples work nicely. For instance, a typical student question may be on the literal level: "What was the name of the ship?" You may want to contrast the question with one that is posed at a higher level: "Why do you think the ship was named *Dark Horizon*? Sharing a little insight on the art of questioning will go a long way.

WRITTEN QUESTIONING STRATEGIES

In the past fifteen years or so a prodigious effort has been made to figure out how written questions work to improve comprehension while students read text material. This effort has led to a frenzy of activity, to say the least, in the world of educational psychology and reading research. As a result, progress has been made regarding how written questions influence learning during reading.

No attempt will be made to recap the rather bulky research literature on adjunct questions, since several reports by Anderson and Biddle (1975) and Frase (1977) have already made this contribution. I will, however, briefly sketch the major characteristics of written questions which have been studied, and the conclusions that have been drawn, so that a perspective can emerge for practical application.

Characteristics of Written Questions

Three characteristics of questions appear to dominate textbook learning: (1) the position of a question in text, (2) the contiguity or proximity of a question to the content being questioned, and (3) the type of question asked. These characteristics are so interrelated that it is difficult to separate their influence.

Summarize the main findings related to each characteristic.

POSITION AND PROXIMITY OF QUESTIONS

Rothkopf (1966) developed an ingenious albeit simple plan to examine what happens when questions are positioned near portions of the text material. He interspersed one or two questions either before or after every one or two pages of a text selection. Questions positioned before each one- or two-page passage were called *prequestions*. Questions inserted after each passage were called *postquestions*.

Upon completing the entire reading selection, which ranged in length from one thousand to five thousand words depending on the experiment, readers were tested on the amount of specific and incidental information they had retained. Specific information included only those facts directly questioned. Incidental information referred to nonquestioned content.

Several things should be kept in mind about most of the research that Rothkopf and subsequent researchers conducted: (1) the questions usually required readers to produce factual bits of information; (2) during the reading of the selection, students were not permitted to turn back to a page once it had been read nor could they take notes while reading; (3) the questions and the text passages were written on separate sheets of paper; (4) "mostly adult" — i.e., college students — participated in the research.

In general here is what was found about the "position effect" of questions interspersed in text material. First, readers receiving factual prequestions retained just about the same amount of information *on questioned material* as those that were given factual postquestions. Second, readers given either prequestions or postquestions demonstrated greater retention of *questioned material* than groups who just read the text selection without the benefit of questions. Of most significance is the third consistent finding of the researchers: readers receiving factual postquestions interspersed in text produced greater recall of incidental information not directly questioned than readers receiving prequestions or none at all.

Rothkopf has characterized this third finding as the "indirect instructive effect" of questions. Postquestions positioned after the passages evidently "shape" the way students study the text. This shaping effect leads both to specific and incidental recall of explicit information in the reading material.

If the crossover from research to real life instruction is to be made, classroom teachers must ask, "So what?" Agreed, factual postquestions do result in greater recall of specific and incidental material than prequestions. But asking questions which direct readers to respond to isolated facts can become a superficial activity in and of itself.

Rickards (1976) recently predicted that a prequestion which requires a response at the interpretive level will prompt readers to perceive relationships in text in the course of deriving generalizations about the material. His prediction held true. "Conceptual prequestions" interspersed in text helped readers to better organize information and to retain it over longer periods of time than factual postquestions. Rickards's research is encouraging. Yet, what basic research on written questions tells teachers is what they have intuitively or artfully known all along: purpose makes the difference.

If your instructional purpose is to help students acquire as many facts as possible, then consider interspersing factual postquestions throughout the reading assignment. If your instructional purpose is to help students interrelate information and derive generalizations, then consider using prequestions that require an interpretive level of response.

Keep in mind the fact that prequestions as they have been discussed do not suggest a batch of questions positioned before the entire reading selection. And postquestions do not imply responding to a batch of questions after the assigned selection. One of the real contributions made by adjunct question researchers is the recognition that a written question is highly effective if it is next to the content being probed. The closer the question to the informative material, the better it is as a stimulant.

TYPE OF QUESTION

Instructional purpose is inextricably tied to the type of questions posed. Most of the written questions devised in the adjunct question research tested readers on their accuracy to repeat factual bits of information. As Anderson and Biddle (1975) asserted: "Of practical interest is the fact that adjunct questions can do more than increase the accuracy with which people are able to repeat strings of words . . . adjunct questions which entail paraphrase and application of principles and concepts to new situations may be especially facilitative'' (p. 103). Anderson and Biddle's contention reinforces what teachers witness whenever they ask questions to provoke interpretive and applied levels of thinking.

Questioning taxonomies identify and classify the types of questions which can be asked to stimulate a thoughtful response (Bloom, 1956; Barrett and Smith, 1975; Cunningham, 1975; Pearson and Johnson, 1978). Bloom's *Taxonomy of Educational Objectives*: *Cognitive Domain* represents the seminal work done in this area. Bloom identified six levels of cognitive performance.

Cognitive Processes	*Student Behaviors*
1. Knowledge	The student recalls or recognizes information.
2. Comprehension	The student changes information into a different symbolic form of language and discovers relationships among facts, generalizations, definitions, values, and skills.
3. Application	The student solves a lifelike problem that requires the identification of the issue and the selection and use of appropriate generalizations and skills.
4. Analysis	The student solves a problem through conscious knowledge of the parts and forms of thinking.
5. Synthesis	The student solves a problem that requires original, creative thinking.
6. Evaluation	The student makes a judgment of good or bad, or right and wrong, according to designated standards.

Taxonomies such as Bloom's underscore the complexity of intellectual activity. They have also led to a greater study and emphasis on the role of questions and question-asking strategies.

Herber (1978) reported that positive relationships existed between the three levels of comprehension construct and Bloom's levels of cognition. Table 7–1 shows these relationships.

Questions designed to elicit responses at the three levels of comprehension can presumably stimulate a full range of intellectual activity among students. Many kinds of response can be agitated by literal, interpretive, or applied questions. A literal question leads to a response that is factual in nature. It helps to prompt recall or recognition of information actually stated in the reading material. An interpretive or applied question, on the other hand, provokes readers to sift through

Table 7–1. A Comparison of Herber's Levels of Comprehension With Bloom's Levels of Cognition

(Based on the 1971 Research of David Honeycutt)

Levels of Comprehension	Levels of Cognition
Literal	Knowledge
Interpretive	Comprehension
Applied	Application Analysis Synthesis Evaluation

and clarify text relationships in order to paraphrase, explain, infer, relate, conclude, contrast, summarize, and so on. Applied questions relate to the textbook content but may actually require readers to go beyond the material under study. Applied questions place the students' knowledge of the world — their core of background experience — at the center of the questioning activity. An applied question may be posed before the actual reading of the assignment to feed students forward. It may attempt to arouse curiosity, initiate problem-solving behaviors, or lead to predictions by helping students to associate previous study and experiences with the new material to be learned. Applied questions may also be asked during reading in order to evaluate, elaborate, predict, or solve problems implicit in the material.

Text questions posed at the three levels of comprehension will reinforce reading performance. As Herber and Nelson (1975) indicated, "Good questions, accompanied by reinforcing feedback on the nature and quality of the response, can raise the students' level of sophistication in their use of reading skills implicit in those questions" (p. 514).

Using Written Questions Effectively

Written questions direct the readers' attention as they study content materials. What you do to guide students through the myriad of relationships woven by the author will mean the difference between students who get bogged down on every word of text and students who read actively and selectively.

Why is reading every word in an assignment described as a "fallacy"?

Teachers must come to grips with the fallacy that every word in a chapter is important to read. In most cases, this just isn't so. Some sections of a text are more important than others. Other sections may be superfluous to your instructional purposes. What's more, there is always a little fluff built into expository writing. Immature and maturing readers have difficulty detecting substance from fluff. You can help them concentrate on relevant, essential information worth reading.

The reason you can do these things better than a reading specialist, or anyone else for that matter, is because you should know your subject matter and how to treat it better than anyone else. You know what the important parts of a chapter are and where to find them. Given this knowledge, you can devise adjunct question guides to impart to students a sense of how to actively respond to information in print and how to organize information around important ideas. Here's how.

QUESTION GUIDES

One way to intersperse questions throughout a text assignment is to

How does a question guide work?

write questions on a separate sheet of paper, providing directions which signal where and when to respond to the questions. The Question Guide Planning Chart — Table 7–2 — synthesizes the information on written questions presented above. The chart provides a quick and easy reference for designing adjunct question guides.

Table 7–2. Question Guide Planning Chart

Instructional Purpose	*Type of Question*	*Position of Question*
1. Recall specific and incidental information during reading	Literal	After the informative text passage
2. Recall specific information during reading	Literal	Before or after the informative text passage
3. Interrelate information and derive inferences during reading	Interpretive	Before the informative text passage
4. Evaluate or elaborate upon information during reading	Applied	Before or after the informative text passage

The question guide in Box 7–3 was developed for a genetics unit in a high school biology course. The teacher's purpose for developing the guide was to allow students who needed assistance with the process of mitosis to utilize text material productively. The questions excerpted from the guide give you the flavor of its format.

Note that some questions in the guide are posed before reading a section of text because they require that students clarify relationships and organize information (the questions for paragraph 3, on page 91 and paragraphs 13–16, on pages 97–98). Those Questions posed after reading are to direct attention to incidental information as well as information keyed by the question. And finally, several of the reading directions do not signal either prequestion or postquestion inspection. The instructor is after questioned material only, and therefore the position of the questions isn't crucial.

Aulls (1978) described an interesting variation to question guides that may be especially appropriate as a learning center activity. He proposed a "hand slide device" which will indicate the pages to be read on one side of the hand slide and the adjunct questions on the other side. To construct a hand slide device, Aulls recommended the following:

Box 7–3

QUESTION GUIDE: — MITOSIS

The primary objective of this assignment is to enable you to isolate the most significant events in the process of mitosis and at the same time to gain an appreciation of the fact that mitosis is a continuous process. You should also gain some appreciation of the rate and control of the process of cell division.

Directions: Read only those parts of the chapter that are listed in the reading directions. Then respond as best you can.

Reading Directions	*Questions*
1. Page 90, paragraphs 1 and 2. First read the paragraphs, then answer the questions.	Do all body cells in mammals constantly divide to produce new cells?
	What are the four basic activities of cells?
	1.
	2.
	3.
	4.
2. Page 91, paragraph 3. Study the questions first, then read page 91, paragraph 3.	As you read about cell division, look for indications that this process does occur in a series of steps.
	What does the word "morphological" mean as it is used in the passage?
3. Page 91, paragraph 5.	List as many specific events of interphase as you can.
4. Page 94, paragraphs 6 and 7.	List the specific events of prophase.
5. Pages 97–98, paragraphs 13, 14, 15, 16. Study the question first, then read these paragraphs.	List below as many differences as you can find between the process of mitosis as it occurs in plant and animal cells:
	Animal Cells Plant Cells

---

use a heavy duty legal envelope and cut a 7″ x 2″ rectangle on the front side and a 7″ x 4″ rectangle on the back side. Prepare a ditto by dividing it into strips slightly smaller than the width of the envelope. Divide each strip into parts equal to the space needed to type the longest adjunct questions to be presented. On one side of the ditto page, write the pages to be read. On the other side, write the adjunct questions (p. 69).

Students should first see which pages are to be read. Before reading, however, the teacher should indicate whether to inspect the adjunct question prior to or after the reading. In all likelihood, the hand slide should be used intermittently, to preserve the motivational quality of the activity as well as serve as a comprehension tool.

A high school business teacher devised questions for a text selection entitled "Face Up to Buying Problems." Several of the questions are highlighted in the hand slide format in Box 7–4.

THE READING GUIDE-O-RAMA

How does a guide-o-rama reinforce selective reading?

Cunningham and Shablak (1975) discussed the importance of guiding students to respond selectively to text. They indicated that content area teachers can impart tremendous insight into how to acquire text information through a reading guide-o-rama.

The teacher begins the Guide-O-Rama by determining the overall purpose for a particular reading assignment. Second, he selects those sections of the reading which are necessary to achieve this purpose. Most important . . . he eliminates from the assignment any and all sections that are irrelevant to the purpose. Third, for those relevant sections that remain, the teacher determines,

Box 7–4

Read page 109, paragraphs 1 and 2. Then turn the slide over and answer the questions.	What is an impulse buyer? What is a smart buyer?
Read the question on the back side first. Then study Illustration 9-1 on page 110.	If you were given a $20 allowance per week how would you spend the money? List the items purchased and the price for each.
Front side of slide	Back side of slide

based on his own model reading behaviors, what a student must operationally do to achieve the purpose — step by step, section by section. (*p. 318*) [italics mine]

The premise behind the guide-o-rama rests with the notion that teachers best understand how to process information from their own subject matter. According to Cunningham and Shablak (1975), the teachers' task becomes "the creation of a step-by-step format for modeling their own appropriate behaviors" (p. 381).

Study in Box 7–5 the examples provided by Cunningham and Shablak to illustrate the types of reading behaviors that can be signaled in the guide-o-rama.

Box 7–5

SIGNALLING READING BEHAVIOR IN A GUIDE-O-RAMA

Page 257, par. 3.
The last sentence of this paragraph states the main idea of the entire chapter. Change the main idea into a question.

Page 61, par. 3 and 4.
These two paragraphs describe (a) what the people of this area were up to, and (b) why they chose this particular spot. Do not read further until you are sure of these two points.

Page 42, par. 1.
The question that is raised at the end of paragraph 1 will be answered in the remainder of this reading. State this question in your own words before reading further.

Page 65, par. 2.
Before attempting to read this paragraph, turn back to page 63 and reread the last paragraph. Does what you read on page 65 give you the facts necessary to solve the problem raised back on page 63? Work with your lab partner to solve the problem. When you think you have the answer, come to me and explain what you did.

Page 61, par. 1.
Read this paragraph quickly in order to get a sense of what is going on.

Page 69, par. 3.
Before reading this paragraph, write down in two sentences what you did in Chapter 1 (don't look back — remember!). Now look at Figure 4.8 and then back to Figure 1.1. Now, do not bother to read the paragraph.

Page 44, par. 3 and 4.
This material is interesting but not essential for understanding. You may read quickly or skip entirely if you wish.

Page 66.
Slow down and read this entire page *very* carefully. It describes the living area in detail. When you have finished the reading, draw the living space as you imagine it in the space provided below.

Page 75, par. 3.
This paragraph summarizes the entire reading selection. Read it slowly. If there is anything you do not understand in this paragraph, go back to the reading and check it over carefully. Ask me if anything still bothers you.

SOURCE: Cunningham, Richard, and Shablak, Scott. "Selective reading guide-o-rama: the content teacher's best friend." *Journal of Reading* 18 (1975): 380–382. Reprinted with permission of Richard Cunningham and Scott Shablak and the International Reading Association.

Guide-o-rama

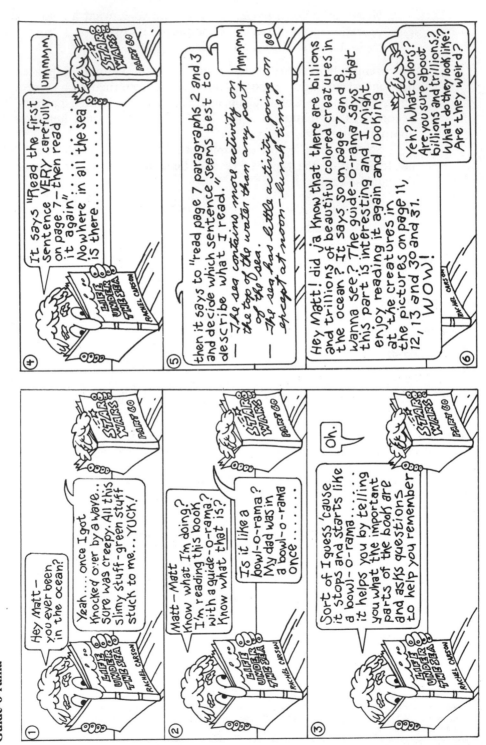

SOURCE: Courtesy of Miriam S. Howard

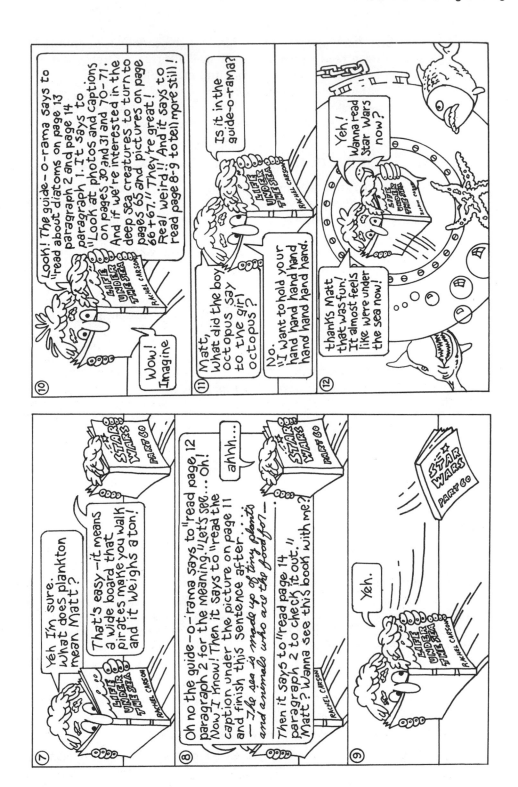

Box 7–6 illustrates how a junior high school social studies teacher developed a reading guide-o-rama which mixes written questions with appropriate signals for processing the material.

Written questions are useful tools when interspersed purposefully throughout selected segments of text material. They encourage an ongoing, active response to content as students read.

LOOKING BACK, LOOKING FORWARD

Oral and written questions can guide and extend reading. But questions become weapons when they are misused in classrooms. This is particularly true in situations where a right-wrong mentality exists, where a Guess What's in My Head game is played, where interrogation checks on comprehension are undertaken daily, or where questions are asked assumptively. How, when, and where questions are asked is the important issue facing teachers.

Four oral questioning strategies were presented to facilitate reading comprehension of content materials. The first two strategies, the DR-TA

Box 7–6

READING GUIDE-O-RAMA TO "ADVERTISING: THE PERMISSIBLE LIE"

Page 128. Read the title. Write a definition of a permissible lie. Give an example of this type of lie.

Page 128, paragraph 1. Do you agree with this quotation? Why or why not?

Pages 128–129. Read paragraphs 2–6 slowly and carefully. What aspects of TV were "borrowed" from radio? Write them down. From personal experience, do you think TV reflects reality? Jot an answer down, then continue reading.

Pages 129–130. Read paragraphs 7–15 quickly. What specific types of commercials are being discussed?

Pages 130–131. Read paragraphs 16–26 to find out the author's opinion of this type of commercial.

Page 131. Read paragraph 7. The author gives an opinion here. Do you agree?

Pages 131–133. Read to page 133, paragraph 45. You can skim this section, slowing down to read parts that are especially interesting to you. What are some current popular phrases or ideas in modern advertising? Think of some commercials you've seen on TV. List another word or idea or fad that's used in a lot of advertising.

Pages 133–134. Read paragraphs 45–50 quickly. Give your own example of a "sex-based" advertisement.

Page 134, paragraph 51. According to the author, what is a good test for an advertisement? Do you agree? Would most advertisements pass or fail the test? Try out a few.

Page 134, paragraph 52. Restate Comant's quote in your own words.

After reading the assignment, summarize what you read in one hundred words or less.

---

and the GRP, are "complete" lesson procedures. They attempt to both guide and extend student reading performance. The remaining two procedures, ReQuest and radio reading, develop student questioning competencies through silent and oral performance respectively.

Written questions are used effectively in question guides when they are purposefully interspersed throughout a text assignment. Nearly twenty years of research on written questions have provided insights into how to position questions in relation to important parts of the text material. Question guides can be devised for practical application, making full use of the knowledge gained from research.

In the next chapter, we'll look at essential study strategies. When does reading become studying? What is essential when it comes to studying content material?

SUGGESTED READINGS

Bloom, Benjamin. *Taxonomy of educational objectives: cognitive domain.* New York: David McKay, 1956.

Greene, Frank. "Radio reading." In C. Pennock, *Reading comprehension at four linguistic levels*, pp. 104–107. Newark, Del.: International Reading Association, 1979.

Guthrie, John, ed. *Cognition, curriculum and comprehension.* Newark, Del.: International Reading Association, 1977.

Hunkins, Francis. *Questioning strategies and techniques.* Boston: Allyn and Bacon, 1972.

Manzo, Anthony. "The request procedure." *Journal of reading.* 12 (1969): 123–126.

Manzo, Anthony. "Guided reading procedure." *Journal of reading.* 18 (1975): 287–291.

Pearson, David, and Johnson, Dale. *Teaching reading comprehension.* New York: Holt, Rinehart and Winston, 1978.

Pennock, Clifford, ed. *Reading comprehension at four linguistic levels.* Newark, Del.: International Reading Association, 1979.

Rickards, John, and Hutcher, Catherine. "Interspersed meaningful learning questions as semantic cues for poor comprehenders." *Reading research quarterly* 13 (1977–1978): 539–553.

Sanders, Norris. *Classroom questions — what kinds.* New York: Harper and Row, 1966.

Stauffer, Russell. *Directing reading maturity as a cognitive process.* New York: Harper and Row, 1969.

Vacca, Richard. "Questions and advance organizers as adjunct aids: implications for reading instruction in secondary schools." In C. Smith and L. Mikulecky, *Secondary reading: theory and application*, pp. 47–77. Bloomington, Ind.: School of Education, Indiana University, 1978.

CHAPTER EIGHT

Study Strategies

*But I tried though — I sure as hell
did that much.*

McMurphy in KEN KESEY,
ONE FLEW OVER THE CUCKOO'S NEST

ORGANIZING PRINCIPLE _____

Mature readers develop their own strategies for studying. Some students, however, never develop any strategies at all. Studying is hard work. It takes a deliberate effort to study. Discipline. A patience with print. Moreover, students need reasons for studying as much as they need reasons for reading. They should study with definite purpose in mind in order to do something with what they have read.

You can show maturing readers how to study content materials purposefully and deliberately. They will learn how to adapt study strategies to their own needs. The organizing principle illuminates the main idea of this chapter: *Studying helps students to do something with what they have read.*

Study the Chapter Overview to develop a set for the organization of this chapter. You might want to first put into words what the chapter will be about. Then ask yourself, "What do I already know about the ideas to be presented? What do I need to know more about?"

During my junior year in high school I had an American history teacher who prefaced every textbook reading assignment by exhorting students to "study the material." And with a great deal of emphasis, he'd make it a point to add, "Notice that I said to *study* the assignment."

In my naiveté I couldn't figure out why the teacher made a big deal out of studying (as opposed to reading). I assumed that he wanted us to memorize the material, which I attempted to do — once. I soon

CHAPTER OVERVIEW

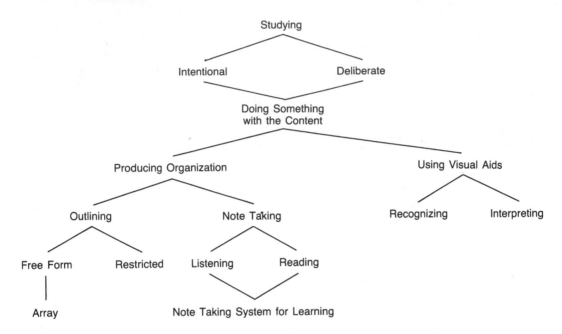

stopped reading American history. If I wasn't about to memorize it, why should I read it? I didn't think too much about reading and studying at the time beyond that pragmatic if not superficial line of reasoning.

When my American history teacher urged his class to "study the material," he probably had something definite in mind. The trouble, however, was that he kept it a secret. He never shared with or showed his students what he meant by studying or how it might have differed from reading, if, indeed, there was a difference at all. Perhaps he assumed that we already knew what he meant. Most of us didn't.

Studying, to my mind, involves reading — plus. We study to learn. Because the bulk of studying is spent reading and rereading, the term "reading-study skills" was probably invented to serve as an umbrella concept. At one time or another, almost all the so-called reading skills have been included under the rubric of studying. Defining study by lists of skills which include everything but the proverbial kitchen sink isn't too helpful in actual practice. Marksheffel (1966) observed the folly of such lists: "A complete tabulation of all the specific skills . . . would be a wearisome, never-ending cataloguing of limited value" (p. 215).

I favor Smith's (1959) straightforward definition of study, because *Why is studying both intentional and deliberate?* it's a simpler and more practical "conceptual rack" to hang one's actions on. She explained studying as skills we use when our purpose is to do something with the content we have read. At least two characteristics of studying are implicit in "doing something with the content": intention and deliberation.

Studying is an intentional act. Students need to have a reason for studying as much as they need to have a reason for reading. Doing something means putting skills to good use by applying them toward purposeful ends. No wonder, then, that study is often characterized by deliberate, diligent work.

The extrinsic reason that most students give for studying is to cover the material or do well in a course. Students will tell you that they study to pass tests. Fair enough. This is why they are quick to associate studying with memorizing information. A concept of study which includes retention has merit. But students run the risk of committing a reductionist fallacy by believing that one part equals the whole, or simply that memorizing is study. Too many students spend too much time using up too much energy on what often becomes their only means of study — rote memorization. Rote learning leads to short-lived recall of unrelated bits and pieces of information. Alternatives to rote memorization should be taught and reinforced when and where they count the most — in a content classroom.

Studying is an unhurried and reflective process. The lack of discipline and patience with print is probably the reason so few adolescents and young adults study effectively on their own in secondary schools or in college. I can remember "arbitrating" a meeting between a sociology instructor and students who were doing poorly in his class during their first semester in college. The purpose of the meeting was to have the instructor discuss ways to study sociology. The students, however, soon turned the meeting into a battleground, venting their own frustrations with the course. The sociologist finally reached his own boiling point: "Listen, the bottom line is this: studying is hard work. You can't read sociological material once and expect to 'get it' through some process of osmosis. You should 'work' the material. Read it. And reread it. First, get the facts straight in your head. And eventually you will make them a part of you."

Although I was an advocate for the students, I found myself agreeing with the college instructor's analysis of the "bottom line." Study is hard work. Cultivating the right mental attitude toward studying is essential. And this is where teachers can help the most. But teaching students how to study has to go beyond the "you should" stage or a litany of imperatives. A learner needs exhortation but also a good model or two.

Plowing through cumbersome text material just once is more than most students can cope with. The prospect of reciting, rereading, or reviewing is downright dreadful. Teachers are in a position to convince students (through example) that "working" with the material doesn't necessarily mean twice inflicting upon oneself the agony of slow, tedious reading.

Sherer (1975) pointed out the value of deliberate study to one of his students:

> She could skim . . . read titles, summaries, topic sentences and headings, first and last paragraphs, or search for major concepts and premises — on her way to locating information . . . Once she had selected the most pertinent part of a reading assignment, she could slow down the pace and read more intensively, secure in knowing she was reading this material to meet a specific goal. (p. 25)

Readers have to be flexible. But knowing when to skim material or slow down or speed up always requires a good sense of purpose.

What is the value of skimming?

Skimming, as we saw in Chapter 4, is a technique for getting general understanding through selective reading. A good studier quickly dispels the myth that you have to read all the words. Skimming should be used to gloss over material, to judge its relevance to a discussion or a topic, or to gain some notions of what a passage is about. As students learn to study text material purposefully and deliberately, they should be encouraged to exercise flexibility, to "sin a little," by reading and rereading selectively.

A teacher has the right to expect students to study a subject — and a responsibility to show them how to. I read once that *effective* means doing the right thing and *efficient* means doing the thing right. When it comes to reading and studying, it's easy to do the wrong things well.

Effective and efficient study strategies can be demonstrated and applied to content area material. Study techniques demonstrated before or after a reading assignment will have a "forward" and "backward" effect: forward in the sense that they will develop an attitude for studying text material that has yet to be assigned; backward in the sense that students can apply skills to study material they have already read.

I've organized this chapter around what I believe to be two essential areas of study: (1) organizing and relating information, and (2) using visual aids. Much of what has already been presented is reflected under these headings. The focus of this chapter, however, is to show how a student can go from reading to studying with support from the teacher.

ORGANIZING AND RELATING INFORMATION

Perceiving the organization of ideas is an integral part of reading comprehension. Producing that organization is an integral part of studying.

Good readers follow the way an author relates ideas. They look for organization in everything they read. Producing the relationships that exist among ideas in a passage is one of the most sophisticated study tasks that secondary students will attempt. Why? Because they must recognize not only that ideas are connected to each other but that some ideas are more important than others. I suggested in Chapter 6 that the hierarchy of concepts in content material must be analyzed and used to good advantage by readers. We saw how some ideas are subordinate to others. Main ideas, however, are always in a superordinate position in the hierarchy. Supporting ideas which have equivalent status are in a coordinate position in the hierarchy. Facts and details are always subordinate to high-level concepts.

Why do some students find it difficult to distinguish important from less important ideas?

The problem of distinguishing important ideas from supportive points and details is complicated by at least three factors. First, direct instruction in reading classes rarely transcends the level of the paragraph when it comes to finding main ideas. Students who are responsible for content area assignments must perceive main ideas over long stretches of text material, yet they are rarely shown how to do this in reading class. Second, some content material is too difficult or just poorly written. If the ideas in a reading selection lack cohesion, are too abstract, or go beyond the experiential grasp of the reader, the reader will not discern relationships. And third, many important ideas in a reading passage are not actually stated but rather implied. When left to their own devices, some students will have trouble making inferences about implied main ideas.

All of these complicating factors point to the necessity for guiding reading. I rehash the importance of perceiving text organization not only because the essence of comprehending lies in seeing relationships, but also because certain study activities such as outlining and note taking demand that students "do something" with the relationships that they have recognized.

Outlining

Outlining helps students clarify relationships. An outline is a product. After readers have sensed or identified relationships, they can produce organization as a means of study through outlining. Developing an outline is analogous to fitting together pieces in a puzzle. In the case of outlining, Hansell (1978) suggested, "The completed puzzle shows the separate identity of each idea as well as the part each idea plays in the total picture" (p. 248). As a study technique, outlining strategies can be used effectively to facilitate a careful analysis and synthesis of the relationships in content material. They can form the basis for critical discussion and evaluation of the author's points.

Problems arise when students are restricted by the means in which they must depict relationships spatially on paper. The word *outlining* for most of us immediately conjures up an image of the "correct" or "classic" format that we have all learned at one time or another but have probably failed to use regularly in real-life study situations. The classic form of outlining has the student represent the relatedness of information in linear form:

   I. Main Idea
      A. Idea supporting I
         1. detail supporting A
         2. detail supporting A
            a. detail supporting 2
            b. detail supporting 2
      B. Idea supporting I
         1. detail supporting B
         2. detail supporting B
  II. Main Idea

This conventional format represents a hierarchical ordering of ideas at different levels of subordination. Roman numerals signal the major or superordinate concepts in a text section; upper-case letters the supporting or coordinate concepts; Arabic numbers the supporting or subordinate details; and lower-case letters sub-subordinate details.

Maturing readers have trouble using a restricted form of outlining. My guess is that, initially at least, they need a more visual display than the one offered by the conventional format. This hunch has some support in the research literature on structured overviews and arrays.

The structured overview is more or less a "free form" outlining procedure. Since we have seen how it helps students identify the interrelationships of key terms, there is little need to discuss its merits further. An *array*, however, is another free-form outlining procedure worth discussing. According to Hansell (1978), students use the array technique to decide how to arrange key words and phrases to produce the relationships in reading material. The student can use words, lines and arrows as symbols to show the nature of the relationships.

A CLOSER LOOK AT FREE-FORM OUTLINING

The only rule in a free-form outline such as an array is that students *How does the array technique work?* must attempt to create a logical spatial arrangement among key words and phrases which connect important ideas to supporting information. This can best be done with straight and uncrossed connecting lines.

Hansell illustrated, using the story of Adam and Eve, how the visual display in an array might be arranged in two different ways depending on one's interpretation of text relationships. See Figure 8–1. The "correct" form of an array, as you can see, is relative. The extent

Figure 8–1. Two Array Depictions

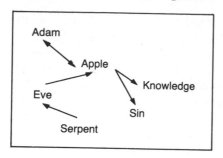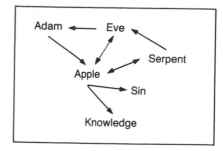

SOURCE: Hansell, T. Stevenson. "Stepping up to outlining." *Journal of reading* 22 (1978): 248–252. Reprinted with permission of T. Stevenson Hansell and the International Reading Association.

to which students can justify a visual display will indicate its appropriateness.

You can introduce the array-outlining procedure to students following these steps:

1. Divide the class into heterogeneous groups of three or four members each.

2. Give each group strips of paper and ask them to copy the key words and phrases that you have previously identified as representing the important and supporting ideas in a text selection.

3. Pronounce each word or phrase; if necessary discuss its meaning. Next, feed students into reading by asking several questions in which they must hypothesize answers. Then assign the reading.

4. Have each group create an array after they have finished reading by laying out the strips of paper and selecting the most important idea, and then arranging the remaining slips around it.

5. Have one member of each group copy the layout on a larger piece of paper and draw lines to show connected ideas and arrows to show the direction of the relationship.

6. Have the groups share their arrays and discuss their reasons for placement and connection.

Once students become familiar with constructing the array, they can move toward more independent production. For example, without help from the teacher small groups can generate their own lists of words and phrases to represent the important and supporting ideas in a text selection. Eventually, making an array can be an individual rather than a group activity.

There are other types of free-form outline constructed with procedures similar to that for the array. Walker (1979) demonstrated two. First, he showed what might be considered a "strict" application of the conventional format, using a chapter on "matter" from an earth science text. See Box 8–1.

How are pyramid, radial, and array outlines similar? Different?

Box 8–1

THE CONVENTIONAL OUTLINE FORM

The Crystals of Earth

I. Identifying Minerals
   A. Investigating Physical Properties
      1. Physical properties
         a. Color
         b. Luster
         c. Streak
         d. Hardness
         e. Specific gravity
   B. Investigating Chemical Properties
   C. Other Tests

II. Crystals
   A. Crystal Structure of Minerals
   B. The Structure of Crystals
   C. Crystal Properties

III. Mineral Groups
   A. A Rock-Forming Mineral: Quartz
   B. Other Rock-Forming Minerals
      1. Silicate
      2. Calcite and Magnetite
   C. Metal-Bearing Minerals
      1. Hematite, bauxite, and sphalerite
   D. Nonmetallic Minerals
      1. Sulphur
      2. Graphite
      3. Halite
      4. Gypsum
      5. Diamond
      6. Corundum
      7. Beryl

SOURCE: Walker, James. "Squeezing study skills (into, out of) content areas." In R. T. Vacca and J. A. Meagher, *Reading through content*, pp. 77–92. Storrs, Conn.: University Publications and the Reading–Language Arts Center, University of Connecticut, 1979.

Then he illustrated how two free-form variations could have been devised: the *pyramid outline* and the *radial outline*. See Figures 8–2 and 8–3.

The disadvantage of using free-form formats such as the pyramid or radial outline is that subordinate details are difficult to organize in the visual display. However, when the teacher's purpose is to show how to distinguish superordinate from supporting or coordinate ideas, the free-form outline is a fitting alternative to the conventional style.

Figure 8–2. The Pyramid Outline

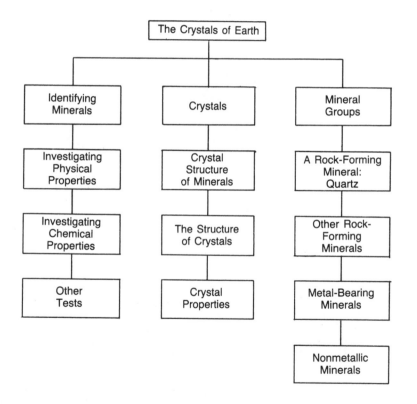

SOURCE: Walker, James. "Squeezing study skills (into, out of) content areas." In R. T. Vacca and J. A. Meagher, *Reading through content*, pp. 77–92. Storrs, Conn.: University Publications and the Reading–Language Arts Center, University of Connecticut, 1979. Used with permission of the author.

Figure 8–3. The Radial Outline

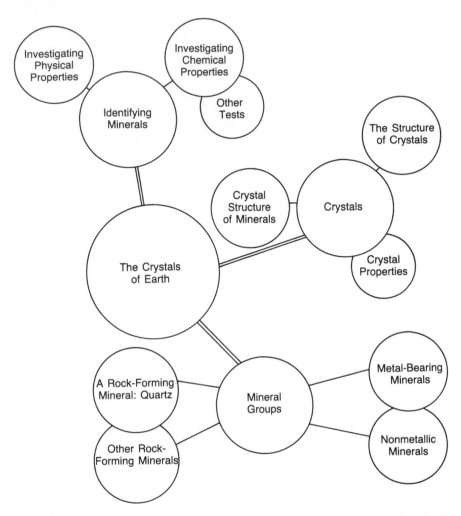

SOURCE: Walker, James. "Squeezing study skills (into, out of) content areas." In R. T. Vacca and J. A. Meagher, *Reading through content*, pp. 77–92. Storrs, Conn.: University Publications and the Reading–Language Arts Center, University of Connecticut, 1979. Used with permission of the author.

RESTRICTED OUTLINING

The conventional outline has a great deal of value and shouldn't be misinterpreted in light of the previous discussion. For although the conventional form restricts students to a definite format, they can use it effectively once they become comfortable with the process of organizing and relating ideas in text. Sufficient application of free-form outlining should precede introduction of the restricted format.

How can the transition to restricted outlining be made gradually?

The transition from free-form to restricted outlining should be gradual and guided. Many reading authorities recommend a progression of restricted outlining assignments. The first assignment provides students with a "skeleton" outline partially completed by the teacher, and the second assignment might provide a skeleton outline less filled out. By the third assignment the teacher may present a "barebones" skeleton but with the main and subordinate information on a separate sheet of paper. Students then match the phrases at the appropriate levels within the skeletal hierarchy. By the fourth assignment the teacher provides the skeletal outline alone.

The level of difficulty of each of these assignments can be set to meet the needs of students in a particular class. The combination of free-form outlining with a gradual progression into restricted outlines should give students enough experience to produce organization in text.

Note Taking

Note taking ranks among the most neglected areas of study instruction. Palmatier and Bennett (1974) observed that note taking is an "accepted phenomenon," particularly of the American college scene. Yet when Palmatier and Bennett surveyed the note-taking habits of college students,

> Only thirty-seven of the 223 students surveyed (17 percent) reported having received any formal instruction in the skills of notetaking. Further, in most cases the instruction was of extremely short duration, thirty minutes or less, and *was in effect more warning as to the necessity for taking notes rather than instruction on how to do so.* [italics mine] *(p. 217)*

If instruction is to be meaningful, students need to be shown how to take notes in actual situations that require taking notes — during listening and reading. Application, consistency, and reinforcement can best be achieved in classrooms that now and then emphasize lecture within the framework of whole-class instruction.

LISTENING: THE ESSENTIAL PROCESS

Consider a very typical classroom scene. The setting is an eleventh grade business education class. The teacher has prepared a lecture on consumerism. How will she be able to tell whether class members are active or inactive participants in the lecture? Let's take a closer look at the dynamics operating in her room.

What is the relationship between active participation and "thinking space" during a class lecture?

A student in the back row next to the window glances briefly toward the football field outside. Yet with pen in hand he seems to be listening. Another student just under the teacher's nose sits back in her chair with arms folded and eyes staring straight ahead. Both students display the two most obvious criteria for active listeners: eye contact and body cues. So do most of the remaining twenty-seven students. The teacher, however, isn't satisfied that the whole class is actively participating. Why? She knows that active listening involves more than physical attentiveness. Active participation involves the productive use of the time in each student's head between hearing the teacher's words and hearing the next words she will utter.

The circle in Figure 8–4 represents each student's total "thinking space" for listening.

A wedge equal to about one-tenth of the total thinking space is reserved for simply hearing the teacher's words. What comprises the remaining nine-tenths of the listener's thinking space? Obviously, the

Figure 8–4. Thinking Space

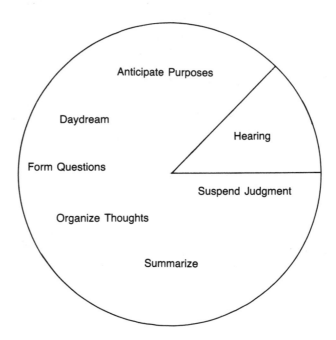

SOURCE: Sarah Lundsteen, *Children learn to communicate*, © 1976, p. 79. Adapted by permission of Prentice-Hall, Inc., Englewood Cliffs, New Jersey.

student's thinking speed far outstrips the teacher's (or any speaker's) talking speed. What students do with this leftover time determines how active and productive their participation will be in the whole-class presentation.

Let's hypothesize that the student in the back row and perhaps fifteen other students in the class were using their thinking space productively. They might be doing some of the following things to enhance learning:

1. taking notes and responding to questions raised
2. anticipating the teacher's next point
3. establishing continuous purposes for listening
4. forming some questions that zero in on what's been said
5. organizing their thoughts into categories of some kind
6. suspending making judgments until more information is received
7. summarizing the bits of information the teacher has presented

Let's assume that the remaining students were not making the best academic use of their thinking space during the lecture. They may have been doing some of these things to impede participation in the presentation:

1. faking attention (staring at the teacher, for example) while daydreaming
2. planning some private activity (such as the next weekend at the beach)
3. jotting down notes to pass along to a friend in the next row
4. failing to screen out irrelevant details and distractions such as the intermittent noise of hallway footsteps or the untied shoe one row over

This scene occurs in every lecture situation, no matter how dynamic a speaker is.

Active listening is the first step toward effective notetaking. The teacher can prime students to listen actively, as the *listening guide* and the *guided lecture procedure* show.

Listening Guide Castallo (1976) maintained that note taking is a two-step process which involves (1) listening for main points in a lecture and (2)

How does a listening guide work? writing those points in an organized manner for later use. He suggested that teachers can use a listening guide as the first step in teaching successful note taking.

To develop a listening guide the teacher must be prepared to give an organized lecture. Or to put it another way, you must know what you're going to say before you say it. This means reviewing lecture notes and deciding what the main and supporting ideas will be and the order in which you will present them. When you accomplish this you should develop a skeletal outline of the lecture, leaving empty spaces for students to fill in during the presentation. The outline in effect becomes the listening guide.

Castallo (1976) provided an illustration of a listening guide from a junior high science class. The science teacher's lecture dealt with two types of learning. His introduction went like this:

> Today's topic is learning. We will be discussing how people learn in two different ways. The first type we shall discuss will be learning through *positive reinforcement*. The second type of learning we shall discuss will be learning through *negative reinforcement*. We shall list at least *three examples* of each type and discuss how they are related. When we finish we shall also discuss how learning takes place through another method which is related to negative reinforcement (*ignoring*). (*Castallo, 1976, p. 290*)

The introduction provided a conceptual overview for the students. The teacher then expanded on the main points of the lecture. Students completed their listening guides as the lecture progressed. The teacher completed the same guide on an overhead projector to "alleviate any possible misunderstandings."

Guided Lecture Procedure Another strategy which promotes active listening and the productive use of thinking space is the Guided Lecture Procedure (GLP). The GLP is the listening counterpart to the Guided Reading Procedure, which was

Explain how to use the GLP.

explained in Chapter 7.

Here's how the GLP works:

1. Students are told not to take notes during the lecture and are encouraged instead to listen with the intent of retaining all information presented.

2. The teacher writes on the chalkboard the three or four main objectives of the lecture. The students read and copy the objectives. Next to each objective, the teacher writes technical terms new to the students which will be used during the lecture.

3. The teacher then lectures for approximately half the class period.

4. After the lecture the teacher directs students to write down individually and quickly everything they recall. They may abbreviate and annotate. The teacher encourages students to use "visual thinking" in order to "see" what interrelationships and categories of knowledge they can form.

5. Students then form small groups to review and discuss the lecture. This is the crux of the activity. They outline their notes in sequential order, identifying major ideas, relating these to pertinent details, and checking to make sure their outline fits with the objectives and new vocabulary the teacher listed.

The GLP provides the structure students need to participate in active listening and study. If questions arise during small-group interaction, the teacher should be ready to help students resolve them.

The originators of the GLP recommended that a writing assignment be given as a follow-up to the class activity: ". . . the student writes in narrative form, independently of her/his notes, the lecture's major concepts, pertinent details, and conclusions. This activity helps the student retain the information and provides an immediate self-appraisal regarding areas that should be studied in more detail" (Kelley and Holmes, 1979, p. 603).

The listening guide and the GLP aren't so much methods for note taking as they are stimulants for active, intensive listening. In the next section, we will examine a note-taking method that can be learned easily.

NOTE-TAKING SYSTEM FOR LEARNING

Every study skills textbook recommends a "classic" note-taking method, but Palmatier's (1973) procedure is one of the few that has been tested empirically and found to be easier to learn than other methods. The *note-taking system for learning* (NSL) is labeled as such because it not only provides for organizing information but also forms the basis for studying for tests.

The NSL makes several provisos for effective note taking. First, a student should use only one side of an 8½-by-11-inch sheet of looseleaf paper with a legal-width margin; (if necessary, the student should add a margin line three inches from the left side of the paper). Second, the student should take lecture notes to the right of the margin.

What are the provisions necessary for effective note taking in NSL?

Although no specific format for recording notes is required, Palmatier (1973) suggested that students "develop a format which uses subordination and space to illustrate the organization of the material. Subordination of items may be achieved through indentation to show continuation of ideas or through enumeration to show series of details" (p. 38). Third, the student is to put labels in the left-hand margin that correspond with units of information recorded in the notes. The labels help to organize the welter of information in the right-hand column and give students the chance to fill in gaps in the notes. The labeling process should be completed as quickly as possible following the original taking of notes.

Finally, the student takes *reading notes* on separate sheets of paper and inserts them into appropriate positions in the lecture notes. According to Palmatier (1973), "This putting together of both reading and lecture notes into a single sequence is one reason for limiting notes to only one side of the paper . . . if the student has taken complete lecture and reading notes, he now has all material organized into a single system for learning" (pp. 37–38).

How can the NSL be used to study for exams?

Once notes are taken and the labeling task is completed, the system can be used by students to study for exams. For example, in preparing for a test, the student can spread out the note pages for review. One excellent strategy is to show students how to spread the pages, in order, in such a way that the lecture notes are hidden by succeeding pages and only the left-margin labels show. The labels can then be used as question stems to recall information — for example, "What do I need to know about (label)?" Accuracy of recall, of course, can be checked by referring to the original notes which were concealed by overlapping the pages.

Outlining and note taking demand that students do something with the content that they have read (or listened to). Another area of study lies in the use of visual information to develop ideas in content material.

USING VISUAL AIDS

Why are visual aids more than mere embellishments?

It's not at all surprising to find five hundred or more visual aids in a single secondary textbook. These graphics are there for a reason. They represent more than icing on the cake; as Robinson (1975) pointed out, publishing costs are too high to sustain mere embellishment. The fact is that graphic materials enhance understanding and interpretation.

A writer has definite purposes in mind in using visual aids to enhance text material. In some cases an aid is used to expand upon a concept developed in the main text. In other cases a graphic might be inserted to serve as an example or an illustration of an idea the writer has introduced. Such aids support points which are sometimes buried in the text. Visual aids, particularly charts and tables, also help readers by summarizing and organizing information. Moreover, visuals such as pictures, cartoons, and maps are "experience builders"; they add a "reality dimension" to the connected discourse. For example, the text description of the points in the arrangement of the entries in the *Reader's Guide to Periodical Literature* is more meaningful and concrete because of the visual the authors provide (see Box 8–2).

Students tend to skip over visual aids entirely or pay only cursory attention to them. Perhaps the sheer number of graphics in a text provides a visual overkill which diverts students from studying any of them seriously. And study skills instruction in a reading class, isolated from real curricular need, doesn't transfer to content area reading assignments as much as we would like to believe. Although students learn the terminology and mechanics of reading visuals, they may see little relation between a "reading lesson" and the application of skills in a "content lesson." Studying visual aids is often a matter of demand and purpose in a meaningful reading situation.

It's a difficult task to read graphic material in conjunction with written text. Students must be shown how to engage in back-and-forth

Box 8–2

ADVERTISING
Art director who has a way with words also has a book coming from Abrams; publication of The art of advertising; interview, ed by R. Dahlin. G. Lois. Pub W 211:55+ Ja 17 '77

Giving impact to ideas; address, October 11, 1977. L. T. Hagopian. Vital Speeches 44:154-7 D 15 '77

News behind the ads. See alternate issues of Changing times

Preaching in the marketplace. America 136:457 My 21 '77

Selling it. Consumer Rep 42:385, 458, 635 Jl-Ag, N '77
See also
Photography in advertising
Religious advertising
Television advertising
Women in advertising
also subhead Advertising under various subjects, e.g. Books—Advertising

Here are some important points to notice about the arrangement of the entries in the *Readers' Guide:*

1. Articles are entered under the author's last name and also under the subject with which the article deals.

2. Author and subject entries are arranged in alphabetical order.

3. The author's name in an author entry is in boldface type, the last name first, in capital letters. Subject headings are also in boldface capitals.

4. The numbers at the end of the entry indicate the volume number of the periodical and, following the colon, the pages on which the article appears. A plus sign (+) means that the article is continued on a later page in the magazine.

5. The issue in which the article appears is shown by the month of publication, abbreviated, the day of the month if the magazine is published more than once a month, and the year.

SOURCE: from THE ENGLISH LANGUAGE 10 by Joseph C. Blumenthal et al., copyright © 1963 by Harcourt Brace Jovanovich, Inc. Reprinted by permission of the publisher.

---

reading, going from print to visual and visual to print. The example of the arrangement of entries in the *Reader's Guide* nicely illustrates how students must study an illustration as they read the corresponding text section.

Teachers can assist students to use visual aids productively through planned guidance. Summers (1965) recommended four conditions that would "maximize" learning from visual aids in a content area. Students should be taught to (1) recognize and interpret separate elements presented in visual aids, (2) analyze and understand the relationships between elements contained in visual aids, (3) pose questions and seek answers through the use of visual aids, and (4) make inferences and draw conclusions from visual aids in light of the problem at hand. The processes involved in reading visual material are basically the same as those tapped while reading connected discourse.

How can open-book discussions help students study visual aids?

Open-book discussions are good times for the teacher to provide the direction that students need to study visual aids successfully. You in effect say to students, "OK, let's take a few minutes to look closely at how the author(s) of our textbook used the (name the graphic) on page 67."

An open-book discussion walks students through an analysis of a visual aid. The teacher models the types of questions students themselves should raise when they encounter a visual in a reading assignment. "Focus questions" will prod students into isolating and identifying important elements in the graphic. A good starting point is always a discussion of the title or caption. "Clarifying questions" will prompt students into analyzing the relationships among the elements and making inferences.

The overhead projector can be put to good use during an analysis of visual aids. Use color markings for emphasis to show relationships and also to show students the inferential connections that they must make to draw conclusions. Participation in several demonstrations will have a positive effect on students' studying.

By way of illustration, let's turn our attention to specific examples which spotlight and extend the points just made.

Charts, Graphs, and Tables

Why can the simplest-looking visual aid pose a potential problem for students?

Pictorial representations are common fixtures in most content area material. The complexity of visual material varies. Yet even the most uncomplicated-looking chart, graph, or table can challenge the student's ability to interpret meaning. Consider, for example, the following illustrations.

Middle-grade youngsters must make many inferential decisions to interpret and understand the "stream" chart illustrated in Figure 8–5.

Figure 8–5. Stages in the Development of Money

1. barter

2. objects used as a measure of value

3. valuable items used as a medium of exchange

4. money coined from precious metals

5. paper money printed

SOURCE: Carter, Robert, and Richards, John. *Of, by and for the people*. Westchester, Ill.: Benefic Press, 1972, p. 360.

They must infer that:

1. The "stages" represent a time sequence with early times depicted in stage 1 and modern times depicted in stage 5.
2. The evolution of money is based on hundreds of years of elapsed time.
3. The contents of the bushels in stages 1, 2, and 3 represent a farmer's grain (or a reasonable alternative).
4. A bushel of grain is a valued item.
5. Bartered "objects" are animate or inanimate.
6. Different objects (such as the steer) have more value than other objects.
7. The equal sign in stage 2 suggests the comparable value of different objects.
8. The contents of the box being held in stage 3 must be of substantial value.
9. Paper money is a substitute for precious metals (gold or silver).

The students must also learn the technical terms *barter, medium of exchange, precious metals* and even *measure of value*. You must translate them into language the students can understand.

The "path of a check" schematic in Figure 8–6 is quite concrete. It illustrates pictorially what may be a difficult sequence of ideas to grasp in the text explanation. Senior high business students can actually "see" the process and the forms used to make the transaction. The chart is an effective experience builder. Nevertheless, in order to make interpretations students must sense the implied chain reaction — the cause-effect pattern. They must know that the arrows indicate the direction of the relationships. In addition, they must read the "fine print" between pictured items.

The general purpose of charts, graphs, and tables is to present and summarize information. Questions or statements should be developed, if none already accompanies a visual, to help students interpret such information. For example, the table in Box 8–3 shows how American history teachers from the Louisville, Kentucky, school system developed a three-level question guide to help students respond to numerical information which summarizes the breakdown of Electoral College votes in the 1960 presidential race in key states.

Since bar and pie graphs are used mainly to make comparisons between sets of relationships, they can be used to identify trends and make generalizations. Notice that in the pie graph in Box 8–4 students must decide whether certain generalizations are correct. The statements serve as springboards to interpretation by helping students identify trends emerging from the comparative data.

Figure 8–6. The Path of a Check

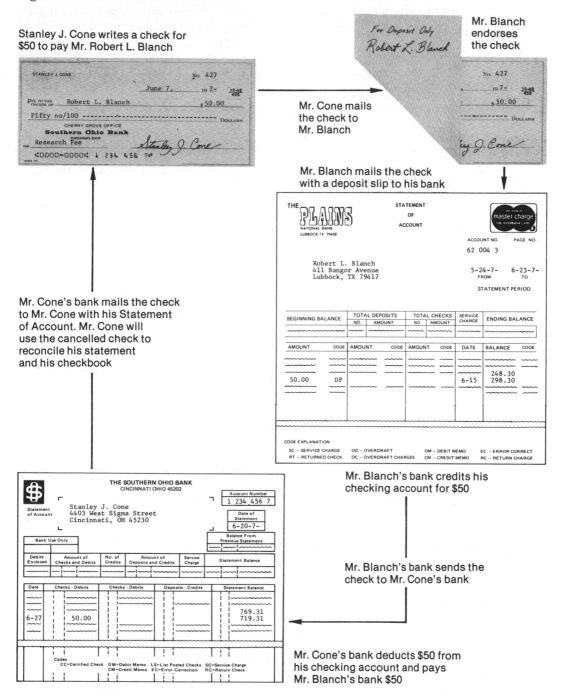

SOURCE: Meehan, James; Pasework, William; and Oliverio, Mary Ellen, *Clerical Office Procedures*. 5th ed. Cincinnati: South-Western Publishing Company, 1973, p. 521.

In contrast to a bar graph or pie graph, a textbook might also use a line graph to compare how two or more sets of data whose relationships are proportional change over time in order to give students a graphic aid to help them predict information. Study the line graph in Figure 8–7, from *Life Science: A Problem-Solving Approach*.

The authors of the text did a fine job of asking questions to help students interpret and apply information from the population graph. Here's a sampling of their questions:

1. In what year was the grasshopper population greatest?
2. In what year was the frog population greatest?
3. Why did the grasshopper population reach a peak immediately after the rye grass?
4. Why was the frog population never as great as the grasshopper population?
5. The population of which organism seems to control all of the populations in this food chain?

Box 8–3

THE ELECTORAL COLLEGE

The Electoral College System suffers several shortcomings. The most serious is that it can produce a President who has won a majority of the electoral votes even though he did not receive a majority of the popular vote.

From the table below:

1. Determine the total number of popular votes cast.
2. Determine the total number of electoral votes each candidate received.

State	Electoral Votes	Kennedy	Nixon	Kennedy	Nixon
California	32	3,224,099	3,249,722		32
Illinois	27	2,377,846	2,368,988	27	
Kentucky	10	521,855	602,607		10
Ohio	25	1,944,248	2,217,611		25
Pennsylvania	32	2,556,282	2,439,956	32	
Texas	24	1,167,932	1,121,699	24	___

Total

Answer the following questions using the chart.

I. Literal Level
   1. In what state did Nixon receive the largest number of electoral votes?
   2. In what state did Kennedy get the largest number of popular votes?
   3. Which candidate received more popular votes?

II. Interpretive Level
   4. Why may the Electoral College be described as a "winner take all" system?

III. Applied Level

    5. Do you think there should be an alternative to the Electoral College System? If so, what?

SOURCE: *Study guides for skill development*. Louisville, Kentucky: Jefferson County Board of Education, 1978.

Box 8–4

PIE GRAPH: BUDGET OF A LARGE AMERICAN CITY

Examine this graph of the budget of a large American city for the years 1969–70.

Total Budget: $6,600,000,000

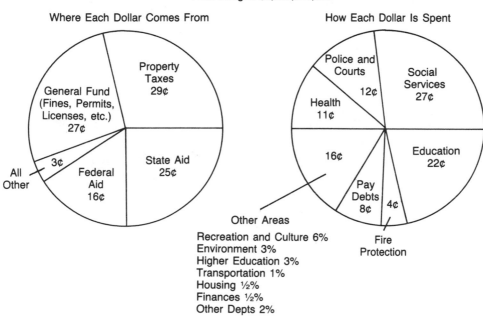

Check your understanding of the budget by telling whether or not the following are correct generalizations.

1. The city depended heavily upon help from the state and federal government to carry out its services.
2. The greatest expense was for aid to the poor and programs to help the poor.
3. Programs for housing and recreation cost more than expenses for health sevices.
4. Transportation costs were one of the largest of city expenses.

5. The greatest source of money for the city was the tax on property.
6. Without federal help, some city services would have had to be cut.
7. Planning for the future of the city was a big expense item.
8. All the money collected from taxes on property could not pay for all the cost of police and fire protection.

SOURCE: O'Connor, John; Gall, Morris; and Goldberg, Robert, *Exploring the urban world*. New York: Globe Book Company, 1972, 403. Used with permmission.

Figure 8–7. Population Graph: The Growth in Population of Three Organisms in a Pond Community

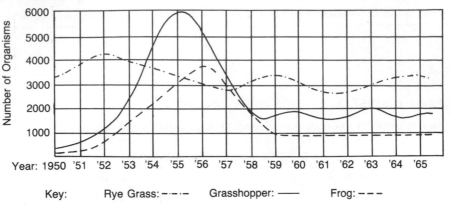

Key: Rye Grass: –·–·–   Grasshopper: ——   Frog: – – –

SOURCE: Carter, Joseph L., et al. *Life Science: A Problem Solving Approach.* Lexington, Mass.: Ginn and Company, 1971, 361–363. © Copyright 1979, 1971 by Ginn and Company (Xerox Corporation). Used with permission.

6. Why were all three populations nearly constant during the last five years?

7. What population would have to be increased first in order to have an increase in the frog population?

8. Which of the three populations will probably show an increase next year?

9. Which population will probably be the last to show an increase due to the addition of the fertilizer?

10. What populations would be affected if an insect-killing chemical were applied to the grass around the pond? Explain your answer.

A steady progression of thought-provoking questions such as these leads students from interpretation to prediction to application. Where questions do not accompany a graphic, content teachers have little recourse other than to develop their own.

Maps, Pictures, and Cartoons

Students need a great deal of interpretive skill to use maps, pictures, and cartoons effectively. Inferences from these aids must be made in relation to the text material.

Pictures in a textbook are invaluable. In Chapter 4 we saw how they can be used to reduce uncertainty, arouse interest, and stimulate questions. A well-timed picture breathes life and adds clarity to the printed word. Through their realism, pictures can expand experience and help avoid misunderstanding. They are particularly effective in showing step-by-step developments, contrasts and comparisons, and the status of things, processes, and events.

Cartoons are fraught with implications based on symbolic representations. Students may lack the background experience or prior knowledge to interpret adequately the symbols and implied meanings in a cartoon. Questions such as those for the cartoons in Box 8–5 will assist students to identify elements and relationships in cartoons. These relationships then will form the basis for interpretation and application. Of course, teachers also should consider the use of declarative statements in a three-level-guide format as another option available for helping students to respond to meaning in cartoons.

Because they are compact and devoid of redundancy, maps also require a great deal of student and teacher attention. A valuable chapter by Summers (1965) contains excellent background material on the nature, complexity, and diversity of maps. It is a "must" resource for content instructors. Summers pointed out the irony that teachers face when working with fairly decent "map readers" who happen to be poor "map thinkers." These students can locate information adequately, for they know terminology. Yet they cannot make the cognitive leap into interpretation. They need to engage in activities similar to those which have already been illustrated in this section.

According to Summers (1965), a map thinker should be aware of the following elements when studying a map*:

1. Map Title — A map title is similar to a book title; it gives the name of the area the map is depicting or the type of information to be shown. Map titles should be read carefully for a brief, succinct introduction to the map and its features.

2. Legend — The legend or key is often compared to the table of contents of a book. Just as the table of contents tells you what the book is about the legend or key indicates what the symbols on the map stand for, the scale of the map and other data. A symbol may be a drawing, pattern or color used to indicate map facts, usually a class of objects rather than a specific object. A variety of symbols may be found on maps although there is a tendency to use standard symbols from map to map. The legend or key is most often found in a separate box on the map. It is extremely helpful for students to

---

Box 8–5

INTERPRETING POLITICAL CARTOONS

Musical Chairs *

"We can get it for you wholesale."

*Redrawn with permission of the McNaught Syndicate.

Directions: Study the cartoons and then complete the exercise below. Put answers on a separate piece of paper.

Identification

1. List three words which best describe what each cartoon shows.
2. What is happening in each cartoon? Who is involved?
3. What issues do these cartoons raise?

Relationships

4. What two things do these cartoons have in common?
5. How is the main character portrayed in each cartoon?

Interpretation

6. Select one cartoon and identify the main character or item portrayed. Identify the other characters or items included in that cartoon.
7. Describe how the main character or item is related to the other character or items portrayed.
8. What observations or conclusions can you make about the problem, based on the information provided by these cartoons?

Application

9. Select two cartoons and describe several of the ideas each cartoon illustrates.
10. Given what you know about the energy problem, what might happen if Congress, the oil companies, or the public reacted as some of these cartoons indicate?

SOURCE: *Study guides for skill development.* Louisville, Kentucky: Jefferson County Board of Education, 1978.

---

visualize the things for which map symbols stand. Looking at the green of a map, one should actually "see" the rugged mountains.

3. Direction — Cardinal direction is indicated or can be inferred in some fashion on all maps. The top of the map usually, but not always, indicates North. It is important that students realize that North is not just a direction but that it is also a concept with the related understandings of true and magnetic North, intermediate distances and the polar regions.

4. Distance — Scale — Any representation of earth on a map or globe is actually a graphic reduction from actual size. The scale of a map indicates what a unit of distance on the map is equal to on the earth itself. Three types of scale are in common use: graphic scale, statement scale and fractional scale. The type of scale is relatively unimportant but the major point to remember is that scale enables you to tell how far something is or how big something is. A small scale map depicts a large area made smaller while a large scale map depicts a small area made larger.

5. Location — Grid systems are useful in locating places on maps. Grids section maps into smaller segments by use of horizontal or vertical lines. Special grids such as township range lines and those used on city maps and Atlases section by use of marginal letters and numbers. Parallels and meridians provide a means of locating places by latitude and longitude from agreed upon fixed points. Projections are devices used to depict a curved area of surface on a flat map and involve distortions. Various projections have been developed and each has advantages and disadvantages.

6. Types of Maps — The major map types are land, elevation, climate, natural vegetation and water features, political, economic and population. Each type provides a different kind of information about an area. Often, combinations of several types appear on one map.

A teacher shouldn't assume that students will attend to these elements independently. Students need to be made aware of the relevant pieces of information such as those described above that are contained in map elements. Nevertheless, a map thinker is not only aware of important information but knows how to use it to make inferences and draw conclusions.

LOOKING BACK, LOOKING FORWARD

Studying was described in terms of showing students how to do something with what they have read. Study was characterized as purposeful and deliberate activity. We explored two areas in particular where studying might have impact: (1) showing students how to produce organization in content material and (2) showing them how to use visual aids in the material to be read.

Outlining and notetaking help students to produce organization in the reading material as well as content lecture. Free form and restricted outlining procedures were discussed. I advised that free form outlining should precede attempts to have students use the conventional, restricted format. Listening is the essential process in taking class notes. Students can be taught to be active listeners. The note-taking learning system is a method that students can learn easily to help them take and study lecture and reading notes.

Visuals are used in content materials to support and enhance the written text. Students easily overlook visual material when they study. Therefore, we examined several instructional procedures that would help readers study visual aids. The questions that content teachers ask to help students focus on and clarify the important points in charts, graphs, tables, pictures, maps, and the like will make a difference.

In the final chapter of this unit, the emphasis will be on vocabulary reinforcement. How does the content teacher extend students' knowledge and use of special and technical terms? The presentation of vocabulary reinforcement will be straightforward. It relies, as you will see, almost totally on example.

SUGGESTED READINGS

Aaronson, Shirley. "Notetaking improvement: a combined auditory, functional and psychological approach." *Journal of reading* 19 (1975): 8–12.

Dunkeld, Colin. "Students' notetaking and teachers' expectations." *Journal of reading* 21 (1978): 542–546.

Herber, Harold, ed. *Developing study skills in secondary reading*. Newark, Del.: International Reading Association, 1965.

Perry, William. "Students' use and misuse of reading skills: a report to the faculty." *Harvard Educational Review* 29 (1959): 193–200.

Peters, Charles. "Perceiving the organizational structure of social studies materials." *Social science record* 14 (1977): 13–20.

Thomas, Ellen, and Robinson, H. Alan. *Improving reading in every class*. 2nd ed. Boston: Allyn and Bacon, 1977.

Walker, James. "Techniques for developing study skills." In G. Duffy, ed., *Reading in the middle school*, pp. 175–182. Newark, Del.: International Reading Association, 1975.

CHAPTER NINE

Reinforcing and Extending Technical Vocabulary

"I hope you won't take umbrage," she said.
"No," he said, "I never take umbrage unless
it's lying around and no one else wants it."

Sally of *PEANUTS*, reading her composition*

ORGANIZING PRINCIPLE

Nice try, Sally. Vocabulary and concept development involves experimenting with language: using, testing, and manipulating words in different contexts and situations. We have already studied in Chapter 3 how to lay the groundwork for vocabulary and concept development. Teachers can plan activities which will help students recognize relationships among concepts, build vocabulary inquiry skills, and become interested in learning the languages of different content areas. Nevertheless, if they are to increase their command of the technical vocabulary in a content area, students need experiences with words beyond the groundwork stage. They need to "work" with technical terms in many instructional situations. Reinforcement is necessary. The organizing principle of this chapter reflects the need to extend students' grasp of content terminology: *Word meanings and concepts are developed through repeated use and manipulation.*

Content teachers establish an environment for vocabulary reinforcement whenever their students participate in classroom activities which require the use of technical terms. One specific means of reinforcement calls for the manipulation of technical terms through teacher-made exercises. As you study the Chapter Overview, note the implied contrast between vocabulary reinforcement exercises which prompt students to make simple and complex associations among words. Simple

*Copyright United Features Syndicate, Inc.

CHAPTER OVERVIEW

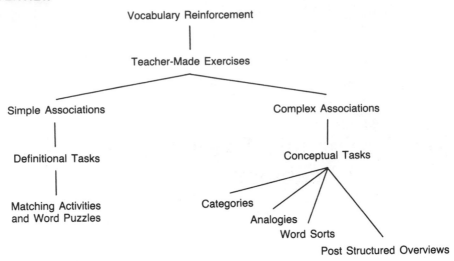

associational tasks reinforce an understanding of definitions. Complex associations foster conceptualization. As you read, sort out the differences between the two types of reinforcement exercises.

Imagine being in the tenth grade again. For the most part you can still recall how middle school teachers seemed to do more "fun things" in class. But now that you're in high school, you can't help but feel that more is expected from you in the way of schoolwork. The ninth grade was a transition year. You learned the ropes. And now that you're in the tenth grade, you know how to cope with academic demands — at least sometimes.

Your biology teacher assigns a lot of reading from your text — let's say it's *Modern Biology* (1973). The textbook shows its age; the cloth cover of your copy is frayed on the corners. Some sections of the textbook are interesting; some are dull. This particular passage is in between:

DARWIN'S THEORY OF NATURAL SELECTION*

In 1859, Charles Darwin, an English scientist, published his *On the Origin of Species by Means of Natural Selection*. His theory of natural selection, while confined to biology, has also influenced other branches of science. According to Darwin, the chief factors that account for the development of new species from a common ancestry can be summarized as follows:

*James H. Otto and Albert Towle, *Modern Biology*. New York: Holt, Rinehart and Winston, 1973, pp. 206–207. Copyright © 1973.

(1) All organisms produce more offspring than can actually survive.

(2) Because of overproduction, there is a constant struggle for existence among individuals.

(3) The individuals of a given species vary.

(4) The fittest, or the best adapted, individuals of a species survive.

(5) Surviving organisms transmit variations to offspring.

Overproduction

A fern plant may produce 50 million spores each year. If all the spores resulting from this overproduction matured, in the second year they would nearly cover North America. A mustard plant produces about 730,000 seeds annually. If they all took root and matured, in two years they would occupy an area 2,000 times that of the land surface of the earth. The dandelion would do the same in ten years.

At a single spawning, an oyster may shed 114,000,000 eggs. If all these eggs survived, the ocean would be literally filled with oysters. Within five generations, there would be more oysters than the estimated number of electrons in the visible universe! There is, however, no such actual increase.

The elephant is considered to have a slow rate of reproduction. An average elephant lives to be 100 years old, breeds over a span of from 30 to 90 years, and bears about 6 young. Yet if all the young from one pair of elephants survived, in 750 years the descendants would number 19,000,000.

Struggle for Existence

We know that in actuality the number of individuals of a species usually changes little in its native environment. In other words, regardless of the rate of reproduction, only a small minority of the original number of offspring reaches maturity.

Each organism seeks food, water, air, warmth, and space but only a few can obtain these needs in struggling to survive. This struggle for existence is most intense between members of the same species, because they compete for the same necessities.

As you read the passage several of the authors' examples capture your interest and hold your attention. You form neat mental images of a world overrun with oysters and mustard plants and begin to get a feel for some of Darwin's ideas. However, some of your classmates form no images.

In retrospect you can give the authors credit for trying to relate some of the abstract concepts in the passage to concrete or familiar examples. But overall, you and your classmates find the material somewhat difficult to read. The technical words get in your way.

In this short passage alone there are at least twenty terms of a scientific nature:

natural selection	competition	descendants
organism	necessities	reproduction
survival of the fittest	spores	ancestors
	visible universe	spawn
overpopulation	species	maturity
variations	transmit	electrons
theory	overproduction	
offspring		

These words and phrases are labels for concepts. Generally speaking, concepts such as these never stand alone. They are bound by relations. Johnson and Pearson 1978) explained that most concepts "do not represent a unique object or event but rather a general class linked by a common element or relationship" (p. 33). This is why concepts commonly have been defined as categories:

> . . . if the learner did not invent categories he would respond to events as unique experiences and quickly overload his information processing machinery. We invent categories to reduce the complexity of the environment, to reduce the necessity for constant learning and to provide us with means to identify events and things in the world. (*Lexier, 1979, p. 51*)

The vocabulary words in the list above trigger meaning. Goodman (1976) put it this way: "Vocabulary is largely a term for the ability of the child to sort out his experiences and concepts in relation to words and phrases in the context of what he is reading" (p. 480).

Step back into the past again. In your biology class, fortunately, you have a teacher who is aware of the problems of reading text. One problem in particular is that of the technical vocabulary which conveys concepts necessary for an understanding of the content under study. Your teacher could have decided to teach the class before assigning the passage every technical term that they would encounter. However, she knew that this would be impractical, time consuming, and fairly boring. She could have assigned you to look up the words and write out their definitions. But this too made little sense to her: looking up lists of words is often a meaningless routine. It more often than not leads to rote memory and verbalization that won't meet the needs of text learners. The teacher even remembers the purposelessness associated with looking up words when she was in school. However, instructional alternatives are within reach.

What does the biology teacher do to prepare the class for reading?

Your biology class has already studied changes in living populations through the ages. A comparison of ancient and modern organisms in fact led to the present unit on theories of evolution. You can bring a great deal of knowledge to the text material from previous study and experiences. Luckily, the biology instructor knows how to activate what you and your classmates know already so that you can bring that knowledge to bear during reading.

Figure 9.1 Structured Overview for Passage on Darwin's Theory of Natural Selection

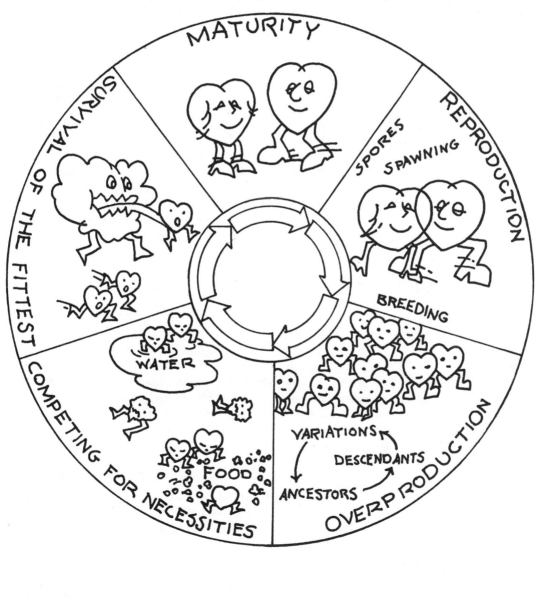

The teacher has the class participate in a discussion of the structured overview illustrated in Figure 9.1 before assigning the passage to read. She lets you students do most of the talking. She asks good questions which allow you to clarify the relationships among the concepts depicted in the overview. As you discuss the structured overview, you analyze structurally the meanings of several of the words: *organism, maturity, variations*. Throughout the discussion the teacher draws on what you know already and helps you to recognize what you need to know as you begin the reading assignment.

Why must vocabulary and concept development go beyond the groundwork stage?

These prereading activities, explained in Chapter 3, build a foundation for vocabulary and concept development. Nevertheless, building a foundation is just that — a foundation or groundwork upon which to construct fuller meanings. Students need many experiences, real and vicarious, to develop word meanings and concepts. They need to use, test, and manipulate technical terms in instructional situations which capitalize on reading, writing, speaking, and listening activities. In having students do these things, the teacher creates the kind of natural language environment that is needed to reinforce vocabulary and concept development.

Germane to this chapter is the development of vocabulary reinforcement exercises for this purpose. Specifically, we will study how to design materials and activities to increase students' grasp of word meanings and concepts. As they work with these activities and materials, students usually discover an attractive bonus: they are fun to do. The manipulative, gamelike structure of reinforcement activities captivates even the most reluctant student in a classroom.

GUIDELINES, COMMENTS, CAUTIONS

Why small groups?

As a rule of thumb, vocabulary reinforcement exercises should be completed individually by students and then discussed either in small groups or in the class as a whole. The oral interaction in team learning situations gives more students a chance to use terms. The increased volume in participation creates an atmosphere for reinforcement. Students can exchange ideas, share insights, and justify responses in a nonthreatening situation. Barron and Earle (1973) suggested the following procedures for small-group discussion of reinforcement activities:

Describe the steps which will facilitate small-group discussion.

1. End small-group discussion only after the group has discussed each answer and every member of the group understands the reasons for each answer.

2. Encourage the active participation of all group members. A student who has trouble with a particular exercise can still make a valuable contribution by asking questions or asking someone to explain answers.

3. Limit talk to the particular exercise or to related questions.

4. Make sure that students use the words and their meanings in discussing the answers, rather than using letters and numbers (for example, "I think the answer to number 1 is C.").

When to assign vocabulary reinforcement activities is an important consideration. Using them before reading has merit in certain situations. Herber (1978) commented, "Logically, it makes sense to have definitions reinforced before reading the material so that meanings can be developed during reading" (p. 159). On the other hand, teachers may also opt to reinforce vocabulary after reading. The issue is really a question of timing and instructional purpose. Postreading vocabulary exercises extend students' ability to use and manipulate concepts attained from reading. In either situation, before or after reading, reinforcement materials will serve to enhance vocabulary and concept learning.

Vocabulary exercises which prompt students to make simple associations between technical terms and their definitions have some value. These activities fall into two broad categories: matching exercises and word puzzles. Simple associational tasks are particularly useful in cases where the reader "does not know or use the word or phrase in his oral language but can grasp the meaning, particularly in familiar natural language" (Goodman, 1976, p. 283). In other words, a technical term may appear to be unfamiliar and troublesome at a surface level but actually represent a meaning familiar to students. In this situation, associating the new with the known through a matching exercise or word puzzle is useful.

However, a note of caution is in order: The learning of definitions is no sure guarantee that students will be able to use or conceptualize the technical vocabulary of a content area. Teachers should discourage students from merely repeating definitions without attempting to approach a conceptual level of understanding. Making simple associations between technical words and definitions is a beginning step in the development of concepts in text material.

Why is learning definitions only a beginning step?

Abstract concepts, such as *square root* or *natural selection,* lack concrete referents. Their meanings often depend on experiences and a level of conceptual development which most maturing learners have not yet attained. Such abstract concepts can be grasped only through a continual process of definition in which students experience words that convey concepts in familiar and meaningful contexts. Good writers know this. Protheroe (1979) observed,

> In regard to presenting unfamiliar or difficult vocabulary, the goal of the author is to use the word in as many familiar contexts as possible or to build an array of familiar contexts into which the word can be placed so that the student will nod his or her head and say, "Yeah, yeah, I know that," or "Oh, is that what that word means?" (p. 103)

To the extent that matching exercises and word puzzles can reinforce the "Oh, is that what that word means?" behavior, they have some use. But recognize that students must work with words on more than just a definitional level in order to conceptualize them.

What do complex association tasks accomplish? Why?

More complex associations involving relationships reinforce an understanding of word meanings and concepts. Vocabulary exercises should be developed not only to reinforce definitions but also to help students manipulate words in relation to other words. *Analogies, word sorts, categorizing activities* and *post structured overviews* are examples of the types of exercises and activities that can be used for this purpose. These conceptual tasks enable students to recognize that pairs of words are related, that is to say, that words can be grouped according to *class, example,* or *attribute* relations.

Class refers to the group to which a concept belongs: *tyrannosaurus* and *brontosaurus* belong to the class *prehistoric animals*. Class and example relations are often reciprocal: *tyrannosaurus* and *brontosaurus* are examples of *prehistoric animals*. Concepts have attributes or properties. The tyrannosaurus and brontosaurus are *extinct*; they had *tiny brains* and *huge bodies*. What did they eat? How did they mate? Answers to these questions reflect our knowledge of some of the attributes or characteristics associated with our concept of prehistoric animals.

Teachers can improve students' understanding of words and concepts by incorporating vocabulary reinforcement activities into their lessons. In the remainder of this chapter, we will examine actual classroom materials developed to reinforce and extend the meanings of technical terms.

REINFORCING DEFINITIONS AND MEANINGS

What insights do the matching exercises provide for developing reinforcement activities in your content area?

One of the best uses of vocabulary exercises designed to reinforce definitions is to associate technical terms with more familiar words that convey meaning. As part of a unit on geography, a social studies teacher developed the vocabulary reinforcement activity in Box 9–1 to help students associate technical terms in the text material with known synonyms and more familiar language. The class first completed the exercise individually and then discussed it in small groups before reading text material.

Technical terms with multiple meanings pose problems to maturing readers. A math teacher anticipated the problem of meeting multiple-meaning words in a geometry unit she had organized. She prepared students for working with these terms through the exercise in Box 9–2.

As in the previous example, class discussion preceded reading. The math students quickly recognized that a given geometry term can refer to a different concept or different concepts outside mathematics.

Box 9–1

SYNONYM MATCH

Directions: In column A are words from the unit. Match the word or words in column B by placing the letter in the correct blank in front of column A.

A	B
_____ 1. cultivate	a. surroundings
_____ 2. erosion	b. change
_____ 3. resource	c. bottom
_____ 4. modify	d. weather
_____ 5. terrace	e. wearing away
_____ 6. environment	f. height
_____ 7. foot (of mountain)	g. use of resources
_____ 8. climate	h. useful supply
_____ 9. elevation	i. raised level land
_____ 10. economic choice	j. work

Box 9–2

MULTIPLE MEANINGS MATCH

Directions: You will find that a word can have multiple meanings. Listed below are words and some of their meanings. Underline the correct meanings for each word as it is related to math.

1. mean — a) signify, b) average, c) bad tempered

2. union — a) a group of workers joined together, b) being united, c) combination of all elements in two or more sets

3. point — a) a sharp end, b) something that has position but is not extended, c) place or spot

4. intersection — a) point where two lines meet or two planes meet to form a line, b) crossing point, c) place where two or more streets meet

5. circle — a) a ring, b) to go around an area, c) a line every point of which is equally distant from a point within called the center

6. range — a) row or line of mountains, b) distance between certain limits, for example high to low, c) land for grazing

A health teacher spent two weeks developing concepts on the effects of cigarette smoking. In that time students had to grasp a number of technical terms to understand the content of the unit. Some of these terms were new words for old meanings. Others were new words for new meanings. The class participated in many activities that provided a natural outlet for vocabulary reinforcement. Toward the end of the unit, the teacher prepared the matching exercise in Box 9–3, which served as a review of students' knowledge of the technical terms.

In addition to their value as definitional tasks, matching activities can reinforce technical vocabulary by helping students make visual associations. Notice in Box 9–4 how a math teacher reinforced technical terms from a geometry unit by having students match them with visual counterparts.

A Variation on Matching: Magic Squares

A *magic square* exercise is by no means new or novel. Yet it has a way of reviving even the most mundane matching activity. I have seen the

How does a magic square exercise work?

magic square used successfully in elementary and secondary grades as well as in graduate courses. Box 9–5 shows how a magic square exercise works. Try it.

The magic number for the exercise on literary terms is 34. Analyze the mental maneuvers that you underwent to determine the correct number combinations. In some cases you undoubtedly knew the answers outright. You may have made several educated guesses on others. Did you try to beat the number system? Imagine the possibilities for small-group interaction.

A magic square need not be used just for vocabulary reinforcement. It can be adapted to fit any learning activity which lends itself to matching — for example, perceiving patterns of organization such as the cause-effect example in Chapter 6, "Jenny." Note the variation that a math teacher initiated in Box 9–6.

Many teachers are intrigued with the possibilities offered by the magic square. But they remain wary of its construction: "I can't spend hours figuring out number combinations."

Box 9–3

CIGARETTE SMOKING

Directions: For the following definitions place the number of a word from the list below which matches the meaning.

— a hairlike growth in the respiratory system that keeps the lungs clean

— a grayish white chemical element that is a violent poison

— a dark brown sticky mixture made up of gases, small amounts of moisture, and tiny pieces of material found in tobacco smoke

— a gas (a compound of nitrogen and hydrogen) found in tobacco smoke

— a very toxic gas found in tobacco smoke

— the uncontrolled growth of unhealthy cells within the body

— a poison in tobacco leaves

— a serious lung condition

— inflammation of the lining of the bronchial tubes (accompanied by a cough)

— any disease affecting the blood circulation system which interrupts or impairs the supply of blood to the heart or brain

— the upper end of the windpipe, where the vocal cords are

1. ammonia	5. carbon monoxide	9. emphysema
2. arsenic	6. chronic bronchitis	10. larynx
3. bronchial tubes	7. cilia	11. nicotine
4. cancer	8. circulatory diseases	12. tar

Box 9–4

GEOMETRICAL TERMS AND "VISUAL DEFINITIONS"

Directions: Place the letter of the figure next to the definition that matches it correctly.

— Line
— Ray
— Angle
— Plane
— Point
— Parallel lines
— Skew lines
— Triangle
— Quadrilateral
— Trapezoid
— Square
— Rhombus
— Parallelogram
— Rectangle
— Circle
— Polygon
— Line segment

Box 9–5

MAGIC SQUARE: HOW WELL DO YOU KNOW LITERARY TERMS?

Directions: Select from the numbered statements the best answer for each of the literary terms. Put the number in the proper space in the magic square box. The total of the numbers will be the same across each row and down each column.

Literary Terms	*Statements*
A. Point of view	1. Mental pictures within a story
B. Symbolism	2. Events and happenings in a story
C. Theme	3. The "when" and "where" of the story
D. Mood	4. The overriding feeling in a work
E. Plot	5. When something stands for something else
F. Metaphor	6. An exaggeration of great proportions
G. Structure	7. That which unifies a story as a whole
H. Myth	8. Saying one thing but meaning another
I. Setting	9. The central insight
J. Simile	10. A comparison introduced by *as* or *like*
K. Hyperbole	11. An implied comparison
L. Allegory	12. Saying less, but meaning more
M. Foreshadowing	13. Clues to future happenings
N. Irony	14. A tale of human life told in supernatural proportions
O. Understatement	15. When objects and characters are equated with meanings that lie outside the story
P. Imagery	16. The vantage point from which everything is known or interpreted

A	B	C	D
E	F	G	H
I	J	K	L
M	N	O	P

Magic number = _____

Box 9–6

MAGIC SQUARE MATH

Directions: Solve each of the following equations to find the value of n. Then place the answer you come up with in the box that corresponds to the letter of the problem. The sum will be the same in each row across and down.

Equations:

A. $57n + 43n = 1000$

B. $(8 \times 3) + (n \times 2) = 8(3 + 2)$

C. $6(9 + 12) = (n + 9) + (6 \times 12)$

D. $3(2 + 6) = (3 \times n) + (3 \times 6)$

E. $6n + 14n = 180$

F. $7n + 8n = 195$

G. $9n + 21n = 360$

H. $4(n + 8) = (4 \times 7) + (4 \times 8)$

I. $(9 \times 6) + (9 \times 5) = 9(6 + n)$

A	B	C
D	E	F
G	H	I

Magic number = _____

This is a legitimate concern. Happily, the eight combinations in Figure 9–2 make magic square activities easy to construct. You can generate many more combinations from the eight patterns simply by rearranging rows or columns. See Figure 9–3.

Notice that the single asterisk in Figure 9–2 denotes the number of foils or distractors needed so that several of the combinations can be completed. For example, the magic number combination of 18 requires one foil in the number 1 slot that will not match with any of the corresponding items in the matching exercise. In order to complete the combination, the number ten is added. Therefore, when you develop a matching activity for combination 18, there will be ten items in one column and nine in the other, with item 1 being the foil.

Figure 9–2. Model Magic Square Combinations

7	3	5
2	4	9
6	8	1

0*   15**

10	8	6
2	9	13
12	7	5

4*   24**

7	11	8
10	12	4
9	3	14

5*   26**

9	2	7
4	6	8
5	10	3

1*   18**

9	7	5
1	8	12
11	6	4

3*   21**

16	2	3	13
5	11	10	8
9	7	6	12
4	14	15	1

0*   34**

19	2	15	23	6
25	8	16	4	12
1	14	22	10	18
7	20	3	11	24
13	21	9	17	5

0*   65**

2	7	18	12
8	5	11	15
13	17	6	3
16	10	4	9

2*   39**

**magic number

*foils needed in answer column

Figure 9–3. More Magic Squares

7	3	5
2	4	9
6	8	1

→

8	1	6
3	5	7
4	9	2

or

6	1	8
7	5	3
2	9	4

Reinforcement Through Word Puzzles

What insights do the varying formats for word puzzles provide for developing reinforcement activities in your content area?

Puzzles are popular devices for reinforcing word meanings. A number of word puzzle formats work well to provide added recall and recognition of key terms. Many word puzzles give the number of letters in each word. Students then figure out the puzzle by working with a variety of meaning clues.

WORD PUZZLE

An effective format for a word puzzle requires students to associate the number of letters in each word with a definitional clue. See Box 9–7.

SCRAMBLED WORDS

Another variation on the word puzzle is scrambled words. Each scrambled word is followed by a definition, which students use to unscramble the word. Study the example in Box 9–8 from an English class.

Box 9–7

WORD PUZZLE ON PHOTOGRAPHY

Directions: Look at the definitions below. Think of a word that has the same number of letters as spaces provided and has the given letter in the position indicated. Write the word on the blanks.

```
1. __ __ __ __ __ __ __ N
                  2. E __ __ __ __ __ __
                  3. G __ __ __ __ __ __ __
                  4. A __ __ __ __ __ __ __
         5. __ __ __ __ __ T __ __ __
              6. __ I __ __ __
              7. __ V __ __ __ __ __ __ __ __ __
        8. __ __ __ E
                  9. S __ __ __ __ __
```

1. light-sensitive coating on film

2. inventor of roll film as we know it

3. material into which the light-sensitive material is suspended

4. made from wood fibers; flexible; transparent

5. silver bromide and silver chloride are light _____

6. Tri-X and Plus-XP anatomic are this

7. protects light-sensitive surface of film

8. flexible and transparent; holds light-sensitive chemicals

9. metal; dissolved; mixed with chloride or bromide

Box 9–8

SCRAMBLED WORDS

Directions: Each word scramble below is followed by a definition of a word that can be made out of the scrambled letters. Read the definition and then unscramble the letters to form a word corresponding to the definition. Each letter in the circled letters will combine to form the key word for this vocabulary unit.

CORRAN	Deep hate	_ Ⓐ _ _ _ _
KNLEAR	To trouble the mind with pain	_ _ Ⓝ _ _ _
GWAERLN	To argue noisily	_ _ _ _ Ⓖ _ _
TEESHE	To be violently agitated	_ _ _ _ _ Ⓔ _
TBULERS	To speak in a rage	_ _ _ _ _ _ Ⓡ

MODIFIED WORD PUZZLE

A modified version of a word puzzle promotes structural word analysis reinforcement as students work with the definitions of key words. In Box 9–9, from a Social Studies class, each term is broken into pronounceable units. Other exercises can easily be adapted to have students work with roots and affixes. Notice that because of the potential difficulty of the exercise, the teacher provided page clues as an added incentive.

Box 9–9

Modified Word Puzzle: The Communist Revolution

1. One word describing the rulers of Russia until 1917 (p. 47):
   T _ _ _

2. Three-syllable word describing a person who is formally giving up a throne (p. 47):
   A _ _ / _ _ / _ _ _ _

3. Two words to describe how Russia was ruled after the last tsar (p. 47):
   P _ _ / _ _ / _ _ _ _ / _ _
   G _ / _ _ _ _ _ / _ _ _ _

4. Three-syllable word to describe the condition factory workers were in because of factory owners (p. 49):
   E _ _ / _ _ _ _ _ / _ _ _ _

5. Two words to describe what Marx called the group of people who exploited the working class (p. 50):
   S _ _ / _ _ _ _
   C _ / _ _ _ / _ _ _ _ / _ _ _ _

6. Three-syllable word to describe the state workers would be in after they had destroyed the capitalistic system (p. 51):
   C _ _ _ / _ _ / _ _ _ _ _

7. One word describing where the roots of the second Russian revolution of 1917 are found (p. 52):
   M _ _ _ _ / _ _ _ _

8. Two three-syllable words describing two major groups (p. 52):
   B _ _ _ / _ _ _ _ / _ _ _ _
   M _ _ _ / _ _ _ _ / _ _ _ _

9. Five-syllable word describing what emphasis Lenin put back into Marxism (p. 53):
   R _ / _ _ _ / _ _ _ / _ _ _ _ _ / _ _ _ _

10. Two words describing in which countries the revolution to improve the workers' lives would first occur (p. 54):
    I _ _ / _ _ _ _ / _ _ _ _ / _ _ / _ _
    U _ _ / _ _ _ _ / _ _ / _ _ _ _ / _ _ _ _

CONTEXT PUZZLES AND RELATED ACTIVITIES

The context puzzle is an interesting variation on the word puzzle format. In Box 9–10, English students are given structural clues but must associate each word with context clues provided in the sentences.

Context activities in general provide more than a definitional task. Students must be able to apply a technical term in a meaningful context. English and reading teachers in particular find context reinforcement exercises valuable because they reinforce and extend an important skill (using context to get meaning) as well as an understanding of vocabulary terms. Small groups of students in a sophomore English class worked with Box 9–11. The sentences were taken from several short stories that they had read.

In the next chapter we will study in some detail how to construct a *cloze passage* to assess the readability of text material. Briefly, you can construct a cloze passage by deleting every nth word from a segment of text. Then you reproduce the passage on a ditto master with a blank space replacing each deleted word. Students must supply the missing words.

Box 9–10

CONTEXT PUZZLE

Directions: Think of a word we have recently studied that fits in the blank space in each sentence below and has the same number of letters as the number of spaces provided in the corresponding line. Fill in the word on the line.

1. H _ _ D R _ _
2. A _ _ _ _ _ Y
3. _ _ _ U I
4. _ _ _ C O N _ _ _ _ _ _
5. _ O _ _ _
6. _ O M _ _ _

a. Charlie Brown tried to give up his _____ existence and lead a life of adventure.

b. Snoopy was in a state of _____ for weeks, showing no interest in anything.

c. Lucy showed her _____ by yawning throughout the baseball game.

d. The serious illness of Linus's grandmother left him _____ ; no one could comfort him.

e. The _____ in her expression was the very image of grief.

f. Such a _____ expression seems out of place on a young child.

Box 9–11

VOCABULARY REINFORCEMENT THROUGH CONTEXT

I. *Directions:* The sentences below are taken from short stories we are studying for this unit. Write a synonym and an antonym for each italic word below:

	Synonym	*Antonym*
1. After hitting the ground, Arvil rose with a slightly *vexed* expression.	_____	_____
2. Because I muffed the winning point, my teammates looked at me *truculently.*	_____	_____
3. Although he had eaten well the last few months, the years of eating just enough to survive made the dog *puny* in size.	_____	_____
4. The house too was *grotesque,* painted gray, its gables hung with daggerlike icicles.	_____	_____
5. In no hurry, I *sauntered* through Grant Park, observing the people as well as the flowers.	_____	_____
6. Usually we don't like people *meddling* with our personal business.	_____	_____
7. Having traveled all the world and lived all sorts of life styles, he was not bound to *provincial* ideas.	_____	_____

8. All the unstated anger caused a *turbulent* silence   _____   _____
between them.

II. *Directions:* The sentences below are taken from the short stories we are studying for this
unit. Using the context clues in these sentences, see if you can figure out the meanings of
the underlined words below. Then record the clues that helped you determine the meaning of
the word.

	Meaning	*Clues*
1. He got down and *pinioned* my arms with his knees.	_____	_____
2. I tried to kick him in the back of the head but could only *flail* my feet helplessly in the air.	_____	_____
3. Georgia made a *cutting* remark that hurt him.	_____	_____
4. . . . before we went to school she *plaited* my hair and I *plaited* hers before the mirror, in the same little twist of ribbons.	_____	_____
5. I liked his ease and the way that he accepted me immediately, *spontaneously* and freely, without waiting.	_____	_____
6. Feeling foolish, he lifted his face, baring it to an expected shower of *derision* from his brother.	_____	_____

Cloze passages can be created in a similar manner to reinforce technical vocabulary. However, the teacher usually modifies the procedure for teaching purposes. Every nth word, for example, needn't be deleted. The modified cloze passage will vary in length. Typically, a two-hundred- to five-hundred-word text segment yields sufficient technical vocabulary to make the activity worthwhile.

Should you consider developing a modified cloze passage on a segment of text from a reading assignment, make sure that the text passage is one of the most important parts of the assignment. Depending upon your objectives, students can supply the missing words either before or after reading the entire assignment. If they work on the cloze activity before reading, use the subsequent discussion to build meaning for key terms and to raise expectations for the assignment as a whole. If you assign the cloze passage after reading, it will help to reinforce concepts attained through reading.

How do modified cloze passages and OPIN exercises reinforce and extend technical vocabulary?

Upon completing a short lecture on the causes of the Civil War, an American history teacher assigned the cloze passage in Box 9–12 before students read the entire introduction for homework. See how well you fare with the exercise.

OPIN is a meaning-extending vocabulary strategy developed by Frank Greene of McGill University. OPIN provides another example of context-based reinforcement and extension. OPIN stands for *opinion* and also plays on the term *cloze*. Here's how OPIN works:

Have the class form groups of three. Distribute exercise sentences, one to each student. Each student must complete each exercise sentence individually. Then each member of a group must convince the other two members that his or her word choice is the best. If no agreement is reached on the "best" word for each sentence, then each member of the group can speak to the class for his/her individual choice. When all groups have finished, have the class discuss each group's choices. The only rule of discussion is that each choice must be accompanied by a reasonable defense or justification. Answers like "because ours is best" are not acceptable.

Box 9–12

MODIFIED CLOZE PASSAGE: CAUSES OF THE CIVIL WAR

What caused the Civil War? Was it inevitable? To what extent and in what ways was slavery to blame? To what extent was each region of the nation at fault? Which were more decisive — the intellectual or the emotional issues?

Any consideration of the __(1)__ of the war must include the problem of __(2)__ . In his Second Inaugural Address, Abraham Lincoln said that slavery was "somehow the cause of the war." The critical word is "__(3)__". Some __(4)__ maintain that the moral issue had to be solved, the nation had to face the __(5)__ , and the slaves had to be __(6)__ . Another group of historians asserts that the war was not fought over __(7)__ . In their view slavery served as an __(8)__ · focal point for more fundamental __(9)__ involving two different __(10)__ of the Constitution. All of these views have merit, but no single view has won unanimous support.

Most historians agree that slavery was one among many issues that separated the two __(11)__ , and that an intertwining of __(12)__ , __(13)__ , __(14)__ , and __(15)__ differences were just as significant. . . . Also, there is the question of the viability of __(16)__ as a form of government. Compromise, so basic to democracy, failed. The __(17)__ — the very concept of __(18)__ — was openly challenged when the South refused to accept Lincoln's __(19)__ .

Answers:

1. causes	7. slavery	14. political
2. slavery	8. emotional	15. psychological
3. somehow	9. issues	16. democracy
4. historians	10. interpretations	17. political system
5. crisis	11. regions	18. majority rule
6. freed	12. economic	19. election
	13. social	

SOURCE: Malcolm S. Langforde, Jr., *The American Civil War*. New York: Scholastic Book Services, 1968, pp. 8–9.

OPIN exercise sentences can be constructed for any content area. Here are sample sentences from science, social studies, and home economics:

Science.
1. A plant's _____ go into the soil.
2. The earth gets heat and _____ from the sun.
3. Some animals, such as birds and _____ are nibblers.

Social Studies.
1. We cannot talk about _____ in America without discussing the welfare system.
2. The thought of _____ or revolution would be necessary because property owners would fight to hold on to their land.
3. Charts and graphs are used to _____ information.

Home Economics.
1. Vitamin C is _____ from the small intestines and circulates to every tissue.
2. Washing time for cottons and linens is eight to ten minutes unless the clothes are badly _____ .

Answers:
Home Economics: 1. absorbed   2. soiled
Social Studies: 1. poverty   2. violence   3. organize
Science: 1. roots   2. radiation   3. rodents

OPIN encourages differing opinions about which word should be inserted in a blank space. In one sense the exercise is open for discussion, and as a result it reinforces the role of prior knowledge and experiences in the decisions that each group makes. The opportunity to "argue" one's responses in the group leads not only to continued motivation but also to discussion of word meanings and variations.

REINFORCING RELATIONSHIPS AMONG CONCEPTS

When students manipulate technical terms in relation to other terms, they are thinking critically. Vocabulary reinforcement activities can be designed to give a class the experience of *thinking about, thinking through,* and *thinking with* the technical vocabulary of a subject. Working with relationships among technical terms provides this opportunity.

Through the aid of vocabulary reinforcement activities, students recognize that they can classify and categorize words which label ideas, events, or objects. In short, they study words critically and form generalizations about the shared or common features of concepts in an instructional unit. Word sorting, categorizing, drawing analogies, and creating structured overviews are activities which get the job done effectively.

Word Sorts

This is an unbelievably simple yet valuable activity to initiate. Individually or in small groups, students literally sort out technical terms which are written on cards or listed on an exercise sheet. The object of word sorting is to group words into different categories by looking for shared features among their meanings. According to Gillet and Kita (1979), a word sort activity gives students the opportunity "to teach and learn from each other while discussing and examining words together" (pp. 541–542).

Gillet and Kita also explained that there are two types of word sorts — the "open" sort and the "closed" sort. Both are easily adapted to any content area. In the closed sort students know in advance of sorting what the main categories are. In other words, the criterion which the words in a group must share is stated. The closed sort reinforces and extends the ability to classify words and fosters convergent and deductive thinking.

Compare and contrast open sorts and closed sorts.

Open sorts, on the other hand, prompt divergent and inductive reasoning. No category or criterion for grouping is known in advance of sorting. Students must search for meanings and discover relationships among technical terms without the benefit of any structure. For example, if you were given the following list of names, how many different arrangements could be made by grouping together two or more names? You must be able to justify the reason or reasons for each arrangement.

Washington	Susan B. Anthony
Alexander the Great	John Kennedy
Rembrandt	Edison
Columbus	De Gaulle
Hitler	Helen Hayes
Caesar	Napoleon
Cleopatra	Einstein
Henry Ford	Margaret Mead

The possibilities are unlimited. Your arrangements probably run the gamut from the obvious (men versus women, modern versus ancient leaders, inventors, artists) to the less obvious (names given to foods and cities, faces on monetary currency worth one American dollar) to the bizarre (suspected of having venereal disease).

Both types of word sorts, open and closed, are useful vocabulary reinforcement activities. Let's take a closer look at each.

CLASSIFYING THROUGH OPEN SORTS

A similar experience to the one you just had awaits students when they are assigned to manipulate a corpus of words in an open-sort activity. Examine in Box 9–13 how an art teacher reinforced understandings with high school students.

CLASSIFYING THROUGH CLOSED SORTS

Closed sorts help students study words critically by requiring them to classify terms in relation to more inclusive concepts. Study Box 9–14 to see how a business teacher helped reinforce concept development from an assignment that students had just read on types of resources.

A junior high math teacher developed a similar closed sort activity for a unit on complex numbers. He developed the exercise in Box 9–15 toward the end of the unit to reinforce understandings learned from reading and class discussion.

Box 9–13

ART OPEN SORT

Directions: Working in small groups of students, classify the words below by arranging them into logical groups. Be prepared to show the rest of the class the logic behind your group's thinking.

jordan	roka	cornwall stone
ball	lead	cone
antimony	chrome	wheel
cobalt	slip	bisque
mortar	scale	stoneware
scrafitto	kaolin	oxidation
	leather	
	hard	

Possible Categories which students may form:
Types of clay
Glaze, chemical
Pottery tools
Coloring agents

Box 9–14

TYPES OF RESOURCES

Directions: Below is a list of words from the unit we are studying. Put each word under the proper category from the three given below the words. Be prepared to justify your classifications.

tools	wildlife
minerals	factories
water	tractors
labor	typewriters
machinery	power plants
trees	buildings

Natural Resources   Capital Resources   Human Resources

Box 9–15

CLASSIFYING NUMBERS

Directions: Place each of the following numbers in the correct region of the Venn diagram below:

A. $\sqrt{7}$	F. 0.72	K. $-4\frac{1}{2}$	P. 13%
B. $\frac{3}{4}$	G. $\sqrt[3]{12}$	L. $\sqrt{26}$	Q. -96
C. 72%	H. 0	M. $\sqrt[3]{-8}$	R. $5\frac{7}{8}$
D. π	I. 14	N. $\frac{4}{5}$	S. $\sqrt[3]{9}$
E. -3	J. $\sqrt{81}$	O. $-\sqrt{49}$	T. $\sqrt{27}$

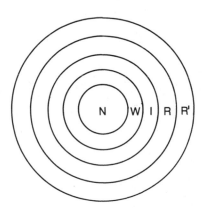

N = {Counting Numbers}
W = {Whole Numbers}
I = {Integers}
R = {Rational Numbers}
R' = {Real Numbers}

Categorization

Explain how categorization and its variations reinforce and extend technical vocabulary.

Vocabulary reinforcement exercises involving categorization require students to determine relationships among technical terms in much the same manner as open and closed sorts. The difference, however, lies in the amount of structure students are given to make cognitive decisions. Put another way, students are usually given four to six words per grouping and asked to do something with them. That something depends on the format used in the exercise. For example, you can give students sets of words and ask them to circle the word in each set which includes the others. This exercise demands that students perceive common attributes or examples in relation to a more inclusive concept, to distinguish superordinate from subordinate terms. Box 9–16 gives sample exercises from different content areas.

Other categorization exercises may direct students to cross out the word that does not belong in each set. This format forces students to manipulate words that convey the meanings of common items. Box 9–17 provides sample exercises.

Box 9–16

CIRCLE THE WORD IN EACH GROUP THAT INCLUDES THE OTHERS

I. Social studies

Directions: Circle the word in each group that includes the others.

1. government	2. generals	3. throne
council	troops	coronation
judges	armies	crown
governor	warriors	church

II. English

Directions: Circle the word that best includes the others.

1. satire	2. irony	3. humor
humor	pun	satire
irony	malapropism	irony
parody	faux pas	tone

III. Geometry

Directions: Circle the word that includes the others.

1. closure	2. irrational	3. function
distributive	rational	domain
property	real	range
associative	complex	relation
commutative	integers	preimage

A variation on this format directs students to cross out the word that does not belong, and then explain in a word or phrase the relationship which exists among the common items. See Box 9–18.

Box 9–17

CROSS OUT THE WORD THAT DOES NOT BELONG

I. Health / Home Economics

Directions: Cross out the word in each group that doesn't belong.

1. fats	2. meat	3. liver
protein	butter	leafy vegetables
nutrients	oatmeal	fruits
carbohydrates	fish oil	minerals

II. Biology

Directions: Cross out the word in each group that does not belong.

1. asexual	2. oögenesis	3. polyembryony
conjugation	fragmentation	fertilization
gamete production	budding	parthenogenesis
fertilization	binary fission	spermatogenesis

III. Language Arts

Directions: Below are words that we have been using while studying the newspaper. Look at each set very carefully. Three words are related in some way. Cross out the one word that does not belong with the other words. Be sure you can defend your answers.

1. AP	2. picture	3. jumpline
wire service	caption	column
UPI	story	caption
ABC	index	page

Box 9–18

TRAGEDY

English

Directions: Cross out the word in each set that does not belong. On the line above the set, write the word or phrase that explains the relationship among the remaining three words.

1. spectacle	2. drama	3. Aristotle	4. time
thought	comedy	Fergusson	character
disclosure	epic	Harris	place
language	tragedy	Marlowe	action

How can a structured overview be used to help develop categorization activities?

Teachers have found that they can construct categorization activities efficiently and effectively when the activities refer back to a previously constructed structured overview. The tie-in between an overview and categories is logical: since structured overviews depict superordinate-subordinate relationships among key terms, it is relatively easy to develop reinforcement exercises involving categorization from them.

For example, turn to the overview on *abnormality* in Chapter 3, on page 64. Study the relationships shown among the key terms. If you were to construct categories in which students would circle the word in each set that included the others, which possible word groups might be formed? Probably groups similar to these:

1. neurosis
   abnormality
   mental
     retardation
   psychosis

2. paranoia
   schizophrenia
   catatonia
   hebephrenia

3. depression
   neurosis
   phobia
   anxiety

A quick perusal of the abnormality overview would also give you ideas for categories in which students would cross out the word that didn't belong in each set. Examples:

1. depression
   anxiety
   antisocial
   phobias

2. catatonia
   mental
     retardation
   paranoia
   hebephrenia

3. neurosis
   psychosis
   personality
     disorders
   schizophrenia

The secret to constructing categories, of course, is to know the superordinate and subordinate relationships among terms in a unit or a chapter.

Analogies

Analogies trigger critical thinking about relationships. Bellows (1980) explained that an analogy is actually a comparison of two similar relationships: "On one side the objects are related. On the other side the objects are related in the same way. Like a mathematical equation, an analogy has equal or balanced sides" (p. 509). Students who are not familiar with the format of an analogy may have trouble reading it successfully. Therefore, teachers should give a short demonstration or two which will walk students through the reading/reasoning process involved in completing an analogy.

For example, a science teacher might write on the chalkboard: "Eating : people :: photosynthesis : _____." The teacher can then point out that the colon (:) stands for *is to* and the double colon (::) stands for *as*. The class reads aloud: "Eating is to people as photosynthesis is to _____.'' The students should be encouraged to complete the analogy and to explain the relationship between the items in each pair. In doing so, they will transform ''Eating is to people as photosynthesis is to plants'' into a new thought pattern which may go something like this: People can't survive without eating and plants can't survive without photosynthesis. Or: Both eating and photosynthesis are essential life-sustaining processes for people and plants respectively.

Ignoffo (1980) explained the practical value of analogies this way:

How do analogies trigger critical thinking and extend the use of technical terms?

''Analogies are practical because they carry an implied context with them. To work the analogy, the learner is forced to attempt various . . . procedures that involve articulation, problem-solving and thinking'' (p. 520). To stimulate articulation, problem solving, and thinking, many types of analogies can be constructed. Several of the more useful types for content areas are included in Box 9–19. As you study these, try your hand at completing each analogy by underlining the word which best fits in each blank space.

Analogies can easily be adapted to the technical terminology in any content area. Examine, for example, Box 9–20, a vocabulary reinforcement exercise from a junior high geography unit.

Box 9–19

COMMON TYPES OF ANALOGOUS RELATIONSHIPS

1. *Part to whole*
   Clutch : transmission : : key :
   (starter, engine, exhaust)

2. *Person to situation*
   Lincoln : slavery : : _____ : independence
   (Jefferson, Kennedy, Jackson)

3. *Cause and effect*
   CB : radio reception : : televison : _____
   (eating, homework, gym)

4. *Synonym*
   Bourgeoisie : middle class : : proletariat : _____
   (upper class, lower class, royalty)

5. *Antonym*
   Pinch : handful : : sip : _____
   (pet, gulp, taste)

6. *Geography*
   Everest : Matterhorn : : _____ : Alps
   (Ozarks, Andes, Himalayas)

7. *Measurement*
   Minutes : clock : : _____ : temperature
   (liters, degrees, gradations)

8. *Time*
   24 hours : rotation : : 365 days : _____
   (Eastern Time, revolution, axis)

9. *Symbol*
   Grim Reaper : death : : _____ : sleep
   (Jack Frost, Father Time, Sandman)

10. *Characteristic*
    Wind : _____ : : hot : fire
    (wave, storm, breeze)

11. *Degree*
    Rotund : _____ : : emaciated : slender
    (tall, ugly, chubby)

Box 9–20

GEOGRAPHY ANALOGIES

DIRECTIONS: Fill in the blank with the word from the list below that best expresses the same relationship with the third word as the second word does with the first.

Example 1: Good : bad : : happy : *sad*. Read the line as follows: Good is to bad as happy is to sad. Both pairs are opposites.

Example 2: Big : small : : large : *little*. Read the line as follows: Big is to small as large is to little. The two pairs express the same idea in different words.

1. Bay : gulf : : cape : _____
2. Latitude : longitude : : Equator : _____
3. Hill : mountain : : sea : _____
4. Tropic of Cancer : Tropic of Capricorn : : Arctic Circle : _____
5. North Pole : South Pole : : prime meridian : _____
6. Water : land : : oceans : _____
7. Tributary : river : : peak : _____

longitude	International Date Line	sea
latitudes	prime meridian	hills
mountain	Antarctic Circle	tropics
Equator	peninsula	continent
river	basin	ocean

Post Structured Overviews

Why will post structured overviews reinforce and extend technical vocabulary?

In the beginning of this chapter I described the structured overview as a prereading vocabulary activity. The structured overview introduces students to the important interrelationships among the key concepts to be studied. Barron and Stone (1973) have also reported the positive effects of what they term *graphic post organizers* — the same as post structured overviews — which students construct after reading.

A graphic post organizer — or post structured overview — allows students to work in groups to relate important content area terms in a spatial arrangement. To do this, students must analyze the relationships among the words.

The post structured overview as a reinforcement activity presumes that students are aware of the idea behind a structured overview. If they are not, you will need to provide them with an example or two. You can then introduce the class to a post structured overview by following these steps from Barron and Stone.

1. Type the key words on a ditto master.
2. Following reading and study of the material to be learned, place students into small groups of about two or three students each.
3. Distribute the list of terms and a packet of three-by-five-inch index cards to each group.
4. Students write each word from the list on a card. They then work together to decide upon a spatial arrangement among the cards which depicts the major relationship among the words.
5. As students work, provide assistance as needed.
6. Initiate a discussion of the constructed overviews.

Before actually assigning a post structured overview to students, the teacher should prepare for the activity by carefully analyzing the vocabulary of the material to be learned. List all the terms that are essential for students to understand. Then add relevant terms which you feel the students already understand and which will help them relate what they know to the new material. Finally, construct your own overview.

The form of student-constructed post structured overviews will doubtlessly differ from the teacher's arrangement. However, this difference in and of itself should not be a major source of concern. According to Herber (1978)

> Form is not the issue; substance is, and that is demonstrated by a clear portrayal of the implicit relationships among key words. . . . Students will see things differently than teachers and from one another. It is good . . . for the teacher to have thought through his or her own arrangement of the words for purposes of comparison, clarification and confirmation. (p. 149)

What is important, then, is that the post structured overview reinforce students' ability to relate essential ideas to one another through the key vocabulary terms in content materials.

LOOKING BACK, LOOKING FORWARD

Vocabulary reinforcement provides the opportunity by which students will increase their grasp of the technical vocabulary of a subject. In this chapter, we went beyond the groundwork stage of vocabulary and concept development by studying how students can use and manipulate words in many instructional situations. Teachers create an atmosphere for vocabulary reinforcement through the kinds of classroom activity which promote speaking, listening, writing, and reading. One specific alternative for instruction is to develop vocabulary reinforcement exercises.

These exercises reinforce word meanings and relationships among technical terms. Definitional tasks help students make simple associations among terms and their meanings. They fall into two broad categories: matching activities and word puzzles. We saw numerous examples of how these reinforcement materials were developed by teachers and incorporated into their lessons.

More complex associations among terms and the concepts they represent can also be reinforced through vocabulary exercises. These conceptual tasks provide the framework needed to study words critically. Various types of categorizing activities such as word sorts, categories, analogies, and post structured overviews reinforce and extend students' ability to perceive relationships among concepts they are studying.

In the next two chapters we will focus on issues related to assessment. Chapter 10 deals with a common concern of content teachers: how to assess the difficulty of text materials. Chapter 11 looks at ways to evaluate student performance to better plan instruction. Both chapters will distinguish between the role of teacher judgment and more "objective" means of knowing — the use of formal and informal measures.

SUGGESTED READINGS

The readings listed at the end of Chapter 3 and the following sources of information are suggested.

Barron, Richard. "Research for classroom teachers: recent developments on the use of the structured overview as an advance organizer." In H. Herber and J. Riley, eds., *Research in reading in content areas: fourth report,* pp. 171–176. Syracuse, N.Y.: Syracuse University Reading and Language Arts Center, 1978.

Barron, Richard, and Earle, Richard. "An approach for vocabulary development." In H. Herber and R. Barron, eds., *Research in reading in content areas: second report,* pp. 101–106. Syracuse, N.Y.: Syracuse University Reading and Language Arts Center, 1973.

Bellows, Barbara. "Running shoes are to jogging as analogies are to critical/creative thinking." *Journal of reading* 23 (1980):507–511.

Carney, John. "Vocabulary and concept development." In R. Vacca and J. Meagher, eds., *Reading through content,* pp. 93–99. Storrs, Conn.: University Publications and the University of Connecticut Reading–Language Arts Center, 1979.

Ignoffo, Matthew. "The thread of thought: analogies as a vocabulary building method." *Journal of reading* 23 (1980):519–521.

Lee, Joyce. "Increasing comprehension through the use of context clue categories." *Journal of reading* 22 (1978):259–262.

Pachtman, Andrew, and Riley, James. "Teaching the vocabulary of mathematics through interaction, exposure, and structure." *Journal of reading* 22 (1978):240–244.

Vacca, Richard. "Reading reinforcement through magic squares." *Journal of reading* 19 (1975):587–589.

PART THREE

Evaluating for Instructional Purposes

CHAPTER TEN

Estimating Text Difficulty

This is the sort of impertinence up with which I will not put.

WINSTON CHURCHILL

ORGANIZING PRINCIPLE ⎯⎯⎯⎯⎯⎯⎯⎯⎯⎯⎯⎯⎯⎯

When a sentence which had ended with a preposition was "corrected" on one of the galley proofs of his memoirs, Winston Churchill restored the original order of the words with the marginal comment quoted above. Writers are funny that way. Their words are important. Their style matters.

The level of difficulty of writing (readability) is never easy to assess. Yet the evaluation of content materials through readability formulas has received a great deal of attention by educators and publishers. Several correlates of writing style can be plugged into a formula to estimate readability. However, the organizing principle of this chapter warns against a narrow view: *The difficulty of text material is the product of factors residing in both the reader and the material.*

An evaluation of textbook difficulty involves both qualitative and quantitative analyses. The main ideas of this chapter can be found in the Chapter Overview. Use the relationships shown in it to organize your reading.

That students have trouble reading content assignments is no longer front-page news to the classroom teacher. Reading workshop leaders invariably call attention to the readability of content material. Teachers know the textbooks they use are difficult. They also know that there's

CHAPTER OVERVIEW

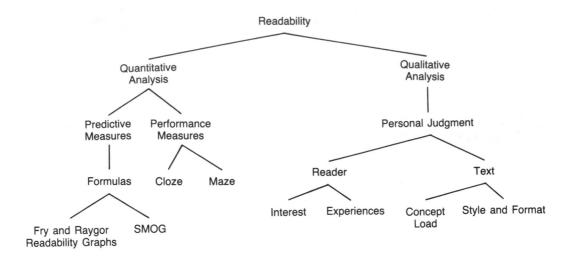

usually a significant mismatch between the reading abilities that students bring to text material and the estimated readability of the text itself. Perhaps this is why teachers have become less dependent upon books in their classrooms. The cartoon below hits home. In some content classrooms books may indeed be the latest educational innovation.

Circumvention is a coping strategy commonly used to deal with students who can't or won't study books on their own. Early (1973) claimed that classroom teachers of the 1970s recognized the reading dilemma that existed; but rather than tackle it head on, their tactic was to avoid the problem:

> The science teacher says: "They can't read the textbook any-way. So I do the experiment, or I set it up for them to do." The social studies teacher says: "They can't read the textbooks. Maybe they shouldn't anyway — the truth is so distorted. So I lecture. Or I set up a simulation." The math teacher says: "I have to read most of the problems to them. . . . We don't have a textbook, most of the kids are on their eleventh LAP. If they can't read the ditto, I explain it to them." *(pp. 367–368)*

The "way out" for some teachers is to abandon difficult materials or to avoid reading altogether as a vehicle for learning. This is unfortunate.

While I'm not suggesting that books are the only source for learning, or that they should be, they will continue to be indispensable tools for increasing knowledge and understanding, sharing the experiences and feelings of others and gaining new insights and perspectives. Avoiding books in the classroom isn't the solution to the reading dilemma that frustrates most content specialists. It only compounds the problem.

I agree with Campbell (1979): "There is no need to discard texts because they are difficult. There is a need for teachers to become aware of possible difficulties" (p. 687). Estimating the readability of content materials helps teachers focus on the potential difficulties that may make reading tough going for students. The best reason I know for evaluating textbooks is that it puts you in a better position to make instructional decisions.

Because of the practical interest in the difficulty of reading materials, readability formulas have received a great deal of attention from educators and publishers. A formula is an indicator of possible difficulty. However, the limitations associated with readability formulas make it necessary for you also to rely on professional judgment to help make decisions about materials. Determining readability continues to be as much an art as it is a science.

USING PERSONAL JUDGMENT TO MAKE DECISIONS ─────────────

Content teachers should evaluate texts from several perspectives: the readers' interests and experiences, concept load, organization, format,

Explain how reading material can be analyzed qualitatively.

and style. A textbook evaluation should be guided by questions that reflect a concern for the nature and number of concepts introduced, the special and technical vocabulary, the continuity among ideas, internal and external or-

"I'm taking an innovative approach to teaching this semester. I'm using BOOKS!"
Source: Reprinted from *Phi Delta Kappan* 59 (1978):416. Copyright 1978 Randy J. Glasbergen.

ganizational aids, the author's assumptions about the intended readership, and the stylistic appeal of the material. Harker (1977) suggested asking:

1. Are the concepts far beyond the student's direct experiences?
2. Are abstract concepts linked to examples and situations that are familiar to students?
3. Are technical terms defined in context as they appear?
4. Does one idea lead logically to another?
5. What does the author assume about the previous learning experience of the students?
6. Are textbook aids provided?
7. Is the material appealing or does it look too "textbookish"?
8. Is the writing brief, concise and to the point?

How can the usability checklist be adapted to your content area?

Answers to these questions are generally not amenable to numerical measurement. The questions, instead, lend themselves to a qualitative analysis of text material. In other words, the content teacher must use personal judgment to evaluate material in these important areas.

To help guide this assessment, check lists are commonly used. Two such check lists are presented in Box 10–1 (general) and Box 10–2 (science). The check list format can easily be adapted to evaluate expository material in any content area.

Box 10–1

GENERAL TEXTBOOK USABILITY CHECKLIST

External Organizational Aids	Has none/ poor	Adequate	Good
1. Does table of contents provide a clear overview of the contents of the textbook?	_____	_____	_____
2. Do chapter headings clearly define the content of the chapter?	_____	_____	_____
3. Do chapter subheadings clearly break out the important concept in the chapter?	_____	_____	_____
4. Do topic headings provide assistance in breaking the chapter into relevant parts?	_____	_____	_____
5. Does glossary contain all the technical terms of the textbook?	_____	_____	_____
6. Are graphs and charts clear and supportive of the textual material?	_____	_____	_____
7. Are illustrations well done and appropriate to the level of the students?	_____	_____	_____

8. Is print size of the text appropriate to the level of student readers?   _____ _____ _____

9. Are lines of text an appropriate length for the level of the students who will use the textbook?   _____ _____ _____

10. Is teacher's manual available and adequate for guidance to the teacher?   _____ _____ _____

11. Are important terms in italics or boldfaced type for easy identification by readers?   _____ _____ _____

12. Are end-of-chapter questions on literal, interpretive, and applied levels of comprehension?

Internal Organizational Aids

1. Are concepts spaced appropriately throughout the text, rather than being too many in too short a space?   _____ _____ _____

2. Is an adequate context provided to allow students to determine meanings of technical terms?   _____ _____ _____

3. Are the sentence lengths appropriate for the level of students who will be using the text?   _____ _____ _____

4. Is the author's style (word length, sentence length, sentence complexity, paragraph length, no. of examples) appropriate to the level of students who will be using the text?   _____ _____ _____

5. Does the author use a predominant pattern of organization (compare-contrast, cause-effect, time order) within the writing to assist students in interpreting the text?

SOURCE: Alaska Department of Education. *Evaluating Textbooks and Reading Materials.* Juneau: 1978.

Box 10–2

SCIENCE TEXTBOOK USABILITY CHECKLIST

Title *Natural World/I*   Fry Graph Readability *varies 6th to 10th*

Publisher *Silver Burdett*   Evaluator *Wallace*

External Organizational Aids	Has none	Poor	Adequate	Good
1. Does table of contents provide a clear overview of the contents of the textbook?			X	
2. Do chapter headings clearly define the content of the chapter?			X	
3. Do chapter subheadings clearly break out the important concept in the chapter?		X		
4. Do topic headings provide assistance in breaking the chapter into relevant parts?		X		

External Organizational Aids	Has none	Poor	Adequate	Good
5. Does glossary contain all the technical terms of the textbook?	X			
6. Are graphs and charts clear and supportive of the textual material?			X	
7. Are illustrations well done and appropriate to the level of the students?				X
8. Is print size of the text appropriate to the level of student readers?				X
9. Are lines of text an appropriate length for the level of the students who will use the textbook?				X
10. Is teacher's manual available and adequate for guidance to the teacher?				X
11. Are important terms in italics or boldfaced type for easy identification by readers?			X	
12. Are textbook questions on literal, interpretive and applied levels of comprehension?				X
13. Are lab experiences integrated with text materials?				X
14. Are lab questions on literal, interpretive and applied comprehension levels?				X

Internal Usability	Has none	Poor	Adequate	Good
1. Do questions raised and concepts presented show familiarity with ongoing research?			X	
2. Are concepts spaced appropriately throughout the text, rather than being too many in too short a space?				X
3. Is an adequate context provided to allow students to determine meanings of technical terms?			X	
4. Are the number of examples, including lab experiences, appropriate for the level of students who will be using the text?			X	
5. Is the author's style (word length, sentence length, sentence complexity, paragraph length) appropriate to the level of students who will be using the text?				X
6. Does the author use patterns of organization (compare-contrast, cause-effect, time order listing) within the writing to assist students in interpreting the text?				X

SOURCE: Alaska Department of Education. *Science/Reading*. Juneau: 1978.

Subjective evaluation is not a substitute for a quantitative analysis of text material but a complement to it. The science of readability prediction and analysis, with its extensive literature spanning a half century, can make some contributions to a teacher's understanding of text difficulty. But aim for a perspective. There are things that readability measures can do and can't do. Let's take a closer look.

READABILITY

There are over thirty readability formulas that can be used by classroom teachers to estimate textbook difficulty. Most of the popular formulas today are quick and easy to calculate. They typically involve a measure of sentence length and word difficulty to determine a grade level score for text materials. This score supposedly indicates the reading achievement level that students need to comprehend the material. Because of their ease, readability formulas are used to make judgments about instructional materials. These judgments are global, to be sure, and are not intended to be precise indicators of text difficulty.

Beware and Be Aware of Limitations

Why are formulas only "rubber rulers"?

A readability formula can best be described as a "rubber ruler" because the scores that it yields are estimates of text difficulty, not absolute levels. These estimates are often determined along a single dimension of an author's writing style: sentence complexity (as measured by length) and vocabulary difficulty (also measured by length). These two variables are used to predict text difficulty. But even though they have been shown to be persistent correlates of readability, they only indirectly assess sentence complexity and vocabulary difficulty. Are long sentences always more difficult to comprehend than short ones? Are long words necessarily harder to understand than short ones?

A series of short sentences in running text may even complicate the reader's ability to comprehend. Pearson (1974–1975) clarified the problem that arises when a readability formula is used to write or rewrite materials. He showed how the inferential burden of the reader actually increases when a long sentence is artificially broken into two short sentences:

> *version 1*: Because the new king clamped down on the public meetings, many residents emigrated to a new land.
>
> *version 2*: The new king clamped down on public meetings. Many residents emigrated to new lands.

Since the causal relationship in version 2 is not explicit, the reader must infer the connection between the separate ideas presented in each sentence. In version 1, however, the connective "because" makes the causal relationship explicit. The inferential burden is greater in 2 than in 1.

And while we're examining inferential burden, keep in mind that a readability formula doesn't account for the experience and knowledge that readers bring to content material. Hittleman (1973) characterized readability as a moment in time. He maintained that readability estimates should include the reader's emotional, cognitive, and linguistic backgrounds. A person's "human makeup" interacts at the moment with the topic, the proposed purposes for reading, and the semantic and syntactic structures in the material. Formulas are not designed to tap the variables operating in the reader. Our purpose, interest, motivation, and emotional state as well as the environment that we're in during reading contribute to our ability to comprehend text.

Why is readability referred to as a moment in time?

Nelson (1978) underscored the importance of viewing a readability formula as a rubber ruler by using the following example:*

What are the implications of Nelson's example?

Take the following social studies sentences as an example: 'The leader often becomes the symbol of the unity of the country. No one will run against him.' These sentences are relatively short and they contain few multisyllabic words. According to readability criteria, the sentences would appear to be appropriate for junior high school text material. However, the difficulty an eighth grade reader might experience in comprehending these sentences has little to do with readability criteria. Consider the information that the student must integrate:

1. The special meaning of *leader* in the social studies content.
2. The word *often* used to mean "in many cases" rather than "repeatedly."
3. The sense of *becomes* as meaning "grows to be" rather than "is suitable to."
4. The abstract concept of *symbolism*.
5. The abstract concept of *unity*.
6. The word *country* as a political unit rather than as a rural area.
7. The idea of *run against* as in an election.
8. The implication of a cause and effect relationship between the ideas presented in the two sentences. *(p. 622)*

The danger, according to Nelson, is not in the use of readability formulas: "The danger is in promoting the faulty assumptions that match-

---

* This and the following quote are reprinted from Joan Nelson, "Readability: Some Cautions for the Content Area Teacher," *Journal of Reading,* April 1978, by permission of Joan Nelson and the International Reading Association.

ing the readability score of materials to the reading achievement scores of students will automatically yield comprehension" (p. 622). She made these suggestions to content teachers:

1. Learn to use a simple readability formula as an aid in evaluating text material for student use.

2. Wherever possible, provide materials containing the essential facts, concepts, and values of the subject at varying levels of readability within the reading range of your students.

3. Don't assume that matching readability level of material to reading achievement level of students results in automatic comprehension. Remember there are many factors that affect reading difficulty besides those measured by readability formulas.

4. Don't assume that rewriting text materials according to readability criteria results in automatic reading ease. Leave rewriting of text material to the linguists, researchers and editors who have time to analyze and validate their manipulations.

5. Recognize that using a readability formula is no substitute for instruction. Assigning is not teaching. Subject area textbooks are not designed for independent reading. The best way to enhance reading comprehension in your subject area is to provide the kind of instruction which prepares students for the reading assignment, guides them in their reading, and reinforces the new ideas through rereading and discussion. *(p. 624–625)*

Within the spirit of these suggestions, let's examine three readability formulas and two alternatives, the *cloze* and *maze* procedures. I selected the formulas because of their current popularity, their ease of calculation, and their high degree of reliability with more complex formulas such as the Dale-Chall (1948).

Fry's Readability Graph

The readability graph developed by Edward Fry (1968, 1977) is a quick and simple readability formula. The graph was designed to identify the grade-level score for materials from first grade through college. Two variables are used to predict the difficulty of the reading material: sentence length and word length. Sentence length is determined by the total number of sentences in a sample passage. Word length is determined by the total number of syllables in the passage. Fry recommended that three one-hundred-word

Describe how to use the Fry readability graph.

samples from the reading material be used to calculate its readability. The grade-level scores for each of the passages can then be averaged to determine an overall readability level. According to Fry, the readability graph predicts the difficulty level of the material within one grade level. The graph and expanded directions for the Fry formula are presented in Box 10–3.

Box 10–3

FRY READABILITY GRAPH

Graph for Estimating Readability — Extended

Average number of syllables per 100 words

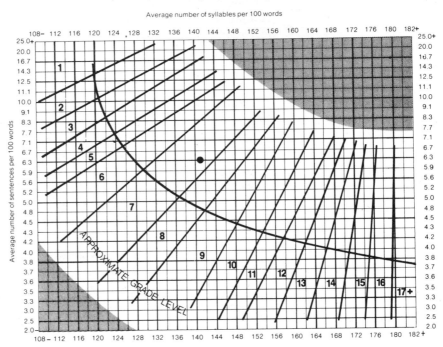

Expanded Directions for Working Readability Graph

1. Randomly select three (3) sample passages and count out exactly 100 words each, beginning with the beginning of a sentence. Do count proper nouns, initializations, and numerals.

2. Count the number of sentences in the hundred words, estimating length of the fraction of the last sentence to the nearest one-tenth.

3. Count the total number of syllables in the 100-word passage. If you don't have a hand counter available, an easy way is to simply put a mark above every syllable over one in each word, then when you get to the end of the passage, count the number of marks and add 100. Small calculators can also be used as counters by pushing numeral 1, then push the + sign for each word or syllable when counting.

4. Enter graph with *average* sentence length and *average* number of syllables; plot dot where the two lines intersect. Area where dot is plotted will give you the approximate grade level.

5. If a great deal of variability is found in syllable count or sentence count, putting more samples into the average is desirable.

6. A word is defined as a group of symbols with a space on either side; thus, *Joe, IRA, 1945,* and & are each one word.

7. A syllable is defined as a phonetic syllable. Generally, there are as many syllables as vowel sounds. For example, *stopped* is one syllable and *wanted* is two syllables. When counting syllables for numerals and initializations, count one syllable for each symbol. For example, *1945* is four syllables, *IRA* is three syllables, and & is one syllable.

SOURCE: Edward Fry, "Fry's readability graph: clarifications, validity, and extension to level 17." *Journal of reading* 21 (1977): 242–252. Reproduction permitted — no copyright.

Raygor Readability Estimate

Describe how to use the Raygor readability estimate.

Raygor (1977) developed a formula using a graph quite similar to Fry's. However, in the Raygor readability estimate word difficulty is measured by counting long words (six letters or more) rather than by counting syllables. Counting syllables can prove difficult and time consuming. It often results in introducing the most human error to an estimate of readability. Baldwin and Kaufman (1979) tested the speed and accuracy of the Raygor formula against that of the Fry. Indeed, they found the Raygor readability graph to be faster to calculate and just about as accurate as the Fry formula. The graph and directions for the Raygor formula can be found in Box 10–4.

SMOG Grading

Compare and contrast the SMOG formula with the Fry and Raygor graphs.

The simple measure of gobbledygook (SMOG) is another quick and easy readability formula to compute (McLaughlin, 1969). Unlike the Fry and Raygor formulas, SMOG Grading doesn't involve plotting points on a graph to yield a grade-level score. It indirectly relies on sentence length and word difficulty to predict the difficulty of reading material.

To compute a SMOG grade level score follow these four steps.

1. Count 10 consecutive sentences near the beginning of the text to be assessed, 10 in the middle, and 10 near the end. Count as a sentence any string of words ending with a period, question mark, or exclamation point.

2. In the 30 selected sentences count every word of 3 or more syllables. Any string of letters or numerals beginning and end-

ing with a space or punctuation mark should be counted if you can distinguish at least 3 syllables when you read it aloud in context. If a polysyllabic word is repeated, count each repetition.

3. Estimate the square root of the number of polysyllabic words counted. This is done by taking the square root of the nearest perfect square. For example, if the count is 85, the nearest perfect square is 81, which yields a square root of 9. If the count lies roughly between two perfect squares, choose the lower number. For instance, if the count is 110, take the square root of 100 rather than 121.

4. Add 3 to the approximate square root. This gives the SMOG grade, which is the reading grade that a person must have reached if he is to understand fully the text assessed.

Box 10–4

RAYGOR READABILITY ESTIMATE

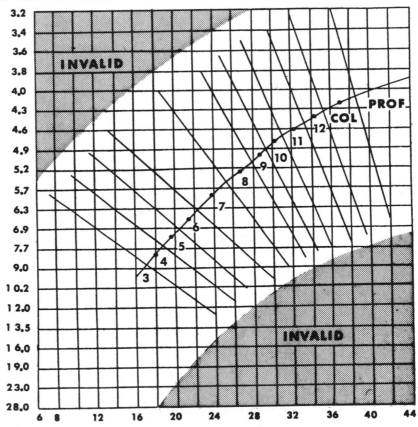

Directions: Count out three 100-word passages at the beginning, middle, and end of a selection or book. Count proper nouns, but not numerals.

1. Count sentences in each passage, estimating to nearest tenth.
2. Count words with six or more letters.
3. Average the sentence length and word length over three samples and plot the average on the graph.

Example:	*Sentences*	*Words*
A	6.0	15
B	6.8	19
C	6.4	17
Total	19.2	51
Average	6.4	17

Note mark on graph. Grade level is about 5.

SOURCE: Scott Baldwin and Rhonda Kaufman, "A concurrent validity study of the Raygor readability estimate." *Journal of reading* 23 (1979): 148–153. This graph is not copyrighted. It may be reproduced. Copies can also be obtained from Dr. Alton L. Raygor, University of Minnesota, 192 Pillsbury Drive S.E., Minneapolis, Minnesota 55455.

A worksheet such as the one illustrated in Box 10–5 can be employed to facilitate the calculation of the SMOG formula.

The SMOG is so incredibly easy to calculate that you may think that it's a put-on. Yet McLaughlin, the originator of SMOG, employed an intricate set of statistical procedures to determine its feasibility as a

Box 10–5

WORKSHEET FOR FIGURING SMOG GRADING

1. Number of polysyllabic words for sample 1 (first set of ten sentences):   ____
2. Number of polysyllabic words for sample 2 (second set of ten sentences):   ____
3. Number of polysyllabic words for sample 3 (third set of ten sentences):   ____
4. Total number of polysyllabic words (add 1, 2, and 3):   ____
5. Nearest perfect square to number 4 above: ____
6. Square root of the perfect square given in number 5:   ____
7. Add 3 to the result of number 6:   ____

Final number is the SMOG grade — the reading grade that an individual must have reached to fully understand the text assessed.

SOURCE: Jerry Johns, *Mimeograph* ed. Northern Illinois University, 1976.

measure of readability. The key to interpreting a SMOG grade level score is the author's claim that the score indicates the reading achievement level students must have to comprehend the material completely. By way of contrast, the Fry graph claims to determine a grade score that is "suitable" for comprehension.

In summary, readability formulas are predictive techniques. Hypotheses about text difficulty are based on an analysis of the material using selected variables which have been statistically determined to correlate with comprehension difficulty. The reader is not a variable in predicting difficulty from a formula. This is one of the reasons why you should approach present readability formulas with a healthy skepticism.

There are readability measures which aren't based on a prediction of text difficulty but on actual reader performance with the material. The *cloze* procedure and the *maze* technique will help you judge students' ability to cope with content material.

Cloze Readability Procedure

The cloze procedure does not make use of a formula to estimate the difficulty of reading material. "Cloze" refers to the psychological principle of closure. Closure is a Gestalt term which applies to the human tendency of completing a familiar but not-quite-finished pattern. An example of the closure principle is for an individual to perceive a broken circle as a whole, or, in the case of listening and reading, to supply a missing word in a familiar language sequence.

The cloze procedure was originated by Taylor in 1953, but its roots can be traced to the work of Ebbinghaus, who developed a "completion method" test in 1897. A cloze test determines how well students can read a particular text or reading selection as a result of their interaction with the material. Simply defined, then, the cloze procedure is a method by which you systematically delete words from a text passage and then evaluate students' ability to accurately supply the words that were deleted. An encounter with a cloze passage should reveal the interplay between the prior knowledge that students bring to the reading task and their language competence. Knowing the extent of this interplay will be helpful in selecting materials and planning instructional procedures. Box 10–6 presents a sample portion of a cloze procedure.

Explain the cloze procedure.

Here is how to construct, administer, score and interpret a cloze test.

1. Construction
   a. Select a reading passage of approximately two hundred seventy-five words from material that students have not yet read, but that you plan to assign.

    b. Leave the first sentence intact. Starting with the second sentence, select at random one of the first five words. Delete every fifth word thereafter, until you have a total of fifty words for deletion. Retain the remaining sentence of the last deleted word. Type one more sentence intact. For children below grade four, deletion of every tenth word is often recommended.

    c. Leave an underlined blank fifteen spaces long for each deleted word as you type the passage on a ditto master.

2. Administration

    a. Inform students that they are not to use their textbooks or work together in completing the cloze passage.

    b. Explain the task that students are to perform. Show how the cloze procedure works by providing several examples on the board.

    c. Allow students as much time as they need to complete the cloze passage.

3. Scoring

    a. Count as correct every *exact* word students supply. *Do not* count synonyms even though they may appear to be satisfactory. Counting synonyms will not change the scores ap-

---

Box 10–6

SAMPLE PORTION OF CLOZE TEST

    Everybody sleeps — everybody, that is, except for an Italian and an Australian. These two men, according __(1)__ twentieth-century medical literature, __(2)__ slept at all. On __(3)__ other hand, not long __(4)__ *The New York Times* __(5)__ on a professor who __(6)__ to have fourteen hours __(7)__ sleep a night. If __(8)__ woke after even thirteen __(9)__ , he spent the day __(10)__ foggy and tense. Apart __(11)__ their sleeping patterns, though, __(12)__ three men, according to __(13)__ experts on such matters, __(14)__ to be perfectly normal. __(15)__ why, by inference, assume __(16)__ their sleep habits were __(17)__ ? Indeed, when it comes __(18)__ sleep, what is normal __(19)__ , by contrast, abnormal? Who's __(20)__ say that what's perfectly natural for me might not be absurd for you?

Answers:

1. to	6. had	11. from	16. that
2. never	7. of	12. these	17. abnormal
3. the	8. he	13. the	18. to
4. ago	9. hours	14. appeared	19. and
5. reported	10. feeling	15. Yet	20. to

---

preciably, but it will cause unnecessary hassles and haggling with students. Accepting synonyms also affects the reliability of the performance criteria since they were established on exact word replacements.

    b. Multiply the total number of exact word replacements by two in order to determine the student's cloze percentage score.

    c. Record the cloze percentage scores on a single sheet of paper for each class. For each class you now have from one to three instructional groups that can form the basis for differentiated assignments. See Box 10–7.

4. Interpretation

    a. A score of forty to sixty percent indicates that the passage can. be read with some competence by students. The material will challenge students if they are given some form of reading guidance.

    b. A score of above sixty percent indicates that the passage can be read with a great deal of competence by students. They may be able to read the material on their own without reading guidance.

    c. A score below forty percent indicates the passage will probably be too difficult for students. They will need either

Box 10–7

CLOZE PERFORMANCE CHART

Subject _____

Period _____

Teacher _____

Below 40%	*Between 40% and 60%*	*Above 60%*

SOURCE: Robert Baker. Mimeographed. Syracuse, N.Y.: Syracuse University, 1972.

a great deal of reading guidance to benefit from the material or more suitable material.

The cloze procedure is an alternative to readability formulas, because it gives an indication of how students will actually perform with course materials. But two potential problems may have a negative effect on the results of student performance on a cloze test. First, the nature of the test itself will probably be foreign to students. They will be staring at a sea of blank spaces in running text, and having to provide words for them can seem a formidable task. Don't expect a valid score the first time you administer the test. It's important to discuss the purpose of the cloze test and give students ample practice and exposure to it.

What may hinder performance on the cloze test?

A second source of difficulty may be students' reactions to the criteria for successful performance. An excellent score on a cloze test means that a student can respond incorrectly to twenty out of fifty test items — a mind-boggling standard of success that may cause unnecessary anxiety among students.

Maze Technique

Because of the above two precautions, the maze technique seems to me to be a promising modification of the cloze procedure. The maze readability technique is similar to the cloze, with one major alteration: instead of leaving a blank space in place of a deleted word, the student can choose from three alternatives. For example: Air comes into the body through the mouth or (1) feet; (2) loses, (3) nostrils. Number 3, of course, is the correct choice. "Feet" is in the same grammatical word class (noun) as nostrils, but it doesn't make sense. The second choice, "loses," neither is grammatically correct nor makes sense. An example of a maze test passage is presented in Box 10–8.

Explain the maze procedure.

Box 10–8

ALICE IN WONDERLAND MAZE PASSAGE

Directions: The following exercise will help determine if you will have any trouble reading *Alice in Wonderland*. Every fifth word in the passage has three choices. Underline the word choice that makes the most sense. The passage begins with our Alice chasing a rabbit right into his rabbit hole.

In another moment down went Alice after it, never once considering how in the world she was to get out.

	turn		rather	
The rabbit hole went straight	somewhere	like a tunnel for six	way	and
	on		some	

```
          blue                                    him                          if
then dipped suddenly    down, so suddenly that boy  had not a moment to
          wonderfully                        Alice                          and
              falling                                  nowhere
think about stopping herself quickly she found herself falling down     what
              before                                  her
      a
seemed to be these very deep well.
          but
      well                                                          it
      Either the house was very deep, or search fell very slowly, for she   had
              given                  she                      think
      or                        run                      wonder
plenty of time dark she went down to candle about her and to sew      what
      as                        look                      homely
      with                      know                        in
was going to happen next. First she tried of    look down and make out
      dive                      to                          them
              under                      dark
what she was coming to        but it was too damp to see anything: then
              sweetly                  rock
drafty                up                  fast
we     looked at the sides an the well, and noticed which they were filled with
she                  of                      that
cupboards                        where                      briefly
cars        and book-shelves: here and until    she saw maps and pictures
wisely                              there                      germs
              took                      twelve                  dirty
hung upon pegs. She jumped down a jar from rusted of the shelves as them
              earth                      one                      she
              "orange                          sour
passed: it was labeled "empty  Marmalade" but to her great disappointment it
              "help                          fly
      iron            inside                  of
was empty: you did not like to learn  the jar for fear this killing somebody
      she                  drop                      until
          sleepy                  me                      shoes
underneath, so colored    to put it into those of the cupboards as him    fell
          managed                  one                      she
```

past it.

"Well!" thought Alice to herself "After such a fall as this I shall think nothing of tumbling down stairs!"

Here is how to construct, administer, score, and interpret a maze test.

1. Construction
   a. Choose a passage from the content material that students have not yet read.
   b. Leave the first sentence intact. Starting with the second sentence, select at random one of the first five words. Delete every fifth or tenth word thereafter, until you have at least twenty deletions.
   c. Substitute three alternative words for each deletion: 1) the correct word; 2) an incorrect word that is *syntactically acceptable* (from the same word class, such as noun, verb, adjective, as the correct word) but *semantically unacceptable* (not meaning the same as the correct word); 3) an incorrect word that is syntactically and semantically unacceptable;
   d. The order of the three word choices should be changed at random for each deletion.
2. Administration (same as in the cloze procedure)
3. Scoring
   a. Count the number of correct word responses.
   b. Determine the student's comprehension score by dividing the total number of deleted words into the number of correct responses made.

$$\text{Comprehension score} = \frac{\text{total number of choices}}{\text{number of correct responses}}$$

4. Interpretation
   a. A score above eighty-five percent indicates the passage can be read with a great deal of competence by students. They may be able to read the material on their own without reading guidance.
   b. A score between sixty and eighty-five percent indicates that the passage can be read with some competence by students. The material will challenge students, but they should be given some form of reading guidance.
   c. A score below sixty percent indicates the passage will probably be too difficult for students. They will need either a great deal of guidance to benefit from the material or more suitable material.

Guthrie (1973, 1974) originated the maze technique, but validated it with primary grade children only. Further validation studies with secondary students may yield a new set of criteria to help make interpretations about student performance. From a common sense point of view, however, the maze technique has much potential.

Also from a common-sense point of view, cloze and maze procedures may be adapted as teaching devices. They will stimulate a close reading of an important text passage that the teacher earmarks for discussion. When used as teaching tools, cloze and maze passages need not have systematic word deletions. As we saw in Chapter 9, you may wish to alter only key concept terms or only a certain combination of word classes to suit your instructional purposes. Synonyms or reasonable word replacements need not be "incorrect" either because you will not be using a passage to test comprehension but to guide its development.

LOOKING BACK, LOOKING FORWARD

Readability is as much an art as it is a science. Subjective judgment can be as useful as numerical analysis in evaluating the difficulty of content material. A teacher, therefore, must be concerned with the quality of the content, format, organization, and appeal of the material and how these factors interact with factors in the reader. With this in mind, the Fry readability graph, the Raygor readability estimate, and SMOG grading were examined. Two alternatives to readability formulas, the cloze procedure and the maze technique, were also reviewed for their utility to estimate text difficulty.

Evaluation takes a different turn in the next chapter. We will explore ways to assess student performance for content instruction. The same dilemma, however, exists. Do you rely solely on quantitative assessment of student abilities? What is the role of personal perception in evaluating for instruction?

SUGGESTED READINGS

Bormuth, John. "Readability: a new approach." *Reading research quarterly* 1 (1966):79–132.

Bormuth, John. "The cloze procedure: literacy in the classroom." In W. Page, ed., *Help for the reading teacher: new directions in research.* Urbana, Ill.: National Council of Teachers of English, 1975.

Burmeister, Lou E. *Reading strategies for middle and secondary school teachers.* Reading, Mass.: Addison-Wesley, 1978, chapter 2.

Fry, Edward. "A readability formula that saves time." In J. Harker, ed., *Classroom strategies for secondary reading,* pp. 29–35. Newark, Del.: International Reading Association, 1977.

Fry, Edward. "Fry's readability graph: clarifications, validity, and extension to level 17." *Journal of reading* 21 (1977):242–252.

Guthrie, John, et al. "The maze technique to assess, monitor reading comprehension." *The reading teacher* 28 (1974):161–168.

Hittleman, Daniel. "Readability, readability formulas, and cloze: selecting instructional materials." *Journal of reading* 22 (1978):177–192.

Klare, George. *The measurement of readability*. Ames, Iowa: Iowa State University Press, 1963.

————. "Assessing readability." *Reading research quarterly* 10 (1974–1975):62–103.

McLaughlin, G. Harry. "SMOG — grading — a new readability formula." *Journal of reading* 12 (1969):639–646.

Nelson, Joan. "Readability: some cautions for the content area teacher." *Journal of reading* 21 (1978):620–625.

Raygor, Alton. "The Raygor readability estimate: a quick and easy way to determine difficulty." In P. D. Pearson, ed., *Reading: theory, research, and practice*. Clemson, S.C.: National Reading Conference, 1977.

Rosenshine, Barak. "New correlates of readability and listenability." In J. A. Figurel, ed., *Reading and realism,* pp. 710–716. Newark, Del.: International Reading Association, 1969.

CHAPTER ELEVEN

Evaluating for Instruction

*Evaluation is one of those "weeds" you
can't get rid of. Administrators view
it as a cash crop. It's also something
we all do all the time anyway.*

BOB SAMPLES, CHERYL CHARLES AND DICK BARNHART

ORGANIZING PRINCIPLE ⎯⎯⎯⎯⎯⎯⎯⎯⎯⎯⎯⎯⎯⎯⎯⎯⎯⎯⎯⎯⎯⎯⎯⎯⎯⎯

Interpreting an indicator of reading performance is analogous to reading a meter on a gauge. The needle on an ammeter of a car, for example, tells us when and to what degree the battery is being charged or discharged. By observing the ammeter, we can make inferences about the internal state of the battery and the charging system. In the same manner, reading indicators in content areas signal how well and to what degree students use reading to learn from text materials. The organizing principle of this chapter builds on this notion: *Evaluation in content area reading is a continuous process involving careful observation during teaching and informal testing on teacher-made inventories.*

Multiple indicators of student performance can lead to effective decision making for instruction. The Chapter Overview will raise your expectations about the material to be presented.

Reading diagnosis — the very concept is formidable, sometimes even bewildering, to content area teachers. The medical connotation of *diagnosis* suggests a search for deficiencies and factors associated with failure in students. Most classroom teachers — sensibly — see their role as one of emphasizing the strengths students bring to learning situations.

CHAPTER OVERVIEW

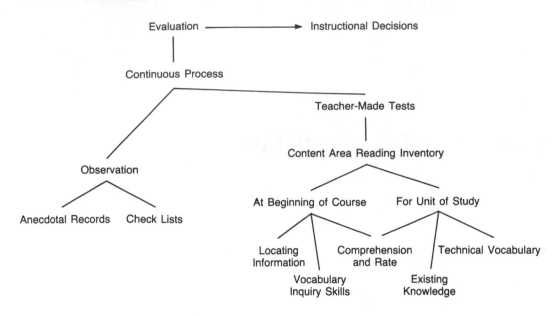

The prospect of diagnosing reading behavior is formidable because it suggests expertise and specialization beyond the domain of the classroom teacher. A diagnostic mystique doubtlessly contributes to whatever bewilderment or misgivings teachers have about evaluating reading performance. What is the diagnostic mystique? Sawyer (1974) described it as "the prevailing attitude that a skill-oriented assessment of . . . reading behavior by a reading expert is the last word in diagnostic workups. That if we can zero in on skill deficiencies the child will progress" (p. 561).

How does the "diagnostic mystique" contribute to faulty assumptions?

The diagnostic mystique is more "mythifying" than mystifying; yet it prevails in school. It also promotes faulty assumptions. As a result, *diagnosis* invariably evokes in the minds of teachers what is wrong with students. According to Hittleman (1977), it "seems to exclude assessing a reading performance that is not marked by failure" (p. 86). Teachers may also assume that they have little to do with assessing reading performance, when in fact their contributions to the evaluation process will doubtlessly enhance reading and learning.

Perhaps it's only a question of semantics, but I prefer to make the distinction between diagnosis and evaluation in content areas. Diagnosis is a restrictive term. It smacks too heavily of examining deficiencies and fragmenting the reading process for instructional purposes. Content area teachers are quick to reject this notion.

Evaluation is continuous, even though on occasion teachers rely on blind faith as a way of knowing. Sometimes we intuitively know that what we are doing in class is effective in light of our objectives. Often, however, evaluation can best be achieved through careful observation of students as they work with tasks that require reading. The strengths and limitations that students bring to content materials can be evaluated in classroom situations through their responses to questions, their performance in class discussions and small groups, or their written work. At times, of course, we shouldn't rely either on blind faith or personal perceptions to make instructional decisions. When a teacher lacks information necessary to plan instruction, he or she may administer a teacher-made test — a content area reading inventory.

Describe three "methods of knowing" about students.

Our conception of the reading process is bound to affect the way we evaluate student reading performance — the form and function of our evaluation. I believe that reading is a meaning-based process and that content area reading makes sense when teachers guide it without fragmenting the process into a wide array of subskills. The same applies to the evaluating process.

EVALUATING THROUGH OBSERVATION

Teachers can garner a wealth of information through the day-by-day classroom interactions that occur between them and students. Observing students' reading and study behavior can help them make good decisions about ongoing instruction. However, unless teachers make a systematic effort to tune in to student performance, they may lose valuable insights. The teacher has to be a good listener and a good watcher of students. Accurate observation should be a natural outgrowth of teaching; it increases teaching efficiency and effectiveness. Instructional decisions based on accurate observation help the teacher zero in on what and how to teach in relation to reading tasks.

How will participant observation contribute to teaching?

However, before this can happen, classroom teachers must view themselves as participant-observers. Participant-observation is a research tool that has been used extensively in the social sciences to understand human behavior. In the classroom setting, participant-observation may be characterized as a period of intensive interaction between the teacher and students when the teacher unobtrusively and systematically collects as much information as possible in relation to specific instructional objectives.

For example, a science teacher is beginning a unit on plants and plant life. She probably approaches the unit with certain preconceptions about the difficulty of the reading material, the work and study habits of the students, and the students' ability to use reading as a vehicle for learning. But she suspends these preconceptions; she purposely tries not to let presuppositions interfere with class presentations until actual classroom events and experiences during the unit suggest that her preconceptions are relevant.

The science teacher responds to the happenings that unfold before her. She guides daily observations by asking herself questions which reflect her objectives: How did students react to the class presentation? Which students had trouble with the reading assignment? How did students respond to instructional procedures and materials? Were students bored with the lesson? Did they grasp the concept related to man's dependence on green plants? What adjustments should I make in class presentations for the remainder of the unit?

This teacher is a participant-observer. She searches for the meanings of events that happen in class. To safeguard against the limitations of memory, the observer-teacher records in a notebook what happens in class. These field notes aid in classifying information, inferring behavior, and making predictions about instructional procedures, and as they accumulate, they become anecdotal records which provide documentary evidence of students' behavior over long stretches of time. Robinson (1975) recommended that

> Students should be observed as they work independently, as they respond to questions . . . and as they interact with their peers. The teacher should concentrate on one or at most a few students at one time and record dated impressions. In this way the instructor is able to compare observations for given students over time while coping with specific reading-study tasks. *(pp. 17–18)*

You can record and date observations on three-by-five-inch cards. A chronicle of informative notes gradually will emerge. According to Robinson (1975), "the instructor then has a product — dated written comments — to view in conjunction with other evaluative evidence" (p. 18).

Check Lists

A check list is different from natural observational techniques in that it imposes an a priori classification scheme on the observation process. A check list is designed to reveal categories of information the teacher has preselected. When constructing a check list you should know beforehand which reading and study tasks or attitudes you plan to observe. Individual items on the check list then serve to guide your observations in a selective manner.

How does a check list guide observations?

The selectivity that a check list offers is both its strength and weakness as an observational tool. Check lists are obviously efficient because they guide the teacher's observations and allow him or her to zero in on certain kinds of behavior. But a check list can also restrict observation by limiting the breadth of information recorded — excluding potentially valuable raw data.

Box 11–1 presents sample check-list items that may be adapted to specific instructional objectives in various content areas.

Box 11–1

SAMPLE CHECKLIST ITEMS FOR OBSERVING READING AND STUDY BEHAVIOR

Reading and Study Behavior	Student Name							
	Fred	Pat	Frank	JoAnne	Jerry	Courtney	Mike	Mary
Comprehension								
1. Follows the author's message	A	B	B	A	D	C	C	C
2. Evaluates the relevancy of facts								
3. Questions the accuracy of statements								
4. Critical of an author's bias								
5. Comprehends what the author means								
6. Follows text organization								
7. Can solve problems through reading								
8. Develops purposes for reading								
9. Makes predictions and takes risks								
10. Applies information to come up with new ideas								
Vocabulary								
1. Has a good grasp of technical terms in the subject under study								
2. Works out the meaning of an unknown word through context or structural analysis								
3. Knows how to use a dictionary effectively								
4. Sees relationships among key terms								
5. Becomes interested in the derivation of technical terms								

Reading and Study Behavior	Fred	Pat	Frank	JoAnne	Jerry	Courtney	Mike	Mary
Study Habits								
1. Concentrates while reading								
2. Understands better by reading orally than silently								
3. Has a well-defined purpose in mind when studying								
4. Knows how to take notes during lecture and discussion								
5. Can organize material through outlining								
6. Skims to find the answer to a specific question								
7. Reads everything slowly and carefully								
8. Makes use of book parts								
9. Understands charts, maps, tables in the text								
10. Summarizes information								

Grading Key: A = always (excellent)
B = usually (good)
C = sometimes (average)
D = seldom (poor)
F = never (unacceptable)

Observation reveals enough information in most cases to help classroom teachers make good decisions about instruction. But observation alone provides a single — albeit ongoing — indicator of student performance. Instructors should also consider other ways of evaluating performance to support their decisions about instructional procedures. In particular, it makes sense at times to analyze student reading performance through the use of tests.

CONTENT AREA READING INVENTORIES

Teacher-made tests are another important indicator of student reading performance in content areas. A teacher-made *content area reading inventory* (CARI) is an alternative to the standardized reading test. The CARI is informal and criterion-referenced. As opposed to the standard of success on a norm-referenced test, which is a comparison between the performance of the tested group and the original normative population, success on a criterion-referenced test is measured by performance on the task itself. The CARI measures performance on reading materials actually used in a course. The results of the CARI can give a teacher some good insights into *how* students read course material.

What steps should be considered in administering a CARI?

Administering a CARI involves several general steps. First, explain to students the purpose of the test. Mention that it will be used for evaluating only — to help you plan instruction — that grades will not be assigned. Second, briefly introduce the selected portion of the text to be read and give students an "idea direction" to guide silent reading. Third, if you want to find out how the class uses the textbook, consider an open book evaluation; but if you want to determine students' ability to retain information, have them answer test questions without referring back to the selection. And finally, discuss the results of the evaluation individually in conferences or collectively with the entire class.

Table 11–1 organizes the objectives and procedures for the development of CARI's based on two different informal testing situations. The objectives and procedures in Table 11–1 are common to all content areas. However, they must be adapted to fit the peculiarities of any particular field. For example, levels of comprehension in mathematics may be evaluated by how students process word problems. Therefore, the literal level will emphasize the facts of the problem; the interpretive level the mathematic concepts or ideas underlying the problem; and the applied level the numerical arrangements related to the problem.

A math teacher may also wish to evaluate whether or not students adjust their rates of reading: Do they read a word problem rapidly or slowly? Do they view the reading of word problems differently from narrative reading? An evaluation of vocabulary skills may also include students' ability to translate words to symbols or to know the meanings of specific symbols in a unit.

A CARI, whether it is developed for use at the beginning of a course or for a unit of study, can be administered piecemeal over several class sessions so that large chunks of instructional time will not be sacrificed. The bane of many content instructors is spending a disproportionate amount of time away from actual teaching.

Beginning-of-Course Inventory

How does a beginning-of-course inventory help to plan instruction?

Informal instructional tests administered in the first two months of a new school year elicit the information a teacher needs to adjust instruction and meet student needs. A beginning-of-course inventory should focus on students' ability to (1) locate information, (2) comprehend text, (3) use vocabulary skills, and (4) read at an appropriate rate of comprehension.

Table 11–1. Informal Test Situations for Content Area Reading Inventories: Objectives and Procedures

	TEST SITUATIONS		
Beginning-of-Course Inventory		Preassessment of Instructional Unit Inventory	
PROCEDURES	OBJECTIVES	OBJECTIVES	PROCEDURES
	To determine if students will:	*To determine if students will:*	
1. Locate Information: Construct 15–20 questions which assess students' ability to use	1. Locate information efficiently and effectively	1. Bring existing knowledge to unit materials	1. Existing Knowledge: a. Ask several open-ended questions that tap students' understanding of important ideas in unit b. Construct a knowledge-based preassessment test that reflects content objectives in the unit c. Construct a prereading guide to assess concepts/attitudes/values related to the important ideas in the unit d. Familiarity with terminology: Construct an inventory of students' knowledge of technical terms

a. Book parts
  b. Textbook aids
  c. Graphic aids
  d. Library resources			

2. Levels of Comprehension: Select a representative text selection of 500–1000 words. Construct 10–15 questions that test students' ability to read at a. literal level	2. Read textbook assignments at different levels of comprehension	2. Read text material at different levels of comprehension	2. Levels of comprehension: Same steps as in Procedure 1 for Beginning-of-Course Inventory

b. interpretive level

c. applied level

3. Vocabulary Skills: Construct questions to test students' ability to analyze technical terms through 　a. context 　b. structure 　c. dictionary/ 　　glossary	**3. Use independent vocabulary skills** to predict the meaning of difficult terms	**3. Read textbook material at an appropriate rate of comprehension**	**3. Rate of Comprehension:** Same steps as in Procedure 4 for Beginning-of-Course Inventory
4. Rate of Comprehension: Determine the number of words in passage that is selected for the levels of comprehension test. Note the time it takes individual students to complete reading. Determine words-per-minute (wpm) performance. Compare rate with percentage of correct comprehension answers.	**4. Read textbook material at an appropriate level of comprehension**		

Some authorities suggest that teachers should also evaluate additional competency areas such as study skills — skimming, scanning, outlining, taking notes, and so forth. I believe, however, that the best use of reading inventories in content areas is on a much smaller scale. A CARI at the beginning of a course should seek information related to basic reading tasks. For this reason, I recommend that outlining, note taking and other useful study techniques be assessed through observation and analysis of student work samples.

LOCATING INFORMATION

Locating information is essential to studying textbooks and to working with library materials effectively. Every teacher should know early in the school year whether or not students can successfully use book parts, library materials, maps, graphs, or charts. Questions which tap students' ability to locate information, such as those asked (about a social studies text) in Box 11–2, can easily be adapted to any content area. The questions can be asked orally or distributed on dittoed sheets. Examine the test items in Box 11–2. A short evaluative session at the beginning of a course screens students who cannot locate information with some degree of competence. These students will profit from instruction.

Box 11–2

TEST ITEMS FOR CARI ON LOCATIONAL SKILLS

I. Using Parts of a Book

1. On what page does the chapter on Southern Europe begin?
2. On what page would you find a population map of Africa?
3. Of what value is Table III in the appendix in helping you understand the material in the textbook?
4. Where would you look to find a list of the longest rivers in the eastern hemisphere?
5. On what pages would you look to find information about the Simplon Tunnel?

II. Using Library Materials

6. What library aid will tell you the library number of a book?
7. What is an almanac?
8. Name one set of encyclopedias. How are the topics in it arranged?
9. Where would you look to find the political boundaries of countries in Europe in 1812?
10. Where would you look to find a picture of a flag of a country and the history of a flag?

III. Using Maps, Graphs, and Charts

11. What information is given on the map on page _____?
12. What does the color red on the map on page _____ represent?
13. Why are longitude and latitude lines drawn on maps?
14. What information is given by the graph on page _____?
15. Using the graph on page _____ tell how many tons of cement were produced in the USSR in 1959.
16. Using the population graph on page _____ , tell which ten-year period Japan's population increased the most.
17. Using the chart on page _____ , list the form of government and the religion of Turkey.

SOURCE: Adapted from David Shepherd, *Comprehensive high school reading methods*. Columbus, Ohio: Charles E. Merrill, 1973.

EVALUATING LEVELS AND RATE OF COMPREHENSION

How can comprehension and rate be evaluated?

Early in the school semester teachers should gauge their students' ability to comprehend text material at three levels of comprehension, as a science teacher did with the inventory in Box 11–3. At this time you can also determine a measure of reading rate in relation to comprehension.

Box 11–3

AN EXAMPLE OF A COMPREHENSION INVENTORY IN SCIENCE

General Directions: Read pages 228–233. Then look up at the board and note the time that it took you to complete the selection. Record this time in the space provided on the response sheet. Close your book and answer the first question. You may then open your textbook to answer the remaining questions.

STUDENT RESPONSE FORM

Reading Time: _____ Min. _____ Sec.

I. A. *Directions:* Close your book and answer the following question.

    1. In your own words, what was this selection about? Use as much space as you need on this page. Continue on the opposite side if you should need more room to complete your answer.

II. A. *Directions:* Open your book and answer the following questions.

    1. An insect has six legs and a three-part body.
       a. true
       b. false
       c. can't tell

    2. Insects go through changes called metamorphosis.
       a. true
       b. false
       c. can't tell

    3. Most insects are harmful.
       a. true
       b. false
       c. can't tell

    4. Bees help flowers by moving pollen from flower to flower.
       a. true
       b. false
       c. can't tell

B. *Directions:* Answers to these questions are not directly stated by the author. You must "read between the lines" to answer them.

Literal Level Response to Main Ideas in Selection

Interpretive Level Response

1. How is a baby cecropia moth different from a full-grown moth?

_____

_____

2. Why does a caterpillar molt?

_____

_____

3. What are the four stages of a complete metamorphosis?

_____

_____

Applied Level Response

C. 1. Why do you suppose the caterpillar spins a long thread of silk around itself?

_____

_____

2. During which season would the full grown cecropia moth leave the cocoon? Why?

_____

_____

3. Why do you think they leave in that season rather than another?

_____

_____

You can construct a comprehension inventory using these steps:

1. Select an appropriate reading selection from within the second fifty pages of the book. The selection need not include the entire unit or story but should be complete within itself as to overall concept. In most cases two or three pages will provide a sufficient sample.

2. Count the total number of words in the excerpt.

3. Read the excerpt and formulate ten to twelve comprehension questions. The first part of the test should ask an open-ended question like "What was the passage you read about?" Then develop three or more questions at each level of comprehension.

4. Prepare a student response sheet.

5. Answer the questions and include specific page references for discussion purposes after the testing is completed.

While students read the material and take the test, the teacher observes, noting work habits and student behavior, especially of those students who appear frustrated by the test. The science teacher of Box 11–3 allowed students to check their own work as the class discussed each question. Other teachers prefer to evaluate individual students' responses to questions first and then discuss them with students either individually or during the next class session.

To get an estimate of students' rates of comprehension, follow these steps.

1. Have students note the time it takes to read the selection. This can be accomplished in an efficient manner by recording the time in five-second intervals by using a "stop watch" that is drawn on the board (see Figure 11–1).

2. As students complete the reading, they look up at the board to check the stop watch. The number within the oval represents the minutes that have elapsed. The number that the teacher is pointing to along the perimeter of the oval represents the number of seconds.

3. Later on, students or the teacher can figure rate of reading in words per minute.

   Example:
   Words in selection: 1500
   Reading time: 4 minutes, 30 seconds
   Convert seconds into a decimal fraction. Then divide time into words.

   $$\frac{1500}{4.5} = 333 \text{ words per minute}$$

4. Determine the percentage of correct or reasonable answers on the comprehension test. Always evaluate and discuss rate of reading in terms of students' comprehension performance.

VOCABULARY SKILLS

Chapter 3 discussed the skills that students need to inquire into the meanings of troublesome content area vocabulary terms. The extent to which they effectively use content and word structure often allows students to continue reading without getting "stuck" on difficult words. A beginning-of-course inventory of vocabulary skills can be helpful to teachers in planning vocabulary activities that will reinforce these skills.

Evaluating Context. Select five to ten difficult words from the textbook passage used for the comprehension inventory or from an assignment that students are about to read. These words should have enlightening context — sufficient semantic and syntactic information clues to reveal meaning. Before students read the selection, write the words on the blackboard and ask

How can context usage be evaluated?

Figure 11–1 "Stopwatch" for Marking Time to Determine Rate of Reading

The teacher marks time in five-second intervals on the chalkboard: 2 minutes and 15 seconds have elapsed. At the end of each 60 seconds, the number inside the circle changes.

students to define each one on a sheet of paper. Then instruct them to read the textbook selection. After the reading, ask them to refer back to their original definitions and to go back to the text to change any of the original definitions in light of information gained through reading.

This procedure is an effective informal way of evaluating students' ability to use context. It quickly tells you which students are proficient, which have some competence but will need reinforcement, and which have trouble and will need assistance to use context effectively.

Evaluating Word Structure. Words carry meaning-bearing units that provide readers with clues. You can select for evaluation content terms which are polysyllabic and are made up of affixes and recognizable English roots. Before testing, be sure students know what prefixes, suffixes, and roots are.

How can structural analysis be evaluated?

Provide each student with a list of representative words from the subject matter and direct the class to underline the recognizable stems and double underline the prefixes and/or suffixes. Then ask them to explain how the prefix and/or suffix affects the meaning of each content area term. Box 11–4 illustrates sample test items using vocabulary terms in various content areas.

Box 11–4

SAMPLE ITEMS FOR WORD STRUCTURE INVENTORIES

Directions: Below is a list of terms from the course. Each word is made up of a recognizable root and a prefix and/or suffix. For each word:

1. Underline the root
2. Double underline prefix and/or suffix
3. Explain in the column next to the word how the prefix and/or suffix influences the definition of the word

Example: undemocratic = not democratic

	Content Area Terms	Meaning Explanation
Social Studies	coexistence	To exist or live together
	postglacial	
	reconstructionist	
	interdependent	
	exploitation	
Science	decompose	
	relationship	
	thermoplastics	
	humidity	
	transformer	
Mathematics	replacement	
	midpoint	
	equidistant	
	conceptualize	
	segmentation	

Business	absenteeism
	malpractice
	unethical
	transaction
	consignment
Industrial Arts	hazardous
	alignment
	electromagnetic
	demonstrator
	countersink
Home Economics	perishable
	biodegradable
	antisocial
	inferiority
	salable
English	demonic
	reiteration
	eccentricity
	infamous
	peradventure

Evaluating Dictionary Usage. Dictionary usage is another valuable skill that aids vocabulary development. During informal testing situations, keep an observant eye on how students actually work with dictionaries in class. Does a student, for instance, select the most appropriate definition from multiple entries in the dictionary entry? Does the student translate formal definitions into his or her own words?

Unit-of-Study Inventory

Information you glean from a CARI at the beginning of an instructional unit will help you organize specific lessons and activities. You can decide the background preparation needed, the length of reading assignments, and the reading activities when you apply your best judgment to the information you have learned from the assessment.

A beginning-of-unit CARI can be designed to evaluate (1) existing knowledge that students bring to the unit, (2) students' familiarity with technical terms, (3) students' ability to comprehend the material to be read, and (4) rate of comprehension.

The procedures for evaluating levels and rates of comprehension are the same as those suggested for the beginning-of-course inventory. The emphasis, therefore, will be on evaluation procedures for existing knowledge and students' familiarity with content terminology.

EXISTING KNOWLEDGE

Explain how to evaluate existing knowledge and attitudes.

The knowledge, experiences, beliefs, attitudes, and values that students bring to a unit of study are invaluable. You can assess existing knowledge in a variety of ways so that you can plan instruction. The most common procedure would simply be to pretest students' knowledge of the material to be learned. The pretest is constructed according to content objectives and reflects the major ideas and concepts in the unit. The pretest can be a short-answer assessment or a set of open-ended essay questions. Many teachers combine short-answer questions with one or two open-ended ones.

Alternatives to preassessment tests of knowledge are instructionally based. For example, you can use many of the prereading activities discussed in Chapter 4 to observe and evaluate students' knowledge and attitudes about a subject. These activities will stimulate discussion about the content to be studied. During discussion, you can draw many insights about the existing knowledge and values that students hold about the topic. Boxes 11–5, 11–6, 11–7, and 11–8 show how teachers have used prereading activities to evaluate existing knowledge and attitudes.

Box 11–5

FILLING OUT APPLICATION FORMS

Subject: Vocational education class for senior high students
Purpose: To evaluate students' beliefs about applying for a job.

Directions: Doing certain things or having certain attitudes can help an individual to secure employment. Read the following statements concerning application forms and decide which statements can help you get a job. Write WH for "will help" and NH for "will not help" on the line next to each statement.

_____ 1. filling in a line on an application form by printing the letters of your answer.

_____ 2. leaving lines unfilled on an application form.

_____ 3. feeling that your completed application form shows how you might perform on the job.

_____ 4. misspelling a word.

_____ 5. typing out your application.

_____ 6. using a pencil to fill out an application.

_____ 7. writing "anything" when asked what position you would like to have in a company.

_____ 8. leaving questions about dates of past employment blank when you cannot remember.

_____ 9. using a former employer as a reference.

_____ 10. using a nickname to sign an application.

_____ 11. turning in an application with a few smudges on it.

_____ 12. bringing a paper containing personal information such as dates, addresses, etc., with you when you go to a company to fill out an application.

Box 11–6

FOOD FADDISM

Subject: Senior high school home economics
Purpose: To determine attitudes and concepts students bring to a unit on food faddism.

Directions: You will be studying about food faddism and some basic misconceptions about foods. Before beginning the unit, read the statements below and put a check mark on the corresponding line for those statements that you agree with.

_____ 1. Eating garlic can reduce high blood pressure.

_____ 2. Chemical fertilizers poison the land and any crops that grow on it.

_____ 3. Yogurt contains no special qualities not found in other foods.

_____ 4. Some people's deaths have been attributed to following certain fad diets.

_____ 5. Natural sugars are better for you than refined sugars.

_____ 6. There are few diseases in the United States today that are caused by dietary deficiencies.

_____ 7. Vitamin E is valuable for fertility, muscular strength and control of heart disease.

_____ 8. Modern food processing methods can preserve or restore foods to their original nutritional value.

_____ 9. Vitamin supplements are usually unnecessary.

_____ 10. Vitamin supplements can be dangerous.

_____ 11. Consumers spend more than a half billion dollars a year on unnecessary vitamin supplements, minerals and health foods.

Box 11–7

STUDYING WEATHER CONDITIONS

Subject: Junior high school science class
Purpose: To evaluate understandings that eighth graders bring to a unit on weather.

Directions: Open the *IET* (*Interaction of Earth and Time,* Rand McNally, Chicago, 1972) text to page 139 and examine the picture on the unit title page. After examining the picture, check the statements below that you think are true.

___ 1. The picture is a photograph of a real condition.
___ 2. The shoreline is on one of the Great Lakes.
___ 3. The shoreline is on an ocean.
___ 4. The land is actually part of a small island.
___ 5. There is a road of some sort visible in the picture.
___ 6. The white area covering the shoreline is a cloud.
___ 7. The white area covering the shoreline is a fog.
___ 8. A breeze is blowing from right to left in the picture (from the water toward the land).
___ 9. The water is cooler than the land.
___ 10. There is a deep valley near the center of the land area.

Note to the reader: At the point where students begin to exhibit some frustration, have them determine what kinds of information/data they would need to know in order to answer the questions and figure out what the picture (a photograph of a real condition) is about. This may be done on paper, in class discussion, or in small groups depending on classroom dynamics.

Box 11–8

CHILD REARING IN FAMILIES OF WORKING AND NONWORKING MOTHERS

Subject: Senior high school social studies class
Purpose: To assess attitudes, values and conceptions students bring to the issue of child rearing in a modern family.

Directions: The neighborhood male chauvinist pig and the president of the local NOW chapter are having a spirited debate on the question of whether or not mothers should work. Since you are known for your great wisdom, impartial judgment and peacemaking abilities, you are asked to mediate the dispute.

Below are presented the major opinions of both sides. Check the items you feel you could *logically* support. Also, add any supportable statements that might contradict (or consolidate) both of their opinions. You must be able to support your answers.

1. __ Nonworking mothers have more confidence in their "mothering" abilities than working mothers.

   __ Working mothers have more confidence in their "mothering" abilities than nonworking mothers.

   You:_____

2. __ Mothers who stay home are more satisfied with their lives than working mothers.

   __ Mothers who work are more satisfied with their lives than mothers who stay home.

   You:_____

3. __ Most women who work do so to gain extra "pocket" money.

   __ Most women who work do so out of financial need.

   You:_____

4. __ Very few working mothers are devoted to their jobs — they just want an excuse to get away from their kids.

   __ Many working mothers find self-fulfillment in their jobs and are very committed to them.

   You:_____

5. __ Not only do working mothers spend too little time with their children, but the time they do spend is too divided among other activities.

   __ Working mothers may have less time to give attention to their children, but the time they do give is devoted exclusively to the family.

   You:_____

6. __ Children of working mothers are undisciplined because their mothers don't spend enough time with them.

   __ Children of nonworking mothers are undisciplined because their mothers are too frustrated to handle them.

   You:_____
   _____

FAMILIARITY WITH TERMINOLOGY

Explain how to evaluate students' knowledge of technical terms.

Closely related to an evaluation of existing knowledge is a procedure which gives the teacher a measure of students' familiarity with the content area terms. An efficient procedure called the *discriminative self-inventory* was recommended by Dale, O'Rourke, and Bamman (1971).

Using the symbols $+$, $\sqrt{}$, $-$, 0, students indicate how well they know a set of terms: $+$ means "I know it well; I use it"; $\sqrt{}$ means "I know it somewhat''; − means "I've seen it or heard of it before''; and 0 means "I've never seen it or heard of it before.''

The teacher lists words related to the unit of study. Box 11–9 illustrates two check lists that teachers developed for assessment.

A BRIEF WORD ON STANDARDIZED READING TESTS ————————

Standardized reading tests are formal, usually machine-scorable instruments, in which scores for the tested group are compared with standards established by an original normative population. The purpose of a standardized reading test is to show where students stand in relation to other students based on a single performance.

Reading researchers have studied the relationships between standardized tests of reading and student performance on reading tasks in specific content areas (Artley, 1948; Peters, 1975). They have generally concluded that specific factors not accounted for on a test of general achievement influence the reading of subject matter materials. In fact, Peters (1975) said a standardized reading test may not provide the information that content teachers desire.

Performance on standardized reading tests can yield only rough estimates at best as to how students will apply reading to textbooks in a particular subject. A student who is a good reader of social studies may be a poor or mediocre reader of math or science. It's safe to say that teachers who consult standardized reading tests should do so judiciously.

Box 11–9

——

EXAMPLES OF DISCRIMINATIVE SELF-INVENTORY CHECKLISTS

I. Mathematics Unit on Quadratic Functions and Systems of Equations (High School Level)

__ 1. exponent	__ 7. intersection	__ 13. origin
__ 2. coefficient	__ 8. abscissa	__ 14. vertex
__ 3. reals	__ 9. domain	__ 15. slope
__ 4. integers	__ 10. intercept	__ 16. parabola
__ 5. irrationals	__ 11. linear	__ 17. solution
__ 6. union	__ 12. mapping	

II. English Unit on the Newspaper (middle school level)

__ 1. wire service	__ 5. copy	__ 9. caption
__ 2. UPI	__ 6. dateline	__ 10. jumpline
__ 3. AP	__ 7. byline	__ 11. masthead
__ 4. filler	__ 8. lead	__ 12. column

LOOKING BACK, LOOKING FORWARD _____

Evaluating for instruction implies a continuous analysis of student reading performance and the difficulty of content materials. The teacher uses evaluation procedures to determine the strengths and limitations that students bring to reading tasks. Observational techniques provide enough raw data, in most cases, to plan instruction effectively. Content area reading inventories, however, may also be used to corroborate or augment the teacher's personal judgment of student performance. These reading inventories can be used at the beginning of a course or at the start of a unit of study.

Enthusiasm over content area reading in the 1970s will be just as dramatic in the 1980s. The attention received by this aspect of reading instruction has resulted in innovative teacher preparation programs, particularly at the preservice level. Colleges and universities are producing more prospective teachers equipped to teach reading within the context of subject matter instruction. But preservice education, at best, is only a beginning, albeit important, step toward learning a craft. Unless new teachers receive support and reinforcement from fellow teachers and administrators, they can soon find themselves eschewing what they have learned in "those method courses."

Taking content area reading into the field will be the key to its success and impact in the 1980s. In general, content teachers already in the field have been slow to change. However, a corner has been turned in their attitude toward reading instruction and their recognition of the problems facing text learners. They want to know how to help students read textbooks effectively.

Inservice staff development is the vehicle by which the strategies and activities offered in this book will become part of the teaching repertoires of content teachers. The Inservice Guide for Content Area Reading in this book provides direction for program leaders who want to plan, implement, and evaluate reading staff development in their schools. Staff development is as important for the new teacher who has had a secondary reading methods course as part of teacher preparation as it is for the veteran in need of renewal. Inservice staff development will give the novice the support and reinforcement that he or she needs. Both veteran and novice will be in a position to study what they do so that they can develop more effectively and efficiently in what they do.

And what they do in the name of content area reading has been the subject of this book. Content area reading has come a long way in a short time. It still has a distance to go before the gap between student and text is narrowed.

There's work to be done.

SUGGESTED READINGS

Estes, Thomas, and Vaughan, Joseph, Jr. *Reading and learning in the content classroom.* Boston: Allyn and Bacon, 1978, chapters 4–8.

Herber, Harold. *Teaching reading in content areas.* 2nd ed. Englewood Cliffs, N.J.: Prentice-Hall, 1978, chapter 10.

Robinson, H. Allan. *Teaching reading and study strategies.* 2nd ed. Boston: Allyn and Bacon, 1978, chapter 2.

Shepherd, David. *Comprehensive high school reading methods.* 2nd ed. Columbus, Ohio: Charles E. Merrill, 1978, chapter 2.

Inservice Guide for Content Area Reading

Working with Content Area Teachers

By JO ANNE L. VACCA
Kent State University

This guide is intended primarily for content area teachers who assume the responsibility for inservice leadership. It will also be useful to reading specialists who find themselves in the same role. The substance for inservice in content area reading is provided in the preceding chapters of this book. But inservice leaders must also have a style: how you work with teachers is as important as the substance of what you teach. The principle that conveys the spirit of this guide is a mixture of philosophy and practicality: *Staff development is part of a change process; no single technique is optimal for all situations.*

"I'd rather correct papers or work with some of the students who are having problems with the material in the unit we're studying."

"I'd rather spend the extra time at lunch. It would be a helluva lot more enjoyable."

"I'd rather go home. Is Jackson taking attendance again?"

So the conversation went. I had unobtrusively slipped into the crowded faculty room an hour before I was to conduct an inservice session on content area reading. Students had been dismissed from school early, and the afternoon belonged to me and the teachers.

If you're an outsider in a school, slipping into the faculty room gives you a feel for the place immediately. I didn't like what I was feeling. What were these teachers saying? I had no doubt that they were probably good at their craft, yet they were dissatisfied.

The school principal (Jackson) had assured me his staff was concerned about the majority of students in the school who couldn't or wouldn't read textbook assignments when he asked me to do a series of workshops on reading in content areas. I had been delighted — mostly by the prospect that this wouldn't be just another one-shot deal. I would have the time to follow up and bring continuity to the inservice sessions.

I interrupted the teachers who were planning their great escape from this afternoon.

"Hi. I'm going to do the workshop on content area reading." I thought to myself: that took guts. It did.

The teachers didn't flinch, although one started to blush. "You overheard our conversation?"

I smiled and nodded.

"Listen, don't take it personally. It's nothing against you. We don't even know you. We're the school cynics. It's just that we're tired of being told about the latest and greatest panacea for improving the ills of our school. We're tired of being told that what we're doing isn't good enough. We work hard. We've had too many bad experiences with inservice."

I couldn't help but commiserate with them. I recalled when I was teaching English in a junior high school and the principal called to order an inservice meeting. I had wished I had been correcting papers.

In spite of the fact that there are many reports and articles about staff development programs in reading, we are dealing with an area which is in a relatively early stage of refinement. The general aim of staff development, other than keeping up to date or improving instruction, is not commonly agreed upon. Until recently, staff development was almost exclusively referred to as "inservice education," a term for many programs which have "tended to be unsystematic, poorly focused and largely ineffective" (Otto and Erickson, 1973, p. vii).

DEFINING STAFF DEVELOPMENT

Not too long ago I conducted in-depth interviews with six nationally recognized reading authorities in order to secure a brief statement that would establish a general aim for staff development in reading (Vacca, 1979). These experts gave fairly lengthy answers to the main interview question: "What is the major purpose of staff development?" The end result of the interviews produced a general statement of the purpose of reading staff development upon which each of the experts could agree: Staff development is a continuous involvement process of developing and utilizing local (and nonlocal) talent to identify and facilitate responses to local needs. What implications in particular does this general aim have for content area reading staff development? Let's take a closer look.

A Continuous Involvement Process

Development of content area reading staff won't just happen because of an administrative mandate. Nor does effective staff development occur as the result of a piecemeal, narrowly conceived effort. Too often teachers feel that inservice is a form of remediation. They perceive change to mean working on weaknesses rather than building on strengths. Instead, the process of working with classroom teachers toward change involves helping them study the things they do instructionally so that they can develop more efficiency and effectiveness. Teachers must be actively involved in an ongoing process from the start.

What does this mean in terms of actual practice? The following:

1. Involve teachers in all phases of planning.
2. Provide follow-up services. A set of inservice sessions on techniques for content area reading isn't the end-all and be-all of staff development. Often teachers need positive support and reinforcement as they implement techniques in the classroom. Are you there when they need you the most?
3. Provide for continuous evaluation and use it, if need be, to redesign future inservice sessions.
4. Allow for flexibility. You can't shy away from immediate or changing concerns.

Using Local (and Nonlocal) Talent

A staff development project in content area reading may make use of outside expertise such as that offered by a college- or university-based consultant. But an inservice program ultimately fails or succeeds because of the professional expertise of local talent — school-based personnel who work "inside" the system. The local inservice leaders for content area reading are often the reading consultants or reading teachers within a school or district. However, total responsibility need not and should not be exclusively theirs. The classroom teacher must play an integral role in content area reading staff development. An ideal situation, for example, may occur when a reading specialist teams up with a classroom teacher to lead an inservice program. The reading specialist may not feel comfortable with the content of a subject area but knows the reading process and how to apply it. The classroom teacher, on the other hand, knows the content but may not feel comfortable with the reading process. Each draws on the other's expertise and strengths to conduct the inservice program.

If you liked what you read in Chapters 1 through 11, why not spread the word? Consider joining with several other content teachers to share the strategies developed in those chapters. One way of getting started is to form an inservice committee of teachers from one or more departments. Invite the principal and the reading specialist and begin to combine your expertise to plan an inservice program.

Identifying and Facilitating Responses to Local Needs

Staff development in reading begins when the needs of teachers are identified. Staff development may at times appear to be a nebulous undertaking; there are no set prescriptions or prepackaged programs that will work for any one school in particular. An inservice program in content area reading is too individual a matter; it grows from within a school system based on the individual needs of teachers and their students.

Effective staff development is never automatically insured; teachers' professional growth is brought about by a planned effort. Throughout this effort the integrity of teachers as adult learners must be maintained. Their feelings and perceptions matter. One of the major emphases of this guide, therefore, is on those characteristics of inservice leaders which have actually been perceived as effective by classroom teachers. Special attention will also be given to strategies and a model for staff development.

WORKING WITH ADULT LEARNERS

Teachers are adults and should be taught as such. And therefore, an inservice leader is an adult educator. Staff development is a learning situation — one in which teachers are placed in a student relationship with the inservice leader. While the dynamics of such a situation are not totally removed from the traditional student-adult teacher instructional paradigm, they merit a different perspective.

The art and science of helping adults learn is called *andragogy* — "to teach adults" — from the Greek word for "man," *ander* and "leader," *agogos*. Use of the word *andragogy* can be traced back to Germany in the 1830s; in the same century the University of Amsterdam established a Department of Pedagogical and Andragogical Sciences. While andragogy is not a new term, Knowles (1973) has maintained that the assumptions and technology it is coming to identify are new.

Andragogy is based on several critical assumptions about the differences between children and adults as learners and differs from pedagogy essentially along four dimensions: (1) self-concept, (2) experience, (3) readiness, and (4) learning orientation.

Self-Concept and Experience

The heart of adultness is independence and self-direction. As people mature, their self-concepts change. They move from a psychological position of dependency to a position of increasing self-directedness. Children and even adolescents often remain dependent on their teachers in learning situations: "teacher knows best." This shouldn't be the case with adult learners.

The staff developer who prescribes what ought to be learned, how it will be learned, and the logical sequence in which it will be learned ultimately works against change, not for it. Newton (1977) was right on the mark when she asserted, "Any adult education situation involving the student in a role of dependency . . . will generate immediate and deep resistance and resentment" (p. 362). When working with fellow teachers, you may best view yourself as a gardener who creates good conditions for the growth of your plants. Once the growth process begins, step back and enjoy the results.

Another basic assumption in adult learning is that adults, with their rich store of experience, become invaluable resources for their own learning. The essence of one's identity is one's knowledge of the world. For many teachers, their teaching experiences are "who they are." The emphasis in staff development should be on techniques which tap those experiences and involve the participating teachers in analyzing them.

Once I observed an inservice leader working with a teaching staff in a suburban high school. The teachers had voiced many concerns, the most ubiquitous being "Our students can't read." The teacher who led the session had anticipated the staff's general level of frustration and planned to clarify exactly what was meant by "They can't read." She asked the large group of teachers to form smaller groups by subject matter and gave each group two problems: (1) What do students actually do in class to indicate that they "can't read" assignments in your content area? (2) What would they need to do as far as you are concerned to successfully read assignments in your content area?

The inservice leader hoped to use the staff's experiences to address some of the important issues related to content area reading. These teachers were facing, perhaps for the first time, the problem of reading their subject matter materials successfully.

The consultant then asked a member from each group to report the group's responses to the entire staff. The resulting banter and wise-cracking was helpful: it broke the ice and led to discussion. Perhaps also for the first time, teachers from different content areas were sharing their opinions and perceptions about reading.

The inservice leader skillfully incorporated the staff members' comments into her agenda. She used their insights to suggest that "teaching reading" is nothing more than good teaching. A third question — "How can we fine-tune our present skills to do what we are presently doing better?" — became the unifying principle for the remaining inservice sessions. The spirit of the staff development effort became "How can we continue to work on our craft?"

Readiness and Learning Orientation

In many cases education for children and adolescents assumes that students are ready to learn things they "ought" to learn based on their biological development and on social and academic pressures. Adult learning, on the other hand, assumes that adults are ready to learn what they "need" to learn in order to meet various situations they encounter throughout various phases in their lives. These situations are products primarily of the evolution of a person's social role as a worker, spouse, parent, or whatever. This is why Newton (1977) observed that "the requirements and demands of . . . the present situation and aspiring roles in real life must dominate and supersede all other considerations . . ." (p. 362).

Teachers respond differently to reading problems primarily because of their backgrounds and experiences, their attitudes toward teaching and learning, their attitudes toward students, and their values regarding education in general. This is why content area reading inservice can't be prepackaged for all the teachers on a staff. By prepackaged I mean each teacher "getting inserviced" by being introduced to the same thing at the same time. Some teachers will be readier than others for certain aspects of a content area reading inservice program. Because of the nature of readiness among adults, the following "do's" for content area reading inservice are appropriate:

1. Individualize inservice through a variety of activities.
2. Respect the values and attitudes of teachers.
3. Offer open sessions for teachers of differing philosophies and values.
4. Make inservice sessions voluntary.
5. Provide released time.
6. Offer incentives for participation — equivalency credit, stipends, recognition, certificates of completion, and so forth.

An adult's orientation to learning is problem-centered and in the here and now. Immediate application of learning is at a high premium since the learner "comes into an educational activity largely because he . . . wants to apply tomorrow what he learns today" (Knowles, 1973, p. 48). Whereas the curriculum for children and adolescents often involves a predetermined logical sequence, a curriculum for adults should be organized around problem areas. Newton (1977) affirmed this assumption by declaring that "postponed, logical, sequentially developed subject matter must be eschewed in favor of field-centered, work related learning" (p. 362). Learning about teaching innovations that cannot be transferred to the immediacy of their classrooms does not appeal to teachers.

"Show me what to do on Monday morning" is a legitimate demand. Often, however, this concern is misinterpreted to mean that classroom teachers are antitheoretical and antiresearch. Don't believe it for a moment. What teachers are actually saying is "Show me how to improve my craft. Let me experience the process you offer first, and if it makes sense, let's discuss why it works."

Inservice programs must be based on insights into teachers' motivations as adults to grow as fully as possible. An inservice leader tries to build an environment in which teachers have the opportunity to make discoveries significant to them. In this environment teachers perceive certain characteristics of an inservice leader as more effective than others.

CHARACTERISTICS OF INSERVICE LEADERS

It's to the advantage of persons responsible for content area reading inservice to judge accurately the perceptions teachers hold about their experiences with staff development. To this extent, I interviewed over one hundred fifty classroom teachers about their opinions and perceptions of effective and ineffective inservice leaders. Out of these interviews I inferred several characteristics of effective and successful inservice leaders.

The teachers I interviewed responded on two separate forms, neither of which required them to name teachers and inservice leaders they were describing. On the first form, teachers were requested to:

> . . . think about your participation in in-service and/or staff development programs in reading. Recall the inservice leader with whom you have been associated. Describe a particular incident that caused you to feel that he/she was an outstanding or very *effective* professional in the performance of his/her job. Tell exactly what the inservice leader did that was effective at that time.

On the second form teachers were requested to judge a situation they could recall as being ineffective.

> If you are currently teaching and have participated in some form of reading staff development (for example, a workshop in school), how would you describe an incident in your experience that caused you to feel that a staff developer was effective? Ineffective? Take a moment or two to describe two incidents you recall in the space provided below.
>
> 1. What did an inservice leader do that was effective?

2. What did an inservice leader do that was ineffective?

Here are some responses on the first (effective) form:
A veteran of many years in a high school:

In a workshop taken in the Spring I had a staff developer who was very effective because he had the participants actively involved playing the role of their students. The ideas were not overwhelming, but the fact that you experienced the technique yourself made it beneficial to the classroom. Due to this incident I was able to bring the ideas back from the workshop and incorporate the technique in my own classroom.

An intermediate grade teacher:

She related personal experiences that were amusing and that we could identify with. This helped add to the relaxed, friendly atmosphere.

A social studies teacher:

This person has touched upon ideas that are quite useful. He has indeed spent time with adolescents and seems to be aware of what we teachers seek to get from this: some good sound ideas and $25.00 per session!

Here are some responses on the second (ineffective) form:
A social studies teacher:

The staff developer was not prepared. Spent one-half hour setting up materials, broke a film screen, and the movie did not operate properly. The person just wasn't necessary. The information that she did give was unorganized and sketchy. I would have been better off correcting homework assignments.

An English teacher conveyed her disenchantment with one staff developer who,

spoke and spoke and spoke on something that was of no interest to me at all. It was a complete waste of time!

I collected a total of 345 separate incidents of effective and ineffective staff development from the 150 teachers I interviewed. My next step was to classify the incidents into meaningful areas and categories. A jury of raters determined that the classification procedure I used was reliable about 90 percent of the time for areas and 80 percent of the time for categories. Area and categories are shown in Table 1.

The area of *content delivery* included all comments on techniques the staff developer used to present the content. Approximately 67 percent

Table 1. Classification of Incidents

Areas	Categories
A. Content Delivery	1. Techniques for involvement or participation
	2. Relevant classroom application; strategy or materials
B. Personal Influence	3. Personal traits or characteristics
	4. Personal actions or responses to situations
C. Professional Competence	5. Background knowledge, preparation, or organization
	6. Proficiency or clarity of directions, adherence to task
D. Structural Arrangement	7. Appropriateness to audience

of all the incidents reported fell into this area. Specific techniques such as small group discussion and role-playing were cited and judged on their usefulness.

The area of *personal influence* (15 percent of the reported incidents) included all comments on the staff developer's personality, manner, or mannerisms ("friendly," "lively") and/or the session environment ("warm atmosphere").

The area of *professional competence* (15 percent) included all comments on the skills or knowledge the staff developer demonstrated ("organized," "informative").

The area of *structural arrangement* (only 3 percent) included all comments on the planning and organization of the inservice program in relation to those attending ("forced to attend").

Effective Behaviors

Once I constructed the areas and categories from the incidents reported by the teachers, I derived the characteristics of an inservice leader — and these characteristics represent effective behavior which can make the difference between success or failure in reading staff development. Here they are:

In the area of content delivery, the effective inservice leader (1) involves the participants actively in the topic, (2) relates the topic directly (through examples) to the classroom, and (3) provides materials or ideas for materials in a classroom.

In the area of personal influence, the effective inservice leader (1) displays a positive attitude and pleasant disposition, (2) is sensitive to the environment or dynamics within the group, and (3) answers questions directly and patiently.

In the area of professional competence, the effective inservice leader (1) is well informed and well organized, (2) has a purpose in mind and adheres to the task at hand, and (3) explains things clearly.

In the area of structural arrangement, the effective inservice leader (1) arranges to assess the needs of the group in advance and (2) provides options in organization matters.

These characteristics are by no means etched in stone. Nonetheless, they provide guidelines to the behavior of inservice leaders. One question of particular relevance involves technique: what are some of the process strategies an inservice leader can use to succeed?

Process Strategies

Certain techniques and strategies which have been effective are stated under each of the major areas and categories of staff development previously discussed.

I. Area A: Content Delivery
   a. Involves the participants actively in the topic.
      1. Brainstorms.
      2. Encourages open-ended discussions.
      3. Facilitates group interactions.
   b. Relates the topic directly (through examples) to the classroom.
      1. Uses role-playing and simulation activities.
      2. Uses visuals and "handouts."
      3. Uses demonstration teaching in classrooms.
      4. Uses videotapes of actual lessons.
   c. Provides materials or ideas for materials useful in a classroom situation. Uses hands-on activities which can range from teachers adapting a technique to fit their students' needs (such as a reading guide) to a series of materials-producing workshops.

II. Area B: Personal Influence
   a. Displays a positive attitude and pleasant disposition.
      1. Interacts with teachers prior to presentation (learn some names).
      2. Keeps teachers on task during small-group work.
      3. Listens for feedback throughout and after a session.
      4. Maintains a sense of humor.
   b. Is sensitive to the environment or dynamics within the group.
      1. Plans "gripe" sessions which do not dominate a program.
      2. Digresses from prepared presentation to respond to a teachable moment.

          3. Responds to body language.
      c. Answers questions directly and patiently.
          1. Respects the audience in order to get its respect. One brusque reply to a question (whether or not it's rude or argumentative) may turn the group against you.

III. Area C: Professional Competence
      a. Is well informed and well organized.
          1. Knows why and how to teach reading in content areas.
          2. Shares an outline or agenda, either verbal or written.
          3. Provides a bibliography of professional sources.
      b. Has a purpose in mind and adheres to the task at hand.
          1. Keeps the proceedings moving and never goes overtime.
          2. For those who want to continue, do so informally.
      c. Conveys explanations clearly.
          1. "Walks" teachers through directions, explaining them fully.
          2. Avoids assumptive teaching.

IV. Area D: Structural Arrangement
      a. Arranges to assess the needs of the group in advance. Plans for informal/formal needs assessment prior to meeting participants. If no assessment has been attempted, assess needs on the spot. Brainstorm at the outset in large or in small groups. Write *all* ideas related to perceived needs on board, organize them into categories. Then choose one category and develop it. The key is in anticipating certain categories of needs in advance.
      b. Provides options in organization matters. Have some options ready . . . especially if something goes wrong. Where can you get more chairs? If there are too many people in the room, where else may they go? If there are a few who have recently heard you and were "forced" to attend . . . can you suggest a feasible alternative for them?

A MODEL FOR STAFF DEVELOPMENT

Numerous opportunities for informal staff development exist in the course of a school day between school-based inservice leaders and teachers. Perhaps the voluntary questions one colleague asks another in hope of securing some advice is the ideal situation for getting teachers involved in content area reading instruction through staff development. Most instances thought of as inservice or staff development, however, are of a more structured nature. They involve program development in which inservice leaders plan change gradually.

A model for staff development in content area reading should be general enough to invite adaptations which the circumstances of individual schools demand. The model should also be systematic enough to move classroom teachers through a planned sequence of activities that identify and facilitate those teachers' needs. And, finally, a program model must have change as its ultimate purpose and product.

The program model which will be explained here is one that Cunningham (1972) proposed. Cunningham identified three phases within a change-oriented model to improve the instructional competencies of content area staff. As Figure 1 suggests, the program model establishes a continuous involvement process for reading inservice in content areas.

Figure 1. Staff Development Model for Reading in Content Areas

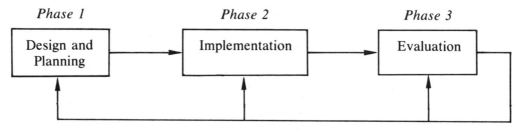

Phase 1: Design and Planning ──────────────────────────────────

Staff development involves cooperation and a long-term commitment to change. (One hopes the era of one-shot workshops is over.) Planning begins with a proposal to initiate a program for reading in the content areas. The proposal may come from the top via administrative mandate and filter down, or it may come from teachers who feel the burden of working with students who they maintain won't or can't read content area materials.

Ruddell (1978) commented that proposal often leads to counterproposal. Counterproposal should be welcomed, not avoided, in designing and planning a staff development program. Planning sessions should involve a committee made up of all parties concerned: teachers, administrators, and reading consultants. Out of proposal and counterproposal comes joint proposal, which culminates in a program design that all participants can accept as theirs.

Planning necessarily relies on information and ideas from a variety of sources, especially the group for whom the inservice is intended. An assessment can help a planning committee collect it.

ASSESSMENT

Assessment helps identify needs, attitudes, interests. and potential resources for the inservice project. It takes many forms.

Attitude Scale. Teachers' attitudes toward reading in their classrooms is important. Vaughan (1977) contended that resolution of students' problems in reading content material "may well begin with the teacher's attitude toward the problem" (p. 606). To this end, Vaughan developed a scale to measure attitudes toward teaching reading in content classrooms and demonstrated through statistical procedures that it was reliable and valid in assessing teachers' attitudes toward reading in context areas.

Attitude scales can be used a number of ways to help plan a staff development project. First, you may agree with Vaughan's (1977) assumption that "teachers who are aware of and sympathetic to the difficulties their students may have reading their textbooks are likely to be the teachers who will learn" (p. 606). If this is the case, the attitude scale can help to determine the immediate target group for the staff development program. Second, the information derived from the attitude scale can indicate the scope and content of the workshop sessions within each of the stages of phase 2, implementation. Teachers with low or below-average scores, for example, may need more time and exposure to activities in implementation stage 1 — unfreezing — than teachers with high, above-average, or average attitudes. And third, the scale can be used as a post-test to measure changes in attitude at the end of a staff development program.

Surveys. Assessment may also include the use of surveys to catalogue the needs, concerns, and interests of a teaching staff. Many formats provide useful tools for data collection; Table 2 categorizes the types of survey instruments available. Look at the two examples in Boxes 1 and 2 of assessment surveys for content area reading.

Table 2. Types of Survey Instrument Categorized Functionally

Type of Survey	Sample Characteristics	Sample Questions
Open-ended	1. Elicit opinion 2. Are often unstructured 3. Request additional information	a. What are some of the things that students find difficult about reading your textbook materials? b. What do you do to help students handle reading assignments more effectively?

Type of Survey	Sample Characteristics	Sample Questions
Check List	1. True/false; yes/no 2. Check as many as apply 3. Structured 4. Demographic information	a. Can your students comprehend their required readings? b. Is the technical vocabulary of your course too difficult to handle?
Ranking	1. Scaled 2. Prioritized 3. Structured	a. Put a 1 in front of the most important experience, a 2 in front of . . . b. Place an x on the following line to indicate . . .

SOURCE: Adapted from Vacca, Jo Anne L. "Surveys: valuable tools for the reading consultant." *Reading horizons* 21 (1981):268–275.

Box 1

SURVEY OF COMPETENCY NEEDS AND RESOURCES

Directions: Listed below are competencies related to reading in content areas. Indicate whether you would like assistance in each area. If you are willing to help others, or if you know of resources that might be used for staff development activities in an area, please indicate this in the Resources column.

Competencies	Needs			Resources
	I feel confident in this area	I would like a little more help here	I would like lots of help here	
1. Differentiate reading assignments in a single text to provide for a range of reading abilities				
2. Plan instruction so that students know how to approach their reading assignments				
3. Help students identify various patterns of organization which a writer uses in text material				
4. Help students set purposes for their reading assignments				

5. Develop reading and study guides to help students comprehend text material
6. Teach technical vocabulary before students meet terms in their reading
7. Reinforce students' understanding of technical vocabulary by providing opportunities for their repeated use
8. Use tradebooks to supplement the basic textbook
9. Determine the difficulty of my content area materials
10. Use informal content inventories to discover students' limitations in reading textbook assignments
11. Develop an instructional unit
12. List additional competency areas accordingly

SOURCE: Adapted from *Right to read manual for community literacy program development.* Springfield, Ill.: Illinois Office of Education, 1975, G-11.

Box 2

SURVEY OF NEEDS AND CONCERNS

Directions: Please number in order of importance the areas you feel you need additional help in order to teach content through reading. Then, answer each question as completely as possible.

___ Determining the reading difficulty level of my content area materials.
___ Guiding students to comprehend their reading assignments.
___ Developing questions for a reading assignment.
___ Reinforcing technical vocabulary by providing opportunities for repeated use.
___ Developing vocabulary skills that will help students unlock the meaning of words independently.
___ Planning instruction so that students know how to approach their reading assignment.
___ Differentiating reading assignments in a single textbook to provide for a range of reading abilities.
___ Guiding students to read graphs, charts, maps and illustrations.
___ Teaching key vocabulary terms before students meet them in an assignment.
___ Showing students how to read content materials critically.
___ Teaching students how to outline text material.
___ Developing a unit which coordinates instructional resources and materials.

1. What is your greatest concern about your students' ability to read textbook assignments?

2. What is your least concern?

3. How many undergraduate or graduate courses in reading education have you taken? Please list them.

4. What contribution do you feel previous course work in reading has made in making you a more effective teacher?

SOURCE: Adapted from *Right to read manual for community literacy program development.* Springfield, Ill.: Illinois Office of Education, 1975, G-9.

Goals, Objectives, and Activities. Once assessment information has been collected and interpreted, the planning committee should set goals and objectives for the staff development program. A goal is a general statement of a desired outcome; goal setting reflects the needs identified during the assessment. Objectives are more precise than goals; they are specific statements of desired outcomes. A goal may subsume several objectives.

The Planning Committee should hammer out in a planning session a realistic and reasonable set of goals and objectives based on the assessment. Here are a sample goal and objectives for the competency area of vocabulary.

Goal: To use subject matter as a natural context for the development of students' vocabularies

Objectives: The teacher will be able to:

1. Identify in text materials key words, interesting words, and words which will help build skills for independent vocabulary development
2. Show students the interrelationships among key terms before they read text material
3. Preteach key vocabulary before students encounter the words in their required reading
4. Guide students toward independence in analyzing unfamiliar words through the use of context, structure, and the dictionary

5. Reinforce and extend students' knowledge of words already learned by providing for their repeated use in a variety of classroom situations

Phase 2: Implementation

An inservice leader works to fine-tune teachers' instructional skills. The implementation phase of the program model emphasizes what is actually done in workshop sessions to bring about changes in teachers' teaching behaviors. The end results of the change process are (1) professional growth and development and (2) the use of content area reading in classrooms.

STAGE 1: UNFREEZING*

Even when the teachers play a role in designing and planning an inservice program, many of them will come into the program with no commitment to participate. Unfreezing enlists their active participation.

Unfreezing is analogous to the readiness stage in a directed reading lesson; its purpose is to build an interest in and a state of readiness for the program steps that are to follow. (Unfreezing cuts across age levels and should be used with adults as well as with children and adolescents.) Inservice leaders use process skills to create relaxed settings, allay fears, and discuss problems, personal reservations, and participants' needs. They are interested in lessening feelings of discomfort and/or hostilities. They are after awareness. Above all, inservice leaders seek the active involvement (mental as well as physical) of participants and their commitment — commitment fostered by a feeling of open-mindedness toward what is to follow in the program.

How does an inservice leader unfreeze rather than "unglue" a group of fellow teachers? I posed this question to a group of more than one hundred fifty specialists, consultants, and supervisors involved in development of content area reading staff who met in April 1979 in Atlanta as part of an International Reading Association Preconvention Institute. During the institute the participants discussed their written responses to my questions, and three distinct categories of activity for unfreezing emerged. What follows is a representative sampling from each category.

1. Ice Breakers. These strategies vary in time from five to twenty minutes (time approximations refer to the application of the strategy and are not meant to imply that unfreezing would be completed within these time frames). They are intended to involve inservice participants. These

* Portions of this section are adapted from: Jo Anne L. Vacca and Richard T. Vacca. "Unfreezing strategies for staff development in reading." *The reading teacher* 35 (1980):27–31.

activities are generally fun. Not only do they get participants involved, but they also get teachers thinking about problems associated with the inservice topic. Examples:

a. Use brainstorming. This strategy can be adapted easily to staff development objectives. Identify a broad concept that reflects the main topic to be discussed — for example, Vocabulary — during the session. Then have participants work in small groups to generate lists of words related to the broad concept in x number of seconds. These two steps will help the staff developer instantly tap into what participants know about the topic.

b. Create conceptual conflict to arouse curiosity about the topic. Present teachers with a "situation that will cause puzzlement, doubt, surprise, perplexity, contradiction, or ambiguity ("case of a fifteen-year-old student who reads text material with perfect oral pronunciation . . . and near zero comprehension"), a situation, for example, that might challenge their present concept of reading. Once aroused, the teachers will be motivated to seek information to resolve the conflict.

c. Lead a magic circle to open up communication by making it possible for each member of the circle (a circle is a must so that everyone can see everyone else) to comment. Intersperse probing questions with questions of a lighter nature. For example, lead off with "What do you like best about your job?" Follow with "Complete this statement: If I had $1,000 to spend in one week in my classroom, I would . . ." Your third question might be "What do you dislike most about teaching _____ ?" (fill in the blank with science, social studies, or whatever).

2. Vicarious Experiences. Strategies in this category are aimed at involving teachers with actual practices or materials that are used with their students. They usually serve as demonstration of a generalization and vary from fifteen minutes to almost an hour in length. Examples:

a. Set up several learning activity centers with examples of content area reading activities. Have teachers follow a minischedule in which they work through all centers in rotation. Allow about ten minutes at each, signaling the switch with a bell or timer.

b. Try out a teaching technique with volunteers in front of the whole group. Then ask pairs of teachers to analyze what has taken place. Share responses, being receptive to statements of "times when this won't work" as well as positive feedback.

     c. Call on a volunteer to read a passage projected on an overhead screen. Choose a passage with unfamiliar vocabulary such as a difficult biology passage or a paragraph using an unfamiliar dialect. Ask first the reader and then the rest of the group to retell it in their own words.

     d. Give a timed test to measure several reading skills of the teachers. Create a formal, quiet, serious atmosphere; use a timer. As the teachers score their tests, generalize about potential problem areas this test uncovers.

3. Problem Solving. In this category are strategies that lead participants to use their own experiences and knowledge in thinking through new concepts. Problem-solving activities can vary in time from fifteen minutes to just over an hour. Examples:

     a. Set up a hypothetical situation. Describe it to the whole group in a concise manner ("It's 1997, and water sources have been discovered in abundance in all parts of this continent, including barren desert areas. How would this discovery change life as we know it?") Divide participants into groups of three or four. Allow about five minutes for group discussion, then pool answers, perhaps forming categories of statements on the board. As a follow-up to 2a above, form small groups and distribute to each a problem related to teaching reading in each content area. Be sure to allow enough time to review each group's answers.

     b. Distribute a ten-statement prediction guide to reading instruction. Have teachers complete the guide independently, then form small groups or pairs and compare answers. Then read each statement aloud, eliciting discussion from the whole group. Part of the guide might look like this:

     Directions: Consider the following statements and determine which are likely and which are unlikely. Check the column under Likely if you think the statement could be true. Check under Unlikely if you think the statement could not be true.

Likely   Unlikely

   —   —   1. Students reading on the twelfth grade level of a reading achievement test will have no difficulty with a physics text written on a twelfth grade level.

Likely   Unlikely

—   —   2. Text pictures and diagrams are self-explanatory.

—   —   3. Silent reading is a habit that can be developed in content classrooms.

—   —   4. Purposes for reading need to be explained by the teacher before students read.

STAGE 2: MOVING FORWARD

In this stage participants are introduced to a range of instructional options and alternatives — the techniques, strategies, and materials developed throughout this book. The inservice program leader arranges a series of workshop sessions to demonstrate them. Involvement is the key to this stage. Teachers sense the process of content area reading by playing the role of student. Once the participants have had the opportunity to experience certain strategies and materials, the leader follows with explanations involving the how and why of them.

Questions should be encouraged in stage 2. "Why should I do this?" "When should I use this approach rather than this one?" "How can I construct these guide materials based on my material?" The effectiveness of stage 2, then, relies on the extent to which it 1) increases the willingness of content area teachers to continue to participate and 2) improves their ability to incorporate functional reading into content area instruction.

Many inservice projects in content area reading screech to a halt at this point. Time, funding, or staffing constraints are some of the reasons typically given for the lack of follow-through and support that is essential in the development of teacher competency. Nevertheless, stage 2 should also provide the time and consultant expertise teachers need to actually produce new classroom materials.

STAGE 3: REFREEZING

Sometimes, nothing can be more frightening than to try out a new idea for the first time, especially when some teachers attempt to incorporate content area reading into their lessons.

> When a teacher tries out a new idea in his classroom for the first time, he needs assurance that the attempt is worth the effort. . . . positive support, along with constructive criticism and willingness to help redesign or modify approaches and materials when necessary, can often make the difference between lasting change and mere lip service followed by a return to less exciting but more comfortable former methods. *(Cunningham, 1972, p. 487)*

The implementation phase assures that staff development will bring real changes in teacher behavior, that readiness, guidance, and follow-up activities will lead to planned change in a gradual manner.

Phase 3: Evaluation

It seems as if at times some school districts have jumped the gun in handling evaluation of staff development programs. In their haste to show the results of staff development programs, they have tended to confuse process with product. For example, are the goals of inservice aimed at showing automatic gain in student achievement even before the teachers' growth and the program designed to influence that growth have been carefully evaluated? One way of avoiding confusion between process and product of staff development is to plan for various levels of evaluation within the process itself. Figure 2 shows three levels for evaluation of a staff development program.

Figure 2. Levels of Evaluation in Staff Development

Level 1	Teacher	
Level 2	Teacher	Classroom
Level 3	Teacher	Classroom	Student

Level 1 evaluates the process by which teacher skills are developed and fine-tuned, answering such questions as: What was the quality of individual workshops? Were the goals and objectives of the inservice program achieved? Was the inservice program leader effective?

Level 2 considers the effect of the staff development process on what teachers are actually doing in the classroom. Are teachers attempting to incorporate or implement content area reading activities into instruction? Have they modified their previous strategies and materials to fit their new purposes? Are their instructional units incorporating a wider range of instructional materials and resources?

Level 3 considers the effect of the staff development process on its ultimate product — improved student attitude toward and performance in content area reading.

Staff development programs too frequently move from teacher and classroom evaluation to student evaluation in a rush to prove their worth.

The push for visible returns is understandable; in the wake of the accountability movement, it's probably inevitable. But programs which center predominantly on evaluation of levels 1 and 2 offer teachers the opportunity to grow professionally and improve the quality of their classroom instruction.

A number of evaluative tools can be used to determine the extent of teachers' professional growth. Pre- and post-testing of teachers' knowledge of reading on tests specifically constructed for the staff development program can yield evaluative insights if it is agreed that knowledge of reading is a good indicator of teacher growth. Changes in teachers' attitudes toward content area reading can be interpreted from pre- and post-tests with an attitude scale. Systems for analyzing and classifying interactions between teachers and students (some good ones can be found in *Second Handbook of Research on Teaching,* 1973) and observation check lists can help evaluate the effect of the program on teachers' classroom activities.

Participants' perceptions of the inservice leader's performance and the individual workshop sessions can also be used to evaluate the quality and effectiveness of the program. Box 3 illustrates a rating scale developed to measure leader performance. You can use one of the survey formats described in the section on assessment to rate the quality and effectiveness of individual workshop sessions in the program. Box 4 shows how this tool can be used.

Box 3

A RATING SCALE FOR STAFF DEVELOPMENT PERSONNEL

Directions: Appraise the staff developer's performance in the present assignment. Consider each statement below. Would you agree or disagree with the statement if you heard it used to describe the person's performance? On a scale of 1 to 6, with *1* being strongly agree and *6* being strongly disagree, check the most appropriate interval. If you wish, use the Remarks section for significant comments.

1. Involves the participants actively in the topic.

2. Relates the topic directly (through examples) to the classroom.

3. Provides materials or ideas for materials useful in a classroom.

REMARKS

1. Displays a positive attitude and pleasant disposition.

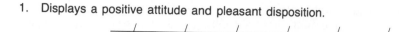

2. Is sensitive to the environment or dynamics within the group.

3. Answers questions directly and patiently.

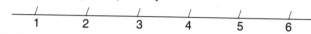

REMARKS _____

1. Is well-informed and well-organized.

2. Has a purpose in mind and adheres to the task at hand.

3. Conveys explanations clearly.

REMARKS _____

1. Assessed the needs of the group in advance.

2. Is cognizant of local organizational procedures and alternatives.

REMARKS _____

Box 4

RATING SCALE FOR WORKSHOPS

Directions: To determine whether this particular workshop met your needs and the established objectives of the program, please provide your honest opinion on its design, presentation and value. Circle the number which best expresses your reaction to each of the items below.

1. The organization of the workshop was
   Excellent 5 4 3 2 1 Poor
2. The objectives of the workshop were
   Clear 5 4 3 2 1 Vague
3. The contribution of the workshop leader(s) was
   Excellent 5 4 3 2 1 Poor
4. The ideas and activities presented were
   Very Interesting 5 4 3 2 1 Dull

5. My participation in this workshop
   should prove

Very Beneficial   5 4 3 2 1   Of no benefit

6. Overall this workshop was

Excellent   5 4 3 2 1   Poor

7. The strongest feature of the workshop was:

8. The weakest feature of the workshop was:

9. Would you like further help on any of the topics presented at the workshop? If so, please list them.

TO THE INSERVICE LEADER

Throughout this guide the emphasis has been on staff development as a continuous involvement process. The success of an inservice program rests squarely on your shoulders. Whether you are a content teacher or reading specialist you must recognize your role as an adult educator when you work with teachers. This means creating a working environment conducive to adult learning. Within this environment you should demonstrate certain behaviors and characteristics which participants in inservice programs have perceived as effective. These behaviors and characteristics are associated with your professional competence and your personal influence, and they reflect your ability to deliver the content of an inservice program and to plan and organize the program in relation to the needs of the teachers involved.

A program model for staff development should be change oriented. You can achieve the continuous involvement process that I described by going through three phases: design and planning, implementation, and evaluation. However, change is gradual and difficult to accomplish; anyone who has ever taken the lead in an inservice program knows the meaning of the words of Machiavelli in *The Prince*: "There is nothing more difficult to take in hand, more perilous to conduct, or more uncertain in its success, than to take the lead in the introduction of a new order of things." Change often means upsetting the status quo. And upsetting the status quo is always a perilous undertaking fraught with uncertainty. Nevertheless, if content area reading is to find its way into the classrooms of teachers, staff development and inservice programs are essential.

SUGGESTED READINGS

Bennis, Warren; Benne, Kenneth; and Chin, Robert, eds., *The planning of change*. 2nd ed. New York: Holt, Rinehart and Winston, 1969.

Bishop, Leslee J. *Staff development and instructional improvement*. Boston: Allyn and Bacon, 1976.

Harris, B. W., and Bessent, W. *Inservice education: a guide to better practice*. Englewood Cliffs, N.J.: Prentice-Hall, 1969.

Hersey, Paul, and Blanchard, Kenneth. *Management of organizational behavior*. 3rd ed. Englewood Cliffs, N.J.: Prentice-Hall, 1977.

Knowles, Malcolm. *The adult learner: a neglected species*. 2nd ed. Houston: Gulf Publishing Company, 1978.

————. *Self-directed learning*. New York: Association Press, 1975.

Otto, Wayne, and Smith, Richard. *Administering the school reading program*. Boston: Houghton Mifflin, 1970.

Rogers, Carl. *Freedom to learn*. Columbus, Ohio: Charles E. Merrill, 1969.

Rubin, Louis J., ed. *Improving in-service education: proposals and procedures for change*. Boston: Allyn and Bacon, 1971.

Rubin, Louis J. *The in-service education of teachers*. Boston: Allyn and Bacon, 1978.

Tyler, Ralph, ed., *Prospects for research and development in education*. Berkeley, Cal.: McCutchan Publishing, 1976.

Bibliography

Anderson, Richard C., et al. "Frameworks for comprehending discourse." *American Educational Research Journal* 14 (1977):367–382.

Anderson, Richard C., and Biddle, William. "On asking people questions about what they are reading." In G. Bower, ed., *The psychology of learning and motivation*. New York: Academic Press, 1975.

Aronson, Elliot. "Busing and racial tension: The jigsaw route to learning and liking." *Psychology Today* 8 (1975):43–50.

Artley, Sterl A. "General and specific factors in reading comprehension." *Journal of Experimental Education* 16 (1948):181–186.

———. "Oral reading as a communication process." *The Reading Teacher* 26 (1972):46–51.

Aukerman, Robert. *Reading in the secondary school classroom*. New York: McGraw-Hill, 1972.

Aulls, Mark. *Developmental and remedial reading in the middle school*. Boston: Allyn and Bacon, 1978.

Ausubel, David. *Educational psychology: a cognitive view*. 2nd ed. New York: Holt, Rinehart and Winston, 1978.

———. *The psychology of meaningful verbal learning*. New York: Grune and Stratton, 1973.

Baker, Robert. "The effects of informational organizers on learning and retention, content knowledge, and term relationships in ninth grade social studies." In H. L. Herber and R. T. Vacca, eds., *Reading in the content areas: third report*. Syracuse, N.Y.: Syracuse University Reading and Language Arts Center, 1977.

Baldwin, Scott, and Kaufman, Rhonda. "A concurrent validity study of the Raygor readability estimate." *Journal of Reading* 23 (1979):148–153.

Barrett, Thomas, and Smith, Richard. *Teaching reading in the middle grades*. Reading, Mass.: Addison-Wesley, 1974.

Barron, Richard. "The use of vocabulary as an advance organizer." In H. L. Herber and P. L. Sanders, eds., *Research in reading in the content areas: first report*. Syracuse, N.Y.: Syracuse University Reading and Language Arts Center, 1969.

Barron, Richard, and Earle, Richard. "An approach for vocabulary development." In H. L. Herber and R. F. Barron, eds., *Research in reading in the content areas: second report*. Syracuse, N.Y.: Syracuse University Reading and Language Arts Center, 1973.

Barron, Richard, and Stone, V. Frank. "The effect of student constructed graphic post organizers upon learning of vocabulary relationships from a passage of social studies content." Paper presented at the meeting of the National Reading Conference, Houston, December 1973.

Beebe, B. F. *African elephants*. New York: McKay, 1968.

Bellows, Barbara. "Running shoes are to jogging as analogies are to critical creative thinking." *Journal of Reading* 23 (1980): 507–511.

Berlyne, David. "A theory of human curiosity." *British Journal of Psychology* 45 (1954): 256–265.

Berlyne, David. *Structure and direction of thinking*. New York: Wiley, 1965.

Betts, Emmett. *Foundations of reading*. rev. ed. New York: American Book Company, 1950.

Bloom, Benjamin. *Taxonomy of educational objectives: cognitive domain*. New York: McKay, 1956.

Bruner, Jerome. "The act of discovery." *Harvard Educational Review* 31 (1961): 21–32.

Bruner, Jerome. *The process of education*. Cambridge, Mass.: Harvard University Press, 1960.

Burmeister, Lou E. *Reading strategies for secondary school teachers*. Reading, Mass.: Addison-Wesley, 1974.

Campbell, Anne. "How readability formulae fall short in matching student to text in content areas." *Journal of Reading* 22 (1979): 683–689.

Capuzzi, David. "Information intermix." *Journal of Reading* 16 (1973): 453–459.

Castallo, Richard. "Listening guide — a first step toward notetaking and listening skills." *Journal of Reading* 19 (1976): 289–290.

Collette, Alfred. *Science teaching in the secondary school*. Boston: Allyn and Bacon, 1973.

Coon, George E. "The reading teacher's lament." *The Reading Teacher* 33 (1979): 154.

Cunningham, James, and Foster, E. "The ivory tower connection: a case for study." *The Reading Teacher* 31 (1978): 365–370.

Cunningham, Richard. "Design, implementation and evaluation of an affective/cognitive model for teacher change through a staff development program. Ph.D. dissertation, Syracuse University, 1972.

Cunningham, Richard, and Shablak, Scott. "Selective reading guide-o-rama: the content teacher's best friend." *Journal of Reading* 18 (1975): 380–382.

Daigon, Arthur. "From reading to writing." In R. T. Vacca and J. A. Meagher, eds., *Reading through content*. Storrs, Conn.: University Publications and the University of Connecticut Reading–Language Arts Center, 1979.

Dale, Edgar. *The word game: improving communications*. Bloomington, Ind.: Phi Delta Kappa Educational Foundation, 1975.

———. "Things to come." *Newsletter* 34 (1969).

Dale, Edgar, and Chall, Jeanne. "A formula for predicting readability." *Educational Research Bulletin* 27 (1948): 11–20.

Dale, Edgar; O'Rourke, Joseph; and Bamman, Henry. *Techniques of teaching vocabulary*. Palo Alto, Cal.: Field Educational Publications, 1971.

Davis, Frederick B. "Fundamental factors of comprehension in reading." Ph.D. dissertation, Harvard University, 1941.

———. "Fundamental factors of comprehension in reading." *Psychometrika* 9 (1944): 185–197.

———. "Psychometric research on comprehension in reading." *Reading Research Quarterly* 7 (1972): 628–678.

———. "Research in comprehension in reading." *Reading Research Quarterly* 3 (1968): 429–445.

Davis, James. *Group performance*. Reading, Mass.: Addison-Wesley, 1969.

Deighton, Lee. *Vocabulary development in the classroom*. New York: Teachers College Press, 1959, 1970.

Devan, Steven, et al. "Priming — a method to equalize difference between high and low achievement students." *Journal of Reading* 19 (1975): 143–146.

Dulin, Kenneth. "Using context clues in word recognition and comprehension." *The Reading Teacher* 23 (1970): 440–445.

Earle, Richard. "Developing and using study guides." In H. L. Herber and P. L. Sanders, eds., *Research in reading in the content areas: first report*. Syracuse, N.Y.: Syracuse University Reading and Language Arts Center, 1969.

———. *Teaching reading and mathematics*. Newark, Del.: International Reading Association, 1976.

Earle, Richard, and Morley, Richard. "The half-open classroom: controlled options in reading." *Journal of Reading* 18 (1974): 131–135.

Early, Margaret. "Taking stock: secondary reading in the 1970's." *Journal of Reading* 16 (1973): 364–373.

———. "The meaning of reading instruction in secondary schools." *Journal of Reading* 8 (1964): 25–29.

Ebbinghaus, H. "Ueber eine neue methode zur prüfung geistiger fähigkeiten und ihre anwendung bei schulkindern," *Zeitsch fur Psych. und Phys. Der Sinnesorgane* 13 (1897): 401–457.

Estes, Thomas. "Use of guide material and small group discussion in reading ninth grade social studies assignments." Ph.D. dissertation, Syracuse University, 1970.

Estes, Thomas, and Vaughan, Joseph, Jr. *Reading and learning in the content classroom*. Boston: Allyn and Bacon, 1978.

Frase, Lawrence T. "A heuristic model for research in prose learning." A paper presented at the annual meeting of the American Educational Research Association, New York, 1971.

———. "Purpose in reading." In J. T. Guthrie, ed., *Cognition, curriculum and comprehension*. Newark, Del.: International Reading Association, 1977.

Frederiksen, C. H. "Representing logical and semantic structures of knowl-edge acquired from discourse." *Cognitive Psychology* 1 (1975): 371–458.

Fry, Edward. "A readability formula that saves time." *Journal of Reading* 11 (1968): 513–516, 575–578.

———. "Fry's readability graph: clarifications, validity and extension to level 17." *Journal of Reading* 21 (1977): 242–252.

Gagne, Robert. *The conditions of learning.* 2nd ed. New York: Holt, Rinehart and Winston, 1970.

Gibson, Eleanor, and Levin, Harry. *The psychology of reading.* Cambridge, Mass.: MIT Press, 1975.

Gillet, Jean, and Kita, M. Jane. "Words, kids and categories." *The Reading Teacher* 32 (1979): 538–542.

Goodman, Kenneth. "The reading process: a psycholinguistic view." In E. B. Smith et al., *Language and thinking in school.* 2nd ed. New York: Holt, Rinehart and Winston, 1976.

Goodman, Yetta, and Burke, Carolyn. *Reading miscue inventory manual: procedure for diagnosis and evaluation.* New York: Macmillan, 1972.

Greene, Frank. "OPIN." Mimeographed. Montreal: McGill University, 1970.

———. "Radio reading." In C. Pennock, ed., *Reading comprehension at four linguistic levels.* Newark, Del.: International Reading Association, 1979.

Greenslade, Bonnie. "Awareness and anticipation: the dr-ta in the content classroom," *Journal of Language Experience* 2 (1980): 21–28.

Guthrie, John. "Reading comprehension and syntactic responses in good and poor readers." *Journal of Educational Psychology* 65 (1973): 294.

Guthrie, John, et al. "The maze technique to assess, monitor reading compre-hension." *The Reading Teacher* 28 (1974): 161–168.

Hansell, T. Stevenson. "Increasing understanding in content reading." *Jour-nal of Reading* 19 (1976): 307–311.

———. "Stepping up to outlining." *Journal of Reading* 22 (1978): 248–252.

Harker, W. John. "Selecting instructional materials for content area reading." *Journal of Reading* 21 (1977): 126–130.

Harste, Jerome. "Instructional implications of Rumelhart's model." In W. Diehl, ed., *Secondary reading: theory and application.* Bloomington, Ind.: School of Education, Indiana University, 1978.

Henry, George. *Teaching reading as concept development.* Newark, Del.: In-ternational Reading Association, 1974.

Herber, Harold. *Teaching reading in content areas.* Englewood Cliffs, N.J.: Prentice-Hall, 1970.

———. *Teaching reading in content areas.* 2nd ed. Englewood Cliffs, N.J.: Prentice-Hall, 1978.

———, ed. *Developing study skills in secondary schools.* Newark, Del.: In-ternational Reading Association, 1965.

Herber, Harold and Sanders, Peter, eds. *Research in reading in the content areas: first report.* Syracuse, N.Y.: Syracuse University Reading and Language Arts Center, 1969.

Herber, Harold, and Barron, Richard, eds. *Research in reading in the content areas: second report.* Syracuse, N.Y.: Syracuse University Reading and Language Arts Center, 1973.

Herber, Harold, and Nelson, Joan. "Questioning is not the answer." *Journal of Reading* 18 (1975): 512–517.

Herber, Harold, and Vacca, Richard, eds. *Research in reading in the content areas: third report.* Syracuse, N.Y.: Syracuse University Reading and Language Arts Center, 1977.

Hittleman, Daniel. *Developmental reading: a psycholinguistic perspective.* Chicago: Rand McNally, 1977.

———. "Seeking a psycholinguistic definition of readability." *The Reading Teacher* 26 (1973): 783–789.

Homer, Cynthia, "A directed reading-thinking activity for content areas." In R. T. Vacca and J. A. Meagher, eds., *Reading through content.* Storrs, Conn.: University Publications and the University of Connecticut Reading–Language Arts Center, 1979.

Huey, Edmund. *The psychology and pedagogy of reading.* New York: Macmillan, 1908.

Ignoffo, Matthew. "The thread of thought: analogies as a vocabulary building method." *Journal of Reading* 23 (1980): 519–521.

Johns, Jerry L., and Galen, Nancy. "Reading instruction in the middle 50's: what tomorrow's teachers remember today." *Reading Horizons* 17 (1977): 251–254.

Johnson, Dale, and Pearson, P. David. *Teaching reading vocabulary.* New York: Holt, Rinehart and Winston, 1978.

Judy, Stephen. "What makes a good teacher." *English Journal* 67 (1978): 6–7.

Kelley, Brenda, and Holmes, Janis. "The guided lecture procedure." *Journal of Reading* 22 (1979): 602–605.

Knowles, Malcolm. *The adult learner: a neglected species.* Houston: Gulf Publishing Company, 1973.

Lexier, Kenneth. "Cognitive learning in the content classroom." In R. T. Vacca and J. A. Meagher, eds., *Reading through content.* Storrs, Conn.: University Publications and the University of Connecticut Reading–Language Arts Center, 1979.

Lundsteen, Sara. *Children learn to communicate.* Englewood Cliffs, N.J.: Prentice-Hall, 1976.

McLaughlin, Harry. "SMOG grading — a new readability formula." *Journal of Reading* 12 (1969): 639–646.

Machiavelli, Nicolo. *The Prince.* In Daniel Donno, ed. and trans., *The Prince and Selected Discourses.* New York: Bantam, 1966.

Malinowski, B. *Magic, science and religion and other essays*. New York: Doubleday, Anchor Books, 1954.

Mallan, John, and Hersh, Richard. *No g.o.d.s in the classroom: inquiry into inquiry*. Philadelphia: W. B. Saunders, 1972.

Manzo, Anthony. "Guided reading procedure." *Journal of Reading* 18 (1975): 287–291.

———. "The request procedure." *Journal of Reading* 11 (1969): 123–126.

Marksheffel, Ned. *Better reading in the secondary school*. New York: Ronald Press, 1966.

Meyer, Bonnie. *The organization of prose and its effect in memory*. Amsterdam: North-Holland, 1975.

Moffett, James. "An interview with James Moffett." *Media and Methods* 15 (1975): 20–24.

Moffett, James, and Wagner, Betty J. *Student-centered language arts and reading K–13*. 2nd ed. Boston: Houghton Mifflin, 1976.

Nelson, Joan. "Readability: some cautions for the content area teacher." *Journal of Reading* 21 (1978): 620–625.

Newton, Eunice. "Andragogy: understanding the adult as a learner." *Journal of Reading* 20 (1977): 361–364.

Niles, Olive. "Developing basic comprehension skills," in J. Sherk, ed., *Speaking of reading*. Syracuse, N.Y.: Syracuse University Reading and Language Arts Center, 1964.

———. "Organization perceived," in H. Herber, ed., *Developing study skills in secondary schools*. Newark, Del.: International Reading Association, 1965.

Olsen, Arthur, and Ames, Wilbur. *Teaching reading skills in secondary schools*. Scranton, Pa.: Intext Educational Publishers, 1972.

Ortiz, Rose Katz. "Using questions as a tool in reading." *Journal of Reading* 21 (1977): 109–114.

Otto, Wayne, and Erickson, Lawrence. *Inservice education to improve reading instruction*. Newark, Del.: International Reading Association, 1973.

Page, William. "Inquiry into an unknown word." *School Review* 83 (1975): 461–477.

Palmatier, Robert. "A notetaking system for learning." *Journal of Reading* 17 (1973): 36–39.

Palmatier, Robert, and Bennett, J. Michael. "Notetaking habits of college students." *Journal of Reading* 18 (1974): 215–218.

Pearson, P. David. "The effects of grammatical complexity on children's comprehension, recall, and conception of certain semantic relations." *Reading Research Quarterly* 10 (1974–1975): 155–192.

Pearson, P. David, and Johnson, Dale. *Teaching reading comprehension*. New York: Holt, Rinehart and Winston, 1978.

Peters, Charles, et al. "A comparative analysis of reading comprehension in four content areas." In G. H. McNinch and W. D. Miller, eds., *Read-

ing: convention and inquiry. Clemson, S.C.: National Reading Conference, 1975.

Piercy, Dorothy. *Reading activities in content areas*. Boston: Allyn and Bacon, 1976.

Preston, Ralph. *Teaching social studies in the elementary school*. 3rd ed. New York: Holt, Rinehart and Winston, 1968.

Protheroe, Donald. "Gi-go: the content of content area reading." In R. T. Vacca and J. A. Meagher, eds., *Reading through content*. Storrs, Conn.: University Publications and the University of Connecticut Reading–Language Arts Center, 1979.

Quealy, Roger. "Senior high school students' use of contextual aids in reading." *Reading Research Quarterly* 4 (1969): 512–533.

Raygor, Alton. "The Raygor readability estimate: a quick and easy way to determine difficulty." In P. D. Pearson, ed., *Reading: Theory, Research and Practice*. Clemson, S.C.: National Reading Conference, 1977.

Rickards, John. "Interaction of position and conceptual level of adjunct questions." *Journal of Educational Psychology* 68 (1976): 210–217.

Rieck, Billie Jo. "How content teachers telegraph messages against reading." *Journal of Reading* 20 (1977): 646–648.

Riley, James, and Pachtman, Andrew. "Reading mathematical word problems: telling them what to do is not telling them how to do it." *Journal of Reading* 21 (1978): 531–533.

Robinson, Frances. *Effective study*. New York: Harper and Row, 1961.

Robinson, H. Allan. *Teaching reading and study strategies*. Boston: Allyn and Bacon, 1975.

————. *Teaching reading and study strategies*. 2nd ed. Boston: Allyn and Bacon, 1978.

Roby, Thomas. *Small group performance*. Chicago: Rand McNally, 1968.

Rothkopf, Ernst. "Learning from written materials: an exploration of the control of inspection behavior by test-like events." *American Educational Research Journal* 3 (1966): 241–249.

Ruddell, Robert. "Inservice reading programs," *Reporting on reading* 5 (1978): 1–4.

Samples, Robert, et al. *The wholeschool book*. Reading, Mass.: Addison-Wesley, 1977.

Sawyer, Diane. "The diagnostic mystique — a point of view." *The Reading Teacher* 27 (1974): 355–360.

Shablak, Scott, and Castallo, Richard. "Curiosity arousal and motivation in the teaching/learning process." In H. L. Herber and R. T. Vacca, eds., *Research in reading in the content areas: third report*. Syracuse, N.Y.: Syracuse University Reading and Language Arts Center, 1977.

Shepherd, David. *Comprehensive high school reading methods*. Columbus, Ohio: Charles E. Merrill, 1973.

Sherer, Peter. "Skimming and scanning: de-mything the process with a college student." *Journal of Reading* 19 (1975): 24–27.

Simon, Sidney, et al. *Values clarification: a handbook of practical strategies for teachers and students.* New York: Hart Publishing Company, 1972.

Smith, Frank. *Comprehension and learning: a conceptual framework for teachers.* New York: Holt, Rinehart and Winston, 1975.

————. *Understanding reading.* 2nd ed. New York: Holt, Rinehart and Winston, 1978.

Smith, Nila B. "Teaching study skills in reading." *Elementary School Journal* 60 (1959): 158–162.

————. "Patterns of writing in different subject areas," *Journal of Reading* 7 (1964): 31–37.

Stauffer, Russell. *Directing reading maturity as a cognitive process.* New York: Harper and Row, 1969.

————. *Directing the reading-thinking process.* New York: Harper and Row, 1975.

Steurer, Stephen J. "Learning centers in the secondary school." *Journal of Reading* 22 (1978): 134–139.

Strang, Ruth; McCullough, Constance; and Traxler, Arthur. *The improvement of reading.* 4th ed. New York: McGraw-Hill, 1967.

Summers, Edward G. "Utilizing visual aids in reading material for effective learning." In H. L. Herber, ed., *Developing study skills in secondary schools.* Newark, Del.: International Reading Association, 1965.

Taba, Hilda. *Teacher's handbook for elementary social studies.* Reading, Mass.: Addison-Wesley, 1967.

Taylor, Wilson. "Cloze procedure: a new tool for measuring readability." *Journalism Quarterly* 30 (1953): 415–433.

Thelen, Herbert. "Group dynamics in instruction: principle of least group size." *School Review* 57 (1949): 139–148.

Thelen, Judith. "Reading textbooks — close encounters of the worst kind?" In R. T. Vacca and J. A. Meagher, eds., *Reading through content.* Storrs, Conn.: University Publications and the University of Connecticut Reading–Language Arts Center, 1979.

Thorndike, Edward. "Reading and reasoning: a study of mistakes in paragraph reading." *Journal of Educational Psychology* 8 (1917): 323–332.

Toffler, Alan. *Future shock.* New York: Random House, 1970.

Travers, Robert, ed. *Second handbook of research on teaching.* Chicago: Rand McNally, 1973.

Vacca, Jo Anne L. "Reading techniques to improve self-concept." *New England Reading Association Journal* 11 (1976): 28–32.

————. "Staff development in reading: what the experts say." *Reading Horizons* 19 (1979): 139–142.

Vacca, Jo Anne L., and Vacca, Richard T. "Learning stations: how to in the middle grades." *Journal of Reading* 19 (1976): 563–567.

————. "Unfreezing strategies for staff development in reading." *The Reading Teacher* 34 (1980).

Vacca, Richard, and Meagher, Judith, eds. *Reading through content.* Storrs, Conn.: University of Connecticut, University Publications and the Reading–Language Arts Center, 1979.

Vacca, Richard T. "A means for building comprehension in social studies." In H. L. Herber and R. F. Barron, eds., *Research in reading in the content areas: second report.* Syracuse, N.Y.: Syracuse University Reading and Language Arts Center, 1973.

————. "An investigation of a functional reading strategy in seventh grade social studies." In H. L. Herber and R. T. Vacca, eds., *Research in reading in the content areas: third report.* Syracuse, N.Y.: Syracuse University Reading and Language Arts Center, 1977.

————. "Development of a functional reading strategy: implications for content area instruction. *Journal of Educational Research* 69 (1975): 108–112.

————. "Reading reinforcement through magic squares." *Journal of Reading* 18 (1975): 587–590.

Vacca, Richard T., and Johns, Jerry L. "$R > s_1 + s_2 + \ldots s_n$," *Reading Horizons* 17 (1976): 9–13.

Vaughan, Joseph, Jr. "A scale to measure attitudes toward reading in content classrooms." *Journal of Reading* 20 (1977): 605–609.

Walker, James. "Squeezing study skills (into, out of) content areas." In R. T. Vacca and J. A. Meagher, eds., *Reading through content,* pp. 77–92. Storrs, Conn.: University Publications and the University of Connecticut Reading–Language Arts Center, 1979.

APPENDIX A

Affixes with Invariant Meanings

AFFIX	MEANING	EXAMPLE
1. *Combining Forms*		
anthropo-	man	anthropoid
auto-	self	autonomous
biblio-	book	bibliography
bio-	life	biology
centro- centri-	center	centrifugal
cosmo	universe	cosmonaut
heter- hetero-	different	heterogeneous
homo-	same	homogeneous
hydro-	water	hydroplane
iso-	equal	isometric
lith- litho-	stone	lithography
micro-	small	microscope
mono-	one	monocyte
neuro-	nerve	neurologist
omni-	all	omnibus
pan-	all	panchromatic
penta-	five	pentamerous
phil- philo-	love	philanthropist
phono-	sound	phonology

AFFIX	MEANING	EXAMPLE
photo-	light	photosynthesis
pneumo-	air, respiration	pneumonia
poly-	many	polygon
proto-	before, first in time	prototype
pseudo-	false	pseudonym
tele-	far	television
uni-	one	unicellular

2. Prefix

apo-	separate or detached from	apocarpous
circum-	around	circumvent
com-	together or with	combine
co-		
col-		
con-		
cor-		
equi-	equal	equivalent
extra-	in addition	extraordinary
intra-	within	intratext
mal-	bad	malpractice
mis-	wrong	mistreatment
non-	not	nonsense
syn-	together or with	synthesis

3. Noun Suffix

Each Noun Suffix Functions to Indicate:

-ana	a collection of various materials that reflect the character of a notable place or person	Americana
-archy	rule or government	oligarchy
-ard	a person who does something to	drunkard
-art	excess	braggart
-aster	inferiority or fraudulence	poetaster
-bility	quality or state of being	capability
-chrome	pigment, colored or color	autochrome
-cide	murder or killing of	insecticide

AFFIX	MEANING	EXAMPLE
-fication -ation	action or process of	classification dramatization
-gram	something written or drawn	diagram
-graph	writing, recording, drawing	telegraph lithograph
-graphy	a descriptive science of a specific subject or field	planography oceanography
-ics	the science or art of	graphics athletics
-itis	inflammation or inflammatory disease	bronchitis
-latry	the worship of	bibliolatry
-meter	a measuring device	barometer
-metry	the science or process of measuring	photometry
-ology -logy	the science, theory or study of	phraseology paleontology
-phore	a bearer or producer	semaphore
-phobia	persistent, illogical, abnormal or intense fear	hypnophobia
-scope	an instrument for observing or detecting	telescope
-scopy	viewing, seeing or observing	microscopy

-ance
  -ation
  -ion
  -ism
  -dom
  -ery
  -mony
  -ment
  -tion
	These noun suffixes are used to form abstract nouns with the meaning of "quality, state, or condition," and action or result of an action.	tolerance
		adoration
		
		truism
		
		matrimony
		government
		sanction

-er
  -eer
  -ess
  -grapher
  -ier
  -ster
  -ist
  -stress
  -trix
	These noun suffixes pertain to living or nonliving agents.	helper
		engineer
		countess
		geographer
		
		youngster
		shootist
		mistress
		executrix

AFFIX	MEANING	EXAMPLE
4. Adjective Suffix	Adjective Suffixes Function to Indicate:	
-est	a superlative	greatest
-ferous	bearing, producing	crystalliferous
-fic	making, causing or creating something	morbific
-fold	division	fivefold tenfold
-form	having the form of	cuneiform
-genous	generating or producing	androgenous endogenous
-ic	a characteristic of	seismic microscopic
-wise	manner, direction or position	clockwise
-less	lack of, free of or not having	toothless
-able -ible	worthy of or inclined to	debatable knowledgeable
-most	a superlative	innermost
-like	resemblance or similarity to something specified, characteristic of or appropriateness to something specified	lifelike
-ous	possessing, having or full of	joyous
-ose	possession of or having similiarity to	grandiose
-acious	a tendency toward or abundance of something	fallacious
-ful	fullness or abundance	masterful useful armful
-aceous -ative -ish -ive -itious	These adjective suffixes mean pertaining to	impish foolish additive fictitious

APPENDIX B

Commonly Used Prefixes with Varying Meanings

PREFIX	MEANING	EXAMPLE
ab-	from, away, off	abhor abnormal abdicate
ad-	to, toward	adhere adjoin
ante-	before, in front of, earlier than	antecedent antediluvian
anti-	opposite of, hostile to	antitoxin antisocial antisemite
be-	make, against, to a great degree	bemoan belittle befuddle
bi-	two, twice	biped bivalve
de-	away, opposite of, reduce	deactivate devalue devitalize
dia-	through, across	diameter diagonal
dis-	opposite of, apart, away	dissatisfy disarm disjointed
en-	cause to be, put in or on	enable engulf

PREFIX	MEANING	EXAMPLE
epi-	upon, after	epitaph epilogue epidermis
ex-	out of, former, apart, away	excrete exposition
hyper-	above, beyond, excessive	hyperphysical hypersensitive
hypo-	under, less than normal	hypodermic hypotension
in- il- im- ir-	not, in, into, within	inept indoors
inter-	between, among	interscholastic interstellar
neo-	new, young	neophyte neo-Nazi
per-	through, very	permanent perjury
peri-	around, near, enclosing	perimeter perihelion
post-	after, behind	postlude postorbital
pre-	before in place, time, rank, order	preview prevail
pro-	before, forward, for, in favor of	production prothorax pro-American
ortho-	straight, corrective	orthotropic orthopedic
re-	again, back	react recoil
sub- sur- sug- sup-	under, beneath, subordinate	subsoil substation
super-	above, over, in addition	superhuman superlative superordinate

PREFIX	MEANING	EXAMPLE
syn-	with, together	synthesis synchronize
trans-	across, beyond, through	trans-Atlantic transconfigura- tion transaction
ultra-	beyond in space, excessive	ultraviolet ultramodern
un-	not, the opposite of	unable unbind

APPENDIX C

List of Resources for Word Histories, Origins, and Derivations

Asimov, Isaac. *Words from history*. Boston: Houghton Mifflin Co., 1968.

_____. *Words from the myths*. Boston: Houghton Mifflin Co., 1961.

_____. *Words of science*. Boston: Houghton Mifflin Co., 1959.

_____. *Words on the map*. Boston: Houghton Mifflin Co., 1962.

Blumberg, Dorothy R. *Whose what?* New York: Holt, Rinehart and Winston, 1973.

Ernst, Margaret S. *Words*. New York: Alfred A. Knopf, Inc., 1950.

_____. *More about words*. New York: Alfred A. Knopf, Inc., 1951.

_____. *In a word*. With drawings by James Thurber. Great Neck, New York: Channel Press, 1954.

Evans, Bergen. *Dictionary of mythology*. Lincoln, Nebraska: Centennial Press, 1970.

Ferguson, Charles W. *The abecedarian book*. Boston: Little, Brown and Co., 1964.

Funk, Charles E. *A hog on ice*. New York: Paperback Library, 1973.

_____. *Thereby hangs a tale*. New York: Harper, 1950.

Funk, Wilfred J. *Word origins and their romantic stories*. New York: Funk and Wagnalls, 1950.

Garrison, Webb B. *Why you say it*. New York: Abingdon Press, 1955.

Lambert, Eloise. *Our language, the story of the words we use*. New York: Lothrop, Lee and Shepard Co., 1955.

Mathews, Mitford. *American words*. New York: World Publishing Co., 1959.

Mathews, M. M. *Words: how to know them*. New York: Holt, Rinehart and Winston, Inc., 1956.

Morris, William and Mary Morris. *Dictionary of word and phrase origins*. New York: Harper & Row, vol. 1, 1962; vol. 2, 1967; vol. 3, 1971.

Norman, Barbara. *Tales of the table*. Englewood Cliffs, New Jersey: Prentice-Hall, Inc., 1972.

O'Neill, Mary. *Words, words, words*. New York: Doubleday and Co., 1966.

Partridge, Eric. *Name into word*. London: Secker and Warburg, 1949.

————. *Origins, a short etymological dictionary of modern English*. London: Routledge and Kegan Paul, 1958.

Severn, Bill. *People words*. New York: Ives Washburn, Inc., 1966.

————. *Place words*. New York: Ives Washburn, Inc., 1969.

Sorel, Nancy. *Word people*. New York: American Heritage, McGraw-Hill Co., 1970.

APPENDIX D

Sample Instructional Units

Our Solar System

Teacher: ELAINE SARGENT
Subject: ASTRONOMY
Grade: FIFTH

This instructional unit is designed for fifth graders with varying reading levels and scientific abilities. Its goal is to help students understand man's efforts to explain the universe through creative and scientific endeavors. Students therefore explore some very basic concepts about the solar system through materials and activities that focus on intellectual, creative, and physical experiences. Grouping arrangements vary from whole class to small groups based on interest and/or ability to "study buddies" to individual study. During this 6- to 8-week unit, students will be expected to take some responsibility for planning, monitoring, and evaluating their learning. They will be expected to keep contracts for projects of their own choice or design and to confer with the teacher at regular intervals.

MAJOR CONCEPTS

1. The science of astronomy has a long history, including early man's various beliefs about the universe.
2. The sun, like all stars, is made up of hot gases that give off light and heat.
3. The sun is the center of our solar system, with the planets revolving in predictable orbits. The order of the planets from the sun outward is Mercury, Venus, Earth, Mars, Jupiter, Saturn, Uranus, Neptune, and Pluto.

4. The planets have both similarities and differences.

5. A satellite is a man-made or natural object that revolves around a planet.

6. The phases of the moon occur as the moon revolves around and reflects the sun's light.

7. There are two kinds of eclipses — solar and lunar.

8. Other members of our solar system include asteroids, meteoroids, and comets.

9. Scientists use different types of evidence to develop a theory.

10. Man has used his knowledge of space to create literature, art, and music.

MATERIALS AND READINGS

Fiction

(All books in this section are listed under Concept 10.)

1. Beatty, Jerome, Jr. *Matthew Looney and the Space Pirates*. Glenview, Ill.: Young Scott, 1972.

2. Campbell, John W. *The Best of John W. Campbell*. Edited by Lester DelRay. Westminster, Md.: Ballentine, 1976.

3. Earnshaw, Brian. *Dragonfall 5 and the Empty Planet*. West Caldwell, N.J.: Lothrop, 1976.

4. ———. *Dragonfall 5 and the Space Cowboys*. West Caldwell, N.J.: Lothrop, 1975.

5. Key, Alexander. *The Forgotten Door*. Philadelphia: Westminster, 1965.

*6. L'Engle, Madeline. *A Wrinkle in Time*. New York: Farrar Straus, 1962.

7. MacGregor, Ellen. *Miss Pickerell and the Weather Satellite*. New York: McGraw-Hill, 1971.

8. ———. *Miss Pickerell Goes to Mars*. New York: McGraw-Hill, 1951.

9. Morressy, John. *The Humans of Ziax II*. New York: Walker and Co., 1974.

10. Philipe, Anne. *Atom, the Little Moon Monkey*. New York: Quist, 1970.

* To be read by teacher to class.

11. Slobodkin, Louis. *The Space Ship in the Park*. New York: Macmillan, 1952.

12. _____ . *The Space Ship Returns to the Apple Tree*. New York: Macmillan, 1972.

13. _____ . *The Space Ship under the Apple Tree*. New York: Macmillan, 1972.

Nonfiction

#	Reference	1	2	3	4	5	6	7	8	9
1.	Adler, Irving. *The Sun and Its Family*. New York: John Day Co., 1969.	1	2	3	4		6	7*		
2.	Asimov, Isaac. *The Moon*. Chicago: Follet, 1966.					5	6	7		
3.	Branley, Franklyn M. *A Book of the Milky Way Galaxy for You*. New York: Thomas Y. Crowell, 1965.	1	2	3						9
4.	_____ . *The Nine Planets*. New York: Thomas Y. Crowell, 1972.	1	2	3	4					
5.	_____ . *What Makes Day and Night?* New York: Thomas Y. Crowell, 1961.									
6.	Carlisle, Norman. *Satellites: Servants of Man*. Philadelphia: Lippincott, 1971.				4	5	6			
7.	Crosby, Phoebe. *Junior Science Book of Stars*. Champaign, Ill.: Garrard, 1960.	1	2		4		6			
8.	Fenton, Carroll Lane. *The Moon for Young Explorers*. New York: John Day Co., 1963.									9
9.	Fenton, Carroll Lane, and Mildred Adams Fenton. *Worlds in the Sky*. New York: John Day Co., 1963.		2	3	4	5	6	7	8	
10.	Feravolo, Rocco. *Wonders Beyond the Solar System*. New York: Dodd, Mead and Co., 1968.	1	2	3	4				8	9
11.	Freeman, Mae, and Ira Freeman. *Fun with Astronomy: Easy Projects for Young Scientists*. New York: Random House, 1953.		2	3	4	5	6	7	8	
12.	Gallant, Roy A. *Exploring the Moon*. New York: Doubleday, 1966.	1				5	6	7		

* These numbers refer to the concepts on pp. 350–351.

Concepts

13. Jobb, Jamie. *The Night Sky — An Everyday Guide to Every Night*. Boston: Little, Brown and Co., 1977.   1 2 3 4 5 6 7 8 9

14. Knight, David C. *Let's Find Out About Earth*. New York: Franklin Watts, 1968.   1 2 3   5

15. Lum, Peter. *The Stars in Our Heaven: Myths and Fables*. New York: Pantheon Books, 1961.   1 2 3 4   9

16. Lyon, Jene. *Astronomy: Our Sun and Its Neighbors*. Racine, Wis.: Western Publishing Co., 1974.   1 2 3 4 5 6 7 8 9

17. Munch, Theodore W., and B. Tiedemann. *What Is a Solar System?* New York: Benefic Press, 1961.   2 3 4

18. Polgreen, John, and Cathleen Polgreen. *The Earth in Space*. New York: Random House, 1963.   2 3 4 5

19. Nussbaum, Hedda (ed.). *Charlie Brown's Second Super Book of Questions and Answers about the Earth and Space*. New York: Random House, 1977.   1 2 3 4 5 6 7 8 9

20. Rey, H. A. *Find the Constellations*. Boston: Houghton Mifflin, 1966.   2   4

21. *Stars and Planets — A Golden Stamp Book*, Racine, Wis.: Western Publishing Co., 1973.   1 2 3 4 5 6 7 8 9

22. Zim, Herbert S. *Comets*. New York: William Morrow and Co., 1957.   1   8 9

23. _____ . *The Sun*. New York: William Morrow and Co., 1975.   1 2   7   9

24. _____ . *The Universe*. New York: William Morrow and Co., 1961.   1 2 3   8 9

Textbooks

1. Gallant, Roy A., and Isaac Asimov. *Ginn Science Program: Intermediate Level A*. Lexington, Mass.: Ginn and Co., 1975, pp. 105–142.   1 2 3   6   9

Concepts

2. Jacobson, Willard. *Thinking Ahead in Science Series: Learning in Science.* New York: American Book Co., 1965, pp. 98–128.   5 6

*3. MacCraken, Helen D., et al. *Science Through Discovery.* Singer Science Series, New York: Random House, 1968, pp. 125–159.   1 2 3 4 5 6 7 8 9

4. Navarra, John, and Joseph Zafforoni. *Today's Basic Science.* New York: Harper & Row, 1967, pp. 88–125.   1 2 3 4 5 6   8 9

5. Rockcastle, Verna N., et al. *Elementary School Science.* Menlo Park, Cal.: Addison-Wesley Publishing Co., 1972, pp. 186–209.   2

Audio-Visual Materials

1. *Earth, Venus, and Mercury.* Jim Handy series, 1971. Filmstrip, intermediate, color.   2 3 4

2. *Eclipse of the Moon.* Film Association of California. Film loop, color.   7

3. *Eclipse of the Sun.* Film Association of California. Film loop, color.   7

4. *Mars.* Jim Handy series, 1971. Filmstrip, intermediate, color.   3 4

5. *Night and Day.* Encyclopaedia Britannica Films, 1955. Filmstrip, intermediate, color.   2

6. *Outer Planets.* Jim Handy series, 1971. Filmstrip, intermediate, color.   3 4

7. *The Earth and Its Moon.* Flannel Board Kit, intermediate.   5 6 7

8. *The Planets: Family of the Sun.* Included in *The Universe,* National Geographic Society, 1972. Filmstrip, cassette, and teacher's guide; advanced; color.   2 3 4   8 9

9. *What a Scientist Sees Through the Telescope.* Educational Reading Service, 1968. Filmstrip, intermediate, color.   1   9

* This is the major text. The others are to be used for advanced or slower study groups, and/or research on individualized projects.

INSTRUCTIONAL ACTIVITIES

Activities	Materials Used†	Concepts
*1. Unit planning with students.	tm	1 2 3 4 5 6 7 8 9 10
*2. Contracts for individual projects.	tm	1 2 3 4 5 6 7 8 9 10
*3. Preassessment survey.	tm	1 2 3 4 5 6 7 8 9
*4. Cloze test and small group discussion.	tm	1 2 3
*5. Structured overview through class discussion.	tm	1 2 3 4 5 6 7 8 9 10
6. Find out about man's early beliefs about the universe. Write a report, make a diorama, give a play, plan a bulletin board.	nf15, nf7, t1, t4	1
7. Look up information on instruments used by early astronomers. Illustrate and tell about the sextant, sundial, celestial sphere, dividers.	t1	1
*8. Read pp. 125–126, directed lesson.	t3	1 2 3
9. Discover about telescopes. Read pp. 93–100.	t4	1 9
10. Experiment with magnifying glass.	t4, nf10, nf11	1 9
*11. Use a telescope (community resource).	t4, 5, nf13, 20	2
12. Make and label models of telescopes.	t4, nf3, 11	1 9
13. Construct a time line for early discoveries in astronomy.	t1, 4, av9, tm	1

* required
† tm = teacher-made, nf = nonfiction, t = textbook, f = fiction

Activities	Materials Used	Concepts				
*14. Read and watch *What a Scientist Sees Through His Telescope*/reading guide.	tm, av9	1				9
15. How did these men contribute to today's understanding of the universe? Individualized project.	t1	1				9
*16. Read pp. 127–128, directed reading.	t3	2				
17. Activity: making a sun calendar.	t1, nf11	1 2				
*18. Read and do three-level reading guide on *Junior Science Book of Stars*.	nf7, tm	1 2	4	6		
19. Project: make a sun camera.	nf11	2				9
20. Experiment: air bends sunlight.	nf11, t5	2				9
*21. Make a model of the sun. Label it. Be able to explain it.	nf23, 3, 9, 16, 21	2 3				
22. Vocabulary: sun word hunt.	tm	2				
*23. read pp. 128–129, directed reading.	t3	2				
24. Structured overview for #25.	tm	2				9
25. Read pp. 186–207 in small group.	t5	2				9
26. Simulate the twinkling of stars.	t5, nf3, 10	2				
27. Make dioramas of the constellations.	t5, nf20, t3, nf13	1 2				10
28. Use a constellation map.	map, nf13, 20	2				9
29. Experiment with light.	t5	2				9

Activities	Materials Used	Concepts		
*30. Draw and label one (minimum) constellation for the bulletin board.	t3, 4, 5, map, nf13, 19, 20	2		
*31. Join in listening while teacher reads aloud *A Wrinkle in Time*.	f6			10
*32. Read pp. 129–132, directed reading.	t3		3 4	
33. Experiment: direct light/reflected light.	t5, 3	2		
*34. Demonstration: orbits of planets.	t3		3	
35. View filmstrip *Day and Night*.	av5	2		
*36. Read pp. 135–136, directed reading.	t3		3 4	
*37. Demonstration: Earth's rotation and revolution.				
38. Haiku: sun, stars, day, night.	tm, nf3, 9, 10, 15	1	3	10
*39. Read pp. 136–139.	t3		3 4	
*40. Learning center: a visit to the planets.	tm		3 4	9 10
41. View filmstrips on particular planet and/or *The Planets*.	av1, 4, 6, 8	1	3 4	
*42. Give an oral report on a planet of your choice.	av1, 4, 6, 8, t4, nf1, 4, 9, 11, 13, 15, 16, 17, 18, 19, 21, 24	1	3 4	9
*43. Using diagrams and tables, three-level guide.	tm		3 4	
*44. Read pp. 98–126, cassette available.	t2		5	9
*45. Word puzzle: satellites.	t11		5	

Activities	Materials Used	Concepts	
*46. Satellites: True or False?	t10	5	
47. Experiment on gravity.	t2, nf11	5	9
48. Make models of satellites: Tiros, Telestar, Pioneer, etc.	nf6	5	9
49. Experiment: paths of falling object.	t2	5	9
50. Experiment: weightlessness.	t2, nf2, 19	5	9
51. Experiment: friction.	t2	5	9
*52. Read pp. 141–142, directed reading.	t3	5 6	
53. Picture study/three-level guide.	tm	5 6	
54. Read pp. 13–17 and write about your walk on the moon. Try to make it as authentic as possible. Tape your story.	nf11, 8, 12, 2, 19, 18, 16, 21	5 6	9 10
55. Learn some legends and folklore about the moon.	nf15, t4		10
56. Find out about moon exploration.	nf2, 12, 16, 19, 21		9
57. Crossword puzzle: the moon.	tm	5 6 7	
58. Observe the moon. Look for seas and craters, different quarters, etc.	nf2, 12, 13, 16, field glasses	6	9
59. Record the times of moonrise.	newspaper nf2	6	
60. Draw a moon map. Locate places the U.S. has explored.	nf12, t4	1	9
*61. Listen to *Clair de Lune*. How did Debussy feel about the moon? Do you think moon explorations have changed the way	recording of "Clair de Lune"	1	9 10

Activities	Materials Used	Concepts		
people visualize the moon?				
*62. DRTA: phases of the moon.	tm, nf2	6		
63. Read pp. 143–144.	t3	6		
64. Read pp. 101–104.	t4	6		
*65. Demonstration: phases of the moon.	t4	6	9	
66. Use the flannel board to show the phases of the moon.	av7	6		
*67. Read pp. 145–146, directed lesson.	t3	7		
68. Watch film loop of lunar eclipse.	av2	7		
*69. Make a model of a lunar eclipse and label. Write a brief explanation.	may use av7, nf2, 19, 11, 21, 15	7		
*70. Read pp. 146–147, directed lesson.	t3	7		
71. Watch film loop of solar eclipse.	av3	7		
*72. Make a model of a solar eclipse and label. Write a brief explanation.	nf23, 19, 11, 21	7		
*73. Read pp. 148–150, directed lesson.	t3	1	8 9	
*74. Categories worksheet: comets, meteoroids, and asteroids.	tm	1	8 9	
*75. Comets: cause and effect.	tm	1	8 9	
*76. Read at least two science fiction works.	f1, 2, 3, 4, 5, 7, 8, 9, 10, 11, 12, 13			10
*77. Post-survey (can use as study device for test).	tm	1 2 3 4 5 6 7 8 9 10		
*78. Final evaluation.	tm	1 2 3 4 5 6 7 8 9 10		

Activity 3 *

SURVEY — BEFORE AND AFTER UNIT

This is not a test! Some of the information here may be totally new for you. However, you may know much more than you think! Place a *T* for true or an *F* for false in front of each statement. If you have no idea what the answer is put a ? in front of the statement.

___ 1. Astronomy is the scientific study of the universe beyond Earth.

___ 2. The science is brand new. It was just developed during the last 50 years.

___ 3. Revolve means to orbit around a central point or spot.

___ 4. The sun is a planet.

___ 5. Stars are made up of hot gases and give off light and heat.

___ 6. The earth is at the center of the solar system.

___ 7. The solar system is a group of planets that revolve around the sun.

___ 8. There are 7 planets in our solar system.

(continued at the top of the next page)

Activity 5

STRUCTURED OVERVIEW OF OUR SOLAR SYSTEM:

Part A

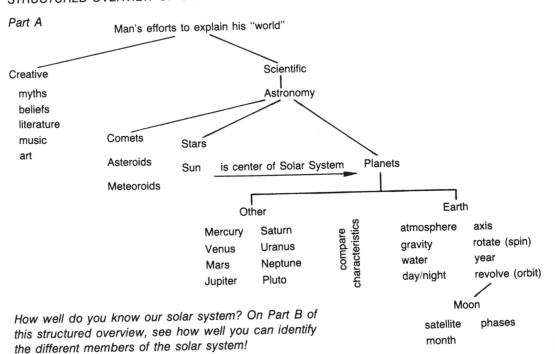

How well do you know our solar system? On Part B of this structured overview, see how well you can identify the different members of the solar system!

(continued on the bottom of the next page)

* The following are sample activities and therefore not necessarily numbered consecutively.

— 9. All the planets are very much alike.

— 10. A satellite is something that revolves around a planet.

— 11. All satellites are made by man.

— 12. The moon does not reflect the sun's light.

— 13. Earth is the only planet that has a moon.

— 14. The moon goes through 8 phases each year.

— 15. The spinning of the earth causes day and night.

— 16. The earth takes one year to travel around the sun.

— 17. When the earth casts a shadow on the moon, we call this a comet.

— 18. A meteor is a piece of metal or stone traveling through space.

— 19. Scientists use facts that they know are true to try to explain things, to make "educated guesses," about things we do not really know for sure.

— 20. Everything you read about space and the universe is true.

When everyone has finished, we will discuss the statements and our answers.

Activity 5

Part B

Identify the members of the solar system and write their names correctly on the lines.

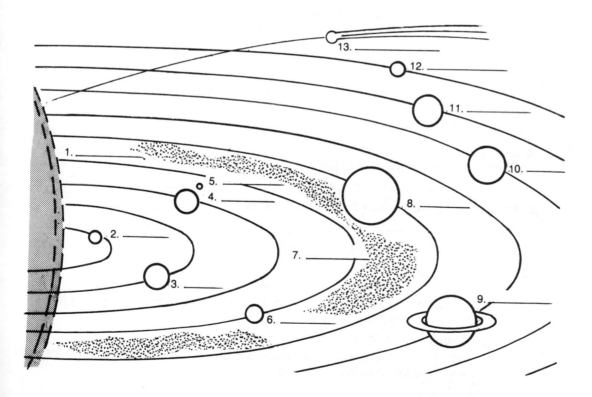

Activity 13

EARLY DISCOVERIES IN ASTRONOMY

Directions: To help you understand the development of astronomy as a science, list the order that the following events occurred. For extra credit, you may include the year the event happened. Check your answers in *Today's Basic Science* or the *Ginn Science Program* book.

_____ The Egyptians made a sun calendar.

_____ Nicholas Copernicus was a Polish astronomer. He introduced the theory that the sun was the center of the universe.

_____ When Galileo improved and perfected the telescope, a new era in astronomy began.

_____ Ancient people had only their eyes with which to study the stars. They had many beliefs about the heavens, but no real evidence for their beliefs.

_____ Tycho Brahe was an astronomer who lived in Denmark. He made the most accurate measurements of the changing positions of the moon and planets known to the world at that time.

_____ The Sumerians used mathematics in their study of the sky. They made accurate records of the changing positions of the stars, sun, and planets. This helped astronomy become a science.

_____ Johannes Kepler was a German mathematician and astronomer. He used Tycho Brahe's careful records to figure the first scale model of the solar system.

_____ As more powerful telescopes were developed, discovery after discovery was made, right up to the present day!

_____ Claudius Ptolemy was a Greek astronomer who lived in Alexandria, Egypt. He believed that the earth was the center of the whole universe. The sun, moon, and planets moved around the earth.

Activity 14

THREE-LEVEL STUDY GUIDE

What a Scientist Sees Through His Telescope

I. Answer all three questions.
   1. Name three famous inventors of the telescope. _____

   _____

   2. List three things Galileo saw through his telescope. _____

   _____

   3. Who first used lenses to make a telescope? _____

II. Check the statements that are true.
   _____ 1. Galileo's use of the telescope was for peaceful purposes.

   _____ 2. Most of what we know about space today would have been known even if the telescope had not been invented.

   _____ 3. Lippenshiem was trying to invent a telescope.

   _____ 4. Marco Polo's discovery of glass lenses used by the Chinese was important for the invention of the telescope.

III. Check the statements that tell what *What a Scientist Sees Through His Telescope* is about.
    ———— 1. A new scientific discovery is often dependent on another earlier discovery.
    ———— 2. Men can use their knowledge to learn more about their world.
    ———— 3. Galileo started a new era in astronomy.
    ———— 4. Astronomy has a long history.

Activity 38

HAIKU

Sun, Stars, Day, Night

Writing a poem is a fun way to express and share not only what you have learned, but also what you thought and felt about those things. An easy and interesting way to write a poem is to use the Japanese haiku (said HI koo). The purpose of haiku is to present a single thought or observation about nature. Try writing a haiku about the sun, stars, day, and/or night. Choose just one for starters. Then you may want to try others. Haiku must follow a special pattern:

Line One = 5 syllables

Line Two = 7 syllables

Line Three = 5 syllables

That's it!

Brainstorm with two or three friends to make a list of words and ideas for a topic you have chosen. Then use these words and phrases to write your own haiku. Share your haiku with the teacher or a friend. Ask for help if you get stuck. After sharing with the teacher, you may want to paint a watercolor to go with your poem. Also, you may want to display it on the bulletin board.

Activity 45

WORD PUZZLE

Directions: Answer the clues by filling in the appropriate spaces. When you have filled in all the blanks, the circled letters will spell the mystery word.

1. ⭕ _ _ _ _ _ _ _
2. ⭕ _ _ _ _ _ _
3. _ _ _ _ ⭕
4. _ ⭕ _ _ _ _ _ _ _ _ _ _
5. ⭕ _ _ _ _ _
6. _ _ _ _ _ ⭕
7. _ _ _ _ _ ⭕ _ _ _ _ _
8. _ _ _ _ ⭕ _ _ _
9. _ _ ⭕ _ _ _ _
10. _ _ _ _ ⭕

1. Radio and television _____ are sent great distances around the earth by satellites.
2. The point in an orbit that is farthest from Earth.
3. Paths in which satellites travel around larger objects.
4. Name for things fired to push a satellite in the opposite direction and slow it down.
5. To push, especially a rocket.
6. To go from one place to another.
7. A force that tends to pull all things together.
8. When a moving object rubs against something and causes it to slow down and/or get hot.
9. Speed.
10. Natural satellites are sometimes called _____ .

Activity 46

SATELLITES

Directions: Determine whether the following statements are true or false. Mark *T* or *F* accordingly in the margins.

_____ 1. Gravity holds satellites in their orbits.
_____ 2. Moons are natural satellites.
_____ 3. You can see earth satellites in the daytime.
_____ 4. All orbits of satellites are shaped ike perfect circles.
_____ 5. Satellites orbit at different speeds at different times.
_____ 6. A satellite moves at a slower speed as it moves toward the earth.
_____ 7. Three-stage rockets are used to put satellites into orbit.
_____ 8. Rockets give satellites a push straight up into space.
_____ 9. Satellites must travel at a speed of approximately 18,000 miles per hour to stay in orbit.
_____ 10. A satellite stays in orbit for only a few days, or a month at the longest.

Now, look over the statements you marked false. Use the space below to rewrite them to make them true. You may check your work by referring back to the book.

_____
_____
_____
_____
_____
_____
_____
_____

Activity 74

COMETS, OR METEOROIDS, OR ASTEROIDS?

Directions: Examine the following phrases and decide whether they describe comets, meteoroids, or asteroids. Write which object the phrase describes in the margin blank. Think carefully, especially in marking one item that seems to apply to all three!

—————————— 1. It is a piece of metal or stone.

—————————— 2. A famous one was named after an English astronomer, Edmund Halley.

—————————— 3. Earth's atmosphere protects it from being hit constantly by them.

—————————— 4. They are located between Mars and Jupiter.

—————————— 5. They usually fall to Earth as fine dust.

—————————— 6. Some are the size of tiny pebbles.

—————————— 7. Their orbits are egg-shaped.

—————————— 8. The first one was discovered in 1801.

—————————— 9. The largest one is named Ceres.

—————————— 10. They revolve around the sun.

—————————— 11. They look like a star with streaming tails.

—————————— 12. They are seen more in August and November.

—————————— 13. Most have diameters of less than fifty miles.

—————————— 14. They are sometimes called "shooting stars."

—————————— 15. No one completely understands what they are made of.

—————————— 16. Friction causes their surfaces to get hot, melt, and turn into glowing gases.

—————————— 17. They are so far away that they can't be seen with a telescope.

—————————— 18. They are considered minor planets.

—————————— 19. People used to fear them.

—————————— 20. They are pulled toward the earth when they come close.

Activity 75

COMETS

Cause and Effect

Match the effects in Part II with the causes listed in Part I.

Part 1: Cause

—— a. In 1910, Halley's comet came very close to Earth so that

—— b. Most comets are so far away

—— c. When a comet moves toward the sun

—— d. By making observations and using early scientific records

Part II: Effect

1. the comet's glowing tail is formed.

2. ices in the head of the comet turn into gases.

3. now people are not afraid of comets.

4. astronomers were able to learn a great deal about comets.

___ e. People thought if a comet came too close it would explode and destroy Earth;

___ f. The earth has passed through the tail of a comet and was not harmed;

___ g. The gases move away from the head of the comet

5. People were afraid of comets.

6. they cannot be seen, even with the aid of a telescope.

7. Edmund Halley correctly predicted the return of a comet.

Survival

Teacher: SHEILA PECKHAM
Subject: LITERATURE
Grade: ELEVEN

This literature unit combines an in-depth class study of a modern American novel, *One Flew Over the Cuckoo's Nest,* with team study of novels whose themes are similar to *One Flew Over the Cuckoo's Nest,* and individual inquiry of themes, topics or issues evolving from class and team study. The lessons move from teacher-centered presentations in the class study to student-centered small group interactions, to individual research projects. Because of the nature of this unit, the teacher uses a content outline to organize learning experiences rather than a system of cross-tabulating concepts, activities, and materials.

CONTENT OUTLINE

I. Major Topics of Study

A. Conflict
   1. man vs. man
   2. man vs. society
   3. man vs. nature
   4. man vs. self

B. Themes
   1. emasculation
   2. alienation
   3. control
   4. dehumanization

SURVIVAL UNIT SCHEDULE

One Flew Over the Cuckoo's Nest

	M	T	W	Th	F
Week 1	Informal preassessment	Prereading activity on metaphor and imagery	Vocabulary Prediction activity for first assignment Assign 1–41 Read aloud	Postreading discussion of prediction activity Guide on imagery and literal statements Vocabulary	Level guide Discussion
Week 2	Prereading vocabulary Prereading guide on emasculation motif Assign 42–91	Postreading activity on emasculation motif: discussion of responses generated from students' lists	Continued discussion Assign 91–115	Postreading array activity: Conflict Make bulletin board (array)	Prereading vocabulary Assign 116–144
Week 3	Rearrange array on bulletin board Three-level guides	Discussion Prereading vocabulary Assign 145–173	Postreading activity: cause/effect guide	Discussion Prereading activity on Christ imagery Assign 174–218	Postreading activity: Christ motif guide
Week 4	Discussion continued using responses from Christ motif guide Assign rest of the novel	Discussion: pull together major themes previously presented	Review activity: poem	Postreading assessment	(composition)

Team Study of 4 Novels

	M	T	W	Th	F
Week 5	Introduction of 4 novels and of team strategy and format Give class schedules Choose books Distribute guides	Reading period	Discussion I Group A Group B (teacher works with each group ½ period)	Discussion I Group C Group D	Reading period

        5. civil disobedience
        6. the Christ figure

   C. Literary Devices
        1. imagery
        2. foreshadowing
        3. motifs
        4. metaphor

II. Reading Materials

   A. Class study: Ken Kesey's *One Flew Over the Cuckoo's Nest*
   B. Group study
        1. Glendon Swarthout's *Bless the Beasts and the Children*
        2. Conrad Richtner's *The Light in the Forest*
        3. James Dickey's *Deliverance*
        4. James Dickey's *First Blood*

III. Instructional Activities

   A. Teacher-prepared adjunct materials for *One Flew Over the Cuckoo's Nest*
        1. structured overview for unit
        2. assessment of students' existing knowledge and attitudes
        3. prereading guide: the uses of metaphor
        4. vocabulary awareness activity: acutes vs. chronics
        5. anticipation guide: mental institutions
        6. reading guide on imagery
        7. interpretive/applied guide
        8. vocabulary awareness: bedlam, berserk, pandemonium, eccentric
        9. vocabulary building: matriarchy, emasculation
       10. prereading guide: masculinity vs. femininity
       11. array depicting conflict between McMurphy and Big Nurse
       12. three-level reading guide
       13. vocabulary building: alienation, technocracy, foreshadow, microcosm
       14. pattern guide: cause and effect
       15. prereading guide: the Savior theme
       16. postreading guide: the Savior theme
       17. review of major themes
       18. assessment of students' understandings
   B. Team study of four novels: general reading guide
   C. Individual projects

Week 6	Discussion II Group A Group B	Discussion II Group C Group D	Reading period	Discussion III Group A Group B	Discussion III Group C Group D
Week 7	Feedback session on each group's novel: Group A Group B	Feedback session Group C Group D	Tie together loose ends: synthesis of all five novels	Introduce individual inquiry ⟶ projects	

STRUCTURED OVERVIEW OF UNIT

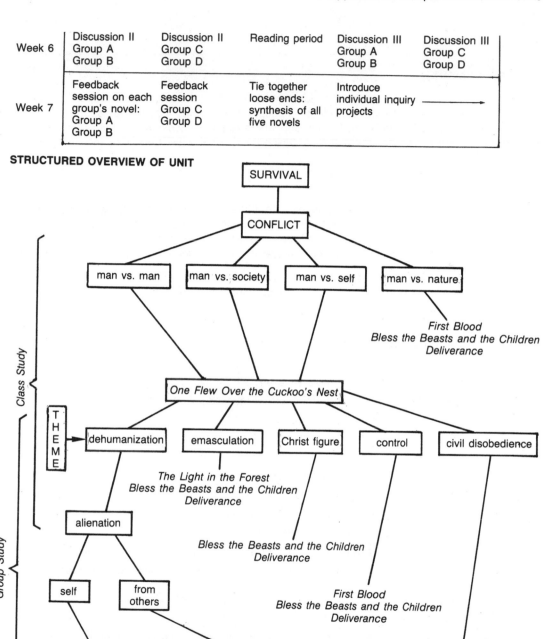

Activity 2

PREASSESSMENT

Purpose: This level guide is designed to function as an informal inventory of students' present understandings of some of the major ideas, concepts, and themes they will encounter throughout the literature unit. Through small group and whole class discussions and reactions, the teacher can informally assess the degree to which these ideas have been thought out by the students.

A. Individual

Directions: Read each of the following statements. Place a check on the numbered line next to those statements you would be willing to defend. Try to think of specific examples you would use to defend those statements you agree with or to refute those statements you disagree with. This is not a quiz or a test. These statements are some of the ideas we will be discussing in the next few weeks.

_____ 1. There is no insanity; only behavior the majority won't tolerate.

_____ 2. A world with risks and choices and pain is worth more than a world of protection and safety.

_____ 3. A person can be alienated from himself.

_____ 4. It is never right to break a law.

_____ 5. It is society that decides who's sane and who isn't.

_____ 6. Power is the sum total of the strength of those dominated.

_____ 7. Modern technocracy softens men.

_____ 8. The majority is usually right.

_____ 9. Most men are sheep.

_____ 10. Every man is responsible for whatever happens to him.

_____ 11. Man creates his own gods and demons to suit his needs.

_____ 12. Violence is an acceptable strategy for change.

_____ 13. Most people dislike what is different.

_____ 14. The difference between right and wrong is largely a matter of point of view.

_____ 15. Few people are really capable of independence; most people seek a leader to follow.

B. Small group

Directions: In your small group, discuss those statements with which you disagree. Try to use concrete examples to convince others of your conclusions.

Activity 3

PREREADING GUIDE

Purpose: This activity is designed to lead students, through the use of metaphor, to understand that reality often exists on other levels than the plane of objective or literal occurrence. This prereading "organizer" is necessary to help students recognize the significance of the recurring mechanical images and motifs essential to their understanding of the first reading assignment in *One Flew Over the Cuckoo's Nest,* as well as of the entire novel.

Procedure: Put the following statements on the board.

Our school is a factory.
It is run by robots.
The student is the product being produced.
The student is being manufactured to fit into a bigger machine.

Divide the class into small groups. Instruct each group to list examples of the daily routine that support or refute the given statements.

Examples:
Everyone is regulated by bells.
Teachers sometimes have no sympathy.
Everyone is expected to do the same things well.

Resume a large group and list the examples the students give. During discussion of their metaphors, introduce Chief Broom's statement:

"It's the truth even if it didn't happen." (p. 13)

Have students react to the statement. Students can use the previous discussion or give other examples to evaluate the credibility of Broom's statement.

Activity 5

ANTICIPATION GUIDE

Purpose: Motivation

Procedure: Introduce the novel *One Flew Over the Cuckoo's Nest* by telling the students it is about a mental institution. Then distribute the following anticipation guide:

Directions: Read the following statements and place a check next to those you believe you'll find to be true in the novel.

_____ 1. Mental hospitals have eliminated all old-fashioned cruelty.

_____ 2. The intention of the therapy is to allow the patients to remain as much a part of their own democratic, free neighborhood as possible.

_____ 3. The inmates are no crazier than anyone on the street.

_____ 4. It is society that decides who is sane and who is not.

_____ 5. The staff is just as interested in the patients' cures as the patients are.

_____ 6. A healthy, sane individual is one who can stand up for his or her own beliefs and rights.

     After a class comparison of prediction statements, assign pages 1–41.

Postreading activity: Reexamine the prediction statements in small groups. Students should be instructed to reevaluate the statements in light of the first reading assignment, and to extract specific examples from the reading to back up their opinions on the statements.

Activity 7

INTERPRETIVE/APPLIED LEVEL GUIDE

Directions, Part A: McMurphy tells Harding, "Nurse Ratchet is trying to make you weak so she can get you to toe the line, and to follow her rules, to live like she wants you to. And the best way she does this, to get you to knuckle under is to weaken you by gettin' you where it hurts worst . . . to sap every bit of strength you got." (57)

Harding tells McMurphy, "Miss Ratchet is a sweet, smiling angel of mercy . . . unselfish as the wind, toiling thanklessly for the good of all . . . and desires our cures as much as we do." (56–58)

Below are some ward procedures and events. Put an *Mc* next to those descriptors which support McMurphy's theory. Put an *H* next to those which support Harding's theory. Use the page numbers given to refer to these procedures and events in context. Work through these together in your group.

_____ 1. the cooperative trophies awarded to the floor (22)

_____ 2. the use of the log book (19)

_____ 3. the therapeutic group session (43)

_____ 4. the orderly time schedule (32–34)

_____ 5. Miss Ratchet's screening procedure for hiring aids (44)

_____ 6. keeping the chronics and acutes separate (36)

_____ 7. Miss Ratchet's charitable deeds on the outside (38)

_____ 8. the staff's gentle coaxing behavior toward the patients (35)

_____ 9. Maxwell Taber's therapeutic treatment (40)

_____ 10. ward rules (28)

_____ 11. Chief Broom's therapeutic treatment (40)

Directions, Part B: Read each of the following statements aloud in your group. Decide whether each can be supported with information from the novel. Consider your discussion of the events in Part A. Put the numbers of those events from Part A which support the statements in Part B in the proper blanks.

_____ 1. The patients are proud of their record for cooperation.

_____ 2. The nurse maintains control by the dictum "divide and conquer."

_____ 3. By confiding their fears to fellow inmates, the patients will gain strength.

_____ 4. The Combine is a conspiracy to regiment the patients' lives, to control them through a hypnotic routine.

_____ 5. The log book is a means to destroy any individuality.

_____ 6. The men serve the "machine," not the reverse.

_____ 7. Nurse Ratchet's biggest fear is that a new admission will destroy her power.

_____ 8. Nurse Ratchet uses fear and hatred to maintain control.

_____ 9. Nurse Ratchet instills feelings of guilt.

_____ 10. Miss Ratchet's charitable deeds destroy the self-esteem of the receiver.

Directions, Part C: Read each of the following statements aloud. Check each statement that you find reasonable and can support by combining ideas contained in the reading selection with your own related ideas and experiences. Be ready to present evidence from both sources to support your decisions.

_____ 1. To the establishment, cooperation with authority is of highest value.

_____ 2. Self-control is a measure of sanity.

_____ 3. The world belongs to the strong. One must accept this as a law of the natural world.

_____ 4. The strong get stronger by making the weak weaker.

_____ 5. It is often painful to admit the truth. It is easier to believe what you want to believe.

Activity 11

ARRAY DEPICTING CONFLICT BETWEEN MCMURPHY AND BIG NURSE

Purpose: At this point the major conflict of the novel has surfaced. Through a visual display of the conflict between Big Nurse and McMurphy and the ideas each character represents, students should be able to see the general movements of the plot as well as the forces at conflict throughout the novel. When students finish constructing the array, it can be posted on a bulletin board and modified throughout the unit.

Directions: Examine the packet of cards in your small groups. Arrange and rearrange the cards into what you agree is a logical display of the story thus far.

conflict	emasculation
McMurphy	laissez-faire
individuality	order and regimentation
conformity	the pioneer
authority	confession
Big Nurse	Chief Broom
Combine	Cheswick
group over individual	Harding
masculinity	Billy Bibbit
femininity	

Students should work in small groups as they develop reasonable descriptions of the relationships between the above elements.

In the large group, compare and discuss arrays. The class should agree upon an array to display on the bulletin board. Throughout the rest of the unit, cards can be arranged according to the plot development, and new cards can be added.

An example of a possible starting array is shown on the next page.

This activity should help students see how ideas as well as people are at conflict.

As students add the names of some of the other major characters to the array, interesting debates may develop in that some of the characters may clearly side with McMurphy but remain under the authority of Big Nurse. Their loyalties will fluctuate throughout the novel. Other students may want to arrange characters' names according to some concepts other than *loyalty*

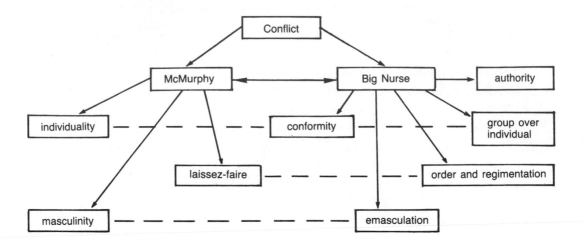

to the two major characters. For example, Harding could be included under *emasculation,* and Chief Broom with *order and regimentation.*

From this point on, a major portion of the novel is fueled by a series of small scale battles between Nurse and McMurphy. Cards should be constructed representing each conflict. Students, through debate, are to decide who was the victor over each issue and place cards appropriately. This should lend itself to much debate because in many cases it may appear that one character is winning the battle, but losing the war.

Activity 13

VOCABULARY BUILDING

1. alienation

Use structural analysis. Students may recognize *alien.*

> *alien:* foreign
> *-ation:* abstract noun ending

Various forms and uses of *alienation* should be discussed (alienation from other, from self, etc.). Use examples from the book. (Chief Broom felt so alienated from society that he stopped talking. Characters who have lost their own will and identity in the novel are self-alienated.)

2. technocracy: management of society by technical experts

Students should recognize the suffix *-cracy* from words such as democracy and autocracy. After establishing that *-cracy* means rule, elicit such meanings for *techno-* as built, craft.

Use the context of the Combine from the novel to build an understanding of a technocracy and manifestations of it.

3. foreshadow: to represent; to typify beforehand

Upon examination of the word's parts, students may be led to see that this word practically defines itself. *Fore-* means ahead; a *shadow* is a representation or image.

Use examples from the novel of foreshadowing in literature:

The story of Uncle Holligan in the first assignment foreshadows McMurphy's treatment of Big Nurse. Ruckley's treatment for rebelling foreshadows McMurphy's treatment.

4. *microcosm*

micro-: little
-cosm: world

Again, start with the meanings the students already attach to this word's parts. They will most likely recognize *micro-* from microscope, etc. They should recognize *-cosm* from cosmos. If they don't, give them the words microscope and cosmos to help them infer the meaning of the word.

Put the word in the context of the novel. One of Kesey's points is that the Ward is a microcosm for the outside society.

Elicit examples from the novel.

Activity 14

PATTERN GUIDE: CAUSE AND EFFECT (pp. 145–173)

Directions, Part A: McMurphy goes through two reversals in this episode. For each change, chart reasons why he changes and the effects of his changes. Choose from the list below. Many are used more than once. For example, an effect of one change can be a cause of another.

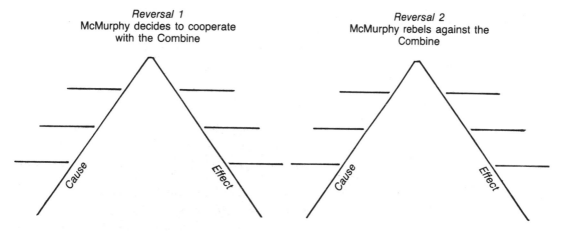

Reversal 1
McMurphy decides to cooperate with the Combine

Reversal 2
McMurphy rebels against the Combine

Cause   Effect   Cause   Effect

Choose from the following events:

1. McMurphy learns that the other inmates have committed themselves.
2. The lifeguard tells McMurphy that committed inmates can be kept in the institution as long as the institution sees fit.
3. McMurphy refuses to help Harding stand up the hydrocephalic patient.
4. Cheswick kills himself.

5. McMurphy scrubs the halls to please the nurse.

6. McMurphy witnesses the shock room.

7. The control panel is adjusted and running smoothly.

8. Big Nurse takes away the tub room privileges.

9. McMurphy breaks through Big Nurse's glass enclosure.

10. The fog thickens around Chief Broom once again.

11. The fog clears from around Chief Broom.

12. McMurphy dreams of faces.

Activity 18

POSTREADING ASSESSMENT

Directions: List I contains some statements that could be reasonable interpretations of the novel *One Flew Over the Cuckoo's Nest.* Read each statement carefully. If you think it is a valid point about the novel, put a *T* in the first numbered space. Then find actual events from the novel in List II which lend support to the statement. Put the number(s) of those events from List II in the second numbered space next to the statement in List I which support that statement. If you believe a statement in List I is not valid, leave the first blank empty, but provide numbers of events from List II in the second blank which support your rejection of the List I statement.

Example, List I: ___T___ ___1,3___ 1. John is married.

List II: 1. John is wearing a wedding band.
2. John likes to hunt.
3. John has a joint checking account.

List I:

_____ _____ 1. The major conflict of *Cuckoo's Nest* is between self-interest and self-sacrifice.

_____ _____ 2. The inmates are victims of a matriarchy.

_____ _____ 3. Influenced by McMurphy, Harding grows decisive and insightful.

_____ _____ 4. Ellis, frozen in crucifixion against the Ward wall, is a live warning to McMurphy and foreshadows his fate.

_____ _____ 5. McMurphy resurrects Billy Bibbit.

_____ _____ 6. Big Nurse is victorious over McMurphy at the end of the novel.

_____ _____ 7. Billy Bibbit plays the role of Judas in this novel.

_____ _____ 8. The inmates will return to their submissive existences with McMurphy's death.

_____ _____ 9. McMurphy's spirit is alive after his death.

_____ _____ 10. McMurphy reveals Nurse's humanness and vulnerability before he dies.

_____ _____ 11. Broom's murder of McMurphy is an act of love.

_____ _____ 12. McMurphy's death is a victory over the Combine.

_____ _____ 13. McMurphy's life is an allegory for the life of Christ.

_____ _____ 14. Broom's battle for sanity and manhood is fought through his surrogate, McMurphy.

_____ _____ 15. At the close of the novel, McMurphy and Broom are morally superior to the other inhabitants of the novel and to their earlier representations.

_____ _____ 16. Broom chooses pain over safety.

_____ _____ 17. McMurphy's tragic flaw is his pride in his own abilities.

_____ _____ 18. McMurphy's tragic flaw is his compassion.

_____ _____ 19. The asylum is a microcosm for the world.

_____ _____ 20. McMurphy is responsible for Billy's suicide.

List II:

1. The men think McMurphy's body, after the lobotomy, is not his but a dummy of him.
2. Harding runs the gambling tables after McMurphy's lobotomy.
3. McMurphy waits for Billy rather than escaping while the time is opportune.
4. Chief Broom kills McMurphy.
5. McMurphy organizes a basketball team and coaches the inmates.
6. McMurphy organizes the game area in the tub room.
7. McMurphy smashes Nurse's glass enclosure after he talks to the lifeguard.
8. Nurse Ratchet threatens to tell Billy's mother about his affair with Candy.
9. The lifeguard warns McMurphy that he cannot release himself.
10. Big Nurse refuses to release McMurphy to another ward.
11. McMurphy refuses to help Cheswick defy Big Nurse.
12. Ellis is destroyed by shock treatment.
13. Broom's fog gradually subsides as the novel progresses.
14. McMurphy unsuccessfully tries to lift the control panel.
15. McMurphy convinces George to go on the fishing trip.
16. Chief Broom's father took his wife's name.
17. George tells McMurphy to be a fisher of men.
18. McMurphy attacks Washington in the shower to defend George.
19. Broom's family sold their land to the white man.
20. Chief throws the control panel through the window to escape from the institution.
21. Billy tells Nurse Ratchet that McMurphy forced him to sleep with Candy.
22. Harding leaves the institution at the end.
23. McMurphy rips open Big Nurse's dress when he attacks her.

List III:

Directions: Listed below are statements which may relate in some way to the novel. Place a plus sign before each statement you believe expresses an idea that is implicitly or explicitly supported by the novel. Place a zero before any statement you believe is not supported by the novel. Below each statement, briefly cite specific examples from the novel to back your conclusion.

_____ 1. Even when there is no hope of victory in terms of the score, if one undertakes an obligation to play against towering odds, he will earn a moral victory — a victory over himself.

_____ 2. A world of pain is better than a world of safety and protection.

_____ 3. We must look beyond the surface when we measure a man.

_____ 4. Violence is an acceptable strategy for change.

_____ 5. Most men exercise little control over their fates.

_____ 6. Men cannot be led to real self-sufficiency; they will always turn to leaders.

_____ 7. When you lose your laugh, you lose your footing, your grasp on life.

_____ 8. Bravado and courage are sources of power.

_____ 9. Modern technocracy holds men in bondage, unawares.

_____ 10. Modern society emasculates modern man.

_____ 11. The American Indian culture was emasculated by the white culture.

Activity 20

PLAN FOR TEAM STUDY OF FOUR NOVELS

Introduction

Introduce *Bless the Beasts and the Children*, *The Light in the Forest*, *First Blood* and *Deliverance*. Each student should select one of the four novels to read. Explain to the class that they will be working in groups, each group being composed of students reading the same novel. Group work will include finding parallels with the themes studied in *One Flew Over the Cuckoo's Nest*.

Give students a schedule of group discussions with the teacher. A general reading guide for all four novels should be distributed. Divide the reading of each novel into three sections for the purpose of group discussion. Assign the first section for the first discussion day, as scheduled.

Group discussions

The schedule allows the teacher three one-half hour sessions with each group, each session after students have read the one-third section assigned. During discussion days, other students can read in class. Those who finish early can begin individual reading on projects when their group isn't meeting.

Reading guide for group work

The following questions can be assigned for group discussion. Some groups will need more guidance and direction from the teacher than others. The teacher can monitor both the use of this guide and its requirements through interaction in the group discussions.

1. In what ways does the author expect us to generalize about the central character(s)?
   a. Who is (are) the central character(s)?
   b. What of importance happens to the central character(s)?
   c. Is it probable that the author wants the reader to extend these central events to all men or to every man in such a situation?
   d. Is the work mainly about the character's development or his deterioration?
   e. What is significant about physical appearance? social status?
   f. What are characteristics of his thought, speech, and action?
   g. What are the character's beliefs and convictions?
   h. Does the author seem favorable, critical, or noncommittal toward the character in question?
2. Who are the secondary characters? What are their chief traits? Are they developed characters or stereotyped ideas?
3. What conflicts constitute the main action of the story?
   Consider:
   a. external conflicts:
      man vs. man
      man vs. nature
      man vs. society
   b. internal conflicts:
      man vs. himself
4. Are the conflicts resolved in the work?
5. Give a summary of the plot. Divide the material to indicate the growth and release of tension according to the following graph:

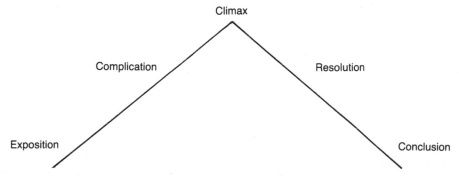

6. What are the various forces that account for the rising action, the turning point, and the climax?
7. Are there significant contrasts in the work between incidents in the plot? between characters? between moods?
8. What is the major theme of the work? Express this in a declarative statement. Theme is the author's judgment about or attitude toward his subject matter. Any expression of theme is correct that can justify itself from evidence in the work. Think of theme as the author's intention that guided him in writing the novel. Consider themes we found in *Cuckoo's Nest*.
9. Does the theme in any way contradict your basic beliefs and convictions about man and the world? Does the theme strengthen your beliefs?
10. How is the setting integrated with the theme? What are the details of the setting?
    Consider:
    historical period, season, etc.

nation, city, or section of the nation
social class and occupation of the characters
mood and atmosphere (e.g., tense, gloomy)

11. What incidents could have happened only in this particular setting? What could have happened at any time or place?

12. Does the environment in the setting bring social, economic, political, or religious pressures to bear on the lives of the characters?

13. How does the author's use of figurative language and symbols affect the development of the theme?

14. How does the author use foreshadowing and suspense to grip the reader and urge him on to future moments in the story?

Activity 21

INDIVIDUAL PROJECTS

A list of suggested readings and projects can be a starting point for individual work. Students may design their own projects after their own ideas and interests. The teacher should, as in the small group study, help steer students to reading selections and research sources that are appropriate to their abilities and interests.

Suggestions may include:

1. reading one of the four novels from small group study.

2. pursuing the question of civil disobedience.
   Suggested readings:
   Thoreau's *Walden* or "On Civil Disobedience"
   Shaw's *Saint Joan*
   Sophocles' *Antigone*
   collected speeches of Martin Luther King, Jr.

3. pursuing the parable as a literary form.
   Suggested readings:
   Steinbeck's *The Pearl*
   selections from the *Bible*

4. pursuing the theme of control.
   Suggested readings:
   Steinbeck's *The Pearl*
   Steinbeck's *The Moon Is Down*
   Orwell's *1984*

5. pursuing the theme of alienation.
   Suggested reading:
   Salinger's *The Catcher in the Rye*

6. pursuing the question of the American Indians versus the white culture.
   Suggested readings:
   Bury My Heart at Wounded Knee
   Little Big Man
   When the Legends Die
   Chief Joseph of the Nez Percé

7. researching the treatment of patients in a mental institution — the questions of lobotomy, legal commitment, shock treatment.

8. reading literature dealing with the conflict man versus nature.
   Suggested readings:
   Jack London's works
   Crane's "The Open Boat"

9. selecting their own literature that is relevant to the survival unit themes.

Credits continued from page iv.

Chapter 3

Henry Coe, department chairperson for social studies in the Middle Schools, Durham, Connecticut, structured overview on propaganda, p. 65, and dictionary exercise, "How Do You Say It?," p. 80.

Ann Russo, business teacher, Coginchaug Regional High School, Durham, Connecticut, structured overview on data processing, p. 67.

Nancy Fishell, art teacher, Coginchaug Regional High School, Durham, Connecticut, structured overview on firing process, p. 67.

William Healy, science department chairperson, Coginchaug Regional High School, Durham, Connecticut, structured overview on human digestion, p. 69.

Chapter 4

Virginia Sazama, junior high school social studies teacher, Connecticut, prereading activity on Massachusetts settlers, p. 97.

Karen Duhig, reading specialist, Deerfield High School, Deerfield, Illinois, prereading activity on "Alas Babylon," p. 98.

Richard McManus, auto mechanics teacher, Coginchaug Regional High School, Durham, Connecticut, prereading activity on clutch situations, p. 99.

Susan Mortensen, high school English teacher, attitude inventory on crime, p. 100.

Robert Ranieri, English and reading specialist, Wheeling High School, Wheeling, Illinois, anticipation guide for Harris column, p. 105.

Mary Lou Getchman, Huntley Middle School, DeKalb, Illinois, anticipation guide on common soldier of Civil War, p. 108.

Chapter 5

Terry Gatlin, reading specialist, Allan D. Shepherd High School, Palos Heights, Illinois, three-level guide on E. E. Cumming's poem, p. 127.

Ray Zeima, English teacher, Peacock Junior High School, Itaska, Illinois, three-level guides on *Flowers for Algernon,* p. 128.

Donald Burzler, doctoral student, University of Connecticut, three-level guide for a mathematical word problem, p. 131.

Darrell Hohmquist, teacher of history and reading, Lincoln Way High School, New Lenox, Illinois, three-level guide on building first cities, p. 133.

Teresa Gaziano, sixth grade teacher, Thompson Elementary School, Rockford, Illinois, three-level guide on growing up, p. 134.

Karen Duhig, reading specialist, Deerfield High School, Deerfield, Illinois, three-level guide on diffusion through a membrane, p. 135.

Rafael Garcia, Jr., Spanish teacher, Coginchaug Regional High School, Durham, Connecticut, three-level guide on "Un Collegio," p. 137.

Chapter 6

Richard McManus, auto mechanics teacher, Coginchaug Regional High School, Durham, Connecticut, pattern guide on power mechanics, p. 147.

Karen Duhig, reading specialist, Deerfield High School, Deerfield, Illinois, pattern guide on "Split Cherry Tree," p. 150.

Dominic Serafino, photography teacher, Coginchaug Regional High School, Durham, Connecticut, concept guide on photography, p. 154.

William Breck, principal, Durham, Connecticut, concept guide on Incas of Peru, p. 155.

Chapter 7

William Healy, Science Department Chairperson, Coginchaug Regional High School, Durham, Connecticut, question guide on mitosis, p. 185.

Lauria Bania, Storrs, Connecticut, question guide on advertising, p. 190.

Chapter 9

Thelma Jenkins, West Palm Beach, Florida, structured overview on Darwin passage, p. 227.

Susan Lupo, math teacher, Medinah Middle School, Roselle, Illinois, vocabulary exercises on multiple meanings, p. 231 and geometric terms, p. 233.

Teresa Gaziano, sixth grade teacher, Thompson Elementary School, Rockford, Illinois, vocabulary exercise on cigarette smoking, p. 232.

Donna Kennedy Manolis, Crystal Lake, Illinois, vocabulary exercise on literary terminology, p. 234.

Karen Duhig, reading specialist, Deerfield High School, Deerfield, Illinois, magic square on Math problems, p. 234.

Dominic Serafino, photography teacher, Coginchaug Regional High School, Durham, Connecticut, vocabulary exercise on photography, p. 236.

Joseph Janoch, social studies teacher, Lyons Township High School, Western Springs, Illinois, vocabulary exercise on Communist Revolution, p. 237.

Nancy Fishell, art teacher, Coginchaug Regional High School, Durham, Connecticut, open sort exercise on pottery, p. 244.

Joseph Campbell, business teacher, Coginchaug Regional High School, Durham, Connecticut, classification exercise on types of resources, p. 245.

Richard DeWitt, principal, Medinah Middle School, Roselle, Illinois, classification exercise on the number system, p. 245.

Robert Ranieri, English and reading specialist, Wheeling High School, Wheeling, Illinois, categorization exercise on tragedy, p. 247.

Debbie Kaprove, social studies teacher, Connecticut, analogy exercise on geography, p. 250.

Chapter 10

Deborah Cooper, reading specialist, Connecticut, Maze passage, p. 273.

Chapter 11

Maureen Wynter, special education teacher, Frederiksted, St. Croix, Virgin Islands, science comprehension inventory, p. 289.

David Gatonska, vocational counselor, Coginchaug Regional High School, Durham, Connecticut, prereading activity on filling out applications, p. 295.

Candice Brickley, home economics teacher, Coginchaug Regional High School, Durham, Connecticut, prereading activity on food faddism, p. 296.

Chet Hollister, Earth Science teacher, Algonquin Middle School, Algonquin, Illinois, prereading activity on weather conditions, p. 297.

Claudia Findley, reading consultant, Glenbard West High School, Glen Ellyn, Illinois, prereading activity on child rearing, p. 297.

Appendix D

Elaine Sargent, graduate student, University of Connecticut, unit on solar system, p. 350.

Sheila Peckham, graduate student, University of Connecticut, unit on *One Flew Over the Cuckoo's Nest*, p. 366.

Index